THE AMERICAN COUNTERCULTURE

THE AMERICAN COUNTERCULTURE

A HISTORY OF HIPPIES AND CULTURAL DISSIDENTS

DAMON R. BACH

 UNIVERSITY PRESS OF KANSAS

Published by the University
Press of Kansas (Lawrence,
Kansas 66045), which was
organized by the Kansas
Board of Regents and is
operated and funded by
Emporia State University,
Fort Hays State University,
Kansas State University,
Pittsburg State University,
the University of Kansas,
and Wichita State
University.

Library of Congress Cataloging-in-Publication Data

Names: Bach, Damon R., author.

Title: The American counterculture : a history of hippies
and cultural dissidents / by Damon R. Bach.

Description: Lawrence : University Press of Kansas, 2020. |
Includes bibliographical references and index.

Identifiers: LCCN 2020011830

ISBN 9780700630097 (cloth)

ISBN 9780700630103 (paperback)

ISBN 9780700630110 (epub)

Subjects: LCSH: Counterculture—United States—
History—20th century. | United States—Social life
and customs—20th century. | Social change—United
States—History—20th century.

Classification: LCC HM647 .B33 2020 | DDC 306/.1—dc23

LC record available at https://lccn.loc.gov/2020011830.

British Library Cataloguing-in-Publication Data is available.

Printed in the United States of America

10 9 8 7 6 5 4 3 2 1

The paper used in this publication is recycled and contains
30 percent postconsumer waste. It is acid free and meets
the minimum requirements of the American National
Standard for Permanence of Paper for Printed Library
Materials Z39.48-1992.

CONTENTS

A photo gallery follows page 172.

ACKNOWLEDGMENTS

Any historian who undertakes a project of this scope inevitably accumulates many debts, and I am no exception. I would like to thank the archivists and librarians at the University of California, University of Wisconsin, University of Michigan, University of Southern Indiana, and San Francisco Public Library for locating the important papers, manuscripts, underground newspapers, leaflets, and pamphlets that constitute the foundation of this study. Several generous grants and fellowships allowed me to travel to archives and provided ample time to complete this work. At Texas A&M, I was awarded a Dissertation Completion Fellowship, College of Liberal Arts Postdoctoral Fellowship, and Charles C. Keeble '48 Graduate Dissertation Fellowship. A Publication Support Grant from the Melbern G. Glasscock Center for Humanities Research covered the costs of images that appear in this book. A research grant from the David L. Rice Library and Center for Communal Studies at the University of Southern Indiana strengthened sections on the "back to the land" movement.

I owe many thanks to several colleagues at Texas A&M. I benefited immensely from the expert mentorship of Terry H. Anderson. Over the years, he provided unflagging support, encouragement, and sincere friendship. He read every chapter multiple times and offered invaluable insights, critiques, and suggestions. The guidance of Andrew Kirkendall, John Lenihan, and James Burk made this study more robust as well. My editors at the University Press of Kansas—Kim Hogeland, David Congdon, and Bethany Mowry—have been very helpful and a joy to work with. Blake Slonecker and the anonymous reviewer at Kansas pushed me to ask more probing questions and contemplate my arguments more deeply. Others also deserve recognition. Chester Dunning, Rose Eder, Jeff Anderson, Gary Boyle, and my uncle, Dan Bach, read the entire manuscript and provided keen commentary and advice. My colleague at Texas A&M, William Collopy, remained steadfast in his support and I thank him for his friendship. My family—Suzanne, Randolph, Jennifer, and Alana—always encouraged me to follow my dreams. My grandparents, Al and Elsie, who did not live to see this publication, often expressed their pride in my successes and took an interest in my life. Their experiences during, and perspectives on, the Great Depression, New Deal, World War II, Vietnam, civil rights movement, and the 1960s, among other influences, provoked my interest in the past and inspired me to become a historian. My friend Nate Altfeather has routinely backed my ambitions and helped me to better articulate my thoughts, feelings, and ideas. Tristan and Joshua Richards provided much love, friendship, and laughter. My greatest debt, however, goes to my wife, Verity McInnis, who loved and supported me throughout graduate school and the publication process. For this, I am eternally grateful.

INTRODUCTION

The American sixties conjure up a variety of images: sit-ins at segregated lunch counters; John F. Kennedy's inaugural address in which the hand-some charismatic president spoke the memorable words, "Ask not what your country can do for you—ask what you can do for your country"; the March on Washington where Martin Luther King Jr. declared, "I have a dream"; soldiers and marines trudging wearily through the sweltering jungles of Vietnam; bloodied student demonstrators clashing with police in full riot gear; exploding ghettos and fire in the streets of Watts, Detroit, and Newark; Robert Kennedy and King lying in blood; Vietcong battling military police in the courtyard of the American embassy in Saigon; as-tronaut Neil Armstrong stepping off the Apollo 11 lunar module onto the moon's surface, proclaiming, "That's one small step for [a] man—one giant leap for mankind."

The sixties also brings to mind another image: colorfully dressed, flowers-in-their-hair youth dancing with wild abandon to the clamorous, psychedelic sounds of Jefferson Airplane or the Grateful Dead at a love-in. This book examines these individuals—hippies—and other cultural dis-sidents of the 1960s era.

Historians began investigating the counterculture when it was at its zenith and their explorations have persisted ever since. Although the available literature has grown by leaps and bounds in the last decade, an orderly and well-defined historiography has yet to emerge. Basic prob-lems and points of contention are not well established. Numerous vol-umes present similar explanations of the counterculture's origins, values, and decline: the traditional interpretation. In this reading, the countercul-ture, traveling a path blazed by the Beats, seemingly appears as a mono-lith—composed of hippies, Diggers, and Yippies—that thrived for a brief period of four or five years (1965–1970) before it met its untimely demise at decade's end or shortly thereafter. Countercultural values are presented as fixed from inception and do not change or evolve. After portraying the "Summer of Love" in 1967 or the famed Woodstock Music and Art Fair of August 1969 as the counterculture's high point, scholars turn to the "dark side" of hippiedom—the decline of Haight-Ashbury, murder of Linda

Fitzpatrick and "Groovy" Hutchinson in the East Village, the Manson Family's bloody killing spree, and the Altamont concert debacle—events, which, for them, represent "mutually reinforcing tombstones." The Kent State shootings, New York City hardhat demonstrations, and Weather Underground townhouse explosion constitute other symbolic "death" events. For these authors, the counterculture did not survive the sixties, and, as a result, little has been written about cultural rebels in the early 1970s. The volumes that do treat this period largely pertain to communes, which gives the inaccurate impression that these features were the only elements to endure the 1960s, when in actuality, urban freaks immersed themselves in a kaleidoscopic array of activism and community building during this time, getting closer to realizing their aspirations of founding a new society.[1]

Many historians have written about the 1960s or the post–World War II era, and they examined the counterculture in a single chapter. Others have studied one local scene or a single element of the phenomenon, including San Francisco, Los Angeles, Ken Kesey, Timothy Leary, drugs, communes, hippie values, underground press, Jesus Freaks, activist entrepreneurs, the "hippie trail," hippie women, counterculture environmentalism, "cosmic cowboys" and progressive country, the intersection of citizenship and rock music, and essays probing hippies' relationship to American Indians, race, feminism, and gay liberation. While all these studies are valuable, they are insufficient in documenting the totality of the counterculture, for it was the sum of its many parts—more than communes, underground newspapers, hip capitalists, LSD, and a few prominent figures.[2]

This book contests the traditional interpretation and expands the boundaries of counterculture history. It endeavors to be comprehensive, investigating the counterculture throughout the United States—from coast to heartland to coast—from its antecedents and origins in the 1950s, emergence in the mid-1960s, massive expansion in the late 1960s, and apogee in the early 1970s to its decline a few years later. It illuminates the counterculture's complexity, continually evolving values, and constantly changing components and adherents, which defined and redefined it throughout its near-decade-long existence. It also explores hippiedom's relationship to, and interactions with, the social movements of the period, including the New Left, civil rights, Black and Red Power, women's and gay liberation, and environmentalism.

This work aims to answer the following fundamental questions: What main forces, themes, and events caused the counterculture's materialization? What circumstances led to its decline? What were its parameters? When did it peak? Were there recognizably distinct periods in its evolution? What values and social philosophies did it manifest and espouse and did they change over time? Where and when did hippie communities sprout forth outside of San Francisco? What themes and developments have not received adequate treatment? What was the counterculture's association to the New Left and other social movements? What are its legacies? How did it change America? Many scholars have neglected to answer these questions in any great detail and many have avoided answering them at all. Yet the answers to these questions are essential for a both an accurate and clearer understanding of the counterculture. A systematic examination of primary sources produced by its participants—the importance of which will be discussed later—yields promising answers to these lines of inquiry.

This book argues that the counterculture evolved in discrete stages, became a national phenomenon, included a diverse array of participants, and experienced fundamental changes from 1965 to 1974. The most significant of these transformations was its transition from the cultural to the political. When the counterculture first emerged in 1965, it consisted primarily of cultural dissidents and it became apparent that there were appreciable differences between it, the antiwar movement, and student New Left. Made up mostly by hippies, the counterculture largely eschewed political involvement and activism, instead turning inward, attempting to achieve self-actualization and adopting new, alternative values. By 1972, however, large segments of the counterculture had taken a decisively political turn. Women's and prisoners' rights, Nixon's bid for reelection, Vietnam, Watergate, labor issues, drug legalization, the American Indian Movement, and struggles against nuclear power preoccupied the counterculture's urban—and many of its rural—adherents. Thus, in its final incarnation, the counterculture was nearly the polar opposite of its former self, exhibiting a conspicuous activist bent, a departure from its original cultural orientation. Moreover, rising local efforts accompanied the counterculture's rising politicization. Activists shifted their focus from the national to the local, convinced that they could effect the greatest societal changes by concentrating on issues within their own communities. This study explains how and why this occurred.

The counterculture underwent extraordinary changes. What began as a phenomenon limited to the coasts in 1965 became a way of life for millions across the country by 1974. The counterculture of the mid-1960s differed from its early 1970s counterpart significantly. It manifested distinct values, practices, and participants at various stages. Often these changes occurred rapidly—even in the space of a year. Comparing the counterculture of 1967 to 1968, for example, reveals meaningful differences. Hippies in 1967 radiated optimism, championed flower power, and created instant communities at love-ins. By 1968, however, some counterculturalists began calling for revolution—perhaps a violent one—while others despaired at and resisted government repression, while still others remained optimistic and joyous, creating the new society in the Aquarian Age. Values changed hastily as well. Consensus was often challenged. In 1965 and 1966, hippies extolled the virtues and possibilities inherent in LSD. By 1968, however, many questioned whether dope could actually induce enlightenment. These seekers looked elsewhere for answers and took up, among other things, transcendental meditation and the guidance of Meher Baba. And the counterculture's overall direction waxed and waned, swaying back and forth between a cultural and political emphasis. Yippies voiced support for political revolution in 1968, but in 1970, large segments of the nation's youth—many of them former or current movement politicos—pursued cultural revolution. Within two years, however, political concerns again became paramount for freaks and activists. Ultimately, a greater understanding of the counterculture will continue to elude us without a close examination of its changing forms and changing definition.

The counterculture's central essence and purpose was profound: to create a new, freer, superior society based on an alternative culture, ideas, values, and institutions. The Diggers, based in San Francisco, favored an anarchistic approach to expedite social change. As Peter Coyote, reminiscing on the motives behind the group, explained, "What we were about was autonomy, finding what authentic, autonomous impulses were. And then being responsive to them, and not making excuses, not waiting for the revolution." The objective was to "create a post-revolutionary society. . . . eternity is now, if you have a fantasy, take responsibility for it and actualize it, build or imply a society around it. And if it's nice, people will join you." And join they did. By the early 1970s the counterculture had successfully created microsocieties in most major cities, building a host of counterinstitutions in the form of free stores, free schools, and free clinics. Such self-sufficient and sustaining communities allowed hippies, if they so desired—and many did—to completely evade majority society and mainstream culture. As rhythm guitarist Barry Melton of Country Joe and the Fish recalled, "We were setting up a new world that was going to run parallel to the old world but have little to do with it as possible." Even those who had no interest in actively creating the new society in an immediate, tangible form through traditional work hoped to bring about a new one by showing alternative possibilities. Sometimes playing in a rock band sufficed. The Grateful Dead saw themselves as "signposts to new space."[3]

A deeper comprehension of the counterculture also provides a unique insight into modern American social conflict during the most tumultuous decade of the twentieth century. The national scope of the counterculture is a testament to the fundamental social, cultural, and political changes that occurred during the 1960s era. Postwar America had a pervasive alienating effect on a substantial portion of the baby boom generation. The counterculture was, at its base, a reaction to Cold War society and culture. Millions of young people revolted against the country's diplomacy, politics, values, laws, morality, religion, government, and institutions. Their solution to perceived societal ills involved adopting remarkably similar alternative values. Counterculturalists believed they had found a better way and attempted to create a new society unencumbered by war, racism, competition, nine-to-five rat race, and authority. Most cities and college towns eventually included a countercultural district; size and population dictated the number of alternative institutions and amenities available to the hip. At a minimum, this district usually entailed a simple landmark or meeting place such as a building, park, or street. Some communities might have had a single hip clothing or poster store. Larger and more elaborate enclaves boasted underground newspapers, concert halls, clubs, and a wide variety of stores, co-ops, head shops, natural food restaurants, and free services. By the late 1960s, even cultural dissenters in the most conservative regions of the nation—like Jackson, Mississippi, and Rapid City, South Dakota—found a welcoming community of like-minded individuals who shared the same interests and objectives.

While hippies tried to usher in a more peaceful, egalitarian, and experimental environment, they disturbed and angered many Americans whose sensibilities were deeply offended by the counterculture's ostensible disregard for traditional institutions, mores, values, and conventions of decency. Mainstream and older citizens could not comprehend—and were appalled by—youth who left behind the abundance and material comforts of suburbia for drugs, sex, communes, squalor, and crash pads. Nixon's "Silent Majority" responded both verbally and physically to the youthful dissidents, denouncing them in newspapers and attacking them in public. Mainstream citizens reaffirmed their faith in long-established codes of behavior, principles, morals, and standards. The establishment, too, harried counterculturalists, as government agencies—the FBI and local police—surveilled, arrested, jailed, and assaulted them.

Ultimately, however, the dominant society and repressive government violence could not vanquish the counterculture's ubiquitous influence, for it left an indelible mark on modern America, spearheading cultural transformation. The majority became less formal. Even those who had once hated hippies relaxed their dress codes, experimented with soft drugs, harbored more permissive sexual attitudes, and became more tolerant of dissenting lifestyles. Other legacies include a populace more inclined to question authority, empowered students at universities, and a more environmentally and health-conscious nation.

Decades later, the sixties and its legacies loom large in the American imagination and politics. The counterculture played a prominent role in the rise of the "culture wars." The ascent of the modern conservative movement was, in part, fueled by a backlash against countercultural activity and the perceived excesses of the sixties. Today's conservatives blame hippies and the sixties for a variety of social problems.

In the larger scope of American history, the counterculture was part of a long tradition of dissent from prevailing societal norms. Although many hippies were convinced that they were a new people creating a whole new social order, nineteenth-century romanticists like the Shakers, Hutterites, and Oneida Perfectionists had preceded them, forming back-to-the-land communes. Residents of New Harmony in Indiana, established in 1825, attempted to form an egalitarian society. Other communitarians founded Brook Farm in Massachusetts, in 1841, where they endeavored to create a new society, sharing labor while putting a premium on individual time for achieving self-realization. Hippies shared a family resemblance with the transcendentalists, too. Henry David Thoreau, who disdained his neighbors' scramble for wealth, secluded himself in a cabin at Walden Pond in Massachusetts where he lived a simple life, enjoyed nature, and engaged in self-reflection. In the twentieth century, 1920s youth challenged traditional morals and sexual standards. The Beats assailed militarism, the Cold War consensus, consumerism, racism, stifling conformity, and the dominant morality in the 1950s. And yet the counterculture was unique, a phenomenon that will not likely be repeated.

This study defines the terms "hippie" and "counterculture." Hippies distinguished themselves by donning eclectic—and from the perspective of outsiders—bizarre clothing that was frequently bright and colorful. Flowers became entities that symbolized love, harmony, and beauty, and many hippies carried them or wore them in their hair. Hippies valued rock music above all other communication mediums and art forms, valorized rock musicians, and celebrated togetherness and community at love-ins. Hippies championed sexual liberation, prized drug experimentation, lived communally, embraced Eastern religions and mysticism, preached and practiced peace and love, and sought more meaningful, authentic lives. The most ardent among them believed vehemently in the transformative qualities and revolutionary potential of dope and rock music. Finally, hippies endeavored to create a better culture based on moral precepts—cooperation, truthfulness, love, empathy, and egalitarianism.

"Counterculture" is a broader term that includes hippies, but also embodies additional young cultural rebels who rejected the traditions, conventions, values, and lifestyles of the American mainstream and middle class. Although the preponderance of counterculturalists up to 1970 were hippies, others were not. Bob Dylan and Andy Warhol, for example, became countercultural icons, but they were not hippies. Warhol—and everyone else at his Factory art studio—hated hippies. Warhol found hippies and their support for free love "boring." Though hippies saw Dylan as a figurehead, his lifestyle and cultural outlook differed starkly from those who held him in such high regard. By 1969 he lived a quiet life with his family in Woodstock, New York. His name never graced the headlines for drug busts, he remained faithful his wife, Sara, and had friendly relations with the local police. "Bob, in my opinion, was a conduit for the divine. That's what [the hippies] were reacting to," commented Dylan's friend Wavy Gravy. "The Bobster, I don't think he was ever [a hippie], never maintained he was that and always turned away from that." Counterculturalists discarded the principles and practices of majority society, but did not necessarily exhibit the hallmarks or values commonly ascribed to hippies such as strange clothing, long hair, communalism, or even love and pacifism. Nor did they necessarily assume the disposition of introspective quietism in the face of pressing political and social issues, or attempt to drop out and turn their backs on the "plastic" society. Many counterculturalists advocated sexual liberation and dope as a pathway to spiritual enlightenment, loved rock music, and adopted macrobiotic diets or vegetarianism, but became politically engaged as well, demonstrating against perceived injustices, or actively building counterinstitutions. Counterculturalists included artists, communards, street musicians, psychedelists, underground filmmakers and journalists, mind and palm readers, guerrilla and experimental theater actors and actresses, Boo-Hoos, Provos, Diggers, "Jesus Freaks," and cultural activists who engineered "smoke-ins" and "nude-ins." Beginning in the late sixties, and continuing into the next decade, the counterculture expanded to encompass political radicals— "politicos"—and activists who also rejected the dominant culture such as antiwar demonstrators, environmentalists, Yippies, Zippies, and some Vietnam veterans and gays.[4]

The counterculture was not merely a set of characteristics and ideologies but a group of real people with the same values and objectives. It must be defined in relation to the social and political movements of the sixties— it cannot be examined in a vacuum. This book defines the counterculture by the individuals, factions, and movements that immediately or eventually adopted an orientation and disposition of rejecting and standing in opposition to the dominant culture and society. It starts from the premise that predominately white middle-class cultural dissenters and hippies defined the counterculture from the beginning and constituted its core moving forward. Other individuals and movements became integrated into the counterculture when they embraced and shared the values, philosophies, goals, and practices of these cultural dissidents and hippies. A collection of disparate movements with no center and common focus, comprising atomized people with different values with little or no contact—perhaps even in conflict with each other—but all actively opposing the dominant social, political, economic, and cultural models, is not a recognizably distinct and cohesive entity that we can call a counterculture. In fact, deep and formidable differences in philosophy, strategy, behavior, and style distinguished the various movements of the sixties. Which constituents of the movement embraced the countercultural ethos, and when did this occur?

Defining the counterculture as primarily white cultural rebels and hippies makes the inclusion of particular individuals and movements for change problematic. Merely being agitated by the status quo and established systems of power did not make one a member of the counterculture. One might be distraught over, or even actively confront, the establishment and not be at odds with the dominant society as a whole. Many people during the sixties experienced discontent with the powers that be, but refrained from living outside the mainstream and generally acceded and conformed to majority society's beliefs and practices. Many conservatives, for example, opposed the liberal consensus, entrenchment of the New Deal welfare state, and domination of the presidency by liberal Democrats and insufficiently conservative Republicans, but they were hardly counterculturalists. America in the 1960s was culturally and politically segregated and "black and white radicals operated more on parallel tracks than on the same track." African American militants never had very amicable relationships with hippies and some of them publicly denounced countercultural icons like Timothy Leary and Abbie Hoffman. Haight-Ashbury was a notoriously segregated community. Few blacks became hippies. New Leftists and antiwar demonstrators in the mid-to-late 1960s also differed from counterculturalists in their comportment and philosophical outlook and many hippies felt indifferent toward, actively opposed, or criticized "politicos" and organized and hierarchical movements. Radical feminists were critical of the counterculture; they eschewed or abandoned hippiedom, chastising it for reproducing the patriarchal structures and sexism of the dominant society. They left the counterculture and New Left behind, forging ahead on their own. Robin Morgan, in fact, caught flak from movement heavies when she began prioritizing women's liberation over the antiwar movement and Yippies. She remembered having "huge arguments in 1968 with [Tom] Hayden, with [Jerry] Rubin, with Abbie [Hoffman] . . . they simply could not believe that I was going to go with these 'dumb broads' to protest against the Miss America Pageant when the revolution was going to be happening in Chicago."[5]

At its peak, millions of people participated in the counterculture, or at the very least, adhered to some of its principles. Such a large group of individuals makes it difficult to draw generalizations since so many held disparate philosophies and worldviews. Nevertheless, several broad forms of cultural dissent can be discerned. "Dropouts" attempted to live on the fringes of mainstream society as much as possible; they included drifters, some communards in rural areas, runaways, and itinerant street people. Hippie "purists" made up a significant part of the counterculture up to 1970. To be sure, purists were not altogether antipolitical or apolitical. Like their New Left brethren, they abhorred the violence, destruction, and immorality of the Vietnam War, racism, nuclear arms race, and bureaucratized multiversity, but they chose not to confront these forces directly; rather, they focused primarily on personal and cultural matters—music, art, theater, dope, mysticism, communal living—exploring themselves and developing particular interests and alternative values. Many believed that personal transformations—with or without the aid of mind-expanding chemicals—would lead to substantive and beneficial cultural, social, political, and economic changes, resulting in a more humane and peaceful society. In sum, hippie purists endeavored to live a life unadulterated by troublesome political issues and vociferous political leaders and movements to the best of their ability. They found political activism to be ineffective, a turnoff, and a waste of valuable time. In an underground article titled "Hippies Are," A. James Speyer voiced his hope that hippies could influence "the structure of our society. . . . without malice, without political protest and without inhibition."[6]

But the behavior and policies of politicians, police, and majority society moved many others to take part in activism of some sort during this tumultuous time. "Hybrid counterculturalists" combined hippie and New Left in equal measure, exhibiting quintessential hippie characteristics while calling for confrontation with the establishment. Hippie activists joined antiwar demonstrations and "cultural activists" built counterinstitutions and protested police harassment and laws prohibiting nudity and drugs.

Others advocated "revolution." "Cultural revolutionaries" believed that fundamental social change could and would occur if enough people "changed their heads" and adopted alternative values and perspectives. A proponent of this approach, for example, excoriated "longhairs" who shouted, "Kill the police!" and "Fuck the establishment!" The "friendly, loving, lawful, peaceful, evolutionary, youthful and inevitable revolution," from his perspective, would be realized only when enough individuals experienced personal transformations: "This society has to be 'turned-on' and this may take time." "Dope revolutionaries" thought that radical and worthwhile changes could be achieved when the masses—or at least young people—"turned on" with hallucinogens and other "mind-expanding" substances. Promoters of "rock revolution" contended that rock music contained within it the power to change individuals and society. Delineating the numerous kinds of counterculturalists is not to argue that each fit neatly into any one category. To be sure, many straddled multiple groups. But, conversely, few, if any, defied classification altogether.[7]

The New Left differed from the counterculture in several respects. The New Left represented a break from the Communists, democratic Socialists, Stalinists, and Trotskyists of the old left. A new generation raised in affluence emerged in the 1960s and created a new kind of political culture. Events beyond America's shores—Mohandas Gandhi's nonviolent struggle to overthrow British rule, emerging independent African nations, and Fidel Castro's Cuban revolution—inspired New Leftists. New Leftists had their roots in student activism; they were mostly young, white, well educated, and opposed to capitalism and imperialism. In 1960 young Southern civil rights workers founded the Student Nonviolent Coordinating Committee (SNCC), an organization dedicated to creating a "beloved community" while working to abolish Jim Crow, which greatly influenced and inspired young white students. That same year, college activists established Students for a Democratic Society (SDS), the organization that best exemplified the white New Left. In 1962 SDS drafted its manifesto, *The Port Huron Statement*, in which it articulated its devotion to the principle of "participatory democracy." The New Left confronted Cold War and Great Society liberalism, demonstrated against the House Un-American Activities Committee (HUAC), protested the arms race, fought poverty and Jim Crow segregation, challenged campus paternalism and bureaucracy, agitated for free speech rights, and later, rallied against the Vietnam War. Activists and students committed to political and social change, New Leftists confronted the existing political structure and establishment, while many hippies, on the other hand—many who were nonstudents or ex-students—dissented against the dominant culture and mainly strived for personal transformations, self-actualization, and expanded consciousness.

New Leftists frequently expressed their disapproval of hippies' philosophies and inaction. "We've learned . . . that dope won't turn Amerika into the land of the free," opined the *Kudzu*, "that just dropping out is a bummer, is lonely, meaningless escapism." Of course, the line separating the New Left and counterculture was not always precise; the two strands of the youth rebellion converged and overlapped at various times throughout the sixties. This dynamic was fluid and varied throughout time and geography. In California, differences between the politicos of Berkeley and hippies of San Francisco were certainly apparent in 1967 and earlier. Yet in 1969 counterculture and New Left fused completely—if only momentarily—at People's Park. Likewise, many people in Madison, Wisconsin, and Bloomington, Indiana, experienced the counterculture and New left as a seamless phenomenon throughout the 1960s and 1970s.[8]

The scholarship, information, and interpretations of this book are based primarily on documents hippies produced themselves: personal correspondence, memoirs, interviews, flyers, pamphlets, and, above all, underground newspapers. These documents provide the most reliable and authoritative sources for discerning the counterculture's rationale for its behavior and actions. They also elucidate its values and the factors behind its origins, expansion, and decline. Moreover, they reveal distinctive periods in the counterculture's historical trajectory. Using establishment sources presents problems. Popular magazine and newspaper articles frequently offered jaundiced and simplistic perspectives of the counterculture, condescending and belittling portrayals written by individuals not involved in the scene. The mainstream press focused extensively on sex, drugs, and rock music, and on the counterculture's most spectacular peculiarities: be-ins, bizarre clothing, public nudity, and drug casualties. Journalists obsessed over hair and cleanliness. A 1967 "firsthand report" from *U.S. News and World Report*, for example, stated, "Weird dress . . . strange talk . . . odd customs. . . . They are the 'hippies.'" After speculating that hippies might be "more than a fad," the article instructs readers on how to identify one: "The hippie is easy to spot. In most cases, he needs a shave, a haircut and a bath. He makes every effort to look bizarre. . . . He is allergic to steady jobs."[9] That said, this book is augmented with establishment primary sources. While it is true that some *Time*, *Newsweek*, *Life*, and *New York Times* journalists wrote speculative and sensational articles, the factual information in these stories is informative and valuable. Underground and mainstream sources, then, examined together, provide crucial evidence for new revelations and interpretations.

Counterculturalists created mountains of documents and had little difficulty lucidly conveying their values and philosophies, which will be evidenced in the pages of this book. In 1965 five underground newspapers existed. A few years later, presses turned out hundreds of titles with a readership that numbered in the millions. Although underground papers circulated openly, they were called "undergrounds" because early rags like the *Los Angeles Free Press* and *East Village Other* appealed to various dissenters, intellectuals, artists, and musicians who considered themselves cultural outlaws. The undergrounds spurned social and cultural norms. Some of them appeared subversive. By the late 1960s numerous undergrounds advocated revolution and the overthrow of the government, and local and federal authorities began to target them. Many hippies and New Leftists did not read establishment newspapers at all, as the mainstream press was largely oblivious to rock and youth culture and its values. Hip individuals read the underground press to understand what was happening in their own communities and the larger counterculture. After Liberation News Service (LNS) was established in 1967, it served as a conduit, uniting the underground press, distributing common news packets to three hundred outlets around the world. Activist Alice Embree called LNS a "huge organizing instrument" that became the movement's "connective tissue." The undergrounds created a sense of cohesion and community among rebellious youth, while providing legitimacy to alternative behaviors, sensibilities, and values. Both hippies and politicos wrote for the underground press, and its pages sometimes highlighted their differences. By the late 1960s, however, most papers covered both political and cultural issues and concerns.[10]

A note on terminology is in order. The "sixties" refers to the chronological decade, 1960–1969. The "Sixties" is employed to signify "the long 1960s," an era of social activism, political and cultural upheaval, and transformation. Though its bookends continue to inspire debate among historians, for our purposes here, its parameters are 1960 and 1974. Because hippies made up a large segment of the counterculture up to 1970, "hip," "hippies," "hippiedom," and "counterculture" are often used interchangeably. Some cultural rebels did not consider themselves hippies, as they found the term imprecise, inadequate, condescending, and media-manufactured. Some denied that there were hippies at all. As Ron Thelin put it, "there's no such thing as hippies. Hippies is a creation of the mass media. Trying to come up with some kind of word that would say what was happening, describe a phenomenon. But it has nothing to do in the world with what's happening. What we are is Americans. We are the real Americans." With this in mind, great care has been taken to name specific individuals when their identities are known, rather than using the general term "hippies." Other expressions commonly used are "longhair," "dropout" and "counterculturalist," words that also signify hippies and others who thought of themselves as part of a counterculture. Some cultural radicals called one another "freaks," or "freeks," words that carried positive connotations. "Head" denotes a heavy dope or drug user. Hippies used most of the terms above to describe themselves. On the subject of drugs, "dope" and "drugs" are used in the sense that hippies understood them. "Dope" indicates mind-expanding, "good" drugs like LSD, marijuana, and peyote, while "drugs" indicates harmful and addictive substances such as heroin, barbiturates, and amphetamines. Finally, other words that appear repeatedly are "establishment," and "the system," terms hippies used to refer to the nation's dominant, entrenched, social, cultural, and political order. The establishment included "straights," politicians, government officials, schools, universities, churches, judges, military, and the police—all the people and institutions that hippies found antiquated, immoral, and oppressive.[11]

This book is organized chronologically. The counterculture's development consisted of five basic periods: its antecedents and origins from 1945 to 1965; inchoate years in 1965 and 1966; flowering from 1967 to 1970; apogee in the early 1970s; and its decline beginning in 1972. A chapter is devoted to each of these distinct stages.

Chapter 1 documents the counterculture's genesis. In the first two decades following World War II, the culture, government, and institutions of Cold War America alienated soon-to-be hippies, precipitating their renunciation of mainstream society's traditions, values, and lifestyles. As hippies themselves understood and testified to in their own newspapers, memoirs, and interviews, suburban conformity and materialism, racism, the arms race, campus paternalism, and bureaucratized multiversity, disillusioned many middle-class kids. Those who became countercultralists questioned and then jettisoned mainstream ideals and values and adopted alternative ideas and lifestyles, while New Leftists confronted and agitated against injustices, the political status quo, and established systems of power.

Chapter 2 analyzes the counterculture in its early years—from 1965 to 1967—when it emerged in large coastal cities and at large universities. During this stage, alienation skyrocketed with the onset of the Vietnam War, causing the counterculture's exponential growth. While the first underground newspapers rolled off the press, the counterculture's fundamental values developed and its forms evolved from "happenings" to dancehall concerts to "be-ins." At this time, hippiedom consisted mostly of cultural dissidents who opposed political activism. For their part, many New Leftists scoffed at hippies who dropped out when important political work needed to be done and pressing social problems warranted attention. "Changing one's head," and individual transformations as a vehicle for social change seemed delusional and ludicrous from the perspective of activists. Meanwhile, the counterculture made inroads into the heartland. While hippiedom's largest centers materialized in San Francisco's Haight-Ashbury and New York's East Village, it also emerged elsewhere, in Los Angeles, Austin, Detroit, Seattle, and Madison.

Chapter 3 examines the counterculture from 1967 to 1970, revealing its unprecedented growth, expansion, and development in every region of America. As freaks anxiously awaited the imminent arrival of what they called the Age of Aquarius—a new era of optimism, faith, and love—the iconic counterculture burgeoned. Hippie values became more numerous, diverse, and complex, as they gathered at love-ins and rock festivals, advocated peace, love, and flower power, and confronted the war makers at the Pentagon, placing daisies in rifle barrels. In the late 1960s, the counterculture expanded and divided, for it never was a completely unified phenomenon. It consisted of cultural dissidents—hippie purists—who concerned themselves primarily with matters of culture. Yet it was an era of protest, especially against racism and the Vietnam War, and so more youths became hybrid counterculturalists, equally devoted to cultural and political radicalism. These individuals joined demonstrations with the New Left, antiwar movement, and by and after the 1968 Democratic National Convention formed groups such as the White Panthers, Youth International Party (Yippies), and Up Against the Wall Motherfucker. At the same time, political activists in the student movement and organizations like SDS became more sympathetic toward hippies and cultural politics. They made up the "New Left's counterculture," which remained separate from the hippie counterculture, as it carried a sharper political edge. Far from facing its demise with the degeneration of Haight-Ashbury, Manson murders, and Altamont, the counterculture survived the 1960s, flourishing—and peaking—in the early part of the next decade.

Chapter 4 explores hippiedom from 1970 to 1972, when it reached its largest and most influential phase. During this period, a number of developments—increasing weariness and disillusionment among antiwar demonstrators, diminishment of hippie purists, and an upsurge in cultural activism—merged alienated counterculturalists and New Leftists into a more cohesive and inclusive "countersociety" composed of students, antiwar activists, Jesus People, Vietnam vets, environmentalists, gays, communards, cultural feminists, advocates of "Red Power," and aging hippies and Yippies. The traditional interpretation that distinguishes counterculture from New Left does not hold true for this period. The ever-changing counterculture hardly resembled what had gone before, as it now cherished organic food, the outdoors, hitchhiking, vegetarianism, simple living, country rock, overseas travel, commune building, and creating alternative institutions. Meanwhile, freaks appeared all over, from Idaho, Oklahoma, and South Dakota to Kentucky. Cultural activism exploded and alternative institution building peaked in 1971 as hippies and political activists came together, establishing co-ops, businesses, free clinics, free stores, free universities, legal services, and community switchboards. The countersociety, immersed in its enclaves, came quite near to achieving its objective of creating a new society.

Lastly, chapter 5 examines the counterculture in its final years, from 1972 to 1974. During this time, some cultural rebels remained dedicated to cultural activism and community building, but many others became increasingly involved in social activism and political protest. Underground newspapers—often in a single issue—carried stories on a cornucopia of political and cultural topics—Watergate, worker strikes at General Motors, lettuce boycotts in support of farm workers, police brutality, American Indian rights, gay pride, dope, sex, organic food co-ops, free universities, art fairs, and multiday rock festivals. While communards aspired to "live the revolution," and Yippies partook in "smoke-ins" to protest unjust dope laws, freaks and activists alike embraced the "new politics," championing George McGovern in the 1972 presidential election, women's and gay liberation, American Indian Movement, and an end to the Vietnam War. Others became dedicated activists in their local communities, supporting workers' rights, prison reform, and agitating against nuclear testing and power. In many respects, then, the counterculture in its last stage was almost the antithesis of its former self, preoccupied with politics and political change through protest, rather than disengagement, which it had favored in the mid-1960s. During this period, various factors and circumstances contributed to the counterculture's decline, such as its commercialization and mainstreaming, a crippling economic downturn, and most importantly, the end of the draft and American involvement in Vietnam. Yet the counterculture left behind a powerful legacy, one that remains with us right up to today: a transformed America. Thus this book chronicles the rise, journey, and decline of the American counterculture, a journey that was, in the words of the Grateful Dead, "a long strange trip."

I

On Saturday, January 14, 1967, the "World's First Human Be-In" took place on a polo field in Golden Gate Park in San Francisco. Billed as the "Gathering of the Tribes," the event drew twenty thousand people. "Perfect. The gods have shined on us . . . The vibrations from this day will extend across the country and turn on millions of people from California to New York," asserted Ron Thelin, co-owner of the Psychedelic Shop in Haight-Ashbury. The crowd, mostly young people, "wore feathers, furs, plumes, floppy hats, tusks, bells, chimes, talismans, beaded charms, tiaras of flowers, animal hides, sequins, and prayer cloths." Others came dressed as "cowboys, pioneer scouts, pirates, angels, devils, Confederate and Revolutionary Army heroes, reincarnated Greta Garbos and Rudolph Valentinos." Many smoked marijuana and dropped LSD. All the while, revelers grooved to the sounds of the Grateful Dead, Big Brother and the Holding Company, and Quicksilver Messenger Service.

The Slocums, tourists from Kansas, gazed upon the gathering. "They're those hippies," said Mrs. Slocum. "Lordy, I never knew there were so many of them. See those girls in long hair and bare feet? They say they never wash. We'd best go someplace else now. I wouldn't be surprised if they— well, they say they have orgies, don't you know."

"I wonder what they're rebelling against?" asked Mr. Slocum, standing confused in his red golf slacks. "I don't understand it. I'd sure like to know where they all came from and why they're here."[1]

Why were they there? Many historians have studied the counterculture, yet few have devoted much analysis to its origins. Theodore Roszak argued that hippies emerged in opposition to the "technocracy," "that society in which those who govern justify themselves by appeal to technical experts who, in turn, justify themselves by appeal to scientific forms of knowledge. And beyond the authority of science, there is no appeal." For Roszak, youthful dissidents sought to undermine the scientific worldview, questioning society's notions of reason and reality. In contrast to technocrats and the technocracy, dissenters exercised the "non-intellective capacities of the personality—those capacities that take fire from visionary splendor and the experience of human communion."[2]

Most scholars emphasize continuities between the Beats and hippies, while some take the connection further, arguing that the Beats "set the stage" for the counterculture or that hippiedom was a "direct outgrowth of the disillusioned beats in the 1950s." Others contend that the Beats exerted direct influence on the younger generation, acting as participants, mentors, and leaders. LSD, it is argued, was the crucial element that facilitated a transformation from Beat to hip. Some have found minimal differences between Beat and hippie, arguing that the major factor distinguishing the two phenomena was sheer numbers.[3]

In addition to the impact of the Beats, researchers have attributed the counterculture's growth to a variety of influences: permissive childrearing, postwar affluence, huge numbers of baby boomers, the "generation gap," and young people intentionally suspending themselves between adolescence and adulthood. Dissenting writers, intellectuals, films, and magazines are stressed, as is the influence of black culture, and the black hipster. "Indeed, without pioneers to point the way," writes one historian, "hippies might never have emerged to fascinate and outrage America." For many scholars, it seems, disaffected youth needed something to galvanize them—throw in Timothy Leary, Ken Kesey, the Beatles, and Bob Dylan, and one apparently has the necessary catalysts responsible for the materialization of hippiedom. Its origins have escaped at least one scholar who has declared, "Beyond its antecedents among the Beats, the emergence of the counterculture has no single satisfactory explanation."[4]

Whether employed in everyday life, science, or philosophy, the term *alienation* has many different meanings. Most of these meanings, when reduced to their base, essentially describe "the act, or result of the act, through which something, or somebody, becomes (or has become) alien (or strange) to something, or somebody, else." In 1844, Karl Marx theorized that man alienated himself from the products of his own spiritual, social, and labor activity, relating to these objects "as a slave, powerless and dependent." Man was self-alienated from the human species and his own essence, failing to grasp "his historically created human possibilities."[5] Although Frantz Fanon employed the term *alienation* infrequently, he was clearly concerned with the phenomenon. He used the word "to designate conditions of separation of the individual from his individuality, his culture, or his existential condition." Moreover, the term indicates a denial or suppression of one's individuality. And Fanon, like others, used it to describe a neurotic condition. Two definitions, one offered by Robert Nisbet and the other by Gwynn Nettler, most fittingly apply to the counterculture. In the preface to the 1970 edition of his *The Quest for Community*, Nisbet defined alienation as "the state of mind that can find a social order remote, incomprehensible, or fraudulent; beyond real hope or desire; inviting apathy, boredom, or even hostility. The individual not only does not feel a part of the social order; he has lost interest in being a part of it." Nettler also described alienation as a psychological state of a normal person. Writing in the *American Sociological Review*, he defined an "alienated person" as "one who has been estranged from, made unfriendly toward, his society and the culture it carries."[6]

Whether as a symptom or a cause, alienation is the most persuasive explanation for the origins of the counterculture. An extensive analysis of counterculture newspapers, memoirs, and interviews indicates that Cold War America—the culture, government, and institutions—*alienated* the young people who became hippies. The estranged rejected society's dominant traditions, conventions, values, and prescribed behavior. Counterculturalists in the 1960s and 1970s understood that they were hippies because they were alienated. "The soul of hip . . . is dysfunction," explained Detroit's *Fifth Estate*. "Defined, *Hip is alienation*." The Los Angeles Diggers also recognized that alienation drove young people into the counterculture's ranks: "Our goals are to help and bring together those segments of society that are alienated."[7]

Historians continue to debate the nature of the 1950s. In one camp are those who argue that stability, happiness, and prosperity made this era distinctive; in the other are those who characterize the immediate postwar years as a stifling time, rife with consensus, conformity, and neglected social problems. This study will not enter that debate because the period's objective essence is not of central concern. What ultimately matters is how later longhairs *experienced* and *perceived* the fifties. At times the observations of future freaks border on a caricature of the period, yet their recollections are nevertheless heartfelt and sincere. The 1950s might not have been a staid and repressive decade—but many middle-class kids *felt* that it was. Alienation—and the counterculture—was the result.

The hippie population numbered in the millions and each countercul-turalist had deeply personal motives for why they abandoned the main-stream. A twenty-five-year-old indulging in the "acid tests" in 1965 most likely dropped out for different reasons than an eighteen-year-old com-munard living at The Farm in 1973. The oldest hippies were born, roughly, between 1935 and 1945. Some were born even earlier. Tuli Kupferberg, a cofounder of the radical band the Fugs, was born in 1923. These elder hip-pies undoubtedly experienced the Red Scare, suburbia, the arms race, and the effects of racial injustice more acutely than their baby boomer peers. Baby boomers likely found the Vietnam War and a coercive draft more alienating than the vestiges of McCarthyism. Some may have been disil-lusioned by a multitude of factors; others, only a few.

Still, all lived through this period and the evidence suggests several common societal and cultural features alienated soon-to-be-hippies. In *Woodstock Nation*, published in 1969, Abbie Hoffman identified the "thorns of the flower children." Young people, he wrote, "were sick of being pro-grammed by an educational system void of excitement, creativity and sensuality. A system that channeled human beings like so many labora-tory rats with electrodes rammed up their asses into a highly mechanized maze of class rankings, degrees, careers, neon supermarkets, military-industrial complexes, suburbs, repressed sexuality, hypocrisy, ulcers, and psychoanalysts." The same year an underground journalist in Indi-ana stated: "Joe McCarthy, Elvis Presley, the N.Y. Yankees and a Humpty Dumpty president characterized the 50's. Niggers were niggers, commies were commies and freedom was the U.S.A." These observations, crude and unsophisticated as they were, accurately represented how future freaks interpreted their surroundings. Now, let us examine the alienating forces that produced the counterculture.[8]

THE COLD WAR, MILITARY-INDUSTRIAL COMPLEX, AND MCCARTHYISM

The first major factors responsible for the counterculture's origins can be found in the immediate events that followed World War II. As the Grand Alliance fractured and the Cold War began, creating a bifurcated world, America and the Soviet Union engaged in an enormous arms buildup that potentially endangered humankind's survival. The Cold War consensus ensured that politicians of both parties supported the military establishment and arms manufacturers. The military-industrial complex wielded a tremendous amount of power and remained largely impervious to democratic accountability. The Cold War eventually turned hot in Vietnam, threatening the moral outlook—and livelihoods—of dissenters who opposed the conflict for any number of reasons. The perceived threat of communism overseas resulted in a Red Scare at home, creating a repressive atmosphere rife with paranoia and suspicion. As a result, the counterculture would champion values antithetical to the ones advanced during their childhoods, including harmony in place of discord and strife, tolerance for dissenting ideas and behaviors, and peace in place of war.

When the world's bloodiest war ended, an estimated sixty million people had perished, including six million Jews in the Holocaust. Over 405,000 Americans died and 670,846 were wounded. Yet for most Americans, it had been a "good war." Material livelihoods improved, the result of industrial mobilization that created prosperity, ending the Great Depression. Citizens had pulled together, working in tandem stateside, doing their part to ensure victory overseas. A just and necessary war, the United States had fought on the side of freedom and democracy, and the troops returned home as heroes. Four years earlier, the publisher of Time, Henry Luce, wrote of the "American Century," and many shared his conviction that the United States could extend capitalism and democracy to the rest of the globe. Some hoped that America, the greatest economic and military power in the world with a monopoly on the nuclear bomb, might prevent further wars, using it as leverage. In August 1945, then, the public looked to the future with high hopes and optimism.

This optimism quickly faded, however, for shortly after the Allied victory, the nation found itself engaged in an ideological, economic, and strategic struggle with the Soviet Union: the Cold War. Joseph Stalin ignored stipulations made at Yalta in February 1945, which called for the division of Germany into four separate zones and for free elections in liberated Europe. With the assistance of the Red Army, communist governments took over Romania, Hungary, Bulgaria, Albania, and Poland, while Russia enveloped East Germany, Latvia, Lithuania, and Estonia. In 1946 George F. Kennan sent his "Long Telegram" from the American embassy in Moscow and a year later, he published an article in *Foreign Affairs* under the pseudonym "Mr. X." Both clarified for US authorities the mindset of the Soviet Union. The foreign service officer asserted that Soviet security, from the Kremlin's perspective, was contingent on America's weakness. Kennan recommended containing Soviet expansionist tendencies politically and geographically. Eventually, the Soviet Union, unable to expand, would succumb to internal strains and collapse. Two weeks later, British prime minister Winston Churchill proclaimed: "From Stettin in the Baltic to Trieste in the Adriatic, an iron curtain has descended across the continent." Stalin charged his former allies with hostility toward his designs for Eastern Europe and predicted an inevitable war between capitalism and communism. The Grand Alliance of America, Great Britain, and Russia fell apart. The Cold War had begun.[9]

President Harry S. Truman was determined to resist further communist expansion. In March 1947, before a joint session of Congress, he articulated the Truman Doctrine, a comprehensive American foreign policy for the postwar world. It encompassed "containment," and set the stage for far-reaching military commitments. Leftists threatened to topple the government in Greece. Turkey faced aggression from Russia looking to establish a greater naval presence in the Mediterranean. Britain could no longer maintain its economic and military commitments in this sphere, so America moved to assume responsibility. The United States, the president declared, would "support free peoples who are resisting attempted subjugation by armed minorities or by outside pressures." Congress authorized $400 million in military aid to beleaguered Greece and Turkey, and America set about rebuilding and stabilizing Western Europe with the Marshall Plan.[10]

Peace had not followed victory, to the dismay of the United States and its people. Having defeated Adolf Hitler, America turned to confront Stalin's "red fascism." World War II had a tremendous impact on the outlook of the men who crafted the nation's foreign policy. America, these men thought, had fought an honorable and necessary war. The United States stood firmly for all that was good. Munich had imparted an important lesson: appeasement encouraged a belligerent Germany to rampage over Europe. Concessions could not prevent further wars, but a forceful confrontation with aggressors could. Two other assumptions guided their foreign policy. First, America must maintain a powerful stance and thus its "credibility." And second, the United States possessed the economic, industrial, and military might to steer the behavior of other nations. Moreover, the world, the establishmentarians believed, was locked in a struggle between democratic capitalism and communism, good and evil, freedom and tyranny. And monolithic international communism—directed from the Kremlin—seemed to be creeping inexorably across the globe. A "victory for communism anywhere" represented a "defeat for noncommunism everywhere." Consequently, policymakers strived to maintain a geopolitical balance of power, countering the Soviets militarily and strategically, fighting communism "wherever the specters of Marx and Lenin reared their ugly heads."[11]

To protect its people, allies, and strategic interests, Washington embarked on a massive military buildup. In the spring of 1950 Truman's National Security Council produced NSC-68, a document that further clarified and defined containment. The paper argued that the Soviets sought to dominate the world, and as such, America should be prepared to extinguish communism wherever it emerged. Not only should the country mobilize its political and economic resources but it should project its power militarily as well, deploying its armed forces to the far corners of the world. To meet the threat, advocates of NSC-68 recommended nearly a fourfold increase in defense spending. Subsequently, expenditures increased from $13 billion in 1950 to $50 billion three years later. In 1940 defense spending constituted 16 percent of the federal budget. By 1959 it accounted for over half. The government increasingly invested in new military technology. In 1952 it exploded the hydrogen bomb, a weapon 750 times more powerful than the one dropped on Hiroshima in 1945. When the sixties began, America had in its arsenal long-range strategic bombers and missiles capable of traversing oceans and continents.

President Dwight Eisenhower combated communism with a fervor equal to Truman's. Ike's secretary of state, John Foster Dulles, criticized containment for being too passive and argued for "rolling back" communism, "liberating" captive nations from its grip. In early 1954 he unveiled his "massive retaliation" policy, the "New Look." Instead of maintaining a large and costly army, the United States could threaten adversaries with less expensive nuclear weapons—"more bang for the buck." Dulles also spoke of "brinksmanship," which entailed pushing Russia to the edge of war so that America might get its way. During Ike's reign, the United States added an average of two atomic weapons to its arsenal every day. Even in the event of a nuclear war, all these instruments of destruction could not be used. With the reintroduction of the draft, the armed forces soared to 3.5 million personnel. Six out of every ten federal dollars went to the Pentagon—an unprecedented amount for a nation not directly fighting a major war.[12]

This obsession with checking communism overseas became an obsession with ferreting out communists at home, leading to the development of the Red Scare. Several factors account for its outbreak. By the late forties, a broad anticommunist consensus had coalesced. Americans of all stripes—conservatives, liberals, Republicans, Democrats, elite politicians, intellectuals, union members, and commoners—shared an anticommunist worldview. This consensus gave politicians and the government ample space to persecute reds as they saw fit. Furthermore, many, if not most, Americans had little concern for the civil liberties of political dissenters. Partisanship also played a major role as the communist issue provided conservatives with an opportunity to claw their way back to power after nearly twenty years of political domination by liberal New Dealers. Finally, ideas of historic American exceptionalism bolstered the crusade. Many strongly believed that divine providence and history had guided the nation since its earliest founders fled the degenerate Old World and established an Eden in the new. Representative government, free markets, individualism, and godliness, they thought, made America a superior civilization, diametrically different from and opposed to Marxism and communism in every conceivable way.[13]

Fears of domestic subversion and anxiety stemming from Cold War developments abroad, combined with the Republican congressional triumph in 1946, led to the creation of a federal employee loyalty program after Truman issued Executive Order 9835 in March 1947. Truman's program eventually investigated 6.6 million people. The standard for dismissal included "reasonable grounds" for "belief that the person involved is disloyal to the Government of the United States." In 1951 the standards were revised when "reasonable grounds" became "reasonable doubt." An employee's "potential" for subversion—based on their thoughts and associations rather than an obvious act of disloyalty—resulted in verdicts of guilt. Standards determining whether an individual posed a threat to security were largely subjective as the criteria were left to the discretions and personal beliefs of board members. The accused received a list of charges, but authorities withheld information deemed secret. Informants—often FBI agents—did not have to testify; neither could the accused challenge them. The board held in its possession the sole "evidence."[14]

Under these circumstances, the program trampled individual liberty. Champions of the First Amendment raised eyebrows. One man was deemed a security risk after he shared his belief that the free speech of communists should be guarded at all times, even in the midst of a crisis. A suspect's perspectives on race relations, sex, religion, and foreign policy could potentially elicit concerns. Officials asked a woman whether she wanted blood banks to segregate blood donated by white and black people. Other investigators inquired, "What do you think of female chastity?" and "Have you provided any sort of religious training for your children?" A typist came up on charges for expressing doubts about the Marshall Plan and supporting an American troop withdrawal from Germany— "Communistic opinions." An African American man who shined shoes at the Pentagon was interviewed by the FBI seventy times before being granted a clearance. Why? Years before, the bootblack had contributed ten dollars to the Scottsboro Boys' defense fund. The federal civil service faced a purge under Truman and Eisenhower. Between 1947 and 1956, one scholar has estimated, loyalty programs terminated 2,700 employees, while another 12,000 resigned.[15]

The cultural and political climate was more than favorable for the emergence of the era's most notorious demagogue: Joseph McCarthy. In February 1950 the junior senator from Wisconsin delivered a speech in Wheeling, West Virginia, in which he proclaimed he had in his hand a list of 205 confirmed communists working in the State Department. He did not actually have a list, but that hardly mattered, for McCarthy was skilled at self-promotion, making false accusations, naming names, and citing numbers. For the next four years, "Low-Blow Joe" denounced "left-wing bleeding hearts," "egg-sucking phony liberals," and "communists and queers who sold China into atheistic slavery." He got ever bolder; no public figure was immune to his attacks. In 1951 he called Truman a "son of a bitch," and referred to the secretary of state as the "Red Dean of Fashion" before implicating General George C. Marshall in a "conspiracy so immense and an infamy so black as to dwarf any previous venture in the history of man." His downfall came in 1954 after he appeared like a slovenly bully at the Army-McCarthy hearings and the Senate condemned him. At career's end, McCarthy had accomplished little more than making headlines, frightening people, stoking impassioned hatred, and destroying lives. He never discovered a single communist that intelligence agencies had not already identified.[16]

McCarthy gave the era its name, but paranoia and hysteria reached an apex between 1949 and 1954 and would have been devastating years for civil liberties even in McCarthy's absence. Several shocking revelations heightened the sense that the country faced imminent danger from reds outside and within. Czechoslovakia fell to communists after rebels seized the government with Soviet aid in 1948. In 1949 the Soviets exploded an atom bomb and China fell to Mao Zedong's communist forces. In 1950 Klaus Fuchs, a Manhattan Project scientist, confessed to passing atomic secrets to the Russians; Julius and Ethel Rosenberg were charged with espionage; and in June the United States went to war with North Korea after the communists moved over the 38th parallel into South Korea. America went from Red Scared to Red Hysterical. Millions were convinced the nation teemed with communists. "There are today many Communists in America," US attorney general J. Howard McGrath warned. "They are everywhere—in factories, offices, butcher stores, on street corners, in private business. And each carries in himself the death of our society."[17]

As anticommunist sentiment arrived at a crescendo, absurd incidents and exploits abounded. In Indiana, a woman advocated the suppression of *Robin Hood* because the prince of thieves stole from the rich and gave to the poor. "That's the communist line. It's just a smearing of law and order." In Wheeling, West Virginia, city managers became alarmed when local children purchased penny candies with the Soviet Union depicted on the wrapper; an official had the dispenser removed. In Mosinee, Wisconsin, American Legionnaires staged a mock coup, educating the locals on the dangers of communist infiltration and in Illinois they warned that subversives indoctrinated the Girl Scouts. A town in New York required a loyalty oath before fishing in city waters and in Washington, DC, officials denied a retailer's license to a used furniture salesman who had invoked the Fifth Amendment. The Cincinnati Reds baseball team attempted to exhibit its patriotism by officially changing the club's name to the "Redlegs" before fans turned down the proposal. Patriotic zealots cleared libraries of "dangerous" materials in many cities. Librarians, often coerced, swept the *Daily Worker* from the shelves, but also jettisoned mainstream and less controversial publications like *National Geographic*, *Time*, and *Life*. Books written by the broad left and black authors, and those favorable to left-wing causes—civil rights, nuclear disarmament, world peace—were often pulled. So, too, were volumes critical of the government and capitalism.[18]

Some later hippies had personally experienced the Red Scare's effects. The House Un-American Activities Committee (HUAC), for instance, had investigated musician Country Joe McDonald's father. "I heard protest songs at home," McDonald recalled, "and I saw in left-wing newspapers stories about lynchings and union strikers being shot." McDonald's bandmate, Barry Melton, had a similar experience: "I became politically aware at an early age because of the persecution my parents were subjected to in the McCarthy era." A college student clarifying and explaining youthful unrest in the 1960s related one of his earliest memories:

I grew up in the Eisenhower era. The most vivid experience of my early life was McCarthyism. My mother apparently couldn't get it into her head that at the time you either had to give up your beliefs or remain silent. . . . I remember her being branded a Communist because she was teaching the Declaration of Independence and the Bill of Rights, along with how important it is to stick to your beliefs. At one point I remember being sent off to another school because someone had written in my brother's religion book, "Your mother is a Red."

Many soon-to-be hippies, then, were well attuned to the politics and forces shaping society in the 1960s because of the repression their parents had experienced during the Red Scare. For future cultural dissidents, hysterical anticommunists had victimized people who maintained their beliefs in the face of persecution and upheld the principles that the nation was founded upon. Few counterculturalists in the 1960s were communists, of course, but they were steadfast proponents of civil liberties, skeptical of the government, FBI, CIA, and self-proclaimed patriots. They condemned McCarthyism's chilling, devastating effects on society. It ruined lives, careers, and trampled civil liberties. Many casualties—liberals, New Dealers, labor leaders, civil rights activists, atheists, and pacifists—were guilty of nothing more than leaning left. A stifling atmosphere of paranoia and suspicion, the Red Scare hampered individual freedom as one thought twice about their personal beliefs, whom they associated with, what kind of activities they engaged in, the books they read, and the music they listened to, for fear of being branded a subversive. The era cast a long shadow. Cultural and political dissenters in the sixties anxiously braced for a "new McCarthyism" they felt might come as a result of the Vietnam War. They also acknowledged that the Red Scare promoted irrational "hysteria" and "throttled the nation with fear."[19]

SUBURBIA, CONSENSUS, CONFORMITY, AND SOCIAL CONSERVATISM

The themes, developments, events, and general ethos of the mid-1950s alienated future freaks to a greater degree than any other factor besides the Vietnam War. The consensus, conformity, and conservatism of this era produced a counterculture that aspired to be completely different from—and opposed to—the "plastic society" in every respect. Many of the "thorns of the flower children" flourished at this time—suburbanization, the military-industrial complex, repressive sexuality, and the promotion of religion, work, and family. The "good war" seemed to establish the United States as a force for all that was right in the world and this put the nation—"God's Country"—beyond reproach in the eyes of many citizens. The counterculture would question whether the country, its culture, people, and policies, were in fact, unassailable.

The Great Fear did eventually recede and a calmer, happier era set in by the mid-fifties. Stalin died, the Korean War ended, and McCarthy fell into disrepute. Americans liked President Eisenhower, a moderate who steered a middle course between the ideologues, preserved the New Deal, and who made them feel at ease. After struggling through the economic hardships of the depression, fighting two wars, and experiencing Cold War anxieties, the time had come to seek security and stability, relax, raise families, and enjoy the good life, while embracing traditional values and religion.

Nearly everyone celebrated marriage and family. Women went to college to find a husband, preferably a financially stable professional. Men faced pressure to wed early; those who did not ran the risk of being labeled a "latent homosexual," or "emotionally immature." People married and started families young. Books and magazines promoted the idea that the stable nuclear family constituted the backbone of a healthy society and trumpeted the importance of "togetherness." "Whether you are a man or a woman, the family is the unit to which you most genuinely belong," counseled *The Woman's Guide to Better Living.* "The family is the center of your living. If it isn't, you've gone far astray."[20]

No family could be complete without children, and the years following the war witnessed an unprecedented growth in births: the baby boom. From 1946 to 1950 women had 3.6 million children per year on average, with this number rising to the 4 million mark by 1954 and peaking in 1957 at 4.3 million, one birth every seven seconds. In all, between 1946 and 1964, over 76 million babies were born.

The baby boom coincided with another significant phenomenon: growing suburbanization. Federal mortgage guarantees protected builders, facilitating construction. Generous Veterans Affairs and Federal Housing Administration mortgage programs, easy credit, no down payments, and no closing costs boosted homeownership. Critic John Keats called suburbs "fresh air slums" and warned, "While you read this, whole square miles of identical boxes are spreading like gangrene throughout New England, across the Denver prairie, around Los Angeles, Chicago,

Washington, New York, Miami—everywhere." Cynics like Keats failed to deter enthusiastic veterans and professionals who purchased homes in record numbers, taking a leap closer to the American Dream. During the fifties, 83 percent of total US population growth occurred in the suburbs and nearly 60 million people—a third of all Americans—lived in suburbia by 1960. After bulldozing over the land—three thousand acres per day— builders constructed ranch, split-level, and Cape Cod–style homes on standardized lots, planted some trees and shrubs and moved on, creating more tract housing. William Levitt, the Henry Ford of house building, per- fected mass construction by preassembling, prefabricating, and precut- ting the most difficult parts of the homes. Large suburban communities called Levittowns appeared in New York, Pennsylvania, and New Jersey. By 1955, three-quarters of all new housing communities took the form of Levittown-like subdivisions.[21]

Conformity flourished in suburbia. Many felt compelled to join politi- cal organizations, parent teacher associations, churches, and a variety of clubs. Building codes and social pressure ensured that residents main- tained manicured lawns and kept up the appearance of their homes. Sub- urbanites studied the buying habits of others and in order to keep up with the Joneses they purchased similar cars and clothes. Most expected their neighbors to fit in. Those who dared to break the mold in thought and intellect—expressing unconventional opinions or reading too much— might be stamped a highbrow or snob and ran the risk of their social ouster. Skeptics disapproved of the suburbanization trend and its uni- formity. Historian and sociologist Lewis Mumford regretted the "mul- titude of uniform, unidentifiable houses, lined up inflexibly, at uniform distances, on uniform roads, in a treeless communal waste, inhabited by people of the same class, the same income, the same age group, wit- nessing the same television performances, eating the same tasteless pre- fabricated foods, from the same freezers, conforming in every outward and inward respect to a common mold."[22]

In the 1960s, hippies expressed their alienation from suburban "up- tight straights" who demanded conformity. "They feel that every action they do has to conform to a ritual, otherwise it's not right," a head con- tended. "You can't do anything that's spontaneous or from yourself. You make love like in the toothpaste ad, talk to your children like . . . 'Father

Knows Best.' . . . they've lost the natural ecstasy of living, man." For the counterculture, spontaneity, individualism, and experience—untethered from security—represented the best kind of life.[23]

The culture expected that women conform to a common mold of wife, homemaker, and nurturing mother. In a 1955 commencement address to the graduates of Smith College, Adlai Stevenson advised women to fight the Cold War "in the humble role of housewife—which, statistically, is what most of you are going to be whether you like the idea or not just now—and you'll like it!" Women had severely limited lifestyle and career choices as colleges prepared them to be the faithful wives of male professionals, ladies who stood behind their organization men. When middle-class women did enter the workforce, they took clerical, nursing, and teaching positions. A woman faced attacks if she veered from the confines of the domestic sphere. The 1947 bestseller *The Modern Woman: The Lost Sex*, for instance, referred to feminism as a "deep illness." Women who pressed for the same opportunities in employment and education, the authors contended, symbolically "castrated" men. Freudian biological theories became influential. An independent woman seeking fulfillment beyond marriage and family was said to exhibit neurosis and "penis envy." Housewives cooked, cleaned, and washed clothes when they were not shuttling children to various activities. A vacation broke up the monotony of daily existence only periodically. Many women with college degrees, dissatisfied with their lives and longing for something more, turned to prescription drugs and tranquilizers to numb their unhappiness.[24]

Consensus was as widespread as conformity and the "liberal consensus" was a prominent feature of Cold War culture. Complacency became pervasive as most agreed that they lived in the greatest country in the history of man. Among politicians, intellectuals, and everyday citizens, consensus prevailed on nearly every issue. In foreign affairs, it was widely believed that America should contain or roll back evil international communism. Most had faith in the government's ability to eradicate social problems and supported the New Deal and government intervention to maintain full employment. Moreover, most thought that capitalism was the fairest and best economic system, that class divisions of the European variety did not apply to America, and that economic growth would continue to eliminate disparities in wealth. Most moved to the broad political center and so did the two major political parties; few still clung to communism and socialism. Class conflict had dissipated considerably since the 1930s and 1940s. Organized labor lacked radicalism, as blue-collar workers strived for pay increases and benefits to attain similar lifestyles of the professional classes.[25]

Historians were no exception, stressing consensus and continuity, taking emphasis off various struggles—ideological, class, and sectional—arguing that historical actors had always shared the same fundamental values and outlooks. Textbooks then promulgated these ideas and interpretations at public schools across the nation. Teachers consigned the history of women, racial minorities, and political dissidents to the shadows as captivated students listened to tales of fearless pioneers, captains of industry, and the great white men Teddy Roosevelt, George Custer, and Daniel Boone. Teachers championed the country's glorious history, stressing that the nation had always been a "melting pot" for various ethnicities and nationalities, that America was the greatest country on earth, that the country was, and had always been, a bastion of freedom and democracy. Each day students dutifully recited the Pledge of Allegiance and in government and civics classes they were instructed to revere the Constitution, Bill of Rights, and Declaration of Independence.

Later longhairs jettisoned narrow conceptions of individualism, which stressed free markets, economic independence, and carried anti-communist connotations. "In Government classes we were taught INDIVIDUALISM, INDIVIDUALISM, INDIVIDUALISM—till it was coming out of my head," wrote an Orange County hippie. "Their concept of 'INDIVIDUAL': Ronald Reagan and apple pie." John Curl, a resident of Drop City, one of the first rural hippie communes, recalled, "Almost all dissent was stifled. History as taught at school was mostly how the US, the fortress of freedom, had saved the world from fascism. Who could disagree? If you didn't have an approved opinion, you kept it to yourself or got in trouble." Future counterculturalists certainly disagreed and voiced their objections not only to Vietnam, but to the dominant morality and traditional lifeways.[26]

Young adults who attended college in the 1950s—"The Silent Generation"—acted and thought much like their parents: they maintained the status quo. In college they eagerly joined frats and sororities. Major concerns included looking good and being popular. They did not confront the nation's festering social problems. The most exciting event on campus occurred when male students stormed the dorms of female students and stole their underwear in "panty raids." Before and after graduation, they centered their lives on finding a spouse and securing a high-paying job. This generation generally did not guard civil liberties, supported book and film censorship, held conservative views on sex, were religious, and conformed to traditional behaviors and conventional thought.

When it came to sex, Americans—on the surface—abided by the dictates of a latter-day Puritanism. Most considered select acts and behaviors—masturbation, homosexuality, abortion, nudism, extramarital affairs, and frank sex talk—deviant. Citizens generally felt that intercourse should be limited between married, heterosexual couples. State laws attempted to enforce sexual "norms," many banning oral and anal sex and homosexual behavior; a few prohibited sex between unwed heterosexuals. Several states banned birth control devices and some imposed laws restricting masturbation. In Indiana, an individual "aiding" or "instigating" a person under the age of twenty-one to commit "self-pollution," could be fined up to $1,000 and serve up to fourteen years in prison. Self-imposed censorship codes ensured that the words *virgin*, *pregnant*, and *seduction* did not escape the lips of performers on the silver screen, and married couples on television slept in separate beds. A long-standing double standard existed for men and women. It was considered "natural" for a man to act on his carnal desires, while women were expected to check male aggressiveness. Nice girls did not let "petting" go "too far" or dare "go all the way" for fear of blemishing or losing their reputations. Sex education teachers left much to the imagination, limiting discussions to the reproduction process. Young people usually discovered sex on their own, often in the backseat of a car in some remote place or at a drive-in movie. Most Americans were buttoned-down and did not stray from socially established sexual behaviors and mores.[27]

Later longhairs threw off majority society's sexual prescriptions. "We were conditioned in self-denial: We were taught that fucking was bad because it was immoral," reminisced Jerry Rubin in *Do It!* "Also in those pre-pill days a knocked-up chick stood in the way of Respectability and Success. We were warned that masturbation caused insanity and pimples.

. . . We went crazy. We couldn't hold it back any more." Counterculturalists celebrated sexuality as a positive and natural impulse. Sexuality was
far from immoral and need not be restrained. Women working on the
staff at the underground *Tiohero* in Ithaca, New York, dedicated to "understanding their lives" and asserting their "new life energy," discussed their
teenage sexual experiences. "The way I was socialized into sex was that it
was evil," reported one. "For the woman it's never any fun. You only do it
to have kids." "In high school I had this boyfriend—we never even took
our clothes off—but I heard this rumor about immaculate conception,"
another confided. "I skipped my period for a few months and I was positive I was pregnant. . . . I used to lie awake and worry. . . . I was so racked
with guilt." Most hippie women separated sex from reproduction, championed sex and pleasure without guilt, and with the introduction of the
pill, worried less about pregnancy.[28]

But consensus, conformity, and social conservatism did not discourage
most Americans as more and more families lived the good life. Indications
of America's surging prosperity and consumerism seemed ubiquitous.
By the mid-1950s, the United States, which constituted 6 percent of the
world's population and 7 percent of its total area, produced nearly half
its manufactured products. Three-quarters of Americans drove at least
one car, 70 percent owned a home, and 87 percent owned television sets.
While only 31 percent of Americans could call themselves middle class in
the 1920s, 60 percent had achieved this status in the mid-1950s. Between
1945 and 1960 the gross national product increased nearly 250 percent,
while per capita income grew by 35 percent. Many had extra cash as dis-
cretionary income doubled and real wages rose nearly 30 percent. Those
investing in the stock market jumped from 6.5 million in 1952 to over
16 million by the early 1960s. Multiple factors made this unprecedented
prosperity possible. Among them were unleashed personal savings that
had been pent up during the depression and war, population growth that
resulted in the expansion of markets, easy credit, installment plans, federal spending that kept the economy vibrant, and the GI Bill, which was
instrumental in sending large numbers of veterans to college, enabling
them to secure well-paying jobs.[29]

The good life entailed consumption. Affluence fostered consumerism
and materialism. Americans had saved $100 billion during the war. After

it ended, they demanded luxuries like imported wines and the latest fashions in clothes. Americans bought things they needed and many more things they did not—homes, cars, kitchen appliances, canned foods, TV dinners, frozen vegetables, paperback books, television sets, high-fidelity stereos, lawn and patio furniture sets, and clothing and footwear for every occasion and purpose. Many suburbanites saw luxuries as necessities. If one family had a new Corvette or swimming pool, then their neighbors wanted those items as well. The children, too, acquired their share of consumer products—radios, records and record players, guitars, cameras, hula hoops, Barbies, comic books, skateboards, cowboy outfits, Davy Crockett coonskin caps. Americans went shopping, the lower middle class at Korvette's and Grant's, the rich at Neiman Marcus. Advertisers spent $5.7 billion a year in 1950 and $11.9 billion by 1960 in order to convince consumers to purchase their products. Many lived on credit and went into debt.

A decade later, many counterculturalists decried such crass materialism and endeavored to live a more uncluttered, simple life. Competition with neighbors to acquire the latest in material goods became anathema to hippies. "What was it I wanted that I traded time so lightly, was it another car or another bit of clothing or the big numbers on the yellow stubs of checks?" wondered Liza Williams of the *Los Angeles Free Press*. "I must have lost myself somewhere in the marble isles of bargains, caught myself on the fine print of time payment, and I don't even know anyone named Jones. But, never again, no more, no more." Hippies tried to spend their time doing something authentic and meaningful rather than chasing new possessions. They saw little to gain in making more money and striving for success performing traditional work.[30]

Unfortunately, the mid-fifties era of repose ended during Eisenhower's second term. Even before Ike's second inaugural, the nation experienced setbacks in foreign relations and affairs. Britain, France, and Israel invaded the Suez region after Egyptian leader Gamal Abdel Nasser nationalized the Suez Canal. Eisenhower pressured Britain, France, and Israel to withdraw, souring America's relations with those countries, while weakening, it seemed, Western unity. At the same time, the Soviet Union crushed an anticommunist uprising in Hungary. Events also upset domestic tranquility. In 1957 Americans and the world witnessed ugly racism in Little Rock,

Arkansas, when white mobs prevented nine black students from entering Central High. The students eventually attended classes under the protection of the 101st Army Airborne. That same year, the Soviets launched a satellite—Sputnik—that renewed fears of nuclear war.

The 1950s with its "little boxes all the same" suburbs, the Silent Generation and organization men, crew cuts and gray flannel, mechanical conformity and unquestioning masses, censorship, conservatism, materialism, traditional lifestyles, and sexual prudery—this was the "plastic society" from which the alienated revolted and the counterculture emerged. Hippies scorned virtually every feature and characteristic of this period. "We have been raised on TV and in schools (read concentration camps) and have been taught to cut our hair, get a job, go to church, and buy buy buy the fake freedom of owning a stupid looking car, a production-line house, a nice wife our-mom-would-be-proud-of and couple of kids, a washing machine, and a color TV set," wrote a freak in the sixties. "That ain't no freedom at all, we said. Fuck that stuff and let's get us a rock and roll band together." Popular entertainment, the education system, religion, material items, and conventional career and family paths constituted a sort of prison for counterculturalists, one that they sought release from. In place of the American Dream, hippies experimented with free love, group marriage, Eastern mysticism and spiritualism, and psychedelic rock music. Rather than aspire to jobs that harmed the environment or people, they endeavored to adopt "right livelihoods," work that advanced the interests of humanity and the well-being of the hip community. Boomers used phrases such as "God," "mother," "apple pie," and "the world of Walt Disney," to succinctly describe their childhood and adolescent experiences. Sometimes they denigrated emblems of the era. "I cut my eye teeth on Donald Duck and Mickey Mouse," a Californian recalled. "But even as a kid I figured Donald Duck would make a great Sunday feed and as for Mickey, I was always hoping someone would build a better mousetrap and remove him from our midst."[31]

Hippiedom had less appeal to women of color. With its focus on sexual liberation and its exoticization of women, the counterculture attracted few black women, as they had long been stereotyped as hypersexual, enigmatic, and sensual—stereotypes they did not want to encourage.[32] Hippie women, as Gretchen Lemke-Santangelo has shown, turned against traditional women's roles, conservatism, and conformity, and cut loose from white middle-class suburbia and its notions of propriety. Even as children, women who became hippies felt alienated from their friends and families. As they grew older, their alienation only increased. Most "described finding the counterculture as 'coming home.'" When they reached young adulthood, they rebelled by hanging out with wild boys, engaged in delinquent behavior, dated ethnic minorities, frequented folk music clubs or became folk artists, experimented with dope, and investigated Eastern religious philosophy. June Millington, a rock guitarist in Fanny—the first all-female rock band to be signed to a major label—defied the strictures that male-dominated society had established for women. "To get married and go live in the 'burbs and raise kids—that to me would have been death," she told an interviewer.

The children of the two-car garage did not look forward to the life that lay ahead of them, dreading the prospect of living a patterned existence, going to college, marrying, securing a nine-to-five job, having children, two cars, dog and cat, a ranch home in the sunny suburbs. They earnestly sought to avoid becoming "Mr. Jones"—a traditional establishment-type character highlighted in the Bob Dylan song "Ballad of a Thin Man," for Mr. Jones "comes home at night, he's tired—he has a beer, he watches TV, and goes to bed. He gets up the next morning and goes through the same thing." "Dad was a perfectly nice man," a Boston doper told a researcher, "but he was politically conservative, and really straight, and, well, he was just wrapped up in the old money and suburbia possession bag, you know . . . a boring life, just—boring."[33]

The young studied their environment and then asked themselves: is this all there is? This question produced millions of seekers in the next decade, those who pursued alternative lifestyles, quested for a deeper and more significant existence, strived to discover themselves, experiment with alternative religions and spiritualties, and to have experiences for experience's sake.

CRACKS IN THE CONSENSUS

In the fifties and early sixties, some began to assault the status quo. And the hippies' origins are partly—but not primarily—rooted in these cracks in the consensus. Although the Beats, rock music, Lenny Bruce, and intellectuals probably influenced some later longhairs to drop out of the mainstream, other forces proved to be more significant; the lived experiences—McCarthyism, Cold War, suburbia, consensus, and conformity—of those who became the counterculture ultimately had the greatest alienating effect. Subsequent events and themes would further alienate the young in the early 1960s. Nevertheless, it is instructive to examine some of the people and influences cited by future freaks as having made an impact on them in their formative years.

From the moment Bill Haley sang "Rock around the Clock" in 1954, a whole generation realized they had something that belonged solely to them, for their parents abhorred rock and roll. Rock's advent "was the first inkling white teenagers had that they might be a force to be reckoned with, in numbers alone." Youths found Frank Sinatra's crooning and sentimental ballads such as Patti Page's "How Much Is That Doggie in the Window?" boring and sterile in comparison to the rollicking pianos, blistering guitars, and thundering drums of rock. Elvis Presley gyrated his hips provocatively, radiating sexuality, and warned his female companion not to step on his "Blue Suede Shoes." Little Richard screamed, "A-wop-bob-a-loom-op-a-lop-bam-boom," while pounding the ivories. In the song "School Day," Chuck Berry proclaimed the arrival of rock and expressed hope that it would deliver him from the past. Buddy Holly stuttered "My puh-Peggy Sue" to a booming beat. The new sounds delighted teenagers and children.[34]

Rock represented something outside the white middle-class mainstream, something new, raw, loud, exciting, and sexual (*rock and roll* was a euphemism coined by bluesmen for the motions made in bed during intercourse). Moreover, it appealed to the young because it was written and performed by artists who spoke to their concerns—dating, cars, sex, school, dancing, and clothing. It also symbolized a protest against the adult world, adult values, and adult music.

Individuals react differently to various stimuli. Hippies would come to see rock as a medium for spreading messages or good vibes, but there was more to it than that. They ascribed to it great power and potential (in the sixties, hippies talked frequently of rock's revolutionary qualities). The new sounds marked the beginning of the sixties era for many. The counterculture maintained that rock and roll, from its inception, possessed the power to liberate body and soul and promote a sense of community. Rubin expressed these sentiments in 1970, writing, "Elvis Presley ripped off Ike Eisenhower by turning our uptight young awakening bodies around. Hard animal rock energy beat/surged hot through us, the driving rhythm arousing repressed passions. Music to free the spirit. Music to bring us together."[35]

Youths tuned into crackling, distant radio stations at the far end of the dial late at night to hear distinctively black urban and rural sounds, and at a time when racism and segregation flourished, white youth listening to black music or cavorting with blacks and black culture smacked of rebellion. Unlike structured and formal Western styles, the dancing associated with rock was physical, emotional, and sexual. Rock's roots in African rhythms alarmed the guardians of morality, the defenders of segregation, and champions of America's Anglo-Saxon heritage. White radio station owners and white audiences often referred to early rock as "nigger music." Adult outrage and consternation made rock and roll all the more enticing to youth. A 1956 editorial in *Music Journal* contended that teenagers were "definitely influenced in their lawlessness by this throwback to jungle rhythms. Either it actually stirs them to orgies of sex and violence (as its model did for the savages themselves), or they use it as an excuse for the removal of all inhibitions and the complete disregard of the conventions of decency." The Citizens' Council of Greater New Orleans, a white supremacist organization, expressed similar views, circulating flyers that read: "DON'T BUY NEGRO RECORDS. . . . The screaming, idiotic words, and savage music of these records are undermining the morals of our white youth in America."[36] But young whites' embrace of rock was not benign and without racial implications. Grace Elizabeth Hale has argued convincingly that white middle-class kids in the 1950s "learned that rebellion sounded black." White fascination with rock, Hale contends, had its roots in nineteenth-century minstrelsy, a medium through which white fans believed that white men in black-face accurately represented African American culture. Early blues artist Ma Rainey, in fact, learned how to employ theatricality and illusion from minstrelsy.[37]

When young whites fell in love with rock—and the rebellion it embodied—"they gave new life to old minstrel definitions of blackness as freedom from social constraints." Whites failed to discern the theatricality of the performance. Teens did not understand black music as an autonomous black individual resisting societal repression. They sensed in the sounds something inherently and authentically black—a form of black transcendence—and used it to enable their own transformations. The "blackness" of rock became the perfect vehicle to express rebellion and demarcate their differences from their parents and their middle-class environments. White teens seeking psychic liberation reinvented themselves by identifying with black music, which they associated with rootedness and autonomy. Yet they simultaneously desired to maintain the social privileges that whiteness provided. And whites acknowledged no contradiction because they could have it both ways—one foot outside and one foot inside white life. Rock and roll created "a whole lot of white Negroes."[38]

Rock music raised concerns among adults and so did unruly juveniles. "Greasers" wore pegged pants, sported "duck's ass" haircuts, guzzled beer, blasted "race records," and had sex with their "loose" girlfriends. They inherited the language of black hipsters, criminals, and the Beats— *dig, cool, chick, pusher,* and *reefer*—words that wound up in the hippies' linguistic repertoire. Juvies modeled themselves on James Dean in *Rebel without a Cause* and Marlon Brando in *The Wild One*: "What are you rebelling against, Johnny?" "Whadda ya got?" Kids rioted, caught up in a rock and roll frenzy while viewing *Blackboard Jungle*. Teen gangs clashed in city streets; other delinquents "boosted" cars and went on joyrides. The FBI reported that police arrested teens for half of all murders, battery, and sexual assaults, and half of all burglaries and robberies. Social guardians blamed the problem on comic books and violent films.

Some are never satisfied with the world they have inherited, and alienated youths moved from subculture to subculture as they grew older. Some rebels of the fifties became rebels in the sixties. "We knew what James Dean was into in the movie because we felt the same way, and we had just as much trouble as he did trying to articulate what it was we felt," wrote John Sinclair, founder of the White Panther Party. "Our parents wanted us to 'straighten up' and go back to the way things were in their day . . . and we knew that was impossible." Abbie Hoffman hung around pool halls with a juvenile delinquent gang after getting thrown out of school.

Likewise, Peter Berg roved the streets of Miami with a violent group of "hillbilly" outcasts as an adolescent.[39]

The Beats represented dissent better than all others. Most knew little to nothing of them. That changed on October 7, 1955, at San Francisco's Six Gallery, when Allen Ginsberg unleashed his rage with the poem *Howl*, taking aim at America's prisons, military, bombs, suburbs, Congress, and sexual stuffiness, declaring it all, "Moloch! Solitude! Filth! Ugliness!"[40] Like Ginsberg, Gregory Corso, Gary Snyder, Robert Duncan, Lawrence Ferlinghetti, William Burroughs, and Jack Kerouac detested 1950s Cold War culture, its complacency, sexual repression, and the Silent Generation. They questioned authority and the dominant religion—McCarthyites, the CIA, Christianity. The Beats established communities in Greenwich Village in New York, the North Beach district of San Francisco, and in Denver, Boston, New Orleans, Berkeley, and Philadelphia. They preferred dark clothing, grew beards and goatees, valued spontaneity, reveled in the be-bop jazz of Charlie "Bird" Parker, crossed the country in flatbed pickups and Cadillacs, mingled in cities with blacks and the poor with whom they associated authenticity, smoked marijuana, popped pills, and swilled booze. Sexually permissive, they engaged in orgies and indulged in interracial and homosexual relationships. They also found inspiration in Hinduism and Buddhism. And they disliked everything conventional, including mainstream entertainment and boring occupations.

Like the Beats, social philosophers and intellectuals assailed the ills of modernity. In his 1964 book, *One-Dimensional Man*, Herbert Marcuse urged his readers to practice the "Great Refusal," to resist being dominated and manipulated by consumerism, abundance, and technology. Earlier, he had published *Eros and Civilization*. In this 1955 work, Marcuse combined Marx and Freud to argue that industrialized society, concerned with maintaining the Protestant work ethic, had become totalitarian, forcing unnecessary sexual repression on its people. Upon the elimination of this repression, Eros would be freed, resulting in man's return to a state of "polymorphous perversity." Norman O. Brown, too, wanted to liberate Eros. *Life against Death*, published in 1959, argued that man repressed his animal instincts. Brown also called for "polymorphous perversity," which entailed pansexualism and a rejection of Western civilization's sexual conduct—straight, monogamous, genital intercourse. He also wrote about discovering the unconscious, creating the "Dionysian Ego," where one could discover unlimited love and pleasure. Sociologist Paul Goodman offered scathing critiques of society as well. His *Growing Up Absurd*, published in 1961, focused on alienated youngsters, teenagers, and juveniles, who came of age in a meaningless society with no legitimate models to follow, no satisfying roles to look forward to. Goodman contended that the corporate, technocratic, consumer culture produced pervasive spiritual emptiness.

Novels contained characters who dented the status quo. Holden Caulfield exemplified alienated youths, railing against adults and their "phoniness" in J. D. Salinger's 1951 novel, *Catcher in the Rye*. Joseph Heller's 1961 book *Catch-22* derided the government, military, patriotism, and the madness of war. The following year, Ken Kesey's *One Flew over the Cuckoo's Nest* appeared. In this novel, wisecracking, free-spirited, R. P. McMurphy leads his fellow mental hospital patients against the authoritarian head of the ward, Nurse Ratched. The novel's message: "People need to get back in touch with their world, to open doors of perception, to enjoy spontaneous sensuous experience and resist . . . manipulative forces." In entertainment, black humorists Lenny Bruce and Mort Sahl assaulted mainstream values and exposed cultural hypocrisy, while *Mad* magazine mocked advertising, movies, television shows, suburbia, and the military.[41]

Gauging the impact of these fractures in the consensus presents a formidable task. To be sure, philosophers and novelists inspired some budding flower children who shared and acted out their ideas, but others did not know of Bruce or read much. Even when they did pick up a book or magazine, the printed page did not possess the power to alter their frame of mind, induce them to smoke marijuana, grow their hair long, join a commune, or journey to a hippie enclave. When a young woman was asked if she had traveled to Haight-Ashbury because of something she read, she answered no: "I never read anything that made me become this way or that way." Books likely confirmed for the alienated what they already knew—war was evil and destructive, they were sexually repressed, society was rife with hypocrisy, and they were not free. "Paul Goodman . . . and all other social scientists concerned with the alienation of youth . . . can only write books notionally about what each of us in the Pepsi Generation knows experientially," explained a Boston draft resister.[42]

The Beats did have significant influence on some who became cultural dissidents. Dylan read *Howl* and Ferlinghetti's *Coney Island of the Mind* before departing the University of Minnesota in 1961 to live in Greenwich Village. As a young poet and artist, Jim Morrison of the Doors found *On the Road* fascinating. John Sinclair read Ginsberg in college. The Beats—Neal Cassady in particular—had a major impact on Kesey's personality and writing. Ron Thelin, Steve Levine, Peter Berg, and Peter Coyote all read Beat literature and a few founders of underground newspapers had Beat associations. All these individuals had one thing in common: they were born before and during World War II, and therefore were impressionable adolescents or adults at the apogee of the Beat renaissance. Many had been Beats in the mid-fifties or immersed in the Beat scene as it waned in the early sixties. A few years later, they became hippies. Ginsberg, Kerouac, and Burroughs had helped youth to make sense of the insanity that surrounded them.[43]

But the Beats influenced the baby boomers—who made up the majority of the counterculture—to a lesser degree. After all, the oldest of the generation were only nine when Ginsberg read *Howl* at Six Gallery and eleven when Kerouac published *On the Road*, hardly an age at which they could read, dissect, and comprehend these sophisticated works. Most probably read Kerouac and Ginsberg years after their books first appeared in print, when they were in the process of dropping out, or after they had already done so. But others were never avid readers. In an interview with the Detroit underground the *Fifth Estate*, Ginsberg appraised the power of his poetry. Reading, he felt, had declined. If people paid attention to poetry at all, Ginsberg maintained, they listened to it through music, the songs of the Beatles and Dylan in particular. He also flatly denied that his poetry created "social awareness."[44]

This is not to argue that the Beats had no effect on baby boomers. They foreshadowed the counterculture with their spontaneous, liberated, hedonistic lifestyles, their interest in alternative spiritualties like Zen Buddhism and Hinduism, and their love of intimate communities. Most hippies were aware that the Beats had preceded them, noting the similarities in how they had attacked the consensus, conformity, and repressiveness of Cold War society. Yet there are important distinctions to be made between the two phenomena, as their characteristics differed. "Beat was dark, silent, moody, lonely, sad—and its music was jazz," a researcher observed, while "hippie is bright, vivacious, ecstatic, crowd-loving, joyful—and its music is rock. Beat was the *Lonely Crowd*; hippie, the crowd that tired of being lonely." Underground journalists recognized these differences, rightfully calling *On the Road* the "bible" for the Beats, while neglecting to assess its meaning for the "flower generation," or the "hopeful generation." Some hippies refused to acknowledge any connection with the Beats: "They were intellectual," argued Louis Rapoport. "They were uptight as hell— so they smoked pot, big deal!—pot's like a cigarette. So you get high. The beats were just another bohemian thing. And this isn't."[45]

The Beats' influence on the counterculture has been overestimated and overemphasized. The Beats undoubtedly anticipated the hippie cultural revolt—but this fact alone does not prove that they paved the way for, or gave rise to the counterculture. The Beats never numbered more than a few thousand and a mere 150 wrote anything. By 1961 they had been broken up and scattered in San Francisco, the victims of police harassment. Their neighborhood in North Beach became a tourist trap. In 1965, latter-day Beats looked down on "imitation bohemians"—"hippie" meant "junior grade hipster." Most Beats disregarded the hippies because the new counterculturalists wasted time getting high and having fun. When Ginsberg and Timothy Leary tried to get Kerouac to take psilocybin, he refused it. Kerouac continued to drink alcohol, shout, and smoke cigarettes. Leary later concluded that Kerouac was "an old-style Bohemian without a hippie bone in his body."[46]

The counterculture functioned full-throttle under its own power, without the assistance of Beats as sages or guideposts. Ginsberg himself dismissed the idea that he occupied "a special position" within the movement as "a lot of crap." The counterculture's nature militated against the rise of prominent leaders. By the late sixties, it was decentralized and widely dispersed throughout the country, and no hierarchy or epicenter existed from which to coordinate and direct it. Furthermore, anarchistic impulses drove the counterculture. Hippies generally distrusted would-be mentors, centralized authority, large structured organizations, and mass political movements. "Be your own leader," a Digger advised, and longhairs agreed, "doing their own thing" without regard to what others did.[47]

THE ARMS RACE, JIM CROW, MULTIVERSITY, AND FREE SPEECH

Although rock and rollers, juveniles, Beats, and dissident writers had challenged the consensus, they failed to substantially alter it. When the sixties dawned, The Silent Generation remained silent and the vast majority of young adults prepared for a traditional life. Men expected to be providers. Women expected to be homemakers. Few had the temerity to question the status quo. This changed when youths got excited about the possibility of transforming their country and the world. The college population tripled from 1960 to 1972, from three to ten million, and the first of the massive baby boom generation arrived at universities in 1964. The youth stratum of society now possessed the potential to become a major social and political force.

The immediate postwar era placed future freaks on an alienated path, and alienation accelerated rapidly in the early sixties. Hippies did not come of age in a vacuum, isolated from the issues that engaged their political, activist counterparts. Jim Crow and racism, proliferation of nuclear weapons, military-industrial complex, and bloated and bureaucratized multiversities, alarmed, angered, discouraged, and disillusioned later longhairs. Hippies and New Leftists shared similar grievances; their reactions to these issues, however, eventually diverged—and sharply.

Some who became hippies engaged in New Left activism before they had epiphanies: protest accomplished little. Hip entrepreneur Chet Helms participated in civil rights activism and joined Students for Direct Action (SDA) at the University of Texas before realizing that "confrontational demonstrations were fruitless." Likewise, Rock Scully, manager of the Grateful Dead, spent two years with the Student Nonviolent Coordinating Committee (SNCC) and served jail time prior to deciding that he "served no real purpose" in demonstrations. San Francisco Mime Troupe member and founding Digger Peter Coyote protested the arms race. He and his friends stopped attending classes, fearing the end of the world during the Cuban missile crisis. He traveled to Washington and picketed the White House. President Kennedy invited Coyote and others in for a meeting after learning of the demonstration. Once inside, they met the president's special assistant for national security affairs, McGeorge Bundy.

"Bundy looked like a chameleon. His eyes were the coldest, most analytical I had ever seen," Coyote remembered. The brief encounter impacted him greatly, hastening a change in his approach to world issues. Coyote thought to himself, "Nothing I say is going to change his [Bundy's] mind. Neither am I going to affect anything by picketing in the streets and carrying a sign. . . . That's when I began to think about culture as opposed to politics." For Coyote and those who became hippies, the intractable systems of power remained unresponsive to democratic forms and tactics. Change would have to come through different means.[48]

Some former student radicals joined hippiedom because they believed in the power of dope revolution. For these burned-out politicos, the dope culture was every bit as political as demonstrations and portended a new movement that could effectively hasten social change. "They're saying it's just as much a political act to turn on as it is to sit in," explained a head, referring to his postpolitical friends and acquaintances. "They're saying we're at the beginning of a new mass movement, a new phase in society, the drug society."[49]

Much of later longhairs' alienation stemmed from the inimical treatment of African Americans in the form of Jim Crow laws and culture. Institutions were segregated—schools, hospitals, prisons, homes for the mentally disabled and blind—and so were public facilities—restaurants, theaters, buses, drinking fountains, zoos, beaches, swimming pools, and ballparks. Even in death, equality escaped blacks as they buried their loved ones in segregated cemeteries. They possessed little to no political power; white Southerners deprived blacks of the vote, instituting literacy tests, good character clauses, and poll taxes. In the South, most whites believed, unquestionably, that "niggers" stank, and were inferior, lazy, and stupid. African Americans were also the victims of extreme acts of brutality. Between 1889 and 1946 white mobs lynched almost four thousand men, women, and children. Blacks fared little better in the North, where de facto segregation was prevalent and blacks had to send their children to separate and underfunded schools. Whites fled the cities for the suburbs as blacks migrated North. Moreover, destitution plagued the African American community. Over 50 percent of two-parent and one-parent black households lived below the poverty line.[50]

Racism angered the young, disturbing their egalitarian sensibilities. The "Land of the Free" had disenfranchised African Americans, instituting near-slavery in the form of Jim Crow. Many whites disagreed with Thomas Jefferson's eminent phrase in the Declaration of Independence: "We hold these truths to be self-evident, that all men are created equal." America failed to live up to the ideals established in its founding documents, which the young had been taught to revere and respect. Soon-to-be counterculturalists understood that blacks faced formidable obstacles to full participation and equality in American life, and that the white majority was responsible. "Most negroes are worse off today than they were in 1960," asserted the *Fifth Estate* in 1967. "More negroes live in segregated housing. More negro children attend segregated schools. A higher percentage are unemployed. . . . The reason is that white people control everything in this society. They do so for their own benefit." Future freaks lamented the slow pace of change in racial attitudes and indifference to black suffering. "This is a country with so little compassion for its black people that police dogs and Ku Klux Klan beatings . . . are needed to 'shock' it into doing something," the *Berkeley Barb* editorialized. "Don't they understand that most black parents want the same things for their children that white parents want for theirs—clean clothes; good housing; good food; a good education; a good job." Blacks needed to have their humanity and needs recognized. The segregated bathrooms and drinking fountains that Grateful Dead guitarist Jerry Garcia witnessed while passing through the South in the summer of 1964 stunned and overwhelmed him. So did the intolerance and hostility of southerners. A cautious Garcia cut his hair and shaved his goatee. Locals made comments about the California license plates on the vehicle.[51]

Activist African Americans moved toward greater equality with the advent of the civil rights movement. It began with the Montgomery bus boycott in December 1955, and gained momentum when young activists, tired of their apathetic elders, participated in direct action and civil disobedience protests with SNCC and the Congress of Racial Equality (CORE). Activists made considerable progress with the Greensboro sit-ins in 1960, Freedom Rides in 1961, and voter registration work in the Deep South. Martin Luther King Jr.'s Southern Christian Leadership

Conference (SCLC) remained active, initiating and leading the Birmingham Campaign in 1963, where Eugene "Bull" Connor's police forces attacked demonstrators with German shepherds and high-pressure fire hoses. King also led the March on Washington the same year, and a trek from Selma to Montgomery, Alabama, in 1965. President Lyndon Johnson signed the Civil Rights Act of 1964 and the Voting Rights Act of 1965. These monumental laws had come at great cost, however, as racist mobs beat, knifed, bombed, assassinated, and murdered activists, movement leaders, and innocent children. White brutality deeply disturbed soon-to-be hippies. When Peter Berg participated in a sit-in at a department store in Richmond, he watched German shepherds attack and rip the clothes from young black women.[52]

Later longhairs participated in the struggle for black equality. Dylan befriended members of SNCC, sang for black farmers outside Greenwood, Mississippi, and performed at the March on Washington. Jefferson Poland, founder of the Sexual Freedom League, registered black voters in Louisiana, and Barry Melton of Country Joe and the Fish joined CORE as a volunteer. Art Kunkin, founder of the *Los Angeles Free Press*, had also been a member of CORE in the late forties. In the summer of 1965, Hoffman went to Mississippi to agitate for civil rights.[53]

The specter of nuclear annihilation—the end of days—horrified youth. The superpowers would eventually accumulate enough nuclear weapons to destroy the world several times over. As children and young adults, the sixties generation participated in "duck-and-cover" drills, cowering under their desks, while others watched their parents construct bomb shelters. Not every citizen, however, feared the use of weapons of mass destruction. To the contrary, many favored it. A 1949 Gallup poll indicated that 70 percent of Americans opposed the government's commitment to "no first use" of nuclear weapons. Another 1951 poll revealed that over half favored dropping atom bombs on Korea. In 1954, Richard Nixon, John Foster Dulles, and Admiral Arthur W. Radford advocated striking the Vietminh with three nuclear bombs during the siege at Dien Bien Phu.[54]

Future counterculturalists protested the proliferation of nuclear weapons. Stew Albert, a Yippie (member of the Youth International Party) and founder of People's Park, attended a "Ban the Bomb" rally at Madison Square Garden. Huw "Piper" Williams, founder of the commune Tolstoy

Farm, was a member of the Committee for Nonviolent Action (CNVA). *Berkeley Barb* editor Max Scherr organized picketing of the Atomic Energy Commission. Rubin distributed flyers that protested the arms race. East Village counterculturalist Ed Sanders protested by climbing aboard a Polaris submarine. "No matter how much of a doper, a weirdo, a wild poet," he remembered, "you could get a sense of righteous indignation and demand that they stop testing in the atmosphere—and then, some people would say, ban all weapons."[55]

The Cuban missile crisis exacerbated fear and anxiety. The United States and Soviet Union had come to the brink of a nuclear arms exchange before narrowly averting disaster. Students and others voiced their concerns. "We are living in an age of insanity. Nothing is immune to the sickness. Party, pulpit and press, far from being above the plague, are participants in its spread," wrote a student at the University of Wisconsin. The extermination of millions had become "acceptable as television, Coca-Cola and tranquilizers." The writer lamented that "Preservation of civilization has become equated with destruction, as men face reality by burrowing into the earth. Life has become death. Peace means war. Defense means retaliation." The episode provoked young people to contemplate alternatives and new possibilities. "We were pretty depressed the night of the Cuban Missile Crisis and stayed up the whole night talking, preparing to die in a nuclear holocaust before dawn," remembered communard John Curl. "If we were still alive in the morning, if the world was still here, we would go away to some isolated place and somehow live there quietly and peacefully. We all felt like giving up on this society. It was too violent and corrupt, too involved with domination and competition." Curl and others founded Drop City in Colorado, which indeed was isolated. And they did live quietly and peacefully for several years. Anxiety over a potential apocalypse continued into the late sixties. "Assuming that human nature is not going to change overnight, how long can we stand on the brink of all-out nuclear war without falling in? Five years? Ten years?" a Californian wondered.[56]

Folk singers addressed the social issues that concerned youth such as racism, Jim Crow, and growing nuclear arsenals. Folk music had been popular during the Depression among unionists, socialists, and communists, but it became marginalized after McCarthyites attacked its supposedly subversive social and political commentary. The early sixties witnessed a folk music revival. College students crowded into coffee-houses to talk politics and to hear folkies sing. Folkniks considered their music authentic, meaningful, and honest. Phil Ochs, Joan Baez, Ramblin' Jack Elliott, Judy Collins, the Chad Mitchell and Kingston Trios, the Brothers Four, the Freedom Singers, Highwaymen, and Tom Paxton became popular and folkniks rediscovered veteran artists Woody Guthrie, Pete Seeger, and the Weavers. Many folkniks gravitated toward the counterculture after the folk craze fizzled. Iconic rock bands and artists the Byrds, the Grateful Dead, Quicksilver Messenger Service, Country Joe and the Fish, Jefferson Airplane, Janis Joplin, and Bob Dylan emerged from the folk tradition.

The largest indication of student unrest occurred at the University of California, Berkeley, in the fall of 1964. The Free Speech Movement (FSM) began when the dean issued a proclamation banning the dissemination of political material on the twenty-six-foot sidewalk off of Sproul Plaza that led to the entrance of campus. Administrators likely instituted the ban because radicals and beatniks lingered around the area. Inspired by the nonviolent civil disobedience tactics of the civil rights movement, demonstrations followed for nearly four months. Students occupied the administration building, held rallies attracting thousands, and gave rousing speeches. Campus activity grinded to a halt, and police made almost eight hundred arrests before administrators and students resolved the conflict.

The movement certainly pertained to free speech, but something more serious unsettled the demonstrators: they were becoming part of a "machine." Inquiring students discovered passages in president Clark Kerr's "The Uses of the University," and believed they had deciphered its real significance. Soon Berkeley would be similar to other business enterprises, advancing and entrenching the Cold War, space race, and the status quo. Faculty and administrators acted as managers, students the managed. The multiversity was the "New Slavery," a "knowledge factory" where students had become "a number on a set of file cards that go through an IBM machine." FSM leader Mario Savio indicted the university for using students as "raw materials" and insisted that they resist:

There's a time when the operation of the machine becomes so odious, makes you so sick at heart, that you can't take part, you can't even tacitly take part. And you've got to put your body upon the gears and upon the wheels, upon the levers, upon all the apparatus, and you've got to make it stop. And you've got to indicate to the people who run it, the people who own it, that unless you're free, the machine will be prevented from working at all.

As individuals, students demanded that administrators respect their humanity. A striker carried a placard that expressed this sentiment well: "I Am a UC Student: Do Not Fold, Spindle, or Mutilate."[57]

Some students involved in the FSM partook in the same activities and held the same worldview as the nascent counterculture. FSM involved social dropouts, those who usually hung around campus and took a class from time to time. Journalist Hunter S. Thompson described the social radicals on the periphery of campus:

> Social radicals tend to be "arty." Their gigs are poetry and folk music, rather than politics, although many are fervently committed to the civil rights movement. Their political bent is Left, but their real interests are writing, painting, good sex, good sounds and free marijuana. The realities of politics put them off, although they don't mind lending their talents to a demonstration here and there, or even getting arrested for a good cause.

The night that students occupied Sproul Hall, some smoked marijuana and made love on the roof. Half the members of the FSM steering committee had used dope. A woman who had participated in civil rights, joined the New Left, and later dabbled in hippie activity, saw FSM as one of the "birthplaces" of the counterculture: "FSM was communal; it was theater and politics; it was play and work. Politics and lifestyle interacted, each creating a context for the other." Some FSM activists became integrated into the counterculture. In October 1965, pop music critic Ralph Gleason, driving back from the dancehall concert "A Tribute to Dr. Strange," noticed lines of longhairs in their Volkswagens plastered with FSM and SNCC bumper stickers.[58]

Instead of grappling with university bureaucrats, becoming a cog in the social machine, some students started dropping out of school and out of the mainstream, liberating themselves from the issues harassing others.

"A lot of students I know are thinking of becoming nonstudents," an ex-student told a journalist. "That student routine is a drag," commented another. "Until I quit the grind I didn't realize how many groovy things there are to do around Berkeley: concerts, films, good speakers, parties, pot, politics, women—I can't think of a better way to live, can you?"[59]

The counterculture believed it had found a better way. Beginning in 1965, the alienated would attempt to create a new culture, a new society—even a new civilization. Other hippies had more modest aims: living a better, simpler, happier life. Cold War America would give birth to a counterculture that opposed it in every respect, valuing libertarianism over authoritarianism, liberation over repression, egalitarianism over inequality, cooperation over competition, the bizarre over the conventional, the precarious over the secure, community over isolation, love over hate, peace over war, life over death.

As the last days of 1964 neared, there were few indications of what was to come. Proto-hippie Karl Franzoni went by the name Captain Fuck, wore a goatee, red tights, a cape with an F emblazoned on it, and lived with his friends Vitautus Alphonsus Paulekas, Zsou, and thirty-five-member free-form dance troupe The Freaks in a communal house in Hollywood. Charlie Brown Artman dressed like an American Indian years before it became fashionable. He built a tipi in Berkeley where he and friends sat around a fire smoking peyote, chanting prayers, and making music with drums and rattles. New York's Holy Modal Rounders put the word *psychedelic* on a record for the first time in their rendition of "Hesitation Blues."[60]

By 1964, then, the seeds were being planted. The next summer, the counterculture began to bloom. "Emerging from the bleak spiritual graveyard of the 50s and early 60s, we have formed a movement that embraces life and seeks enlightenment and joy for all our brothers and sisters," proclaimed an Arizona hippie. Made up of youth who had endured the alienating effects of Cold War America, the counterculture became ever larger with the onset of a war in Southeast Asia.[61]

SOMETHING HAPPENING

THE EMERGENCE OF THE
COUNTERCULTURE, 1965 TO 1967

2

Discussing Vietnam, San Francisco poet Lenore Kandel told a researcher, "There's war. . . . And if you don't want it to happen, you've got to have another direction. If you don't want the world you're pushed into, you have to find another world."[1] Hippies endeavored to create "another world" in their counterculture. Several significant characteristics, developments, and themes characterized the counterculture from 1965 to 1967. First, it consisted primarily of cultural dissidents. Differences between hippiedom and the New Left in philosophy and style became apparent. Second, alienated by harassment, campus paternalism, and bureaucracy—and especially the brutal war in Vietnam—the counterculture burgeoned on the coasts, and later in the heartland. Formidable hippie communities emerged in New York, Los Angeles, San Francisco, and Seattle. By the fall of 1966, a counterculture enclave had appeared in Austin, Madison, and Detroit as well. Third, hippie values materialized. Longhairs lived for the moment and valued spontaneity and taking chances. While an alarmist press publicized its concerns about growing drug use—marijuana, LSD, and amphetamines—on the nation's campuses, cultural activists and students struggled to promote sexual liberation and the eradication of repressive laws. Fourth, hippies founded the first countercultural communes, Drop City in Colorado and Hog Farm in California among them. Fifth, to counter the biases of the establishment and mainstream media, underground newspapers emerged to inform and unite rebellious young people. Finally, the counterculture made itself visible. What began as "happenings" and "acid tests" in 1965 progressed swiftly into dancehall concerts and "be-ins" by 1966.

VIETNAM, THE DRAFT, CAMPUS PATERNALISM, AND HARASSMENT

No single factor proved more alienating for later longhairs than America's involvement in the Vietnam War. Not only did the war kill and maim millions of Vietnamese but the draft potentially threatened the lives of youth opposed to the war and military service for myriad reasons. As students entered the nation's universities rules and regulations governing their behavior in loco parentis compounded existing alienation. Many resisted, while others dropped out of college to augment hippiedom's growing numbers. Meanwhile, police and school authorities harassed rebellious youth for wearing their hair long, opposing the draft, and loitering around their favorite establishments. The counterculture's ranks swelled exponentially as a result.

In 1965 President Lyndon Johnson committed the first combat troops to Vietnam, but the nation's entanglement there started at the end of World War II, when Communist leader Ho Chi Minh expelled occupying Japanese forces with the aid of the American intelligence agency the Office of Strategic Services. Committed to thwarting the incursion of communism into Southeast Asia and to prevent the toppling of noncommunist nations like "dominoes," America helped France regain and maintain its colonial position in Indochina in return for its support as a bulwark against communist encroachment into Europe. Between 1945 and 1954 the United States provided three-quarters of the funding for France's war against the communist Vietminh. After France's disastrous defeat at Dien Bien Phu in 1954, Vietnam was divided along the 17th parallel with Ho Chi Minh exercising power in the North and fiercely anti-Communist Ngo Dinh Diem at the head of the government in the South. Firmly committed to protecting the South Vietnamese regime, President Eisenhower dispatched military "advisors" to Vietnam. By the time of John F. Kennedy's assassination in November 1963, over sixteen thousand troops were stationed there. In the summer of 1964 North Vietnamese torpedo boats supposedly attacked two American destroyers. This encounter led to the Gulf of Tonkin Resolution, which authorized President Johnson to take "all necessary measures to repel any armed attacks against the forces of the United States and to prevent further aggression." Johnson escalated the war, putting 184,300 troops "in-country" by the end of 1965. In 1968, that number had leaped to over half a million.[2]

Legions of youth hated the war, characterizing it as "beyond brutality," an "obscenity," an "atrocity," and "pure madness," resulting in countless "incinerated, gutted, bayoneted and bombed human bodies." The United States dropped napalm, poisonous gas, and fragmentation bombs on Vietnamese men, women, and children—people Washington officials claimed to be protecting. By 1967 the United States had unleashed more bombs on Vietnam than it had in all theaters during World War II. Antiwar youth found the suffering, killing, and death on both sides unconscionable.[3]

The war's detractors did not constitute a monolith, as they offered multiple and diverse justifications for their opposition. Many simply opposed war on principle, especially pacifists. Others thought the war unjust, waged primarily to spread America's sphere of influence in Southeast Asia where it had no rightful place. Young Americans died for a "delusion." They did not fight for freedom, the war's foes asserted, but aided an "immoral" and "imperialist" war, propping up a corrupt and illegitimate South Vietnamese government in Saigon.

Many opposed the war on pragmatic grounds: preserving an independent, noncommunist South Vietnam had no bearing on US citizens or world security. Contrary to the arguments of Harry S. Truman and others, Americans would not have to fight communists in New Orleans and Chicago even if the nation refrained from fighting them overseas. The government, asserted an East Lansing, Michigan, underground, had "lied to the American people in a calculated and terrible way to convince us that we must kill these people to protect us from some never-defined, never-proven, never-realized menace, the international communist conspiracy." Those who became hippies found official government explanations, theories, and documents related to the Cold War and communist threat unpersuasive if not completely fabricated.[4]

America's enmeshment in Vietnam further alienated those who had experienced the shocks of the 1950s and early 1960s, but the war alone, alienating baby boomers coming of age in the mid-to-late sixties, produced new counterculturalists, hundreds of thousands, perhaps millions. Indeed, in a letter to an underground newspaper, an insightful writer argued, "There probably would be no Haight-Ashbury without the war." Youths who under other circumstances might not have joined the counterculture, found themselves resisting the dominant society. "From Vietnam, I learned to despise my countrymen, my government, and the entire English-speaking world, with its history of genocide and international conquest. I was a normal kid," wrote cofounder of the Liberation News Service (LNS) and back-to-the-land communard Raymond Mungo.[5]

The draft also alienated students—especially men—who opposed a government that coerced young men to commit violence and to die in an abominable, unnecessary—and, after the Tet Offensive in 1968—seemingly endless war. Undergraduate students (and graduate students until the summer of 1968) could avoid conscription with a deferment, but lived in fear of losing that deferment should they fail to maintain an adequate grade point average. Men who resisted induction or burned their draft cards faced incarceration. Many applied for conscientious objector status, some went to jail, while perhaps a hundred thousand made their way over the Canadian border. Draft opponents pilloried the director of the Selective Service System. "General Hershey wants you to drop napalm on Vietnamese children, distribute candy bars and liberate the entire subcontinent back to the Stone Age," wrote a Seattle youth. Many resisted military service because it violated their ideals and value systems. A California draft resister declared, "[I] shall not . . . submit my person nor my intellect to any organization (in this case the United States Armed Forces) which deals in the subversion of love and life and which teaches death and hate above understanding."[6]

Vietnam and the draft bred disillusionment, as did rules and regulations that governed students' lives in loco parentis. Universities and colleges mandated codes of conduct in an effort to usher the young into responsible adulthood. Many found the university repressive, a place where they had no rights. Rules dictated where one ate, slept, and lived, and what one wore. Guidelines attempted to prevent students from going to bed together. A significant portion of the student handbook at the University of Michigan outlined women's hours and curfews. Men who visited women's dorms were required to keep three of four limbs on the floor at all times to comply with the rules. Underage drinking, smoking marijuana, curfew violations, inappropriate contact with the opposite sex, a traffic ticket, even throwing an errant snowball might result in suspension or expulsion. Offenders often had no right to appeal. Students contested campus paternalism, calling universities "institutions of repression." Student newspapers referred to dorms for female students as "detention homes." The Princeton student newspaper argued, "The University has absolutely no moral right to regulate the private morality of its students." "In loco parentis is suffering from rigor mortis," *Time* reported in the fall of 1966. "On almost every campus, students are either attacking in loco parentis—the notion that a college can govern their drinking, sleeping, and partying—or happily celebrating its death."[7]

Like campus paternalism, university bureaucracies and curriculums frustrated students. The 1960s witnessed the unprecedented growth of the multiversity. Its antecedents dated back to World War II when the government and institutions of scientific knowledge colluded to produce the Manhattan Project's atom bomb. This partnership continued into the Cold War. The military and manufacturers required trained experts to develop new technologies and consumer products and the university became increasingly important to these centers of power. The science faculties at major universities such as Stanford and Massachusetts Institute of Technology came to rely on military funding. In 1946 *Time* magazine wondered, "Is the military about to take over U.S. science lock, stock, and barrel, calling the tune for U.S. universities and signing up the best scientists for work fundamentally aimed at military results?" Then in 1957 the Soviets launched Sputnik, igniting the space race. Public dollars poured into higher education. Total spending on universities spiraled from over $740 million in 1945 to nearly $7 billion in 1965. The massive baby boom generation also fueled expansion. From 1963 to 1973, college enrollments doubled, from 4.7 to 9.6 million. Annual growth rates quadrupled. In the 1940s not a single university registered more than fifteen thousand students. By the 1960s fifty universities enrolled thirty thousand or more. The "megaversity" subjected students to huge bureaucracies, computerized student records, and impersonal televised lectures designed to improve educational efficiency.⁸

The students who eventually dropped out of the mainstream perceived universities as "sick," remote-feeling "factories" where they constituted mere numbers, herded "from class to class like cattle." Many undergraduates had disliked high school but continued on to university anyway, going through the motions, doing what their parents expected of them. Eugene Bernofsky, cofounder of the first rural hippie commune, Drop City, recalled his experience at Erasmus High: "It seemed as if youth, when not chained to the walls of the classrooms, were dragging chains with them down the hallways. The adults, by insisting on quiet and regiment, seemed like prison wardens." Bernofsky believed that "college was just a glorified extension of high school." He and others felt that the education system imposed prisonlike conditions that precluded personal and creative growth. In university and underground newspapers, students complained about irrelevant course curricula and "class standings . . . evaluated test scores and fulfillment of requirements left over from the 19th century." Some found assigned books beyond their comprehension without frequent class meetings, while others argued that instructors failed to appear at office hours, that they had little to no personal contact with professors and other students, and that exams did not accurately test students' knowledge. Faulty told them "what to read, what to write. . . . what's true and what isn't." "Tell the man what he wants to hear or he'll fail your ass out of the course," asserted a sympathetic instructor at California State–Los Angeles, Jerry Farber, in his widely circulated article, "The Student as Nigger." Many had the impression that they endured "programmed boredom," only to obtain a diploma and "a dull, secure job." Jerry Garcia found students' efforts to reform universities "laughable": "Why enter this closed society and make an effort to liberalize it when that's never been its function? Why not just leave it and go somewhere else? Why not act out your fantasies, using the positive side of your nature rather than just struggling? Just turn your back on it and split—it's easy enough to find a place where people will leave you alone."⁹ Many shared Garcia's sentiments, abandoning the university, refusing to grapple with bureaucrats and administrators, joining an environment where they could do whatever they wanted and develop as human beings. College dropouts augmented the counterculture's ranks.

If the war, draft, and a repressive university were not disconcerting enough, the young felt increasingly harassed and intimidated by authorities. The police, FBI, and school administrators executed their duties, but it did not appear that way to the rebellious; cultural and political dissidents felt that the establishmentarians aspired to extinguish their freedom. In Los Angeles, newly enacted ordinances restricted the playing of music on the city's beaches and at public parks. On both coasts, city safety officials teamed with police to oust bohemians and beatniks from housing. In Berkeley, the FBI tailed and interrogated antidraft organizers. Police searched for loiterers and curfew violators to arrest at hip hangouts and businesses denied service to men with longer hair.[10]

Underground newspapers counseled youth on their dealings with law enforcement, emphasizing that their lives possibly hung in the balance. "Your life and future depend on how you handle yourself in your contacts with the police," advised the *Los Angeles Free Press*. "If you handle yourself poorly you will go to jail, be subjugated to police harassments, get beaten up or perhaps even killed. If you handle yourself well, you will be permitted to continue your life as a free citizen." For the hip, the police became instruments of repression; only by following nonsensical and superfluous laws—from their perspective—would they be free from harassment or bodily harm.[11]

At high schools throughout the country, authorities ordered students who wore sandals, boots, short skirts, mustaches, beards, or Beatle cuts to go home until they had more of the "hallmarks of an All-American Girl or boy." A prep school in Omaha even hired a barber for compulsory hair clipping. "A public school. . . . is not a joint or a pad where beatniks gather, drink espresso coffee and substitute offensive behavior and bizarre dress in lieu of brains," stated the assistant attorney general of North Carolina, and his attitude was typical.[12]

Students urged their classmates to question authority rather than remain uncritical, unthinking "machines." "We are told that regulations are merely a part of growing up and are made to be obeyed *without question*. Any inquiring individual must question *this*," expressed a California high school student. "We are destined to go through life like machines, acting but rarely thinking about our actions. . . . Rules are made to be obeyed; but we must always keep in mind . . . they can be changed."[13]

As alienation among the sixties generation skyrocketed, the counterculture bloomed, and so did the underground press. New Leftists and counterculturalists dispensed with the mainstream press and founded papers of their own. Freaks and students picked up copies at head shops, alternative bookstores, poetry readings, art galleries, and light shows. Underground writers sought to provide ample coverage to the avant-garde and bolster radical politics. Underground rags highlighted the perniciousness and injustice of racism, and the immoral, destructive war in Vietnam. Such newssheets aimed to make politicians responsive to the people and touted the rewards that accompanied commitment to important causes. Cultural critic Louis Menand contends that underground newspapers "were one of the most spontaneous and aggressive growths in publishing history." The underground press proved integral to the movement: it provided the intellectual framework, brought people into its ranks, cultivated a sense of community, inspired community building, and urged its members to make greater democratic demands. Underground newspapers likely prodded youths in the conservative hinterlands into the counterculture and movement. John McMillian maintains that the underground press "played a crucial role in helping youths to break away from the complacency and resignation that prevailed in postwar America, in order to build an indigenous, highly stylized protest culture." Indeed, without underground journalists and newssheets, "much of what we associate with the late 1960s youth rebellion . . . might not have been possible."[14]

Max Scherr founded the *Berkeley Barb* in August 1965. It reported on various aspects of the movement: antiwar rallies, New Left activism, civil rights, and alternative lifestyles. Two months later, former artist Walter Bowart established the *East Village Other*. Less politically oriented than the *Barb*, the *Other* featured freaky comic strips and stories on local "happenings," ran sexualized personal ads, included nude photos of "Slum Goddesses," and printed endless articles on marijuana and LSD. In November, the *Fifth Estate* rolled off the press in Detroit; it gave prominence to rock music and the activities of government agencies like the FBI and CIA. The *Paper* in East Lansing followed closely on the *Estate*'s heels in December, covering developments at Michigan State University.[15]

THE EMERGENCE OF COUNTERCULTURE VALUES

Underground newspapers elucidated the values and social philosophy of the counterculture. "Sex, drugs, and rock and roll," usually comes to mind when one reflects on hippies, but their numerous, complex, and widely varying principles cannot be encapsulated in such a cliché and simplistic phrase. To be sure, counterculturalists revered this triad, especially during its nascent period. However, even from the outset, freaks expressed principles beyond the so-called holy trinity, including living for the present, community, and having new lived experiences. Within a couple years, counterculture values would become more abundant, sophisticated, and comprehensive, as hippies articulated perspectives on everything from daily existence to work to religion.

Counterculturalists held values and social philosophies diametrically different from the American majority. They reacted against establishment ethics, deliberately engaging in behavior that ran counter to the mainstream, for they believed they had discovered a new and better way to live. The system valued militancy and war, hippies valued peace; the system sexually repressed society, hippies championed free love; the system attempted to squelch the use of narcotics, hippies smoked dope and dropped acid; the system was clean-shaven, hippies grew beards. The counterculture thus became the "Disloyal Opposition to Establishment culture."[16] While hippies encouraged a culture of love, the behavior of the powers that be—drug busts and efforts to derail rock concerts or prevent the founding of communes—often necessitated confrontation with the establishment.

Hippies embraced community, holding togetherness in high regard. A community of likeminded individuals provided a sense of comfort and familiarity as well as a refuge from majority society. The community ethic also entailed cooperation, eschewing competition, working toward common goals, and building a new culture based on moral precepts. "I love you all, whoever you are. Come, let's work together," wrote a frequenter of the Sunset Strip in Los Angeles. Community also involved care and nurture, and hippies assumed such a value would work to the benefit of everyone. Moreover, community acted as a force for good, countering sinister elements in society. "Things are bad all over, the saying goes, and the only hope is people getting together with other people for the good of all the people," commented John Sinclair in Detroit. "That IS what's happening, and it's the most beautiful thing in the world." The emphasis on community intensified in the late sixties and was applied to every aspect of life. "In this time, in this place, brothers and sisters, we gotta get our shit together!" urged Mungo from a Vermont commune, "we gotta write together, paint together, sleep together, have children together, study together, build together, love together, publish together, play together, make music together, say YES YES YES together!" The new society could only come to fruition through the efforts of the community from the counterculture's perspective. Rock music, festivals, dope use, and, most importantly, communes also fostered a sense of community.[17]

Another central characteristic of the hippie lifestyle and attitude included a preoccupation with the present. The present represented what mattered, the only position on the time-continuum with significant value. "Who cares about tomorrow and yesterday?" Bob Dylan proclaimed, "People don't live there; they live now." Hippies advocated living life to the utmost, experiencing as much as possible at the moment. From their perspective, too many people spent their lives reflecting on the past or planning for the future, "dreaming and scheming instead of DOING." Ringo Starr would often say, "Tomorrow Never Knows," which stressed the importance of living in the now. John Lennon named one of his psychedelic songs after the phrase. Some hippies believed that their project had no precedent and asserted that the past, in effect, was of little consequence. As one commented, "the hippie development is of a totally new order, wherein the past, in a sense, is irrelevant."[18]

Furthermore, the hip valued direct experience. They took chances, threw caution to the wind, and lived life to the fullest, no matter the risks involved. Living was dangerous, "a win or lose game with happiness and personal fulfillment as the stakes." The hip thought that people spent too much time worrying about their material security, letting life slip by. They championed the idea that one should experience, as much as possible, "the joy, love, and pain of living . . . even if he is hurt more in the process."[19]

The sexual ethics of counterculturalists emerged simultaneously with a larger trend in the sixties, the burgeoning "sexual revolution," which was actually "evolutionary" in many respects. A sexual revolution of sorts began in the 1920s, when youths challenged Victorian culture. Decades later, in the forties and fifties, Alfred Kinsey's studies on human sexual behavior exploded the myth of a puritanical America. The "Kinsey Reports" revealed that 50 percent of women and 84 percent of men with high school diplomas had had premarital intercourse. The media became more sexualized as well. Following World War II, the Supreme Court started striking down censorship laws, and in 1953 Hugh Hefner's *Playboy* hit the newsstand, topless women gracing its pages. Three years following its inception, its circulation numbered one million. The straightforward *Playboy* philosophy directed male readers to have many sexual trysts and steer clear of relationships that necessitated settling down. The magazine broke sexual codes regarding monogamy and nudity, and brought sex out into the open. Helen Gurley Brown published *Sex and the Single Girl* in 1962, a book that promoted sexual liberation for women. Brown urged her female readers to heed their biological urges and have intercourse whenever they wanted. And new contraceptive technology carried great implications for the sexual revolution. Approved by the Food and Drug Administration and made available for the first time in 1960, the pill contributed to women's adoption of sexual liberation, as they worried less about getting pregnant. Researchers made breakthroughs studying the physiology of sex. In 1966 William Masters and Virginia Johnson published the bestseller *Human Sexual Response*, which revealed that women could achieve multiple orgasms, and that the clitoris—not the vagina—was the primary site of female orgasm.[20]

More than any other subset of youth within the sixties generation, the counterculture spearheaded the sexual revolution, attacking established principles and mores. From the outset, hippies held permissive attitudes. They considered sex fun, pleasurable, natural, and healthy, a form of expression to be celebrated, not shunned or concealed. The counterculture aimed to transcend barriers to practicing sex freely. Intercourse did not have to be confined to marriage, a stable partnership, or even between people in love, although hippies highly prized sex within a loving relationship. Counterculturalists preached the idea that individuals needed to discard their sexual "hangups" and repressions, especially feelings of guilt and shame. They also insisted that the human body was beautiful, not obscene or dirty. Others found masturbation completely acceptable and not inferior to intercourse. Hippies explored their sexuality and different sex positions outlined in the *Kama Sutra*, a text that originated in ancient India. Some welcomed group sex or "orgies," provided no individual coerced another into participating. Freaks contended that group sex allowed one to pursue spontaneity and authenticity. Additionally, one could indulge their fantasies and assert their individuality. Most counterculturalists, however, rejected coordinated and organized group sex because they associated it with middle-class "swinging." Hippies promoted spontaneous pleasure and loving relationships, principles violated by seemingly shallow swinging suburbanites.[21]

The counterculture dropped society's "hangups" and "taboos," bringing sex into the open, writing about it, discussing it, depicting it, and doing it. Hippies readily accepted casual sex. Dropouts passed over "games" and traditional rituals such as dating, getting to intercourse quicker than those in straight society. They were often forthright and honest about their intentions. "Well, like here it's different," explained a woman in Haight-Ashbury. "If I meet a boy I like, I can tell him and he can tell me, and then we just make love, that's all. Nobody gets uptight about it. I don't have to go to a shrink." Likewise, a hippie man remarked, "The girls don't play so many games. They play a few, but they don't play so many. You just ask a girl and she'll say yes or no." For many hippies, sex was not a big deal, not worthy of argument, or warranting deep soul searching. Ideally, one should be allowed to communicate their sexuality however they wanted. But this ideal was not consistently lived up to in reality. Some in the counterculture—in the mid-1960s especially—did not welcome forthright expressions of homosexuality, and celibacy likely would not have been a viable option in many scenarios and would have drawn hostility.[22]

Counterculturalists of the cultural activist persuasion, exemplified by the Sexual Freedom League, intended to smash traditional moral codes and legal obstacles impeding sexual liberation. The organization's founder, Jefferson Poland—who later legally changed his middle name to "Fuck"— was a flowers-in-his-hair beatnik who anticipated the counterculture's back-to-nature values and its melding of protest and theatrics. While he was living in a group house in San Francisco his female roommates educated him on the anarchist doctrine "free love," and by the time he moved to New York City in the fall of 1963 he had embraced anarchy and the cause of sexual freedom. After his arrival, Poland founded the New York League for Sexual Freedom with Leo Koch, a biology professor who had been fired from the University of Illinois for advocating premarital intercourse. Other founding members included Allen Ginsberg, Peter Orlovsky, Ed Sanders, Paul Krassner, and Diane Di Prima. The real leaders, however, were Poland, Randy Wicker, and Tuli Kupferberg.[23]

Early league activities consisted primarily of discussion. Poland, Kupferberg, Wicker, and others met weekly in Greenwich Village to debate the meaning of "sexual freedom." Their discussions often revolved around hypothetical situations, making the organization, in part, an abstract, intellectual enterprise. They argued over the morality of prostitution and pedophilia and decided that bestiality was permissible provided the animal did not resist. Public masturbation elicited some of the most intense conversations. Members decided that as long as a man's semen did not come into contact with others, it was a legitimate practice.[24]

At a speak-out at Columbia University in April 1964, the league demanded the decriminalization of prostitution, interracial marriage, oral and anal sex, bestiality, and transvestism. They also assaulted stringent laws against divorce, censorship, public nudity, abortion and birth control, and railed against police harassment of gays. Other league demonstrations included picketing the New York Public Library, protesting the segregation of books about sex. In addition, the league raised objections to obscenity charges slapped on the underground film *Flaming Creatures*. On September 19, 1964, Poland and Wicker sponsored the first public demonstration for gay rights in New York City. The league soon disbanded and Poland traveled back to San Francisco.[25]

Back West, Poland renamed his organization the Sexual Freedom League, and it began assaulting the dominant sexual culture. Imitating the civil disobedience tactics of the civil rights movement, the league defied local laws, striking a blow for personal freedom. Poland believed the naked human body was not obscene and that laws prohibiting public nudity bolstered a repressive sexual culture. In August 1965, Poland and three others—a young man and two young women—held a nude "wade-in" at Aquatic Park municipal beach in San Francisco. In front of cameras and a crowd of spectators, the four entered the freezing ocean and three shed their bathing suits. An anarchist on the beach waved a banner that read,

"Why Be Ashamed of Your Body?" while supporters standing in a picket line chanted, "Sex is clean! Law's obscene!" Authorities sent Poland to jail for five weekends and the women received suspended sentences. The wade-in received national news coverage.[26]

In addition to attacking traditional sexual mores, youth experimented with dope. An increasing number of college students from coast to coast smoked marijuana, dropped lysergic acid diethylamide (LSD), and swallowed stimulants—"pep pills"—although their numbers were relatively few compared to the numbers that turned on in the coming years. Dope spread as nonstudents and former students brought mind-expanding substances onto campus from hip urban enclaves in the vicinity of the universities. Students huddled together in dimly lit dorm rooms, put on records, strummed guitars, lit candles and incense, and passed around joints or LSD. In Texas, chewable peyote buttons could easily be obtained. Professors, researchers, and students gave widely varying estimates in 1966 as to how many people used dope. *Time* estimated that ten thousand California youth had tried acid, while a professor at the University of Southern California guessed that 10 percent of students at large universities had used marijuana. Others offered higher estimates. At Harvard and New York University, students judged that a fifth of the campus had tried marijuana or LSD. A graduate student at San Francisco State believed that a quarter of the student body had "some contact" with pot. Authorities cracked down on users. At Brown University and San Francisco State, administrators expelled or suspended students for possession. Arrests mounted as police discovered possession at major universities in California, New York, Massachusetts, Ohio, Wisconsin, Colorado, and North Carolina.[27]

The press trumpeted and sensationalized the spread of drug use, whipping up a public frenzy. Magazines and newspapers ran articles with the titles "An Epidemic of Acid Heads," "Psychosis Peril Seen in Marijuana," "Girl, 5, Eats LSD and Goes Wild," "Thrill Drug Warps Mind, Kills." In late 1965 the federal government banned LSD distribution. At the same time, Sandoz, the company that originally produced acid, recalled all existing supplies. The establishment press's coverage tended to be negative and made a point of portraying acidheads as society's rejects. *Time* quoted Los Angeles psychiatrist Sidney Cohen, who posited that LSD enthusiasts were "life's losers—dissatisfied, restless people, afflicted with problems they can't handle." Cohen continued, "A lot of them wallow in self-pity and denigrate those who have made it in the 'square' world." The media emphasized acid casualties—suicides, hospitalizations, people who thought they could fly and plummeted to their deaths, a young man who tried to stop traffic on a busy boulevard killed by a car. The press also stressed that marijuana smokers naturally "graduated" to harder drugs like LSD and heroin.[28]

Life's "losers" disregarded the establishment press, as the counterculture's perspectives on the values of dope were antithetical to the establishment's. Most hippies made distinctions between "dope" and "drugs." Heads considered dope to be nonaddictive, "mind-expanding" substances—LSD, peyote, mescaline, psilocybin, and marijuana. Conversely, drugs were thought to be dangerous and addictive—amphetamines, heroin, opiates, and barbiturates. Other drugs hippies associated with the middle-class and their parents—nicotine and alcohol. Generally, hippies believed good substances expanded consciousness and bad substances made one stupid. But individuals interpreted what constituted good and bad drugs differently. No single set of criteria existed for parsing dope and drugs. Tom Coffin, a writer for the Atlanta underground *Great Speckled Bird*, made distinctions between the two:

> DOPE, not DRUGS—alcohol is a drug, pot is DOPE; nicotine is a DRUG, acid is DOPE; DRUGS turn you off, dull your senses, give you the strength to face another day in Death America, DOPE turns you on, heightens sensory awareness, sometimes twists them out of shape and you experience that too, gives you vision and clarity, necessary to create Life from Death.[29]

Love for dope within the counterculture was nearly universal. Few hippies counseled against its use. Heads criticized its illegality and lamented drug busts, and sometimes dealers peddled substances of poor quality at high prices—but dope generally presented few problems, and its positive attributes outweighed its downsides. Ram Dass and others credited dope with growing the counterculture, as young people threw off the shackles of the postwar era after ingesting mind-altering chemicals. Many believed that dope made the counterculture passive and amiable. The Woodstock festival in 1969, for instance, witnessed little violence. Most importantly, dope demarcated the hip from straight society and the establishment. Heads saw it as revolutionary precisely because its use confounded so many ordinary Americans. Its criminalization made heads cultural outlaws who risked incarceration in pursuit of higher consciousness or mere fun. Society deemed everyone who dropped acid a criminal, and by the late 1960s parents and police considered dope users members of an amorphous "counterculture"—regardless of whether their dope experiences had caused them to oppose the status quo. Dope use, then, symbolized rebellion against majority society.[30]

The counterculture commonly smoked its staple drug: marijuana. More readily available than LSD, hippies could get it cheap. Marijuana was one of the oldest mind-altering substances known to man. Chinese literature had described it nearly five thousand years before hippies began smoking it. *Cannabis sativa*—the plant that marijuana came from—grew wild in most parts of the world. Heads especially prized the best-quality, most powerful weed—Acapulco Gold and Panama Red. They also valued hashish, a more potent form of marijuana, five to eight times stronger. Hippies enjoyed the pleasant, peaceful, euphoric, and relaxing sensations marijuana produced. Many claimed it provided a portal to expanded consciousness and enlightenment. While some found themselves isolated in deep contemplation, others engaged their friends in ecstatic, philosophical debates with new insights they felt marijuana had given them. Users reported that all their senses became heightened. They experienced sounds and colors more acutely, which made music and art more fascinating. Not surprisingly, marijuana enthusiasts parried establishment claims concerning the dangers of dope. They denied that grass was addictive and argued that dopers were not responsible for rising crime rates. They also maintained that marijuana was not a gateway or stepping-stone to harder drugs. Marijuana advocates, especially those who pushed for its legalization, pointed to medical evidence to substantiate their claims that it was less addictive and harmful than alcohol.[31]

Hippies indulged in LSD as much as they smoked dope. Acid had been in use for two decades before the counterculture got its hands on it. The psychedelic revolution's beginnings can be traced back to 1938, when Swiss chemist Albert Hofmann accidentally synthesized LSD while experimenting with a rye fungus intended to relieve migraine headaches. Five years later, on April 16, 1943, he absorbed some of the substance through his fingertips. Hofmann proceeded to administer self-experiments and noted that the drug altered the state of consciousness and produced wild hallucinations: "Kaleidoscopic, fantastic images surged in on me, alternating, variegated, opening and then closing themselves in circles and spirals, exploding in colored fountains, rearranging and hybridizing themselves in constant flux." Sandoz, the giant pharmaceutical company that employed Hofmann, began shipping LSD to American psychiatrists.[32]

North American psychiatrists subjected patients to "psychedelic therapy" in the 1950s and 1960s. It involved a large dose of LSD coupled with intensive psychotherapy. The objective was to bring forth a psychedelic experience that could potentially improve one's self-image, outlook, and values. Frequently used to combat alcoholism, it had other applications as well, employed to treat patients with narcotics addictions and neurotic and terminal illnesses. Psychedelic therapy administered to alcoholics proved remarkably successful. According to an analysis of eleven North American studies, it improved the condition of over 50 percent of patients. Only 30 percent experienced no change. And although the US government criminalized LSD for recreational purposes, it largely neglected to interfere with psychiatric experiments and research involving LSD, which continued into the 1970s.[33]

Others got hold of acid, including the CIA, which tested it throughout the 1950s, hoping to unleash its potential mind-control capabilities. In a research program known as ARTICHOKE, the CIA administered LSD to soldiers, convicts, the mentally and terminally ill, ethnic minorities, general population, and their own agents. In 1953 the agency initiated further experimentation with secret project MK-ULTRA. Agents speculated whether LSD given to a prisoner of war might have the effect of a "truth serum," reducing that individual's reluctance to divulge secret intelligence. Exploration backfired when CIA personnel dosed unsuspecting army technicians at a conference in backwoods Maryland. Later, one of the dosed, a biological warfare researcher, Frank Olson, became depressed and despondent, throwing himself through a tenth-story Hilton hotel window, an incident the agency covered up for twenty years. Despite Olson's suicide, the CIA continued its research; the army tested LSD on nearly 1,500 soldiers by the mid-sixties.[34]

But the government did not have a monopoly on acid. A former World War II intelligence officer, Captain Alfred Hubbard—the "Johnny Appleseed of LSD"—traveled North America and Europe distributing it to friends, statesmen, churchmen, and scientists. *Brave New World* author Aldous Huxley published *The Doors of Perception* in 1954, a book that extolled mescaline's ability to open the mind to new sensations and mystical experiences. Interest in psychedelics grew and the famous turned on. The publisher of *Time*, Henry Luce, and his wife, Claire Booth, dropped acid with Huxley. Luce later took LSD on a golf course, where he claimed he spoke to God. Actor Cary Grant claimed the drug enabled him to love women more fully and genuinely.[35]

Timothy Leary researched psychedelics in the early 1960s and eventually became the decade's undisputed champion of their virtues. Leary's initiation into the world of psychedelics occurred in the summer of 1960 after he ingested *Psilocybe mexicana*—magic mushrooms—in Cuernavaca, Mexico. He returned to Harvard in the fall, determined to conduct systematic experiments with the mysterious fungus. Leary and Richard Alpert (later Ram Dass) set up the Harvard Psilocybin Project. Within two years, the professors had moved on to LSD. Harvard fired Alpert in May 1963 for doling out acid to students. Leary failed to attend an honors program committee meeting and Harvard authorities dismissed him, too. The pair continued investigating LSD at Millbrook, a sixty-four-room mansion in Dutchess County, New York, with their organization, the International Federation for Internal Freedom (IFIF), which was soon disbanded, replaced by the Castalia Foundation. Thirty men and women lived there communally, regularly flying high on LSD—some for ten days straight—seeking mystical awareness and aiming for permanent spiritual transformations.[36]

Leary came to be the drug's greatest proselytizer, an acid evangelist. He believed that psychedelics distributed to the masses would have the effect of creating a new world. "Wars, class conflicts, racial tensions, economic exploitation, religious strife, ignorance, and prejudice were all caused by narrow social conditioning," Leary postulated. "If we could help people plug into the empathy circuits of the brain, then positive social change could occur." Leary tried to make his utopian social vision a reality, skillfully using the media to promote LSD, presenting lectures at universities, encouraging potential followers to "Turn On, Tune In, and Drop Out."

Turning on involved activating one's "neural and genetic equipment," becoming "sensitive to the many and various levels of consciousness." Tuning in entailed "interacting harmoniously with the world around you," externalizing, materializing, and expressing one's "new internal perspectives." Dropping out required "detachment from involuntary or unconscious commitments," and favoring "mobility, choice, and change."[37]

Leary probably swayed some heads to turn on, and others certainly shared his revolutionary vision. Most hippies, however, discovered psychedelics on their own as smugglers brought LSD into the United States from Canada, Europe, and Mexico. By the late sixties, those interested in taking acid could obtain it in most college towns and in large cities at affordable prices. Many acid users did not know of Leary and few were dedicated followers. Even in Haight-Ashbury—the nation's LSD capital—Learyites constituted a minority of acidheads. According to writer Charles Perry, most did not endorse his style and philosophy in the district. When Leary visited in late 1966 and communicated his "turn on, tune in, drop out" mantra to a group of youth, they did not comprehend his message. And few became hippies under the high priest's influence. "I don't need Timothy Leary or LSD," Garcia told an interviewer. "Nobody in the Haight-Ashbury follows Leary. The people here would have done this thing without acid, without Leary. I would have been a member of some weird society wherever I went. . . . This is our trip."[38]

LSD enthusiasts found it difficult to describe acid's effects in words: "I cannot convey the idea of a nuclear explosion by lighting a match." No two people experienced it exactly the same way. A typical trip lasted eight to twelve hours. Users claimed to have entered new worlds and dimensions that seemed more real than reality. LSD sharpened the senses, making colors more intense and sounds more distinct. When hippies did write and speak about acid's effects and its potential uses, most asserted that it opened the mind to mystical experiences and expanded consciousness, although some believed that it did not offer miraculous visions but only facilitated the discovery of dormant knowledge that already existed in each person. Some believed that during an LSD trip, the mind shattered and then reassembled itself, changing the user forever, enriching their sense of self-worth and expanding their spiritual horizons. Some hippies argued that dope could produce religious experiences and bring religious communities closer together. Others contended that it could make users act in moral ways. Dope's champions referenced older, established religions in the Americas that treated peyote and mushrooms as sacraments. Likewise, fervent heads saw dope as a sacrament and favored rituals to administer it. Many felt that acid acted as a vehicle for achieving harmony with humanity and the universe, or finding God. A twenty-one-year-old head described his experience this way: "The universe around you comes upon you with such a blinding flash that it really seems . . . it gives you the opportunity to attain . . . 'divine presence'. . . . You see all the embodiments of people. You see your place among these people . . . for me it's a very clarifying experience and gives me a profound sense of joy." To counter unfavorable publicity, defenders contended that the psychedelic was not dangerous or addictive and that bad trips were the exception, the result of misuse.[39]

Not content with merely turning inward, having personal mystical and enlightening experiences, cultural insurgents championed "dope revolution" as a panacea for the world's problems, contending that marijuana—and especially acid—could precipitate fundamental social change. Actively turning others on represented a political act within the social sphere. Psychedelics, cultural radicals maintained, possessed the power to transform one's values. The more dope indulgers there were, the logic went, the more peace, love, and understanding there would be. Dope had the power to instigate a revolution in consciousness and induce a new way of thinking. One could never go back to the person they were before, because dope allowed people to see new possibilities, to live a life based on individual choice. People did not have to stay confined to mainstream culture but could break free to pursue a more meaningful existence. Once the masses realized that they were part of an all-encompassing universe and had something akin to a religious experience, they would drop the national, political, and racial loyalties that prevented humanity from living in harmony. They might also dispense with material items and jettison middle-class lifestyles. Will Albert proclaimed that this revolution in consciousness would have an "ultimately beneficial effect on our society." "People in the drug scene," a student explained, "think it is a revolutionary act to turn on everybody they can find. This is like a religious movement. You knock on my door, come into my home, we turn on together and you see that we're better people for having given up all this plastic junk we're surrounded with." Psychedelists went as far as to assert that acid could end wars. "Everybody wants to turn Lyndon Johnson on," a student told an investigative reporter. "If he'd take a 500-milligram trip, the war in Vietnam would be over when he got back."[40]

Perhaps the most zealous dope revolutionaries were the Brotherhood of Eternal Love. A group of surfers and former street toughs, John Griggs and others founded the brotherhood near Laguna Beach, California, in the summer of 1966. Griggs successfully recruited Leary, who supposedly called Griggs "his guru." The brotherhood worshipped LSD as a divine instrument of God, and committed themselves to turning on the world, convinced that it could and would create a new, better, enlightened society. Beginning the mid-sixties, David Hall brought marijuana into California from Mexico, first in boats pulled by pickup trucks, then by airplane. The brotherhood found an enabler in a corrupt Mexican police chief, who rented them a house to stay in while they were in Mexico. Hall also introduced California to some of its first hashish, smuggled from India in a hollowed-out surfboard. Eventually, the brotherhood became the biggest hash-smuggling organization in America, establishing a pipeline from Afghanistan to California. Griggs had at his disposal a fleet of vehicles— Volkswagen buses, Land Rovers, campers, Porsches—that sailed on container ships from India and Pakistan, weighted down by "primo hash, the good stuff" from Kathmandu and Kandahar. Several members had connections with legendary acid producer Augustus Owsley Stanley III in San Francisco and by the summer of 1967 Laguna Beach had become a center for LSD distribution in southern California. Rick Bevan began working for Stanley in 1968, smuggling ergot—the rye fungus and chemical basis for LSD—from London into California. In turn, Bevan supplied acid to London. In 1969, the brotherhood distributed over 3.5 million tablets of potent LSD—"Orange Sunshine"—that was ingested by the Manson Family, Hell's Angels at Altamont, and the legions at Woodstock. Orange Sunshine found its way to the heartland, including Manitowoc, Wisconsin, and Lancaster, Pennsylvania. The brotherhood became a major supplier of marijuana to the East Coast as well; Glenn Lynd delivered thousands of pounds of weed by car to New York City that fall, netting $98,000. The drug trade financed the brotherhood's headquarters, Mystic Arts World, which doubled as an art gallery, health food and bead shop, and metaphysical bookstore. In 1970, two of the brotherhood appeared in the film *Rainbow Bridge*, featuring Jimi Hendrix. The group also raised the cash that paid for Leary's prison break.[41]

Other surfers became involved in the international marijuana trade. As Peter Maguire and Mike Ritter write in *Thai Stick*, "The surfers who became smugglers were mostly Dionysian men of action who rejected all things political in favor of a sensual, hedonistic life." The chief motivation for smuggling pot was simple: accruing enough money to hit the road for surfing destinations—perhaps for years. By the late 1960s an international market had developed for marijuana and surfing provided excellent cover for smugglers who could be found in Europe, Africa, and Mexico, among other exotic locales. Surfer Terry Dawson became legendary in Hawaii for selling potent "Golden Voice" ganja from Laos at $1,000 per pound.[42]

For some, LSD eased integration into the counterculture. Ron Thelin, coowner of the Psychedelic Shop in Haight-Ashbury, had such an experience. Acid revealed society's problems to him and exposed the fact that he was merely an interchangeable part in a system that perpetuated war and a dull existence. "When I first turned on," he told author Burton Wolfe, "it pulled the rug out from under me. Suddenly I saw all the bullshit in the whole educational and social system, and that's where I was. The Vietnam War was pressing in on me. I couldn't justify going to school with this war on." Psychedelics helped him to understand that schools turned out "robots to keep the social system going and to keep the war going." LSD, then, pointed Thelin in new directions.[43]

Ron's brother Jay held acid in such high regard that he claimed it facilitated the adoption of countercultural values:

> I had had sex problems that were hanging up my life. I couldn't relate to another person that way. . . . Then I had this experience with LSD, and I saw that this is what people do—they fuck—and there's really nothing to it. . . . there's nothing to be ashamed of, these are human things, and you're all part of the same universe, the same patterns of life, and they're groovy!

Hallucinogens helped Thelin to leave behind his reservations about sexual intimacy and realize that sex was natural, made him part of the human community, and brought him closer to nature.[44]

Many heads explored dope as a result of their alienation, searching for answers, the truth, authenticity, and a pathway to enlightenment. Not every counterculturalist, however, was a seeker. To the contrary, many just wanted to have a good time. In the freewheeling and insouciant atmosphere of hippiedom, one did not need a justification for reveling in dope nor did anyone ask for one. The massive hype surrounding LSD, perpetuated by newspapers, magazines, television, and radio compelled many to turn on. A woman recalled that "the media were advertising it, saying things like 'heightening your perception,' 'seeing things like you've never seen them before,' 'getting to the roots of religion and ritual,' 'playing with madness.' All that was just fascinating to me. I thought, WOW! Give me some." Simple curiosity, then, offered enough reason to try acid. As dope use and hippiedom burgeoned, growing in popularity, an increasing number of young people got high for kicks. A head who had used acid as a means to expand his consciousness and to reach God recalled a conversation he overheard between "teenyboppers." "I was shocked to hear these kids talking about using LSD that weekend," he remembered. "They weren't searching. They were going to have a great party, and they were going to have great records, and they were going to have great sex. . . . I mean, I saw it as a sacrament, and they were going to drop LSD for the sheer partying of it." As this episode demonstrates, counterculturalists approached dope with disparate intentions and philosophies. For many, the pleasure principle and hedonism were paramount, while others elevated acid to the level of a sacrament that could produce religious experiences.[45]

The most ardent acidheads established psychedelic churches to worship LSD. Former clinical psychologist Arthur J. Kleps—who called himself Chief Boo-Hoo—created the Neo-American Church in 1965. Kleps, whom Leary called a "mad monk," did not take himself seriously; he intentionally joked on institutionalized churches and religion—the Neo-American Church was a "'non-church' church." The Neo-Americans differed from Leary in their approach to dope. Kleps likened Leary's view of LSD to a "religion" with Leary acting as "spiritual leader." He, on the other hand, functioned "like a pope who is nothing more than a super-business man." Kleps set no concrete doctrines or moral codes. A satirical and silly organization, the church's "strategic concepts" included "Relax and act goofy as you like—play the game of cops and robbers comically," and "Infiltrate and take over the communication and entertainment industry." Rituals consisted of several individuals reading from random books simultaneously and dancing with stroboscopes to activate mind expansion. Later, in 1967, the Boo-Hoos married couples in ceremonies that combined Buddhist prayers, tantric yoga, and Mohawk moccasins. The church's motto was "Victory over Horseshit" and Kleps deemed Bob Dylan the organization's official poet. Payers of the small monthly dues received a psychedelic coloring book and the church bulletin, *Divine Toad Sweat*. Membership climbed to over a thousand.[46]

The only thing the Boo-Hoos took seriously was their devotion to LSD. Acid had "religious" connotations for them as members used it in a group setting in an effort to better appreciate "God," by which Kleps meant a deep psychological, mystical experience, whereby the "ultimate Truth" could be ascertained. Kleps claimed acid was a "sacrament," a part of the Boo-Hoo religion. He therefore argued that his church's use of LSD should be protected under law. The Boo-Hoos lost their case in court. The judge pointed to the organization's official theme song—"Row, Row, Row Your Boat"—and ruled that Kleps's outfit did not qualify as a church.[47]

Dope was important, but rock and roll proved equally central to the counterculture. Dylan became one of its most revered artists. In 1963 he burst onto the musical and political landscape, greatly influencing the young political activists in particular. Dylan wrote deeply personal lyrics yet became a generational spokesperson, a position and title he came to regret and reject. New Leftists admired the albums *The Freewheelin' Bob Dylan* and *The Times They Are a-Changin'*, released in 1963 and 1964, respectively, because the lyrics spoke to their concerns: racism, Jim Crow, Cold War militarism, and the prospect of nuclear apocalypse. "Whether he liked it or not, Dylan *sang for us*. . . . We followed his career as if he were singing our song; we got in the habit of asking where he was taking us next," recalled Todd Gitlin. "The Death of Emmett Till," "The Lonesome Death of Hattie Carroll" and "Only a Pawn in Their Game" addressed racially motivated murders, the latter pertaining to the assassination of civil rights leader Medgar Evers. "Masters of War" and "With God on Our Side" skewered Cold War ideology and the military-industrial complex. Written in the midst of the Cuban missile crisis, "A Hard Rain's a-Gonna

Fall," described a nightmarish world in the aftermath of a nuclear war. Dylan sang that the answer to war and racism was "Blowin' in the Wind," and, in "The Times They Are a-Changin'," he spoke of a new generation that would bring new morals and values to a country that failed to live up to its creed.[48]

In 1965, to the chagrin of New Leftists and folk purists, Dylan abandoned "finger-pointing" songs and his acoustic guitar in favor of a Fender electric, amplifiers, a head of fuzzy disheveled hair, and introspective and surrealistic lyrics. And it was at this juncture when Dylan made a significant impact on the counterculture. The Beatles had influenced his shift to electric music. Dylan knew that the Fab Four represented more than a passing fad, and that rock was the wave of the future: "I really dug them. Everybody else thought they were for the teenyboppers, that they were gonna pass right away. But it was obvious to me that they had staying power. I knew they were pointing the direction of where music had to go."[49]

His transformation to rocker expanded his appeal to a far broader audience. At the Newport Folk Festival in 1965, backed by the Paul Butterfield Blues Band, Dylan burst into chugging amplified rock. Veteran folk singer Pete Seeger seethed with anger and the crowd booed. Outraged folkniks felt that Dylan had lost his authenticity. His break from politics and protest music mirrored a larger trend: an evolving schism between the New Left and counterculture. The young man from Hibbing, Minnesota, rejected the role of spokesperson—The Great Cause Fighter—that had been foisted upon him. "All I can do is be me—whoever that is," Dylan told an underground journalist. Politicos charged him with "selling out," scorning his shift to political indifference. "He is seen as a threat to the left, representing an anti-political response to the increasing crises in American life," commented a Bay Area Californian. Like the growing army of hippie dropouts, Dylan had had enough of politics. "The stuff you're writing is bullshit, because politics is bullshit," Dylan told Phil Ochs. "It's all unreal. The only thing that's real is inside you. Your feelings. Just look at the world you're writing about and you'll see you're wasting your time. The world is . . . just absurd." The lyrical content of his songs pertained no longer to politics but to his own sentiments and dilemmas, and the theme of personal freedom. "The left has been mistaken," wrote a Dylan supporter. "It is not only the negroes who are in chains, but all Americans who are trapped by uneasy boredom, by loneliness, and god knows what else. These are the chains that Dylan wants to break."[50]

His fourth album, *Another Side of Bob Dylan*, released in 1964, foreshadowed the thematic substance of albums to come. In "My Back Pages," Dylan repudiated his politically oriented artistry and proclaimed that he was younger now than he had been only a few years earlier. "I Shall Be Free No. 10" contained an early reference to dope. In 1965 and 1966, Dylan produced three of his best—and most influential—albums: *Bringing It All Back Home*, *Highway 61 Revisited*, and *Blonde on Blonde*. Along with the Beatles, he transformed popular music into an intellectual art form by applying serious, surreal, poetic lyrics to rock and roll. Listeners contemplated, analyzed, and debated the meaning of his songs. Dylan's records reflected the values of the counterculture, while spreading its message. *Bringing It All Back Home* featured an ode to dope, "Mr. Tambourine Man," and on *Blonde on Blonde*'s "Rainy Day Women #12 & 35," Dylan gleefully encouraged everyone to get stoned. *Highway 61*'s hit single, "Like a Rolling Stone," romanticized breaking away from traditional values, the quest for freedom, and the precarious, freewheeling lifestyle. But it was also a cautionary tale. The song's protagonist, "Miss Lonely," went to the finest schools and threw change to bums on the street, but ends up losing her fortune and has to pawn her diamond ring, while making deals with shadowy characters. Commentators have speculated whether the song was about Edie Sedgwick, an actress at Andy Warhol's Factory, who died of a drug overdose in 1971. "Ballad of a Thin Man" mocked the straight and square world. "Mister Jones," confronted with nudity, geeks, one-eyed midgets, and freaks, has no idea what is happening around him and cannot fathom the social changes that are taking place.[51]

The Beatles influenced the counterculture as much as—if not more than—Dylan. From the moment John Lennon, Paul McCartney, George Harrison, and Ringo Starr set foot in America, mothers, fathers, and especially youths sensed a certain strength and energy in their music and personalities. On February 9, 1964, the Beatles appeared on *The Ed Sullivan Show* before an estimated 73 million viewers, more than 60 percent of the television audience. By early April the Fab Four held the top five positions on the *Billboard* singles chart and two of their albums sat at the top of the

LP bestsellers list. In July teenagers across the nation crowded into the-aters to see the Beatles on film in *A Hard Day's Night*. They had "invaded" and conquered America, causing Beatlemania. Girls screamed, tore at their hair, fainted. Beatles-obsessed consumers purchased a dizzying array of merchandise with the band's name on it—hats, T-shirts, wigs, pajamas, plastic guitars, boots, dolls, board games, soda, and ice cream sandwiches. Two enterprisers even sold one-inch pieces of the unwashed sheets each Beatle had slept on.[52]

America felt the force and effect of the Beatles immediately. Several fac-tors account for their enormous success and the ecstatic reception they received. With their humor and wit, the Beatles helped revive the flagging spirits of a nation still mourning the death of President Kennedy, killed a few months before their arrival. Furthermore, youth found the working-class lads from Liverpool attractive because they were a rarity in America. Moreover, the Beatles rejuvenated rock and roll, filling the void left by the departure of rock's early heroes. Buddy Holly had been killed in a plane crash and Chuck Berry, Elvis, and Bo Diddley had dropped off the charts. The Beatles brought African American music back to its homeland, rein-troducing it to young whites, with raucous, hard-driving covers of Berry's "Rock and Roll Music," the Isley Brothers' "Twist and Shout," Larry Wil-liams's "Dizzy Miss Lizzy," and Little Richard's "Long Tall Sally." But the Beatles did not merely cover the songs of others; they wrote their own tunes and possessed a distinctive, original, and exciting sound incorpo-rating minor chords and sevenths, producing hits like, "Please, Please Me," "From Me to You," "She Loves You," "I Want to Hold Your Hand," and "Can't Buy Me Love."[53]

The hip clearly recognized with whom the band aligned themselves, for the Beatles eschewed adult values and behavior, ridiculed the press, and directed their message explicitly at youth. "And mockers they are," proclaimed the *Los Angeles Free Press*. "They are hip, disrespectful, carefree, anti-patriotic, irreverent. . . . They challenge older generations to earn the respect they demand from kids—and so seldom deserve." Some right-wing religionists found the band dangerous. The Reverend David A. Noe-bel authored a pamphlet titled "Communism, Hypnotism and the Beatles: The Communist Music Master Plan," in which he asserted that John, Paul, George, and Ringo intended to provoke a communist revolution through their music. "Throw your Beatle and rock and roll records in the city dump," Noebel urged his readers. "Let's make sure four mop-headed anti-Christ beatniks don't destroy our children's emotional and mental stability and ultimately destroy our nation." For many young people, the arrival of the Beatles heralded the beginning of the Sixties. "When I heard the Beatles for the first time, I knew something was happening. Something new. Something different. It was the first signal," a baby boomer recollected.[54]

But the Beatles did not make a substantial impact on the counterculture until they released the albums *Rubber Soul* and *Revolver*. Lennon began speaking out, espousing controversial opinions. He called the war in Vietnam "lousy" and "wrong" and said it "should be stopped." The band also started to compose under the influence of Dylan, LSD, and pot, all of which had a critical effect on its sound and lyrics. They consciously made artier songs and wrote more introspective lyrics. Fewer formulaic love tunes appeared on their albums, as the group treated a wider range of topics, experimented with new studio techniques, and incorporated new sound effects, and backward guitars, brass, and strings.[55]

The Beatles released *Rubber Soul* in late 1965. The album's cover featured a surrealistic, distorted portrait of the group, the title stamped in bubbly, bulging psychedelic lettering in the corner. Lennon sang about himself in the third person on "Nowhere Man," and the hip interpreted it as a put-down of traditional, conformist suburbanites who lacked a point of view. On "Norwegian Wood," a song about a covert affair, Harrison introduced the sitar, an instrument that became familiar on many psychedelic albums. The Beatles had something to say on this record and prophetically proclaimed that "The Word" was love and that it could set people free. Millions of kids eventually agreed with this message.[56]

With *Revolver*, released in 1966, the Beatles delved into the psychedelic. "Eleanor Rigby" made social commentary on alienated lonely people. On "Tomorrow Never Knows," Lennon sang lyrics inspired by Leary's *The Psychedelic Experience*, a guidebook for acid trips based on *The Tibetan Book of the Dead*. McCartney's "Got to Get You into My Life" celebrated marijuana. "She Said, She Said," was a cryptic retelling of an acid trip Lennon had taken with Peter Fonda, and "Doctor Robert" lauded an LSD dealer who could make one a new and better man.[57]

The Rolling Stones invaded America through the breach the Beatles had opened. The band recorded African American music, covering songs by Chuck Berry, Marvin Gaye, Wilson Pickett, and bluesmen Slim Harpo and Howlin' Wolf. Manager Andrew Loog Oldham purposefully cultivated an image for the Stones that ran directly counter to the Beatles' squeaky-clean public perception. In contrast to the innocent, lovable moptops who only wanted to hold a girl's hand, the Stones came off as scowling, menacing, ugly, street-toughened, cynical, and rude. They played blues-based rock that was dark, unsentimental, and overtly sexual. Their mega-hit "Satisfaction" appealed to youth because it spoke to teenage frustration, aggression, and the need for freedom and sexual fulfillment. They became one of the most popular bands in America. Like the Beatles, the Stones experimented with psychedelic sounds and made references to dope. "Paint It Black," was gloomy, Eastern-flavored, sitar-driven psychedelia. On the song "19th Nervous Breakdown," the band mentioned a drug trip and an attempt to alter a young woman's mind. "Mother's Little Helper" pointed out the hypocrisy of the respectable middle-class that condemned marijuana use among the young while its members abused prescription drugs.[58]

Other artists recorded music that reflected countercultural anxieties, values, thoughts, and sentiments. Los Angeles quintet the Byrds birthed folk rock with "Mr. Tambourine Man," combining Dylan's poetic lyrics with the Beatles' jangly, electric sound and harmonies. Folk artist Phil Ochs recorded the anti-Vietnam songs "I Ain't Marching Anymore," and "Draft Dodger Rag," while condemning America's role as global police in "Cops of the World." Buffy Sainte-Marie castigated war and killing with "Universal Soldier." Barry Maguire sailed to the top of the charts with "Eve of Destruction," which damned war, racism, hatred, and violence, and asserted that the world teetered on the brink of annihilation. The Who exploited the emerging generation gap with "My Generation," asking their elders to fade away and hoping to die as relatively young men. Eric Burdon and the Animals declared, "We Gotta Get out of This Place" and noted that the older generation worked and slaved their lives away.[59]

Rock songs also increasingly made allusions to dope and dope experiences. British band the Pretty Things recorded a song in which they shouted, "I need LSD!" Texas rockers the 13th Floor Elevators released the first album to explicitly call itself "psychedelic," *The Psychedelic Sounds of the 13th*

Floor Elevators. The liner notes included a nod to acid, celebrating humanity's ability to "chemically alter his mental state[,] restructure his thinking and change his language." The Byrds flew "Eight Miles High," and so did Donovan Leitch's "Sunshine Superman." Donovan also helped initiate a highly unproductive banana-peel smoking craze with "Mello Yello." Hip listeners were convinced that artists were shrouding references to marijuana in the name of a woman—the Stones' "Lady Jane" and the Association's "Along Comes Mary." The folk trio Peter, Paul, and Mary recorded "Puff the Magic Dragon," and listeners speculated whether "puff" was a verb. Peter Yarrow, however, maintains that the song is about innocence lost. Paul Revere and the Raiders—the house band on Dick Clark's television show—recorded the first antidrug song, "Kicks," which made the top ten.[60]

Popular musicians spearhead the counterculture in many respects, anticipating its styles, attitudes, and values. Dylan, the Beatles, the Rolling Stones, and San Francisco acid rockers assumed the hippie persona during the counterculture's infancy, before it became a continental phenomenon. And because youth greatly valued rock and revered its performers, some imitated their heroes. A female dropout from San Francisco State described her transformation and those of her peers: "And there was Dylan and the Beatles and they were doing that electronic thing. And it sort of made us change," she explained. "They kept us running after them, and running into a happier thing, and into a more joyful thing, a more colorful thing." Similarly, a baby boomer woman saw the Beatles as catalysts for bringing about the counterculture: "They seemed to pave the way for most of the changes in the '60s—psychedelics, meditation, protest."[61]

Michael J. Kramer assigns great significance to rock. During the 1960s, "rock music became a crucial cultural form," he argues. "It sustained a hyper-charged interplay of identity and community, personal experience and public participation, self-expression and collective scrutiny, cultural exploration and political engagement." For hippies in San Francisco and GIs in Vietnam, Kramer contends, "rock heightened the stakes of democratic life during wartime." Participants in the musical landscapes of San Francisco and Vietnam—the "republic of rock"—called the "very nature of citizenship into question." Rock helped young Americans navigate issues such as freedom and its limits and the nature of rights and obligations at the same moment that Cold War liberalism faced its dissolution.[62]

THE ADVENT OF FREE UNIVERSITIES
AND COMMUNES

While practicing its distinct values, the counterculture established alternative communities and that entailed founding counterinstitutions.
Dissatisfied graduate students and professors set up "free universities"
as an alternative to what they believed was the complete inadequacy of
academia. Attendees usually paid no tuition or the lowest tuition rate possible. Largely unstructured, free universities focused on students, not research dollars, final exams, grades, credits, or syllabi. Classes offered to
students and nonstudents—beatniks, hipsters, dropouts, and radicals—
taught "new and radical scholarship analyzing American society in all
its manifold sicknesses." By spring 1966, Columbia, UC Berkeley, Stanford, Michigan State, the University of Florida, and colleges in Detroit,
New York City, and Chicago had established a "Free U." These alternative
educational institutions instructed on a wide variety of subjects such as
anarchism, Christian existentialism, psychedelic drugs, American imperialism, and modern cinema.[63]

Other freaks founded communes and they did so for many reasons.
Most wanted to construct communities different from majority society in
every conceivable way, environments where everyone worked and shared
together, where people could be themselves, act on their impulses, do
whatever they fancied. Another major early force was escapism, as alternative communities provided refuge from a society plagued by the military-industrial complex, war, racism, competition, consumerism, and
daily drudgery. Building a new society was another chief motivation. "We
felt that the society about us had degenerated to such a point we couldn't
live within it," recalled a founder of Drop City. "But we felt people were
good enough and under the right circumstances could live a good life. We
wanted to build a society from the ground up—that would develop kind
human beings." Communards had great faith in their ability to construct
new realities and grow as individuals.[64]

In 1962 a woman named Amelia Newell opened up her land at Gorda
Mountain near Big Sur to whoever wanted to live there, and by the mid-
1960s it became known as a good stopping point, crash pad, and drug-
trading location for hippies traveling between Los Angeles and San

Francisco. By 1967 Gorda Mountain had at least two hundred residents. Newell provided free bulk foods. Transient communards faced hostility from neighbors who cut the water lines and wanted Newell committed for insanity. A local gas station owner carried a handgun and denied service to anyone from the community. Gorda Mountain's inhabitants—mostly consisting of ex-convicts and derelicts—dwelled in tents, caves, and on the edges of cliffs. In 1968 Gorda Mountain closed down.[65]

Huw Williams started Tolstoy Farm in Washington state in 1963, one of the first Sixties communes guided by anarchist principles. Williams, active in the anti–Polaris submarine and nukes movement as a member of the New England Committee for Nonviolent Action (CNVA), had encountered the protest organization's communal farm near Voluntown, Connecticut, in 1962. He decided to establish a West Coast counterpart and bought land thirty miles west of Spokane. The next year, he and nine others resolved to live peacefully and avoid military service, courts, and jail. The communards adopted one rule for Tolstoy Farm: no one could be forced to leave. This edict forced members to work out conflicts the "right way." Tolstoy's residents lived near subsistence level, made decisions based on consensus, and pooled their money. They grew their own food and had a communal center called Hart House. Total acreage ballooned to two hundred, and by 1966 hippies dwelled there, attracted to a community where one could grow marijuana and where no restrictions on sexual behavior existed. Naked hippies strolled the grounds and refrained from pointing out each other's physical flaws. Freedom seemed boundless. "I like it here because I can stand nude on my front porch and yell, 'Fuck!'" commented a young woman. "Also, I think I like it here because I'm fat, and there aren't any mirrors around. Clothes don't matter, and people don't judge you by your appearance like they do out there." An unstable teen burned Hart House to the ground in 1968. Williams taught kids at an alternative school on site, but eventually left the farm himself with his wife and two children. Despite counterculturalists' best efforts to transcend sexual hangups and possessiveness, anarchical sexual practices led to jealousy, suicide, and undermined the community.[66]

The creation of Drop City inaugurated the era of back-to-the-land hippie commune building. Drop City, Timothy Miller has written, "brought together most of the themes that had been developing in other recent communities—anarchy, pacifism, sexual freedom, rural isolation, interest in drugs, art—and wrapped them flamboyantly into a commune not quite like any that had gone before." Drop City originated when founders Eugene Bernofsky and his wife, JoAnn Bernofsky, along with Clark Richert, purchased five acres of goat pasture near Trinidad, Colorado, on May 3, 1965. Bernofsky and company quested to create a new "civilization" where life and art intersected. The residents—"Droppers"—took new names, eschewed everything conventional, and welcomed others who sought to expand their cultural perspectives. After attending a lecture by Buckminster Fuller, the Droppers built Drop City's defining features: geodesic domes. The communards worked diligently and creatively, constructing their homes with old telephone poles, tarpaper, bottle caps, stucco, and materials pulled from junkyards, including car tops. They even took apart abandoned railroad bridges for supplies. Droppers shared everything—money, vehicles, clothing, and decision making. They opposed leaders of any kind; members saw anarchy as good thing and individuals did as they pleased. Most busied themselves creating art, comic books, films, paintings, statues large and small, sculptures, and artistically painted furniture and clothing. Drop City opened its land to anyone and everyone. Time magazine featured the commune in a cover story on hippies in July 1967. That summer, resident Peter Rabbit orchestrated the Joy Festival at Drop City, featuring rock music and art. The publicity overwhelmed the Bernofskys, who departed. Richert followed in 1968, after his wife became pregnant. By 1970, despite reversing the open-door policy, motorcyclists, speed freaks, overflowing outhouses, and hepatitis put Drop City on a downward trajectory and it closed in 1973. In 1978 neighbors bought the land.[67]

HIPPIEDOM IN SAN FRANCISCO

In 1965 hippies appeared in San Francisco's Haight-Ashbury, the most publicized and celebrated counterculture enclave. Counterculturalists recalled the early days with affection, before media publicity inundated the district with weekend hippies, reporters, criminals, and tourists during the Summer of Love in 1967. Early manifestations of the counterculture included happenings, superseded in short order by acid tests, dancehall concerts, and be-ins.

The San Francisco scene began to gain steam four hours away, just over the Nevada border. Virginia City, a renovated ghost town, was home to the Red Dog Saloon, where a couple dozen artists and dopers from Haight-Ashbury congregated in the summer of 1965. The house band, the Charlatans, wore cowboy boots, straw boaters, and Western apparel, and played rock and roll, blues, country, and folk, that they extended into long jams. They also carried guns, not only to emphasize their Western appearance but to fend off potentially hostile straights, as they were a group of long-hairs playing in Nevada. The staff of the Red Dog, dressed in Edwardian clothes, bodices, net stockings, and ten-gallon hats, dropped psychedelics together on Monday evenings after the Red Dog closed. Bill Ham provided an early version of a liquid light show and Owsley Stanley offered LSD. Soon hippies started to come to Virginia City from San Francisco, Reno, Seattle, and Portland.[68]

The Virginia City experiment soon fizzled and the hippie scene in San Francisco started to come to life in the fall of 1965. In the early sixties, latter-day beatniks and students from San Francisco State began residing in the low-rent Victorian houses in the slightly dilapidated Haight-Ashbury district on the periphery of Golden Gate Park. To the Haight's north was the black Fillmore, and to the east, a commercial center. Many had migrated there after tourists, gangsters, and narcotics agents overran their hangout in North Beach. Over the next several years, Berkeley radicals, artists, and musicians filtered into the area.

Residents of the Haight looked back fondly on the district's early days before the media began to publicize "hippies." Denizens felt part of something significant, exciting, and special—and largely unknown to the public. Gary Duncan, the guitarist of Quicksilver Messenger Service, recollected:

> What was really going on in San Francisco in the early sixties was a whole other thing most people don't know about. The underground scene was really a lot heavier than what was publicized and what people think happened, you know, hippies playing music with flowers in their hair, all that crap . . . I first started hanging out there back when there were no hippies. There were beatniks, and crash pads, poets and painters, every kind of drug imaginable and every kind of crazy motherfucker

in the world. It was kind of cool to be in on something that nobody else knew about. Early on, there was a big scene that was totally invisible. If you knew the right address and knocked on the door, you could walk through that door into a whole other world. You'd go to, say, 1090 Page Street, open up the door, and there'd be a fourteen-bedroom Victorian house with something different going on in every room: painters in one room talking to each other, musicians in another room. It was really cool, and to all outward appearances there was nothing happening. It was like a secret society.

Duncan's description is a testament to the wide variety of dissenters who called the Haight their home. Those involved in this "secret society" understood that something of great importance was transpiring in the district.[69]

Describing the action on the Haight, the San Francisco Examiner put the term hippie into print for the first time on September 6, 1965, in an article about the Blue Unicorn, a coffeehouse on Hayes Street near Golden Gate Park that had a chessboard, books, music, art, free clothes, and a comfortable old sofa. It served as a meeting place and one could find friends coming to San Francisco from out of state. Hippies could get food in exchange for washing dishes. The organization LEMAR—short for Legalize Marijuana—met there, as did the Sexual Freedom League.

Dope was plentiful in the "Hashbury." Many denizens made a living selling marijuana and LSD. The district's principal LSD manufacturer was college dropout and Air Force veteran Owsley Stanley, who gained legendary status in the Haight as a "bootleg chemist." Stanley traveled with the Merry Pranksters, a zany group of proto-hippies who hung out with author Ken Kesey, before he and his apprentice Tim Scully established an underground lab. The pair invested in a pill press and began turning out 250-milligram colored tablets—"white lightning," "blue barrels," and "orange sunshine." Heads revered Stanley's LSD for its purity and potency. Stanley is estimated to have produced some four million hits of acid in the mid-sixties. Profits motivated Stanley, but he and his assistants also believed in the power of psychedelics and wanted to help Hashbury residents with their "consciousness raising."[70]

FROM HAPPENINGS TO DANCEHALL CONCERTS

As San Francisco emerged as a hippie center, the hip took to clubs, theaters, and art galleries, orchestrating happenings. In 1965, happenings usually involved art, film, theater, music or poetry. The producers of these events flooded spectators' minds and senses with sights and sounds intended to provoke an emotional experience. The artists endeavored to produce something authentic. Others wanted to enlighten their audiences, though many remained confused. "It doesn't matter whether you 'understand' or not," asserted the *Open City Press*. "Sometimes the only thing to understand is that somebody is doing something—and you're watching him do it."[71]

Avant-garde artists in New York City created many happenings. Among them was Yoko Ono, who would later marry John Lennon. In November 1961, Ono staged her first uptown piece at Carnegie Recital Hall. She performed one movement from her "opera" titled "A Grapefruit in the World of Park," in complete darkness with nearly no sound, to the astonishment, if not indignation, of spectators. Later, two men, tied together, slowly made their way across the stage, empty bottles and cans clanging around them. Ono wanted the small audience to hear people perspire, so the dancers wore microphones. After a stint in Japan, she returned to New York and put her career on solid footing in 1965 with "Stone Piece." For this performance, Ono crawled into a bag—alone or with someone else—disrobed, and engaged in a sex act. Sometimes she sat for hours, only moving to elicit the interest of passersby. "Inside there might be a lot going on," Ono explained. "Or maybe nothing's going on."[72]

In Los Angeles, youth gathered in a natural outdoor amphitheater to hear Hindu and experimental music. Others watched psychedelic films involving several movie and slide projectors operating simultaneously. Poets recited their work amid a cacophony of instruments and sounds— drums, whistles, flutes, horns, tapes played at half and double speed. Folk singers performed while speeches, sound effects, and commercials blasted from a tape player.[73]

In San Francisco, a theater company put on a one-act play as a "kaleidoscopic web of changing colors" projected on the wall pulsated to music behind the performers. The Laughing Stock Gallery showed an experimental film accompanied by a variety of sounds—"scrapings, squealings . . . unearthly wailings." The Open Theater did liquid projections on nude bodies.[74]

Happenings at New York art galleries involved flashing neon lights, nude films, wigs hanging from ceilings, old phonographs playing ancient records, a partial motorcycle painted bright red, a pair of glass eyes in a cup. In a New York basement club, the Psychedelic Theater simulated an LSD experience. Jazz musicians improvised while images of Mount Rushmore, a floating frog embryo, and the Buddha moved in and out of focus.[75]

Dancehall rock concerts began to eclipse happenings by the end of 1965. After the Trips Festival in January 1966, dancehall concerts were held regularly on weekends and became countercultural institutions in San Francisco. The first major show was held on the evening of October 16, 1965. Put on by the Family Dog, an organization that produced concerts, at Longshoreman's Hall, "A Tribute to Dr. Strange," true to its name, drew a slew of strange characters indeed—Hell's Angels and people dressed in mod, Old West, Victorian, pirate, and free-form outfits and costumes. The performers were also in costume. Jefferson Airplane wore mod clothes. The Charlatans sported long hair and cowboy gear. And the lead singer of the Great Society, Grace Slick—soon to join Jefferson Airplane—appeared in a purple miniskirt and stockings. A poster of an eagle clutching bombs and dollar bills hovered above Slick. The bombs were labeled "peace," the bills "freedom." Above the eagle, the poster read "Bad Taste." For artist Alton Kelley, the dance was a major revelation: "Everybody was walking around with their mouths open, going, 'Where did all these freaks come from? I thought my friends were the only guys around!'"[76]

Probably the most important concert promoter was Bill Graham. Born Wolfgang Grajonca, Graham escaped Nazi Germany as a child and grew up in the Bronx. After a bitter struggle to obtain a permit, he started producing shows at the Fillmore Auditorium. Although he became central to the San Francisco counterculture, Graham did not take dope; he wanted to make money and saw a lucrative opportunity in boosting the dancehall scene.[77]

One of Graham's earliest promoted shows involved the San Francisco Mime Troupe, for which he acted as business manager. After its obscenity bust in August 1965, the troupe's financial problems increased. The San Francisco Arts Festival excluded them and Bay Area police decided that their plays could not be preformed publicly. A court found director R. G. Davis guilty for performing without a permit on November 1. In stepped Graham, who promoted an "appeal" benefit for the troupe to be held at the loft on Howard Street. Jefferson Airplane, Allen Ginsberg, the Fugs, and folk singer Sandy Bull all offered their services. On November 6, the appeal turned out to be a great success. People painted the loft's walls in bright colors and hung bananas and grapes from the ceiling. Filmmakers contributed sixteen-millimeter film loops and screens. Large crowds turned out for "the biggest bohemian gathering to date."[78]

Chet Helms was another hip capitalist. He had hitchhiked from Texas to the Haight in the early 1960s with a young blues singer named Janis Joplin, who would later join Big Brother and the Holding Company, a group Helms would manage. Unlike Graham, Helms lived the hippie lifestyle, integrating himself fully into the Haight-Ashbury community. He was the third manager of the Family Dog. Helms used dope, operated his business like a commune, and did not charge some people admission to shows. He started his business activity holding Tuesday night jam sessions at 1090 Page Street. He then presented shows at the Fillmore in conjunction with Graham. After falling out with Graham, Helms opened the Avalon Ballroom to compete with the Fillmore.[79]

The dancehall concerts provided an impetus for a psychedelic art movement in San Francisco. Influenced by LSD, the surrealists, Dada, and pop art, Kelley, Wes Wilson, Stanley Mouse, Rick Griffin, and Victor Moscoso created brightly colored, swirling, kaleidoscopic art. Such images appeared most prominently on concert posters, but elsewhere as well, including underground newspapers and comics. Hippies who purchased rolling papers found Mouse and Kelley's Mr. Zig-Zag on the packet. At the Fillmore and Avalon, freaks reveled in psychedelic light shows produced by Bill Ham, Elias Romero, Roger Hilyard, and Ben Van Meter. The artists created them by projecting light through liquid pigments, which, when beamed on a wall, appeared as strange, radiant, swirling, abstract images that changed constantly.[80]

The freaks attending shows at the Fillmore, Avalon, Winterland, Matrix, and dancehalls elsewhere had similar experiences. The dancehall concerts were social happenings where the hip community came together, psychedelic drugs flowed freely, and heads experienced cosmic visions. Bands played eardrum-shattering psychedelic rock as hippies engaged in "expressionistic writhing and free-form twirling, in the dark or under stroboscopic lights that might hit a hypnotic rhythm as they turned the dancers into a series of flashing snapshots." People covered in Day-Glo paint grooved under ultraviolet lights. High on dope, they wore strange costumes, bright clothing, beads, and buttons bearing messages such as "Alice designs her face on my mind." Light show artists beamed liquid projections, colored lights, kaleidoscopic patterns, and slides of faces or flowers onto the walls.

But despite the light shows and eclectic crowds, youth came to see the main attractions, the local bands that gained notoriety for producing the "San Francisco sound": Big Brother and the Holding Company, Grateful Dead, Quicksilver Messenger Service, Country Joe and the Fish, Jefferson Airplane, Moby Grape, and Sopwith Camel. Guitarists improvised, playing meandering forty-five-minute solos and audiences enjoyed feedback emanating from the musicians' amplifiers. Acid rockers explored and experimented with sounds to create an atmosphere. "With the use and control of feedback we can get the sound so big that you don't hear the music, you feel it; and you don't dance to it; you dance in it," explained Robin Tyner, the vocalist for the Detroit band MC-5. John Sinclair testified to the magic created by the interactions between the crowd and the artists: "The vibrations coming at the musicians from the audience merge with their own vibrations to form a huge human pulsation that surpasses what most people know as 'music' to take over the whole hall and turn everyone there, finally, into pure human freaks."[81]

Hippies experienced a sense of community—felt part of a family—at the shows. They grew accustomed to seeing familiar faces, which enhanced the community sentiment. "Going to the Fillmore and the Avalon and all those places was probably the most fun I ever had in my life," recalled participant Florence Nathan. "Considering that I personally probably knew a couple of hundred people at the Fillmore on a given night, the shows seemed more like parties than concerts, and there was a wonderful sense of community, and great music obviously." Jerry Garcia echoed this perspective. For him, the bands did not perform; rather, they became integrated with the audience. "The best thing about it was that the audience all danced. We were part of that world. We were not performers. We were playing for our family, in a sense."[82]

DIFFERENCES BETWEEN THE COUNTERCULTURE AND NEW LEFT

Although some of the most heavily politicized issues—the Vietnam War, the draft, and campus paternalism—resulted in the counterculture's significant expansion, hippies did not share the New Left's approach to combating these perceived social and political ills. While the New Left joined protests and picket lines, most hippies opted to drop out of the mainstream, focus on personal matters, or actively build counterinstitutions and communes. Counterculturalists favored cultural revolution or dope revolution as expedients for change—which activists considered both delusional and laughable. Observers noted obvious differences in appearance between the two camps. The counterculture was not merely an entity that opposed and offered alternatives to majority society's cultural, economic, and political paradigms, but a group of real people with similar values and philosophies. And in the mid-1960s, hippies—who essentially constituted the counterculture—and New Leftists were not the same people.

New Leftists protested the escalating war in Vietnam. At the University of Michigan in late March 1965, the first "teach-in" drew fifteen thousand students. Although all perspectives were welcomed, the vast majority opposed the war. The war's detractors argued that foreign countries—China, Japan, and France—had dominated Vietnam for centuries and that America was now intent on imposing its authority over the Vietnamese people. Vietnam, they emphasized, fought for national liberation. Democracy as opposed to communism had little to do with the escalating conflict. Debate ensued for eleven hours, disrupted periodically after prowar forces called in three bomb threats. Over one hundred other campuses soon held teach-ins.

In April, twenty-five thousand people appeared at a Students for a Democratic Society (SDS)–sponsored antiwar demonstration in Washington. Formed at the University of Michigan in 1960, SDS had been active in opposing Jim Crow, sending members to participate in sit-ins, voter registration drives, and Freedom Rides in the South. SDS also helped organize auto workers in Michigan. Influenced by the writings of Herbert Marcuse, C. Wright Mills, and Frantz Fanon, New Leftists pilloried the American government for promoting imperialism in Vietnam. They criticized capitalism and the doctrine of containment, while castigating American support of right-wing dictators. The United States, from this perspective, hoped not to spread democracy and combat communism but to maintain economic hegemony over Vietnam and Southeast Asia.

Almost one hundred thousand people protested in eighty cities in October 1965 during the International Days of Protest. In November, thirty-five thousand protestors marched from the White House to the Washington Monument in a demonstration organized by the Committee for a Sane Nuclear Policy, supported by Women Strike for Peace, National Coordinating Committee to End the War in Vietnam, and SDS. Carl Oglesby, SDS's president, gave a speech in which he denounced the Cold War consensus. Liberals, he argued, not right-wing ideologues, were the architects of the war, promoting corporate capitalism overseas. The National Liberation Front, he contended, were not unlike the Americans who had thrown off Britain during the revolution. Although, Oglesby acknowledged, "good men" implemented these policies, they were guilty of aiding corporate and business interests at the expense of Vietnamese national self-determination. Oglesby indicted ordinary Americans in this policy, for they had been willing participants and consumers in the country's corporate system. The war's objective, in other words, was not about fostering liberty, freedom, democracy, or containing communism. The following spring, antiwar activists in Europe, Australia, New Zealand, Tokyo, Rome, New York, Boston, and San Francisco participated in the Second International Days of Protest.[83]

Most Americans did not differentiate between political activists and the counterculture and conflated long hair, drugs, beards, and beads with the antiwar movement. In reality, significant tensions existed between the New Left—whose members engaged in overt political activism—and the counterculture—hippies who generally rejected political protest in favor of cultural radicalism and the quest for personal liberation.

These divergent approaches to dissent became obvious at the Berkeley Vietnam Day Committee (VDC) rally in October 1965. Activists persuaded

Ginsberg to ask Dylan to lead a demonstration. Dylan, like other counterculturalists, had no interest in protesting, and remarked, "There's no left wing and right wing, just up wing and down wing." Ken Kesey, however, participated. As he waited to speak, Kesey grew disturbed by the self-righteous rhetoric of the activists. There was no humor and the acerbic speeches seemed incongruous with a peace rally. Kesey took to the microphone wearing an orange Day-Glo windbreaker and World War I helmet. He compared the speaker that preceded him to Mussolini and lit into the crowd—"You're not gonna stop this war with this rally, by marching." He then took out a harmonica and played "Home on the Range." The Pranksters—dressed in Day-Glo, helmets, goggles, and flight suits— accompanied him on horns and guitars. "Who invited this bastard?" shouted a VDC member. Kesey then leaned forward into the microphone and shouted, "There's only one thing to do . . . And that's everybody just look at it, look at the war, and turn your backs and say . . . Fuck it." The crowd was stunned and confused and some booed. Kesey's philosophy was similar to that of other cultural dissidents, those engaged in personal pursuits, reforming themselves, and changing the culture rather than government policy.[84]

The counterculture and New Left found fault with the other. Many New Leftists saw counterculturalists as self-indulgent and silly, and doubted whether the counterculture and drugs could be revolutionary. Oglesby recalled his hostility toward hippies: "I was always annoyed at people who thought that the counterculture was in and of itself the revolution and that all we needed to do was all get high and listen to rock music. . . . [C]hange your head, that wasn't a revolution." Radical politicos viewed the counterculture as a diversion, its "isolating," inward-turning tendencies impeding the organization of popular movements for change. Activists believed much was at stake. Consequently, hippies' political indifference and their dropping out rankled demonstrators: "The cool world's answer is 'Do nothing,' but that won't do."[85]

The counterculture opposed the New Left's approach to America's problems. Although most hippies leaned left, they generally opposed participating in political activism. Most counterculturalists believed that protest failed to hasten change, that it was a waste of time and effort as demonstrations failed to influence the power elite. "I don't see that anything is to be gained by marching around with a sign or anything," Jim McGuinn of the Byrds told a reporter. "I have sympathy for those people, of course. And so the hair [the reporter noted that here he touched his own long hair] is kind of a badge, to show which side I'm on, it comes to that." In the San Francisco Bay Area, four poets proposed "Gentle Thursday" as a way to protest the war, distributing leaflets that read: "Nobody listening to you? Stop yakking . . . Spend the day calmly. Be gentle. Be kind." The strident ideology and militancy of protestors, combined with the negative energy that they produced, turned off passive hippies. Furthermore, the counterculture's more radical members advocated cultural revolution—not political protest—as a better means of changing society. "Changing peoples' heads" would lead to a more peaceful and harmonious world. Politics, culture, and society, cultural revolutionaries reasoned, would change only after individuals experienced personal revolutions, after their perceptions, values, and lifestyles changed. An ideal world free of hate, suspicion, jealousy, and competitiveness would emerge following mass personal revolutions. "I see political revolutions as only changes in power bosses," explained a writer for the Aquarian Herald. "Peace will only come upon the earth as each of us strives for inner peace." For many hippies, political revolutions ended with corrupt and authoritarian rulers in power. Real change started at ground zero, at the individual level.[86]

Hippies and New Leftists looked different, too. While hippies wore their hair long, donning beads and strange and eclectic clothing, male New Leftists and activists looked conventional, wearing ties and maintaining short hair—even crewcuts. Female demonstrators wore neat shirtwaists, nylons, and flats. Many students were embarrassed by movement longhairs, as they disliked the beatnik image that the press attempted to stamp on the New Left. Many SDSers were outraged, for example, when the New York Times Magazine featured a story on the organization in November 1965 and published a photo of the only long-haired member in the office. The rest of the leadership was clean cut. Furthermore, some activists, especially those who had worked with the destitute, made a point of looking "like ordinary people" as in their view "dressing in rags" was tantamount to "ridiculing poor people."[87]

In addition, New Leftists and hippies viewed dope and drugs differently. In early 1966, authorities busted an Oklahoma chapter of SDS for smoking marijuana. As a result, most of the national leadership wanted to dissociate the organization from the renegade Oklahomans. Vivian Rothstein, an early activist, became "very frightened" of drugs and "moved away from the drug culture" after some of her friends "fried their brains on LSD." Other activists felt that drugs obscured the political vision and harmed the movement; therefore, they did not want drugs to be "associated with politics." Tom Hayden, the best-known New Leftist, did not respect the drug culture. A fellow activist recalled that Hayden felt the counterculture was a "joke." Hayden did not attend many rock concerts, owned few albums, and remained a "straight man" all through the cultural revolution.[88]

KEN KESEY AND THE MERRY PRANKSTERS

Ken Kesey's experimentation with mind-altering chemicals started in 1960 when he volunteered to be a guinea pig for a federally funded CIA psychotomimetic drug experiment; doctors introduced him to the psychedelics LSD, mescaline, Ditran, and a substance called IT-290. Soon Kesey and friends—including a young Jerry Garcia—were taking doses of LSD mixed with venison chili in the bohemian community Perry Lane in Palo Alto, California. With his royalties from his novel *One Flew over the Cuckoo's Nest*, Kesey purchased a home fifty miles south of San Francisco in La Honda. There, he and his Perry Lane friends ingested LSD. To be sure, Kesey enjoyed his drug trips, but he also recognized acid's capacity to reveal one's true inner self. LSD removed unconscious barriers, allowing him and others to experience the present more fully. As Kesey explained it, "The first drug trips were, for most of us, shell-shattering ordeals that left us blinking kneedeep in the cracked crusts of our pie-in-the-sky personalities. Suddenly people were stripped before one another and behold: we were beautiful. . . . We were alive and life was us."[89]

The Merry Pranksters formed at La Honda. On June 14, 1964, Kesey and friends set out across America in a psychedelic 1939 International Harvester school bus with the word "FURTHUR" painted across the front and a sign on the back—"Caution: Weird Load." Travel, they felt, provided a means to spiritual enlightenment; all were prepared for "the great freak forward." The purpose of the journey was to go "furthur," discover the unknown, experience whatever thoughts and actions might come as the result of an LSD trip, and to leave reality behind. They also intended to blow the minds of straights; they called it "tootling the multitudes." As Kesey explained it, "The purpose of psychedelics is to learn the conditioned responses of people and then to prank them. That's the only way to get people to ask questions, and until they ask questions they're going to remain conditioned robots." The Pranksters created new identities for themselves by painting their faces, dressing in masks, buckskin, and capes, and taking new names—Sir Speed Limit, Mal Function, Swashbuckler, Intrepid Traveler, Doris Delay, Sensuous X, and Mountain Girl.[90]

While on this freaky LSD-drenched voyage the Pranksters happened to drop by Millbrook, New York, to visit acid guru Timothy Leary. But the former Harvard psychologist did not come out of his sixty-four-room mansion to greet them. He had been tripping for three days and did not want to be interrupted. They did eventually meet in an affable atmosphere but it became apparent that a schism in attitudes and styles existed between the Pranksters and Leary's IFIF. Serious behavioral scientists worked for IFIF. They took notes on their drug experiences, delivered lectures, and published a journal. They had "nothing to gain by associating with a bunch of grinning, filthy bums wearing buckskins and face paint." The feeling was mutual, as the Pranksters scoffed at IFIF's scholarly stuffiness. Kesey abhorred structured acid-taking sessions, finding them unnecessary as the drug's effects could be unharnessed anywhere—among family, at a rock concert, at a party, on a bus. Although Kesey and Leary disagreed on some aspects of LSD, both believed in the drug's transformative and therapeutic potential. Turned off, the Pranksters drove home. Back at La Honda, Kesey hosted legendary LSD parties for the Hell's Angels motorcycle club in the summer of 1965. The Pranksters and the Angels dropped acid, drank beer, and blasted Dylan albums.[91]

Kesey and his crazy coterie were protohippies, some of the first counterculturalists. Yet the importance of Kesey and the Pranksters to the counterculture's genesis has been consistently overemphasized by scholars. They certainly exhibited hippie values before most others because they revered dope as a pathway to enlightenment and valued experience, spontaneity, theatrics, colorful costumes, and living for the present, while maintaining an apolitical disposition. But the Pranksters weird behavior did not generate many converts to the counterculture. As we have seen, the lived experiences of youths alienated them from the mainstream.

THE ACID TESTS

Happenings evolved, becoming less arts- and poetry-oriented by the fall of 1965. Organizers introduced LSD and rock and roll into their events, transforming happenings from something that people experienced passively into events in which individuals actively participated. "The general tone of things has moved on from the self-conscious happenings to a more jubilant occasion where the audience participates because it's more fun to do so than not," read a press release for the Trips Festival. "Audience dancing is an assumed part of all the shows."[92]

Although San Francisco has been celebrated as the major center of counterculture activity, the first happening involving LSD, rock, and hippies occurred in Los Angeles. The "Lysergic A Go-Go," organized by Hugh Romney and Del Close, took place at the American Institute of Aeronautics and Astronautics Auditorium in November 1965. *Los Angeles Free Press* columnist Paul Jay Robbins called the Go-Go "an organized trip through the senses—an entertainment predicated on the psychedelic experience . . . voided of value judgments." Over five hundred people attended the event, and upon entering the venue, each was handed a capsule of LSD—referred to as "Solar Meat Cream"—by Romney throughout the evening. The organizers made "a friendly mockery" of Leary and Richard Alpert's lecture techniques, evidence that rank-and-file hippies did not take the LSD experience nearly as seriously as its most visible proponents. As the band Summer's Children played, an ultraviolet light was projected on stage, and people danced in mist among twirling ropes and waving serapes, as a weather balloon was being inflated. The *Free Press* concluded that "'Lysergic A Go-Go' is so right and so groovy that it has to happen again."[93]

Kesey wanted to share the LSD experience with others and to create an alternative reality, resulting in the "acid tests." Held from November 1965 through January 1966, they became legendary. "They were attempts to engage people in their senses so totally as to make it a transformational experience through sensory overload," Alpert remembered. "It was an attempt to overload one dimension so much that it forced people into another dimension." Kesey and the Pranksters advertised their LSD parties, asking prospective participants, "Can You Pass the Acid Test?" Youth responded enthusiastically. The first test occurred on private land outside Santa Cruz on November 27, 1965. Everyone got high and shared music, LSD, drink, art, and food. Nearly four hundred showed up at the second test held at a private home in San Jose; two hundred attended a third in Mountain View. A fourth unfolded at Muir Beach north of San Francisco. Over two thousand appeared for a test at the Fillmore Auditorium in January 1966. The atmosphere was similar at all the events. Chemist Stanley supplied plenty of LSD and the Warlocks—soon to be the Grateful Dead—provided music. Lights bounced on walls, tape machines sputtered strange noises, and kids tripping on acid danced. Ginsberg sang Buddhist and Hindu mantras, while Neal Cassady and Ken Babbs rapped and chanted into microphones. The Pranksters played avant-garde music and showed the film they had made on their cross-country bus trip over a year earlier. "The room is a spaceship and the captain has lost his mind," Kesey proclaimed at one of the tests.[94]

A three-day LSD extravaganza took the acid tests to a new level: The Trips Festival. Organized by biologist Stewart Brand—who later compiled the *Whole Earth Catalog*—the festival unfolded at Longshoreman's Hall on the San Francisco waterfront in January 1966. The Trips Festival was an experience complete with wild, liberated dancing, strobe lights and black lights, microphones that anyone could speak into, high-decibel psychedelic rock, painted bodies, costumes of all kinds, trampolines, guerrilla theater, and five film projectors operating simultaneously. Kesey, dressed in a silver spacesuit and bubble helmet, made random comments into a microphone; he also put up a message on the projector: "Anyone who knows he is God please go up on stage." Dopers stayed high, dipping into tubs of acid-spiked Kool-Aid. "Thousands of people, man, all helplessly stoned, all finding themselves in a room of thousands of people, none of whom any of them were afraid of. It was magic, far-out beautiful magic," recalled Garcia. Months later, on Halloween night, roughly two hundred patrons watched the Pranksters receive diplomas at the "Acid Test Graduation."[95]

While hippies grooved to eardrum-shattering acid rock, the inaugural issue of several underground papers appeared in 1966. In an effort to share "the news that the middle-class press won't print or can't find," the Underground Press Syndicate (UPS) was established in the summer. In August, the first underground in the Southwest appeared, Austin's *Rag*, which appealed to political hippies and hip politicos. In October, a group of poets and artists started a paper explicitly devoted to matters of culture, the *San Francisco Oracle*. It printed articles on everything from yoga to eastern mysticism to astrology. By the end of the year *Underground* had appeared in Arlington, Virginia, as had the *Washington Free Press* in the nation's capital; the *Illustrated Paper* in Mendocino, California; *Vanguard* in San Francisco; *Grafiti* in Philadelphia; and Richard Fairfield's the *Modern Utopian*, a publication focused on experimental communities.[96]

COUNTERCULTURAL COMMUNE BUILDING INTENSIFIES

The countercultural commune building that began with Drop City intensified in the lead-up to the Summer of Love. Near Los Angeles, in Sunland, Romney established Hog Farm in 1965. Though most of the best-known hip communes originated hundreds of miles north, Hog Farm achieved legendary status after its members acted as a "Please Force," feeding and medicating the legions at Woodstock in 1969. Romney and others took the initiative in founding the commune after they were offered a farmhouse and thirty acres on a mountain. The communards were given free rein over the property, but they had to look after the owner's hogs and pay the taxes in exchange. They pitched tents and built geodesic domes. In the free-form hippie community, diets consisted of brown rice and veggies, community clothing was stacked in the back of an abandoned car, communards freely indulged in dope, and on Sundays they staged happenings. Though visitors were rarely ousted, the Hog Farmers did expel Charles Manson and his girls. In 1967, the residents acquired a few busses and hit the road, providing light shows and support at rock concerts. Three years later they attained national notoriety after appearing in the Woodstock film. Observers noted that the Hog Farmers performed admirably at the festival, attending to hippies freaked out on bad drug trips. At a Texas music festival, blues guitarist B. B. King gave Romney his more familiar name: Wavy Gravy. In 1979 a large contingent of Hog Farmers, including Wavy, moved to Berkeley.[97]

To the north in Sonoma County, ex-professional-musician Lou Gottlieb opened his land to settlers, creating one of the most storied hippie communes: Morning Star Ranch. Only a handful of people lived there for the first summer in 1966. In November, seven people from Haight-Ashbury arrived. Hundreds visited by the Summer of Love. At Morning Star residents engaged in yoga, free love, and meditation, read the works of Asian spiritualists, and took psychedelic drugs. Reporters fixated on the casual nudity, and female communards greeted authorities in the nude. Some people discarded their clothes upon arriving only putting them on again when going into town. Although some of the residents were attached to someone, many others were single, and free love was practiced without hesitation. "Part of the deal was that, clearly, when I went to Morning Star, I was supposed to have sex with everyone," a woman who lived there for a period recalled. "There was kind of an underlying assumption of free love. . . . It was just kind of an assumed thing that everybody wanted to have sex with everybody else." Spiritualism was a major theme as well. Swami A. C. Bhaktivedanta visited in April 1967, engaging the communards with Hare Krishna chants, and six people converted instantaneously. By the late 1960s visitors described ramshackle structures, overcrowding, overflowing toilets—even rape. After authorities shut down Morning Star for sanitation violations in September 1967, a series of arrests followed, and Gottlieb eventually deeded the land to God in 1969. Despite buildings being razed multiple times, hippies continued to populate the commune until 1973.[98]

Thousands of urban crash pads came into existence, providing a place where people could stay for a night, a day, a month. Very disorganized, crash pads often consisted of an empty space where anyone could live or sleep among perhaps dozens of others. They varied greatly in terms of conditions. Diseases, rampant sexually transmitted infections, and chaotic childrearing characterized some. But others were well run, serving regular meals and assigning sleeping places. Some provided comprehensive social services. In New York City's East Village, hippies bedded down at Galahad's Pad. Ronald Johnson—Galahad—hailed from Kansas City. He acquired a run-down tenement on East 11th Street, and had twenty to thirty hip people—mostly teenagers—staying there on most days. On the West Coast, crash pads abounded in Haight-Ashbury, where they often served as counterculture induction centers. According to Jay Stephens,

"Your first night in the Haight was usually spent in one of the many communal crash pads, sandwiched together with a dozen friendly strangers. Your inhibitions and frequently your virginity were the first things to go, followed by your clothes and your old values—a progressive shedding that was hastened along by your first acid trip." Crash pads allowed counterculture values—dope use, free love, new perceptions, brotherhood and sisterhood, communal living—to thrive in a small space.[99]

Antiwar protests, civil rights demonstrations, "beatniks," and hippies triggered a backlash from majority society, though it was relatively tame compared to the late 1960s when it flared with much greater intensity. Many middle-class Americans found protestors and shaggy kids dirty and questioned their patriotism. "If they'd only take a bath, I wouldn't care what they did," one commented, while another asserted, "I think if they really believed in America they'd shave." Former president Eisenhower, too, expressed displeasure. "All this long hair, this lack of decorum. . . . I've always thought that sloppy dress was indicative of sloppy thinking." Ike was also disgusted by the appearance of young women whose hair hung down "over their faces so they look like baboons." Many others shared similar opinions. A Harris survey taken in the fall of the 1965 revealed that Americans disapproved of nonconformists. Two-thirds of the adult public thought that antiwar and civil rights demonstrators were "harmful to the American way of life." Over half felt the same way about men with long hair and beards. Of course, not everyone disapproved of social and political dissidents. Some adults sympathized with the young as they, too, expressed concerns about the issues facing the country. "It is difficult to tell a kid he may lose his mind with LSD when he knows he can have his whole head blown off in Vietnam," a professor remarked. An Iowa truckdriver commented, "I get a big kick outa hearin' about 'em, the drugs and shacking up together and givin' the big guys hell. Maybe the kids will come up with something good if they give 'em a chance."[100]

THE BURGEONING OF THE COUNTERCULTURE
IN LOS ANGELES, NEW YORK, AND SEATTLE

Countercultural activity that began in San Francisco expanded on the coasts in Los Angeles, New York, and Seattle. "There are literally thousands of young people," declared the *East Village Other* in the summer of 1966, "who have, in one form or another, dropped out of the system to the extent of just barely existing on its borders and who would benefit once and for all by seceding from the union."[101]

In Los Angeles, the Sunset Strip and the surrounding area became a focal point for the hip community, a "battlefield of the current social revolution," as one frequenter called it. Hip youth hung out at Whiskey A-Go-Go, the Trip, Ciro's, Barney's Beanery, the Galaxy, Ben Frank's, Pandora's Box, Cantor's, Bido Lito's, the Fred C. Dobbs, and the London Fog. At the "acid bars," hippies tripped, meditated, and danced. Youth also crammed into clubs to see the local bands: Love, the Doors, the Byrds, Frank Zappa and the Mothers of Invention, Buffalo Springfield, and the Lovin' Spoonful. Concertgoers packed the Shrine Auditorium, where acid rock bands jammed. The crowd shouted, "Freak out! Freak out!" as they grooved, strobe lights flashing, swirling colors and drawings projected on the walls. A dope culture developed at nearby UCLA where an estimated 20 percent of the campus had tried marijuana and 5 percent had taken LSD.[102]

Merry Prankster Ken Babbs and Hugh Romney organized a series of acid tests in Los Angeles in early 1966. Again, Stanley provided the LSD. The first took place at a Unitarian Church, where attendees ate acid-spiked bowls of pineapple chili. The second unfolded near Watts and it did not go well. There were many "bad trips," the result of overdoses. Other tests took place in Hollywood.[103]

The Byrds rehearsed in a room where Vito Paulekas taught clay sculpting. Paulekas had been a marathon dancer decades earlier. In the 1940s he spent four years in prison after a botched movie theater robbery. Upon his release, he moved to Los Angeles and assembled a group of protohippies. Paulekas formed a dance troupe and operated a crash pad for wayward youth. When the Byrds began a residency at Ciro's beginning in March 1965, Vito's troupe—the Freaks—danced along to the music and became an attraction themselves. Paulekas's wife Zsou ran a women's clothing store and dressed the female dancers in see-through lace and velvet—and the women rarely wore underwear. In July 1965 the Byrds departed on a tour through Colorado, South Dakota, Kentucky, Minnesota, Iowa, Illinois, Florida, Missouri, and Ohio. The Freaks accompanied the band on a sixty-passenger bus and danced during the shows. The coterie of protohippies shocked the people they encountered and were rebuffed. "They thought we were from outer space," remembered Lizzie Donahue, one of the troupe dancers. "In Paris, Illinois, they actually threw us off the dance floor." In states where counterculturalists had yet to be seen, the sight of long hair on men elicited hostility from straights. Such aggressiveness facilitated greater cohesion among the band. "We had to stick together because we were about the only thing that looked like us around the country," Michael Clarke said. "[In the South] they wouldn't serve us in restaurants. 'Hey, did your barber die?' Are you a boy or a girl?'"[104]

Like the counterculture in San Francisco, the Los Angeles counterculture had an artistic contingent. Four actors and writers made up the Firesign Theatre, which specialized in recording and radio. They made multilayered surrealistic recordings featuring the works of James Joyce mixed with sound samples from television shows and old films. They also hosted a late-night free-form talk radio show titled "Radio Free Oz" on channel KPFK that showcased prominent artistic people.[105]

In New York City, the Lower East Side—known as the East Village— became a vibrant counterculture enclave complete with experimental art, film, music, and theater. When hippies arrived, they moved into ramshackle tenements alongside Poles, Ukrainians, and Puerto Ricans. The corner of Third Avenue represented the entrance to the hippie community. Along the sidewalks, freaks preached free love and pacifism, and pontificated on the benefits of LSD. Others sang songs, read poetry aloud, or engaged in street theater. In Tompkins Square Park, longhairs pounded on bongo drums, danced, and chanted Krishna mantras daily. Popular hangouts included the bars Old Reliable, the Dom, and the Annex; artists and writers preferred Stanley's. Numerous coffeehouses, avant-garde theaters, and underground movie venues also dotted the Village. Along Saint Marks Place, hip youth scored dope and drugs and purchased items at specialty shops—beads, posters, drug paraphernalia, secondhand books, and clothing. Heads procured bells, beads, rolling papers, incense, and pipes from Morocco at the Psychedelicatessen.[106]

Artists thrived in New York. Claes Oldenburg and Robert Rauschenberg staged happenings, inviting audiences to participate. Andy Warhol was the most famous artist in the Village. He used art as a vehicle to question conventions and accepted norms. His famous paintings of Campbell's soup cans critiqued consumer culture, mass production, and the mundaneness of everyday life. Warhol employed images—a Brillo box, Marilyn Monroe, Jacqueline Kennedy Onassis, and Mick Jagger—to provoke viewers into questioning whether they were leading fulfilling lives. He demonstrated that even individuals could be mass produced in a consumer society. The artist surrounded himself with young rockers the Velvet Underground. The Velvets were different from West Coast hippies, as they dressed in black, wore black sunglasses, and popped amphetamines. Frontman Lou Reed shot heroin. Warhol hired the band to provide the music for an experiment he called the *Exploding Plastic Inevitable* that included the simultaneous use of films, lights, projections, and dancing.[107]

Experimental theater was an important element of the counterculture. Americans invented it to a large degree and Europeans gave American productions their greatest acclaim. Experimental theater's chief intellectual inspiration came from Jerzy Grotowski and the Polish Laboratory Theatre, which pioneered the concept of "minimalist" theater—stripping down the stage, doing without props and scenery. Julian Beck and his wife Judith Malina founded Living Theatre in New York in 1946. The company achieved national notoriety in 1959 with *The Connection*, a play about drug dealing. Beck and Malina were radicals; they took their performances to the streets in the service of various political causes. Beck's World-Wide General Strike for Peace, for example, involved a sit-down in Times Square in March 1962 to protest Kennedy's nuclear testing.[108]

Between 1964 and 1968, Living Theatre performed in exile. In September 1965 its production, *Frankenstein*, opened in Venice. The play led Italian authorities to deport the company. *Frankenstein*, according to distinguished director James Roose-Evans, was a collage of "yoga, meditation, gymnastics, howls, grunts, and groans." Audiences watched acts of "crucifixion, lynching, guillotining, and heart transplants." Back in New York in 1968, the Living Theatre became increasingly extreme. By that time international hippies dominated the company. Spectators described its audience-involving performances as "Dionysian." First the actors took off their clothes, followed by the spectators. Malina led her naked audiences out into the streets, crying: "I demand everything—total love, an end to all forms of violence and cruelty such as money, prisons, people doing work they hate. We can have tractors and food and joy. I demand it now!"[109]

New York was also home to the Fugs, whose members included Ed Sanders, Tuli Kupferberg, and Ken Weaver. Publisher and poet Sanders owned the Peace Eye Bookstore that served as the band's headquarters. Kupferberg, a pacifist-anarchist, published the magazine *Yeah*; its slogan was "Fuck for peace." The Fugs fused cultural radicalism with political protest, a melding the Youth International Party (Yippies) would accomplish later. The self-described "fantastic protest rock n' roll peace-sex-psychedelic singing group" merged the artistic with the vitality of the civil rights and antiwar movements. Their lyrics challenged authority. The Fugs wrote and performed the sexually themed songs "Group Grope," "Coca Cola Douche," and "What Are You Doing after the Orgy?" Numbers like "Horny Cunt-Hunger Blues" were integral to what Sanders called a "Total Assault on the Culture (anti-war/anti-creep/anti-repression)." Their repertoire included the satirical antiwar tunes "Kill for Peace" and "Strafe Them Creeps in the Rice Paddy, Daddy." One evening at the Bridge Theatre, the Fugs held a "Night of Napalm," performing their political antiwar numbers. Over loud feedback, the Fugs screamed, "Kill! Kill!" before heaving red-dyed spaghetti over themselves and the audience. "For a joke, the Fugs were OK," concluded Sanders.[110]

In Seattle, young men with shaggy hair and beards began appearing on the University of Washington campus. These "beatniks," as they were called in 1965, loitered around University Way Northeast—"the Ave"—the main business district near campus. A growing contingent of longhairs hung out in the Adams Forkner Funeral Parlor parking lot, strumming guitars, dealing dope, and "making the scene." The assistant King County prosecutor denounced hippies as "unbelievable bums." Police presence increased on the Ave. In the fall of 1966 Jack and Sally Delay opened up a bookstore they named the Bookworm, and let homeless kids stay at their home. The Delays also formed an organization, "The Brothers," which fed hippie dropouts. In a loft above Coffee Corral, the "Free University of Seattle" held its first classes. Students could choose courses on topics ranging from anarchism to Zen.[111]

THE COUNTERCULTURE IN
DETROIT, MADISON, AND AUSTIN

New York, Los Angeles, and San Francisco were the largest and most visible countercultural centers, but hippies started appearing elsewhere. A dope culture developed at major coastal universities like Harvard, Berkeley, UCLA, NYU, Brown, and San Francisco State. And by 1966, the counterculture had made inroads into the heartland.

John Sinclair greatly influenced the hip scene in Detroit. The enclave's gestation began in 1964 after Sinclair moved to Detroit to attend graduate school at Wayne State University. He quickly integrated himself into the "hipster" community near campus, hanging out with jazz musicians and poets at beatnik establishments such as the Red Door Gallery. Sinclair also met his future wife, Magdalene "Leni" Arndt, an artist and photographer.[112]

Sinclair and Arndt and friends began discussing setting up an organization for poets, musicians, and artists that fall. The first order of business was establishing a meeting place outside of campus. The group drafted a "document of self-determination." It proclaimed the virtues of resisting the "square" culture. Soon the Artists' Workshop was founded. It published *Guerrilla*, one the first underground papers in the Midwest. *Guerrilla*'s masthead read, "A Newspaper of Cultural Revolution." The collective disdained the dominant society; its members isolated themselves, loafed around, smoking dope and listening to jazz. The Artists' Workshop also interacted with hip communities on the coasts. Sinclair attended the Berkeley Poetry Conference in 1965, where he met Ginsberg and Sanders, among others. The Detroit Police Narcotics Bureau soon took an interest in the fledgling "beatnik" enclave and arrested Sinclair for marijuana possession. He was sentenced to six months in the Detroit House of Corrections.[113]

Despite this setback, the Artists' Workshop flourished. In August 1966 it hosted a "Festival of People," or "a summer ecstasy of the contemporary arts." The festival celebrated "PEOPLE—ourselves," and featured several bands, poetry readings, a photography exhibition, and films. Detroit, like San Francisco, developed a psychedelic dancehall scene. Bands such as the MC-5, the Chosen Few, and the Woolies jammed at the Grande Ballroom, while the light-show artists High Society beamed "throbbing amoeba-like" projections behind the performers.[114]

A counterculture also formed in Madison, Wisconsin. Even before a hippie enclave developed on Mifflin Street in the late 1960s, the University of Wisconsin was a center for bohemianism. In the late 1950s and early 1960s, political and cultural radicals—existentialists and hard-core leftists—gathered at the Rathskeller, a space modeled after a German tavern and known as the "rat," in the Memorial Union. Beginning in 1957 members of the Student Peace Center coordinated annual "antimilitary balls" to counter military festivities on campus. In 1965 four students founded the Ad Hoc Committee for Thinking. Three of the four had taken part in the civil rights movement in the South. Upholding a "sacred oath of antiauthoritarianism," the group engaged in cultural pamphleteering, placing documents that read "Your Professor Does Not Really Exist," on students' desks. In 1966, students gathered in dorm rooms for weekly "pot parties" and they also hung a sign on a fence: "LSD: YOUR CAMPUS TRAVEL AGENT—ONE TRIP IS WORTH A THOUSAND WORDS." *Connections*, the campus's first countercultural newspaper, blended cultural and political concerns and new forms of journalism.[115]

Likewise, a counterculture enclave burgeoned in Austin near the University of Texas. The 13th Floor Elevators, a local band, celebrated the use of drugs. Austin hippies smoked marijuana and had access to peyote buds, which they either ate or cooked. Texas counterculturalists did not dispense with all the habits of their elders, however, as they consumed beer in large quantities. At the University of Texas, "Gentle Thursday" became a weekly ritual gathering. It represented a synthesis of dissident politics and dissident culture. Jeff Shero of Austin's SDS chapter proposed the idea and the local underground, the *Rag*, publicized and defined the event. Organizers urged students to "do exactly what they want," and that included having fun, picnicking, playing music, reading poetry, and flying kites. At the very least, the organizers insisted, students should "wear brightly coloured clothing." In November 1966 over two hundred people gathered on the West Mall, where they relaxed, played music, held flowers, drew peace symbols on the sidewalks, and blew bubbles. Others stood gawking at the revelers. Hip students wrote "Fly in peace, gentle plane" on a permanently fixed aircraft outside the Reserve Officers' Training Corps building and danced around it. Gentle Thursday caught on, as SDS chapters put together similar gatherings in Colorado, Iowa, Kentucky, Missouri, Oklahoma, and New Mexico.[116]

STUDENTS FOR SEXUAL FREEDOM AND THE DIGGERS

As counterculture communities developed, organizations devoted to sexual freedom proliferated. Richard Thorne, a twenty-nine-year old African American and head of the East Bay Sexual Freedom League, promoted and organized orgies attended by UC Berkeley and San Francisco State students. At least six orgies, involving between twenty and forty-five participants each, occurred in the spring of 1966. Advocates of "nude parties" cited intellectual and philosophical motivations for initiating such events. Thorne stressed that people needed liberation from socially imposed sexual guilt and repression. "Man will only become free when he can overcome his own guilt and when society stops trying to manage his sex life for him," Thorne told *Time* magazine. He believed that any sexual act that did not "impose on the desire of other people" was acceptable. The University of California Sexual Freedom Forum sold buttons—"TAKE IT OFF" and "I'M WILLING IF YOU ARE"—and handed out information on birth control, abortion, and sexually transmitted diseases. Other sexual freedom committees and organizations formed at Stanford and UCLA. In Austin, the Texas Student League for Responsible Sexual Freedom called for an end to taboos and "archaic" laws. The organization's policy maintained that "any consensual sex act between adults which did not involve force or physical harm" should not be illegal. The league applied this policy to fornication, sodomy, miscegenation, and adultery. Senior Tom Maddox called limiting birth control pills to married women "ridiculous." He also singled out society for its "hypocritical" attitude toward gays. The university eventually expelled the group from campus.[117]

The most serious and revolutionary counterculturalists at this time were the Diggers. Their story began with R. G. Davis's San Francisco Mime Troupe, an organization that combined "avant-gardism with radical politics, Artaud's Theater of Cruelty with Brecht's social didactism." The "mime" in the outfit's name referred to a kind of broad gestural acting. Davis modeled the troupe on theatrical elements found in the Renaissance Italian form commedia dell'arte. Refusing foundational money and the politics that came along with it, the Mime Troupe stayed afloat by spending little on props and sets and relying on receipts and donations from spectators who attended their performances in the parks. Although the Parks and Recreation Commission had revoked their permit for alleged obscenity, the troupe continued to operate, risking arrest.[118]

A faction of actors within the Mime Troupe broke off to form the Diggers in the summer of 1966. Several of the Mime Troupe actors had become disgruntled with the troupe's political satire and well-trodden left-wing ideas. The Diggers took their name from a seventeenth-century anarchistic group that had confiscated common land in Surrey, England, in protest of high food prices. They ridiculed leftists who championed Cuba, China, and Vietnam as social models, but they also scoffed at acidheads and their mystical visions. Emmett Grogan called Leary and Alpert "charlatan fools," but reserved additional vitriol for the "puritanical" left that diverted attention from community-building in the Haight. The dozen men and women who founded the Diggers were cultural revolutionaries and activists working to make their alternative social vision a reality. They believed that capitalism had produced unprecedented wealth, which was horded by the few at the expense of the many. Additionally, politicians squandered wealth on unnecessary wars. Diggers were convinced that the answer to this predicament was for the masses to experience radical psychological transformations. The Diggers would lead the way as "life actors," enlisting hippies in their project, building a countercultural community, and these alternative institutions and ideas, they thought, would eventually infiltrate and permeate the mainstream. No one person acted as leader or spokesperson. If someone asked who was in charge, they responded, "You are!"

The Diggers believed that people could make a better world if they tried. They wanted more than to redistribute wealth to the masses; they sought freedom from what they considered to be the foundations of civilization: hierarchy, money, profits, power, and private property. And free was a basic principle—free food, free clothes, free everything. Beginning in the autumn of 1966 and continuing on a daily basis for over a year, the Diggers handed out free meals in the Panhandle. Hungry hippies and dropouts walked through an orange scaffold—a "Free Frame of Reference"—to get their grub. They also set up a free store, a free medical service, and crash pads for the multitudes of young dropouts who flooded the Hashbury. Opposed to profits, the Diggers even set out a basket containing "free money," while urging hippies to resist the "money game." They endorsed ignoring the law; they called this "assuming freedom." The media got the Diggers wrong. They were not a charity organization but were indeed attempting to initiate an alternative collectivist society. By inserting "free" into all their activities, the Diggers engaged in artistic street theater as "free" represented a kind of "social acid" that provoked revelations, making people question the dominant culture's consumerism and morality.[119]

LOVE PAGEANT RALLY, RIOT ON SUNSET STRIP, AND DEATH OF MONEY PARADE

Hippies held the first outdoor celebrations—"be-ins" or "love-ins"—shortly after the dancehall concerts began taking off. Dropouts had gathered on the hills behind Haight-Ashbury at dawn on June 21, 1966, to usher in the summer solstice, but the first major outdoor gathering of consequence was the Love Pageant Rally. Sitting near a café window in September 1966, *Oracle* editor Allen Cohen had an epiphany after witnessing a group of demonstrators pass by. He and Michael Bowen believed protest created negative energy and caused a negative response. Why not hold a celebration instead? "If people aren't demonstrating for civil rights violations, it's the war in Vietnam. We should be able to turn some of that negative energy into something more positive." Cohen's sudden revelation evolved into the Love Pageant Rally, held on October 6, 1966, the same day California outlawed LSD. The "666" of the date held special significance for the *Oracle* staff. In the Bible 666 symbolizes the Anti-Christ, and the Love Pageant's planners saw this as a portent—the government's criminalization of acid was demonic! Flyers advertising the event included a "Prophecy of a Declaration of Independence," a clear articulation of hippie values: "We hold these experiences to be self-evident, that all is equal, that the creation endows us with certain inalienable rights, that among these are: the freedom of the body, the pursuit of joy, and the expansion of consciousness." The Love Pageant Rally, according to the leaflet, would be "the first translation of this prophesy into political action." Like happenings and dancehall concerts, the rally brought hip people together, strengthening the sense of community. The rally was also an open celebration of psychedelic drugs. The organizers encouraged people to bring children, flowers, flutes, drums, beads, flags, incense, and joy. A few thousand people made merry in the Panhandle next to Golden Gate Park as the Grateful Dead and Big Brother played for free. As the master of ceremonies read a manifesto, hundreds swallowed a tab of acid at the same time. In New York City on the same day, psychedelists gathered at Tompkins Square Park for "Love: A Psychedelic Celebration." They brought children, flowers, flags, incense, and sang Hare Krishna with an elderly swami from India.[120]

In Los Angeles middle-class youth and police clashed on the Sunset Strip in November 1966, which alienated more kids—creating more freaks for hippiedom. Teenagers and students gathered at Pandora's Box, a popular coffee shop, to read poetry and play folk music. In an effort to widen the street, city planners decided to demolish the building. The closing of Pandora's Box, coupled with stringent curfew laws and police harassment, set off a week of demonstrations and riots. Young adults protested police harassment, carrying signs saying, "Freedom for All on the Strip," and "Don't Hurt Us; We're Your Children." On the most violent night, two thousand young people flooded the street. Musical duo Sonny and Cher sat down with others, causing massive traffic jams. Police formed flying wedges, charged the crowd, and arrested three hundred, including Peter Fonda. Rioters overturned a car, threw rocks and bottles, and tried setting fire to a bus. Filmmakers hastily shot the movie *Riot on Sunset Strip*. John Wilcock, publisher of the underground *Other Scenes*, believed he had witnessed the initial stirrings of a social revolution after viewing the film and prophetically proclaimed: "The opening shots were fired in California last month in a war that is going to engage America's attention increasingly in the next few years. It is going to be a civil war that may or may not be bloodless, but that will certainly revolutionize the lives and habits of everybody in America." Inspired by the events, Stephen Stills of Buffalo Springfield penned "For What It's Worth": "There's something happening here," sang Stills, "what it is ain't exactly clear." The lyrics highlighted growing tensions between young people and police. Moreover, Stills noted that youth faced formidable resistance from the establishment. But the song contained a measure of ambiguity, too. Stills raised the possibility that everyone was wrong.[121]

To the north in San Francisco, the Diggers staged their "Death of Money and Rebirth of the Haight" Parade on December 16, 1966. At five p.m. they began handing out "rearview mirrors, flowers, lollipops, incense, bags of grass (lawn clippings) and signs reading 'Now!'" Three people in hoods "carried a silver-dollar sign on a stick," followed by six pallbearers in animal masks bearing a coffin. The Gargoyle Singers, dressed like "cripples and dwarves from the Middle Ages," chanted "oooh," "aaah," "sssh" and "be cool," while spectators blew on pennywhistles. A thousand people gathered, suffusing the sidewalks, stopping traffic. A Hell's Angel led the parade with a "Now!" sign on the handlebars of his motorcycle. A Digger woman wearing a cape stood on the bike, holding up a "Now!" sign. Cops took two Angels into custody, provoking the crowd to picket the police station. Hippies paid for the Angels' bail.[122]

The Diggers and many other counterculturalists opposed commercial pursuits. Operating in this environment, hip capitalists became targets for criticism and scorn. Hippie businesses struggled on several levels. Low profit margins, lack of capital, intense competition, and rapidly shifting fashions posed difficulties, not to mention hostility from straight businesses determined to push them out of the market. On top of this, contradictions abounded. Hip capitalists, though counterculturalists, had to maintain strict business practices. Moreover, many of the people they strived to serve were indigent. Some refused to pay for items at all. Digger Emmett Grogan was especially critical of hip entrepreneurs, believing that they had "no business charging hippies for their daily needs." For Grogan, the Diggers' free store was the best model, a statement against materialism and profits and a demonstration of their commitment to the welfare of the community. Hip businesses' social position undermined Grogan's vision of the new society and that of many other counterculturalists. "They just want to expand their sales, they don't care what happens to people here," Grogan explained. "They're nothing but goddamn shopkeepers with beards."[123]

Some hippie women stole or "liberated" items from businesses in order to avoid working "shit jobs" or to keep themselves afloat. They abided by a code of ethics that allowed for stealing under certain conditions. First, one must truly need the goods. Second, the business had to be a large, for profit enterprise that overcharged consumers and paid workers low wages. Crescent Dragonwagon, for example, remarked, "I never rip off things around the corner and I won't at any country store where people treat you like a human being."[124]

By late 1966 the Haight was booming. By then, brothers Ron and Jay Thelin had opened the Psychedelic Shop, determined to disseminate information on acid. The shop was a doper's dream, where a head could buy records, books, smoking implements, fabrics, bamboo flutes, and psychedelic poster art. It soon became a hippie hangout, a refuge for street people, a place to trade and talk dope, or browse the community bulletin board. Hippies enjoyed a cup of coffee at I/Thou and ate at the Drog Store Café, Bob's Restaurant, and Quasar's. They bought jewelry, incense, and rolling papers at the Phoenix, posters at the Print Mint, and hip clothing at In Gear, Mnasidika, and the Blushing Peony. Far Fetched Foods sold health food. Annex 13 sold books, and Chickie P. Garbanza Bead and Storm Door Company sold supplies for bead stringers. To get away from the hustle and bustle of the city, youth retreated to "Hippie Hill" in Golden Gate Park to play guitar, smoke a joint, make friends, and score dope.

As 1966 drew to a close, the counterculture was poised to explode. Buffalo Springfield was right: there really was "something happening" and keen observers in San Francisco, New York, Seattle, Madison, Detroit, and Los Angeles knew it. The next spring, the rest of the nation would know it, too.

3

In August 1969, between four and five hundred thousand counterculturalists gathered at the Woodstock Music and Art Fair on Max Yasgur's six-hundred-acre dairy farm near Bethel, New York, for "three days of peace and music." Michael Lang, one of the festival's producers, contended that Woodstock symbolized the new culture's break from the old generation and the old culture. He also strongly insinuated that the festival represented a blueprint for the new society. "You see how they function on their own—without cops, without guns, without clubs, without hassles. Everybody pulls together and everybody helps each other." Whatever transpired when the people returned home, Lang asserted, "this thing has happened and it proves that it can happen." A few years earlier Woodstock would have been unimaginable.[1]

In the late sixties, the iconic counterculture bloomed; hippiedom appeared in its most memorable, publicized, and celebrated form—the Human Be-In, Haight-Ashbury, Summer of Love, flower power, the I Ching, *Sergeant Pepper*, Woodstock, Altamont, daisies in rifle barrels. Hippies diligently constructed the new society during what they called the Age of Aquarius—a time of optimism, faith, peace, and love.

Numerous changes distinguish the years 1967 to 1970 from the previous era. First, a partial blending of the New Left and counterculture occurred as the movement confronted obstinate national political leaders committed to prolonging the Vietnam War. More hippies joined antiwar protests, while more New Leftists embraced hippie practices and styles. On the whole, however, the counterculture and New Left remained separate and distinct strains of the youth rebellion. In the late 1960s the counterculture consisted of cultural dissidents—hippie purists—and hybrid counterculturalists—those who welded political and cultural radicalism, who were equal parts hippie and New Leftist, such as the Youth International Party (Yippies) and White Panthers.

Second, a contentious debate within the counterculture ensued as factions grappled with one another over the question of how best to change their world. Purists championed dope and love as panaceas for the world's ills, communards sought refuge from urban malaise, hybrid counterculturalists called for revolution, cultural revolutionaries urged people to "change their heads," and cultural activists demonstrated against laws criminalizing dope and nudity. Some feared a civil war as Americans became more polarized and divided over social, cultural, and political issues, fighting for—or so many felt—the very soul of the country.

Third, hippiedom spread across the country in 1967, taking root in nearly every city and large university. At mid-decade, hippies numbered in the tens of thousands. According to press reports, that number increased to a core of about two hundred thousand "full-time hippies" by 1968, with an additional three hundred thousand that held and practiced hippie values. By 1969 the counterculture grew ever larger, as Richard Nixon ascended to the presidency, the war continued, and political revolution and politics seemed a dead end. By the turn of the decade, millions of freaks, dropouts, cultural activists, and communards populated every region of the nation, including the Mountain West and Deep South.[2]

Fourth, as the counterculture burgeoned, its values became more numerous, sophisticated, and nuanced. Hippie values expanded well beyond a belief in the primacy of the present, community, and sex, drugs, and rock music. While some questioned whether LSD and marijuana could produce spiritual enlightenment, others embraced harder drugs such as speed, heroin, and cocaine. Hippies celebrated nudity, seeking, meditation, and took up Eastern mysticism and religions, overseas travel, and commune building. A few counterculturalists even made overtures to minority communities in an attempt to share their lives with marginalized peoples in California, New York, and New Jersey.

Fifth, the counterculture's manifestations evolved. In the spring of 1967 hippies all over the nation participated in love-ins. Massive multi-day rock festivals became all the rage by 1969—"the year of the festival." "Back-to-the-land" commune building grew ever more intense and demonstrations against the war included hippie factions.

THE HUMAN BE-IN

San Francisco's Human Be-In announced the arrival of the countercul-ture, while marking the start of its unprecedented growth. The Be-In's organizers—a group associated with the underground paper the *Oracle*—hoped to bring Berkeley political activists and the "love generation" of Haight-Ashbury together, groups that disagreed on approaches to libera-tion. Painter Michael Bowen and the *Oracle* staff also sought to turn Berke-ley's radical left on to psychedelics. Bowen suggested that Jerry Rubin, a leader of the Vietnam Day protest, represent the activist community. The promoters made grand predictions for the Be-In. "In unity we shall shower the country with waves of ecstasy and purification," announced the *Berkeley Barb*. "Fear will be washed away; ignorance will be exposed to sunlight; profits and empire will lie drying on deserted beaches; violence will be submerged and transmuted in rhythm and dancing." Bringing the New Left and counterculture together was only one of the Be-In's objec-tives, for it also celebrated the hip community, psychedelic way of life, and the "reaffirmation of the life spirit."[3]

On January 14, 1967, "A Gathering of the Tribes for a Human Be-In" took place at the Polo Grounds in Golden Gate Park. Over twenty-five thousand people eventually congregated around the stage. The festivities on this bright and clear day commenced in the afternoon after Gary Sny-der blew long and loud into a white conch shell, summoning the tribes. Other Beat poets—Michael McClure and Lawrence Ferlinghetti—sat next to him. Lenore Kandel read sexual poems from her *Love Book*, while Allen Ginsberg, dressed in white, sang mantras. Timothy Leary, wearing white pajamas, urged those who would listen to "turn on, tune in, and drop out" and the revelers responded tepidly.

The audience constituted the main attraction at the Be-In. Around the stage, people did their thing. *Newsweek* described the scene as "gentle anarchy." Revelers wore animal robes, feathers, tusks, beads, and flowers, and held balloons, banners, fans, flags, and chimes. Women donned long skirts and colorful blouses. Longhairs played bongos, flutes, and tambourines and burned incense. Others sat in the grass, sharing food and wine. The Diggers distributed free turkey sandwiches and Owsley Stanley donated free LSD tablets—"White Lightning." Many openly smoked marijuana and police on horseback did not make arrests. Hippies danced to Quicksilver Messenger Service, the Grateful Dead, Jefferson Airplane, the Sir Douglas Quintet, Big Brother and the Holding Company, and the Loading Zone, while the Hell's Angels stood guard over the sound equipment. At one point, a parachutist made a dramatic entrance, landing on the field. As the sun started to dip below the horizon, Gary Snyder blew on the conch once again, and the crowd began to disperse. "The be-in was a blossom. It was a flower," recalled McClure. "It was perfect in its imperfections. It was what it was—and there had never been anything like it before."[4]

The Be-In, though executed quite successfully overall, failed to achieve one of its main objectives: uniting politicos and hippies. The gathering of the tribes had actually revealed significant divisions between the factions. When it came time for Rubin to speak, he made the only political speech, an appeal for bail money for jailed activists. He ranted angrily about the war in Vietnam, which seemed out of place at the peaceful gathering. The crowd mostly ignored him and some made sarcastic remarks. Tensions between activists and psychedelists became heightened a few days later when the *Oracle* staff held a hip "houseboat summit" conference. Leary attended and elucidated a perspective held by the growing legions of dropouts. "Don't vote. Don't politic. Don't petition," Leary said. "You can't do anything about America politically." For Leary and many counterculturalists, politics brought people down and were a bummer. Power-hungry individuals dominated all political systems and all political systems were similar and equally oppressive. Leary called activists "young men with menopausal minds" and concluded that a "completely incompatible difference" divided the counterculture and leftist radicals. Outraged by Leary's comments, the editors of the *Berkeley Barb* urged antiwar activists to protest his presence when he returned to the Bay area to speak.[5]

BE-INS AND LOVE-INS IN THE SPRING OF 1967

The Human Be-In was only the opening salvo in what was to be the year of the be-in and love-in: 1967. Be-ins started on the coasts in March and moved inland by April. Hippies joined them for several reasons. First, the be-ins presented an opportunity for hippies to indulge in two of their foremost values: community and love. Second, they allowed countercultural-ists to escape the establishment and the troubles of straight society for a few hours. Hippies at the Chicago Be-In, for example, "relaxed, forgot the cold, the police, the hate, war, and all the petty flaws that keep men's scat-tered souls from uniting in love." Finally, such gatherings represented the essence of the countercultural project. Hippies created—albeit for a short period—ideal, instant communities, which allowed them to engage in their unique values together without obstruction.[6] Newsweek and the New York Times publicized the Human Be-In in February and alienated hippies far and wide became aware of San Francisco's "love feast" and "psyche-delic picnic." That spring, be-ins materialized in almost every region of the country.

Inspired by the Human Be-In, hippies in New York City put together their own. On March 26, 1967, Easter Sunday, ten thousand people crowded into Sheep Meadow in Central Park from dawn to dusk. The New York Times called the event "noisy, swarming, chaotic, and utterly surreal-istic," noting the clothing and accessories of the young who painted their faces and who wore bedsheets, tights, flower petals, paper stars, and tiny mirrors. "Love" was an omnipresent sentiment: girls painted it on their foreheads, kids surrounded police chanting it, while others jumped up and down, shouting it. The participants shared feelings of openness, ten-derness, and trust. Hippies clad in robes strummed guitars and banjos and blew bubbles and, as a gesture of goodwill, they offered a police of-ficer jelly beans.[7]

At the same time, at least four thousand hippies grooved at the Easter Sunday Love-In at Elysian Park in Los Angeles. The earliest attendees ar-rived at daybreak, watching the sun come up. A youth sat atop the stage reading aloud an American Indian prayer titled "Seeking the Return of the Great Spirit." Strangers handed each other lilies and balloons, and hip-pies wearing shawls and robes sat in tents or on blankets listening to rock bands the Turtles, New Generation, Rainy Daze, and the Peanut Butter Conspiracy.[8]

The prospect of huge numbers of youth dropping out of the mainstream—and out of politics—raised concerns on the political left. While hippies smoked grass, sailed on acid, and preached love and peace, Americans and Vietnamese continued to die. Activists disdained apolitical and antipolitical individuals while so many lives hung in the balance. From their perspective, hippies had misplaced priorities. The war needed to be stopped and dropouts did nothing. Activists targeted the hippie value love. Addressing the "Love Generation," a woman wrote to an underground paper, "Turn off for a while and show some love for the women and children being napalmed by the hate people." "Love is great, I love it—but it's not enough," remarked another. For New Leftists and activists, the countercultural emphasis on love was irresponsible. Meaningful change required real structural changes in the political system. *Ramparts* published a story on hippies, identifying the potential threat they posed to activism. "The danger in the hippie movement is more than over-crowded streets and possible hunger riots this summer," wrote Warren Hinckle. "If more and more youngsters begin to share the hippie political posture of unrelenting quietism, the future of activist, serious politics is bound to be affected."[9]

But activists did not give up on dropouts, because they saw in them substantial untapped resources. Peace, love, flower power, rock music, and be-ins could be steered to political purposes. Protest organizations made strong efforts at luring hippies to their cause, utilizing counterculture trademarks. Student activist organizations scheduled rock concerts and light shows to raise funds for the antiwar movement. The Washington Spring Mobilization for Peace Committee enticed dropouts to participate in a demonstration by organizing a "happening," complete with guerrilla theater. "We want the Mobilization to serve as a focal point for fresh avenues of expression of opposition to the war," remarked a female coordinator. "Diverse approaches have to be tried to get people on the Peace Train to New York."[10]

As a result of activist efforts, some counterculturalists began joining antiwar protests. The Spring Mobilization Committee to End the War in Vietnam, a loose confederation of pacifists, radicals, and liberals seeking to unify the antiwar movement, sponsored major protests. On April 15, some fifty thousand people demonstrated in San Francisco, and two hundred thousand marched with Martin Luther King Jr. and other notable figures in New York City. In San Francisco hundreds of marchers wore costumes and carried flowers. Although some people were skeptical about mixing be-ins with politics, several thousand young men and women gathered for a be-in at Central Park organized by activists. Hippies with painted faces and legs danced to guitars, flutes, and drums in Sheep Meadow before the demonstration commenced. During a draft card burning, some of the demonstrators wore or carried daffodils, while others chanted, "Flower power."[11]

Meanwhile, love-ins continued to sprout. On Saturday, April 22, at least seven thousand counterculturalists attended a be-in at Franklin Park Zoo in Boston. Women wore floppy hats and other mod women strolled the grounds in miniskirts. Hippies handed out flowers and burned incense, while balloons marked with the words "Love Everybody" floated around.[12]

Love-ins soon spread to the Midwest and South. More traditional and conservative than the coasts, hip celebrations in these regions were considerably smaller with fewer participants. Hippies clustered around urban centers and near universities, places more eclectic, cosmopolitan, and socially and politically liberal than the surrounding countryside. On Sunday, April 23, Texas hippies loved-in at Houston's Hermann Park. The crowd grew to nearly 1,500 at its peak. Young people sported flowers and danced to jug bands. A man wearing a black cape and gas mask suggested that the participants march to the zoo, which they did. The Austin *Rag* called the love-in "spontaneous and happy."[13]

The next Sunday, April 30, over four thousand gathered at Detroit's Bell Isle Park. After his release from jail for marijuana possession in August 1966, John Sinclair began the legwork that culminated in the formation of Trans-Love Energies (TLE) in 1967, an organization that brought together Detriot's hippies, students, and other alternative groups. Inspired by the Human Be-In and similar gatherings elsewhere, TLE promoted the love-in as a meeting place for Detroit's straight and hip populations. Together they would celebrate peace and love and a new vision of society. At Belle Isle, Detroit's hip coalesced for six or seven hours of dancing, singing, sharing, and picnicking. Strangers fed each other, passing around eggs, oranges, and tomatoes. Flower children smiled at each other, called each other beautiful, and presented each other with gifts. A woman passed out cards with "love" written on it. Other smoked grass, dropped LSD, and chanted. In what proved to be the "great banana hoax of 1967," heads passed around "banana joints," believing, incorrectly, that the inside lining of banana peels had psychoactive potential. As a band jammed, hippies danced or rolled around in the grass together. For the most part, the be-in was a placid affair. As nightfall approached, however, the gathering turned into a full-scale riot after law enforcement arrested a motorcyclist. The press portrayed TLE as mindless hedonists and sided with the police.[14]

On the same day in Seattle, the underground paper *Helix* promoted "The Chief Seattle Flower Potlatch Power & Isness-in," which took place at Volunteer Park. The crowd of four thousand was mostly made up of hippies, but others attended as well. A marine from Fort Lewis wore a painted flower on top of his head and a silver-haired woman wearing an orchid on her poncho exclaimed, "I haven't had so much fun in YEARS." The young danced, flailing wildly to the sounds of local bands Clockwork Orange, Crome Syrcus, and Magic Fern. They also picnicked, blew soap bubbles, flew kites, and played conga drums and wooden flutes.[15]

On Mother's Day, May 14, hippies assembled on North Avenue Beach for Chicago's Human Be-In. The be-in, the *Chicago Seed* proudly proclaimed, was "the Midwest's confirmation that She, too, belonged within the folds of Love that have gathered the tribes together everywhere across the continent." Despite the cold and wind, nearly five thousand joined in the fun. Hippies held balloons, flew kites, wore and passed out flowers, and openly expressed their love for one another along the beach. Some built small fires to keep warm.[16] Philadelphia's "Happy Un-Birthday Be-In" also unfolded on Mother's Day, when approximately 2,500 hippies met in front of Independence Hall. The organizers passed out five hundred joints made from a half pound of marijuana. A hippie family distributed balloons, while others gave away candy, magazines, and incense.[17]

Underground newspapers multiplied as quickly as be-ins. In 1967, many inaugural issues rolled off the press—*Helix* in Seattle, the *Seed* in Chicago, *Open City* in Los Angeles, and *Avatar* in Boston. Marshall Bloom and Raymond Mungo established a hip press service in the fall, the Liberation News Service (LNS). By the end of the year, John Kois had started the *Milwaukee Kaleidoscope* and Don DeMaio had produced Philadelphia's

Distant Drummer. In 1968, other major undergrounds appeared such as New York's *Rat* and *Other Scenes*, Boston's *Old Mole*, and the antiwar, antiracist *Great Speckled Bird* in Atlanta, one of the first papers to emerge in the South. By the close of the sixties, nearly every city with over a hundred thousand residents had an underground paper, as did fifty college towns. Eventually there would be three wire services, five hundred underground papers, and more than five hundred dissenting high school papers, with a total circulation of about five million.[18]

ALIENATION IN THE LATE 1960S

The underground press proliferated and the counterculture expanded at an unprecedented pace for one central reason: alienation was on the rise. Government leaders and policymakers caused immense discontent. The older generation, in the view of youth, had started a war and expected young men to serve in the armed forces. Those opposed to the war might be coerced to fight and die, while the people responsible for the conflict did not make any sacrifices. "Obscene and senile people . . . sit on draft boards and slaver at the sight of all the young ass that's eligible for being stuffed into uniform and sent away to fight obscene and evil wars for the obscene and evil old ones. . . . why the hell don't YOU go out and fight?" asked the *Los Angeles Free Press*.[19]

Moreover, democracy did not seem to exist. The young wondered, "Who represents us in Washington?" Both major political parties had made the commitment to fight a global Cold War and communism in Vietnam and both parties represented special interests, especially the defense industry. Those who yearned for peace had no viable political options. Men could be drafted and sent to war at age eighteen, yet they could not make an impact on government policy as the voting age was twenty-one. "This country is supposed to be a democracy—but there is no real control over one's own life," lamented a youth from upstate New York. A Californian expressed a similar sentiment, writing, "No matter who wins, the wars will continue, and the conditions surrounding the lives of most Americans will not change."[20]

Furthermore, hypocrisy and an intolerant majority caused disillusionment among those who became hippies. Traditionalists and conservatives charged peace advocates with treason and communist subversion. Many adults championed the First Amendment but supported censorship of materials they deemed obscene. Others revered the American revolutionaries of 1776, while staunchly opposing "unpatriotic" and "un-American" student revolts against authority on campuses. Youth found the condemnation of drugs by adults to be the height of hypocrisy. The epitome of the establishment—the US Army and the CIA—did not disparage its own dope use, experimenting with LSD long before the counterculture came into contact with it. Adults smoked cigarettes, got loaded on alcohol, and abused prescription drugs—tranquilizers, barbiturates, and amphetamines—drugs more powerful and dangerous than marijuana. By the mid-sixties, about three thousand people died of prescription drug overdoses each year. Yet these drug-addicted and dependent adults condemned drug use by youth.[21]

The young found ironies in relation to Christianity especially disturbing. The majority of Americans claimed to be Christians, but supported wars and killing, while standing opposed to people who followed the actual teachings of Christ, a "radical sort of character who told people to love one another and live together in peace." If Jesus came back to earth, the young argued, he would be wanted by law enforcement for practicing medicine without a license, loitering around synagogues, and wearing "typical hippie attire—long hair, robes, and sandals." Furthermore, Christ would likely have been an antiwar demonstrator, the kind of individual professed Christians condemned as irresponsible, unpatriotic, and bad for the country.[22]

The majority's definition of what constituted obscenity also confounded the young. Youth vehemently contested the establishment's idea of what qualified as obscene. The government and Silent Majority seemed to accept, condone, and perpetrate hate, killing, and war—the epitome of obscene, they argued—while censoring sex—a natural, healthy, and beautiful act. A Nebraska underground paper articulated this frustration:

Is it obscene to fuck,
or
Is it obscene to kill?

Is it more obscene to describe
fucking,
An act of love,
or,
Is it more obscene to describe
killing,
An act of hate? . . .

Which is really obscene?²³

Alienated hippies appeared everywhere as be-ins proliferated throughout the spring and Summer of Love. Los Angeles hippies held a series
of gatherings in Griffith and Elysian Parks in which tens of thousands
participated. A couple of be-ins complete with "bright smiles," "bells"
and "strange thoughts" occurred in Cleveland near the lagoon in front of
the art museum and two love-ins "sputtered along" in Milwaukee's Lake
Park. In the nation's capital, 1,200 came together for a be-in at Rock Creek
Park, while Oklahoma flower children held a love-in in Tulsa. Freaks who
had access to the ocean hit the sandy shores. Florida experienced its first
love-in when 1,500 hippies and motorcyclists descended on tiny Lantana
Beach. An estimated ten thousand sang, danced, and made music on Seal
Beach in California in late June, and in early July, three thousand hippies
congregated in Audubon Park in New Orleans. Flower people in Spokane,
Washington, came together for at least three be-ins at Cliff Park.²⁴

HAIGHT-ASHBURY HEADING INTO
THE SUMMER OF LOVE

Yet no single hip enclave or scene was larger, more vibrant, or more celebrated than Haight-Ashbury in San Francisco. Over twenty-five new businesses had opened in the district the year before. In the spring of 1967
runaways, poets, artists, Christian missionaries out to make converts,
beggars, Hindu hippies, and people who claimed to be from UFOs packed
the Haight. People smiled everywhere. A mailman went by the name Admiral Love, and hippies knew the local policeman as Sergeant Sunshine.²⁵

Haight hippies established counterinstitutions. Lawyers founded the Haight-Ashbury Legal Organization (HALO). The Switchboard helped dropouts find crash pads, temporary employment, and assisted concerned parents of runaways. Doctor David Smith opened the twenty-four-hour Free Medical Clinic. Part-time doctors and volunteers staffed it, treating ailments such as venereal disease, foot sores, and adverse drug reactions.

The national news media became obsessed with Haight-Ashbury. Nearly every major television network and publication showcased the psychedelic community. For a time it seemed as if the entire country was fixated on hippies, mesmerized by their alternative lifestyles. Descriptors such as "flower children" and "love generation" entered the mainstream lexicon. Reporters from all over the world descended on the Hashbury and hippies joked about bead-wearing *Life* and *Look* journalists interviewing each other.

"If you're going to San Francisco," sang Scott McKenzie, "be sure to wear some flowers in your hair." McKenzie sensed that something was astir; later he sang, "All across the nation / Such a strange vibration / People in motion." When summer began, hordes of middle-class youth from all over the country enthralled by incessant national news stories poured into the Haight; eventually seventy-five thousand would arrive during the Summer of Love. The problem of runaway teens reached epidemic proportions. The Juvenile Justice Commission apprehended and returned to their parents two hundred runaways each month. Tourists inundated the area, too. Carloads of wide-eyed gawkers, bumper-to-bumper, came down Haight Street. So did Gray Line Bus Company, taking its passengers on a "Hippie Hop"—"the only foreign tour within the continental limits of the United States." Businesses immediately began transforming the counterculture into a commodity, selling Day-Glo posters, "lovedogs," and "hippieburgers." Tourists bought "Love Guides" at the Print Mint.[26]

THE COUNTERCULTURE AND RACIAL MINORITIES

The counterculture did not have a clear-cut relationship with racial minorities. Certainly, the young whites who embraced hippiedom abhorred racism and expressed sympathy for African Americans facing poverty and discrimination and radical black organizations confronting government repression. Cultural radicals like the Diggers, White Panthers, and Yippies admired and lionized militant African Americans and leaders who struggled to attain equality for blacks. Some counterculturalists reached out to African Americans, Mexican Americans, and Puerto Ricans by staging be-ins and smoke-ins, and assisting residents of riot-ravaged cities. Freaks and activists became steadfast supporters of the American Indian Movement. Yet strains existed. Many longhairs likened themselves to American Indians or blacks in order to invent new identities and make dubious claims to minority status and state victimhood. Hippies eschewed the middle-class niceties and lifestyles that many minorities aspired to, and African American activists found it difficult to take the countercultural aspects and actions of the white antiwar movement seriously. In Taos, New Mexico, violence flared between communards and Chicanos, the result of culture clash. These contacts were fluid and even volatile. Eldridge Cleaver of the Black Panthers, for instance, wrote approvingly of hippies in his 1968 book, Soul on Ice; by the early 1970s, however, Cleaver denounced the Yippies and larger counterculture as silly and useless.

As the flower people flowed into the Hashbury, racial tensions emerged. White middle- and upper-class individuals primarily constituted the counterculture. Approximately one-quarter, however, belonged to the working class. Many hippie runaways in America's cities came from blue-collar and even poor families. Few hippies of color moved among their white counterparts, a great irony given that the African American hipster of the early twentieth century influenced the counterculture's style, language, and oppositional nature. And African American musicians were mostly responsible for developing the hippies' beloved rock and roll.[27]

In the Hashbury and elsewhere, longhairs referred to black people as "spades." Many African Americans held hippies in contempt because hippies had abandoned the comfortable middle-class life that they struggled to attain. Additionally, blacks resented that the flower children could escape their self-imposed poverty at any time, while they could not. They resented hippies' claims of being an oppressed minority even more. Black residents complained that their kids were exposed to hippie drug taking and lovemaking in the parks. For their part, hippies had difficulty understanding black aspirations. "The negroes are fighting to become what we've rejected," commented a white Haight resident. "We don't see any sense in that." Culture clash also exacerbated the friction. Many "freaked-out WASPs" had never had any contact with minorities before arriving at the Haight.[28] Confrontations occurred elsewhere. In New York, on the Lower East Side, hippies clashed with blacks and Puerto Ricans at Tompkins Square Park. Hippies and Mexican Americans engaged in physical hostilities on the edges of Elysian Park in Los Angeles. Other freaks contended with rock- and bottle-throwing Mexican American gangs. In New York, Eastern European Americans—Poles, Czechs, and Ukrainians—also disliked the hippies' noise, disorder, and antiauthoritarianism.[29]

Some counterculturalists reached out to minorities in an effort to bridge racial divides and form friendships. This happened most frequently in urban centers. In San Francisco, Chester Anderson, writing for the *Communications Company*, lamented, "HAIGHT/ASHBURY IS THE FIRST SEGREGATED BOHEMIA I'VE EVER SEEN!" He recognized similarities between the hippie and black communities, claiming that both were "oppressed minorities." Anderson reminded white and black hip alike that they fought for the same ideal: freedom. He also urged hippies to unite with African Americans against their common enemy: "the Man." Anderson asserted that the Man knew hippies and blacks were "brothers." Consequently, the Man worked hard to drive a wedge between the races in order to maintain power. If hippies and African Americans worked together, sharing resources and experiences, they could deal a major blow to the Man. Anderson encouraged white hippies to visit the black Fillmore district, to share their lives with the people there. If black and white formed strong bonds, Anderson argued, "Freedom Power" would reign. "Freedom Power is Soul Power is an Army of Brothers. Let us love each other and be free." Similarly, Tuli Kupferberg, in New York, argued that hippies harbored no racial prejudice, especially when it came to sex: "The hippy just fucks beautiful chicks (or men) of any color or nationality & just lives & shares with chicks & men of any nationality or color, naturally. By naturally I mean without thinking twice."[30]

In Los Angeles, hippies organized be-ins for the explicit purpose of bringing whites and minorities together. In July, freaks staged a love-in that drew seven thousand people in Watts. Taj Mahal and the Chambers Brothers provided musical entertainment and the organizers declared the event a success. Hippies and others joined in the music making with bongo drums and flutes. Vito and the Freaks showed up and danced with African Americans. *Open City's* Bob Garcia praised the infectiousness of the counterculture, writing that "hippies short-circuited the ghettos' mental hate syndrome with smiles, freaky renaissance clothes, bare feet, free food, and an open attitude which became more contagious as the day wore on."[31]

Some efforts, however, brought disastrous results. On August 30, hip groups Green Power and Vito's Fraternity of Man sponsored a be-in in the East Los Angeles Aliso Village Projects, where African and Mexican American families lived in poverty. A rock band provided entertainment. Green Power distributed stale food, displeasing the poor residents, and later there was a confrontation between black adults and a white hippie woman after she chased a black child. "Hippies have quite a bit to learn about people in general and this is especially true if they are poor and not white Anglo-Saxons," reported *Open City*.[32]

Counterculturalists came to the aid of black ghetto residents in Newark following the July 1967 riots. A dozen people, including Abbie Hoffman, a former civil rights organizer turned hippie, staged a be-in for the community. Hoffman heard that hippies had rioted in Newark and Detroit alongside African Americans, which made him very happy. Flower children were becoming tough. Hoffman scoffed at academics who tried to understand the underlying reasons for urban unrest. He wanted less analysis and more action. In an article titled "Diggery is Niggery," Hoffman wrote, "Riots—environmental and psychological—are Holy, so don't screw around with explanations." For Hoffman, riots created a revolutionary consciousness. Dressed in "jump suits, miniskirts, safari hats, buttons, and painted faces," the New York Diggers gave black children piggyback rides and handed out flowers, candy, baby food, canned goods, bread, and meat. Hoffman played touch football with kids. He also staged a guerrilla theater skit parodying an antebellum slave auction with Hugh Romney. As Hoffman flexed his arms and opened his mouth to bare his teeth, kids placed bids. Hoffman's point was that Diggers were like black people: "Spades and Diggers are one," he wrote. An African American woman understandably sensed that her well-meaning visitors might not be formidable allies, remarking, "I don't know if it's going to do us any good to have people like you on our side."[33]

In addition to reaching out to African Americans, longhairs made efforts to ameliorate tensions between themselves and Puerto Ricans. Dope went a long way toward achieving this goal. "The hippies and the Puerto Ricans have one thing in common—grass," remarked a smoke-in participant. "From that, a great relationship is being built up." In August, the New York Diggers arranged a conga rock and roll party for nine hundred Lower East Side hippies and Puerto Ricans at the Cheetah night club. Free tickets had been distributed at the Diggers' free store in the East Village. The party brought together two communities that had been recently warring at Tompkins Square Park. The Players and the Strawberries, along with Mongo Santamaria Jr. provided music. In spite of the efforts of the Diggers and others in the Haight, Los Angeles, and elsewhere, relations between minorities and hippies would never be very amicable.[34]

The counterculture also had an ambiguous relationship with the Black Power movement. Black Power's beginnings dated back to the mid-sixties, when the Student Nonviolent Coordinating Committee (SNCC) began to turn away from the principles of integration and interracialism. SNCC unveiled its new militant stance during the "March against Fear" in the spring of 1966 when Stokely Carmichael stood before a rally and proclaimed, "What we are gonna start saying now is Black Power." For the rest of the march, SNCC activists periodically asked crowds of black supporters, "What do you want?" and they responded enthusiastically with shouts of "Black Power!"

Black Power did not necessarily entail the revolutionary transformation of American society. For some, it simply meant "black pride"—a reverence for a distinct African American heritage and culture. Many viewed this pride in racial identity as similar to the ethnic cohesion that had helped earlier groups such as the Jews and Irish attain upward mobility. Pan-Africanism also became integral to Black Power. American blacks embraced African culture, donning dashikis. They also played or listened to traditional African music. The bonds went beyond culture, however, as the Pan-African element linked black African freedom with black American freedom. Black Power encompassed additional meanings as well. Carmichael and others rejected nonviolence; if violent whites attacked blacks who refused assimilation, blacks would return violence. Above all, Black Power involved self-empowerment.

The Black Panther Party for Self-Defense was perhaps the most visible and controversial manifestation of Black Power. Bobby Seale and Huey P. Newton, students at Oakland City College, founded the Panthers in October 1966. A community action group rather than a political party, the Panthers, in their manifesto, "What We Want, What We Believe," made several demands of white America—freedom, full employment, decent housing, the release of black prisoners, and "an immediate end to POLICE BRUTALITY and MURDER of black people." The Panthers did more than talk, providing services for the black community—food, shelters, education, and alternate housing. They promoted self-defense and advised black people to arm themselves for protection. Wearing black berets, leather jackets, and dark sunglasses, the Panthers formed self-defense groups and openly brandished loaded weapons.

Initially, the Panthers viewed hippies as allies. They understood that rebellion among white youths constituted a threat to the establishment. In Soul on Ice, Cleaver wrote, "The characteristics of the white rebels which most alarm their elders—the long hair, the new dances, their love for Negro music, their use of marijuana, their mystical attitude toward sex—are all tools of their rebellion. They have turned these tools against the totalitarian fabric of American society—and they mean to change it." Cleaver recognized that hippies intended to transform society. His interest in hip white culture and radicalism made him a rarity among the Panther leadership. After the Weather Underground helped Timothy Leary escape from prison in 1970, he traveled to Algeria, where he formed an uneasy alliance with Cleaver. Leary extolled the Panthers, telling a reporter from Rolling Stone, "Read the writings of Huey P. Newton or look into his eyes when you see him. He's a complete turned-on holy man, a golden black Aquarius tuned into the central energy. It was always an acid dream of ours to find turned-on blacks who could leap over the whole middle-class integration trip and define a new culture. That's what the Panthers are." In a letter to "Beloved Brother" Ginsberg, Leary called the Panthers "the hope of the world," and Cleaver a "genial genius."[35]

The San Francisco Diggers also forged a nominal partnership with the Panthers. The Diggers viewed bourgeois middle-class white men as emasculated figures who cowered behind law enforcement, afraid of masculine men of color. They believed that African American men possessed a more authentic, "primitive" manhood, which sustained them in the face of white supremacy and oppression. They, too, valorized black masculinity and virility while repudiating their own white identity, heeding poet Gary Snyder's exhortation to "kill the white man" within. Emmett Grogan delivered free food to the Panther headquarters and the Diggers printed the first issue of the party's newspaper. The Diggers also held a fundraising benefit for boxer Muhammad Ali when he resisted his military induction. Furthermore, they supported the Black Man's Free Store, which was opened by Panther Roy Ballard, and worked closely with the party in trying to ease racial tensions in Haight-Ashbury. Black street toughs had been robbing white hippies. The Panthers published a notice in the party's paper ordering "Black brothers" to "stop vamping on the hippies. They are not your enemy. . . . Your blind reactionary acts endanger the BLACK PANTHER PARTY. . . . LEAVE THEM ALONE. Or—THE BLACK PANTHER PARTY will deal with you!"[36]

Black Power never made up part of the counterculture. While opposed to the establishment, African American militants strived to attain the middle-class comforts hippies had abandoned. Furthermore, black nationalists advocated racial pride and separatism, which isolated them from the counterculture. Black radicals shared far more commonalities with the New Left than with hippies, as New Leftists stood against imperialism and viewed poor blacks as potential revolutionary proletarians.

THE SUMMER OF LOVE, HAIGHT-ASHBURY'S DECLINE, AND "DEATH OF HIPPIE"

Moving into the Summer of Love, the Beatles released *Sergeant Pepper's Lonely Hearts Club Band*. The album effectively heralded the blossoming of the counterculture. After the Fab Four quit touring in 1966, they devoted themselves completely to creating a musical masterpiece in the studio. *Sergeant Pepper* was to be a new kind of album, a work of art. "In 1967," a Beatles scholar has written, "odd-chord progressions, elusive lyrics, unusual instruments and bizarre studio effects would lend to the Beatles' music a sense of magic and mystery that defied rational interpretation." By the time the Beatles recorded *Sergeant Pepper*, all four members had taken LSD; acid heightened the creative abilities of the songwriters. John

Lennon and Paul McCartney made greater demands of producer George Martin. For the song "Being for the Benefit of Mr. Kite," Martin incorporated swirling circus sounds and Victorian steam organs. For the cut "A Day in the Life," the album's finale, a forty-one-piece symphony orchestra produced a cacophony of noise after Lennon informed Martin he wanted "a sound building up from nothing to the end of the world." At the end of the album, the group added a note at 20,000-Hertz frequency, which could be heard by dogs but was inaudible to the human ear. Production costs soared. The band's first record had cost about $2,000 and was recorded in a single day. *Sergeant Pepper* cost $100,000 and took four months to complete.[37]

The record's motifs and lyrics were eminently countercultural, addressing drugs, community, and the search for authenticity. The Beatles made references to acid. "Lucy in the Sky with Diamonds," an alleged mnemonic for LSD, evoked surrealistic images of a psychedelic otherworld. Lennon always maintained that the song was inspired by a painting made by his son Julian. Lennon also sang about wanting to turn people on to LSD and an individual blowing his mind in a car in "A Day in the Life." Other lyrics pertained to hippie values and recent developments within hippie culture. "She's Leaving Home" referenced a runaway girl who flees the safety and security of middle-class life to fill a void in her life. "With a Little Help from My Friends," expressed communal values of getting by and getting high with the aid of one's brothers and sisters.[38]

The album's release in June 1967 was a watershed moment in the lives of many people. Thousands to this day—especially former hippies—remember where they were and what they were doing the first time they heard *Sergeant Pepper*. Critics showered the record with praise. Kenneth Tynan called it a "decisive moment in the history of Western Civilization." Leary went the furthest in extolling the band. "The Beatles are Divine Messiahs," he declared, "The wisest, holiest, most effective avatars (Divine Incarnate, God Agents) that the human race has yet produced." Like Leary, many hippies took the album seriously, analyzing it with great intensity—like they would the I Ching, astrological charts, and tarot cards—searching for prophesies, messages, and signs. During the Summer of Love, *Sergeant Pepper* was ubiquitous, its songs floating out of open windows, passing cars, and transistor radios from Los Angeles to London to Paris to Rome.[39]

An equally significant counterculture event occurred in mid-June, the first major rock festival of the Sixties: the Monterey International Pop Festival. On the second day the crowd swelled to fifty thousand. Others placed the number at one hundred thousand. Some of the most talented groups and artists of the era performed: Eric Burdon and the Animals, Simon and Garfunkel, Country Joe and the Fish, Butterfield Blues Band, Moby Grape, the Grateful Dead, Jefferson Airplane, Buffalo Springfield, Electric Flag, Quicksilver Messenger Service, Otis Redding, Ravi Shankar, Canned Heat, and the Mamas and the Papas. Brian Jones of the Rolling Stones introduced Jimi Hendrix. Nico, who sang on the Velvet Underground's first album, also attended. Some gave more memorable performances than others. Hendrix carried out a sacrificial ritual of his guitar, dousing it in lighter fluid and setting it aflame. Janis Joplin and Big Brother and the Holding Company gave an arresting performance of "Ball and Chain," which resulted in a record deal with Columbia. Joplin and Big Brother became the first San Francisco act to top the charts with *Cheap Thrills* in 1968. At the conclusion of the Who's set, a smoke bomb exploded, Keith Moon kicked his drums over, and Pete Townshend rammed his guitar into an amplifier before demolishing the instrument in front of stunned and bewildered onlookers.

A countercultural atmosphere pervaded the festival. A spirit of brotherhood, sisterhood, and love was in the air. Although they did not agree with the admission prices, the Diggers came and served food to hungry kids. Booths decorated in strange designs and bright colors covered the festival grounds and flowers were everywhere. The police looked askance as musicians smoked marijuana backstage and concert revelers smoked it openly. Free tabs of LSD—"Monterey Purple"—were given out. Hippies handed flowers to police, burned incense, and gave the peace sign, and everyone seemed to be smiling.[40]

While Monterey Pop was a resounding success, Haight-Ashbury took a downward turn. The national mainstream media played a major role in bringing about the Hashbury's problems, for it began defining the hippie image, culture, and values, and as a result, the legions of individuals that flooded the Hashbury differed significantly from the district's original denizens. These individuals merely assumed the image the media created; they did not embrace or practice authentic hippie values. Suddenly, anyone could be hip. "Plastic hippies" and weekenders from the suburbs did not seek spiritual awakenings or hope to build a new and better world—they threw on beads, smoked dope, and rapped about "doing their own thing." Many men came in the hopes of picking up a "hippie chick." Alienated and aimless teens arrived with no plan, no place to live, no job, no food, and no means of supporting themselves. They quickly took to begging on the street and sleeping in doorways, while getting heavily loaded on drugs.[41]

The Haight declined rapidly. Delinquents, drug pushers, and criminals from the Tenderloin district migrated to the area. Amphetamines, STP ("Serenity, Tranquility and Peace," 2,5-dimethoxy-4-methylamphetamine), heroin, and PCP (phencyclidine), contended with pot and acid as the drugs of choice. Rapes and assaults increased and so did cases of sexually transmitted diseases. Homeless and hungry speed freaks went crazy and some became violent. Junkies lacked all moral restraints in their quest to acquire funds for their next fix. Assailants murdered two well-known acid dealers, John "Shob" Carter and William Thomas—known as "Superspade"—in August. A *Communications Company* leaflet described the brutal reality of what the Haight had become by September: "Pretty little 16-year-old middle-class chick comes to the Haight to see what it's all about & gets picked up by a 17-year-old street dealer who spends all day shooting her full of speed again & again, then feeds her 3000 mikes & raffles off her temporarily unemployed body for the biggest Haight Street gang bang since the night before last. . . . Rape is as common as bullshit on Haight Street." By the end of the year, seventeen murders, one hundred rapes, and nearly three thousand burglaries had been reported. Lieutenant James Ludlow believed that the real rates were twice as high.[42]

Veterans of the Haight—those who considered themselves authentic counterculturalists—decided to start anew and lay the media-manufactured "hippie" to rest forever. On Friday, October 6, the "Death of Hippie" and "Rebirth of Free Men" ceremony was held. All the local stores closed in observance of the pageant and the Psychedelic Shop closed its doors for good. The Free Medical Clinic had temporarily ceased operations three weeks earlier. The Grateful Dead and Jefferson Airplane migrated out of the district and so did many of the Diggers. A funeral procession carried hippiedom in a black coffin down the street. Approximately eighty "mourners" tossed hair, wilted flowers, beads, sandals, and posters into the coffin and later, hippies exorcised and burned it in the Panhandle. "Hippies are dead: now the Free Men will come through!" they shouted.[43]

Additional bad news came from New York that fall. Within days of the "Death of Hippie" parade, a handyman discovered the nude and bloody bodies of James "Groovy" Hutchinson and Linda Rae Fitzpatrick in a dirty boiler room in the East Village. Their heads had been bashed in with a blunt instrument and Fitzpatrick had been gang-raped. The two hippies had met a tragic end. Fitzpatrick was only eighteen and from a wealthy Connecticut family and Groovy was a friendly drifter from Central Falls, Rhode Island.[44]

The national press declared the end of hippie. "Trouble in Hippieland," proclaimed *Newsweek*; "Hippies—A Passing Fad?" wondered *U.S. News & World Report*; while the Associated Press trumpeted that the "Hippie Movement Has Lost 'Spirit.'" The *New York Times Magazine* bluntly contended, "Love is Dead. . . . The hippie movement is over." The average citizen reading mainstream publications was likely convinced that the counterculture had lasted only a few months. *Time* had introduced hippies in July with a cover story. By October it asked, "Where Have All the Flowers Gone?"[45]

Perhaps the evidence was compelling at the time, or maybe the mainstream wanted desperately to believe that hippiedom was declining precipitously. Whatever the case, the press was mistaken. The great irony is that at the very moment the media proclaimed the counterculture was either dying or coming to its end, it was actually growing at an astronomical rate. Hippies, of course, knew that the media had it all wrong. "Well, it's over," joked *Open City*. "How do I know? The Establishment newspaper is how. Would you believe I wasn't even aware it was time to quit until I heard on the radio everyone else was [quitting]?"[46]

CONTINUING COUNTERCULTURAL ADVENTURES IN LOS ANGELES, NEW YORK CITY, AND DENVER

Despite Haight-Ashbury's problems and the gruesome murders of Fitzpatrick and Hutchinson, the counterculture thrived. Millions of counterculturalists built the new society outside of San Francisco, and the Haight itself survived into the early seventies. As for Fitzpatrick and Hutchinson, their deaths shocked and dispirited the East Village community. Yet the murder of two individuals, though tragic, did not represent the end of the counterculture or its project.

Los Angeles's hip community flourished, abounding with coffee-houses, rock clubs, and hip clothing boutiques. By 1967 the scene had expanded from the Sunset Strip and Venice into Fairfax and the Malibu, Topanga, and Laurel canyons. Hundreds of garage bands and psychedelic groups formed. Communes thrived in the canyons—250 in Laurel Canyon alone during the Summer of Love. The most famous commune was Gridley Wright's Strawberry Fields/Desolation Row. Kids stayed at the many crash pads available. Like San Francisco, Los Angeles became an immensely popular hippie dwelling place. In 1967 the police department estimated that seventy to one hundred thousand counterculturalists lived there. Thousands of dropouts came to Los Angeles during the Summer of Love and the local Diggers, despite financial difficulties, fed and housed them. Leary and Richard Alpert delivered many sermons on the wonders of LSD in the area. Though most hippies came from white middle-class backgrounds, some African Americans and Chicanos in LA became counterculturalists; multiracial bands War and Love played around the city's many clubs, and blacks and Chicanos wrote for the *Los Angeles Free Press* and *Open City*. Differences between freaks and hip politicos were less pronounced, as they shared the same political causes and spaces, coming together in the summer of 1967 to protest the war in the Century City district. Laurel Canyon and Los Angeles, according to Michael Walker, "wrested from New York and London the bragging rights of musical capital of the world and held them through the 1970s." During the canyon's "golden era," Joni Mitchell, David Crosby, Stephen Stills, Frank Zappa, Love's Arthur Lee, Micky Dolenz of the Monkees, Nick St. Nicholas of Steppenwolf, John Densmore and Robby Krieger of the Doors, and members of the Mamas and the Papas lived there.[47]

The East Village scene remained lively as well, experiencing demonstrations, hippie gatherings, and street theater. An estimated two thousand dropouts moved into the tenement buildings near Tompkins Square Park during the Summer of Love. In August five hundred hippies turned out to celebrate nature over concrete, planting a tree in the intersection of Saint Mark's Place and Third Avenue. The East Village acquired a music venue when Bill Graham opened up the Fillmore East in March 1968, which hosted such acts as the Who, the Grateful Dead, and Santana. Dance shows and performances by the Fugs took place at the Astor Place Playhouse. Hip people looking for androgynous threads shopped at the Limbo. Hippies collected items for their pads at the Diggers' free furniture store, and went regularly to the avant-garde theater, Café La Mama E.T.C., while teenage runaways favored the City Living Center on East Tenth Street for a hangout. The offices of the *East Village Other* served an information center, aiding runaways with food, transportation, and shelter. And like Haight-Ashbury, the Village scene deteriorated when runaways began begging and stealing and tourists and hip "weekenders" flooded the area.[48]

Earlier that autumn the counterculture had penetrated the Rocky Mountains. On Sunday, September 24, "Denver's First Human Be-In" got underway in City Park, west of the Natural History Museum. The crowd, clad in feathers, beads, and bells, felt "good vibes from beginning to end," according to the *Solid Muldoon*. "Everyone a child at play, and family of Man was there and no one can put such a festivity down." Youths carried signs, one of which read: "I AM A HIPPIE. I AM FOR LOVE. FOR LEGALIZED POT. AGAINST WAR OF ALL KINDS." Members of the New Buffalo commune formed a circle around Leary. Numerous rock bands performed, including the Boenzee Cryque, the Grateful Dead, the Crystal Palace Guard, Mother Earth, Beggar's Opera Company, and Captain Beefheart and his Magic Band. Freaks blew soap bubbles, played flutes, drums, and hand cymbals, and at least one couple made love—"cool seated position balling"—out in the open. Hippies flooded Denver. Members of the Denver Provo—an organization of self-described "dope fiends"—fed and housed runaways and assisted parents looking for their children. Dropouts could sleep at one of twenty crash pads. San Francisco's Family Dog, under the direction of Chet Helms, opened a branch in Denver. The Dog featured a four-track recording studio and dance floor.[49]

As the counterculture became firmly ensconced in the nation's cities and universities, some hippies engaged in cultural activism. Freaks typically resorted to cultural protest when authorities or laws obstructed, hindered, or violated the hip lifestyle or values. The most common cause for demonstrations related to dope. While some hippies may have been reluctant to lend a hand to antiwar activities, others may have found cultural activism worthwhile. Angry hippies protested in New York in August 1967 against arrests for selling and possessing narcotics. After a cop busted three youths for selling dope, about a hundred protested in front of the Manhattan Criminal Court building and a day later, some five hundred longhairs dressed in sandals, colorful clothing, and beads staged a protest march from Tompkins Square Park to a Federal House of Detention following a Fugs concert.[50]

Hippies staged "smoke-ins," which served a dual purpose: first, they were demonstrations against what hippies believed were unjust laws against marijuana; and second, smoke-ins allowed hippies to smoke grass openly, as police did not bother making arrests. In July, in New York, about two hundred hippies and their Puerto Rican friends sat in Tompkins Square Park and smoked for over three hours. Provo sponsored the event. A band called the Pteradactyls jammed on electric guitars and five Puerto Ricans joined them onstage to play drums. Two young men threw joints into the air, sending the participants scrambling. Seven policemen stood by and heads gave them an ovation. In the fall, in Cambridge, Massachusetts, between eight hundred and a thousand hippies held a smoke-in for more than three hours on the Common. A smoke-in on the Boston Common was even larger, as three thousand heads participated in that event surrounded by police and television cameras. Around the same time, at least three hundred demonstrators lit up at San Francisco's Golden Gate Park.[51]

Others contested discrimination. After the manager of a Marc's Big Boy hamburger restaurant in Milwaukee made it his intention to deny entry to anyone wearing beads, beards, sandals, or funny glasses, hippies formed picket lines outside the business. A similar protest occurred in Bloomington, Indiana, when the owner of the Pizzaria began denying service to students who loitered in the restaurant. Police arrested several demonstrators. Students claimed that they were discriminated against because they had long hair.[52]

ABBIE HOFFMAN, JERRY RUBIN, AND THE MARCH ON THE PENTAGON

While hippies engaged in cultural activism, antiwar activists organized some of the largest demonstrations in the nation's history. In October, the newly created National Mobilization Committee Against the War—the

MOBE—made up of students, civil rights workers, moderates, liberal intellectuals, and radicals, sponsored "Stop the Draft Week." The antiwar movement became increasingly militant; some began moving "from protest to resistance," determined to "confront the war-makers." In Oakland, ten thousand demonstrators battled police in the streets, and at the University of Wisconsin, students sat-in at a building to block Dow Chemical, a company that produced napalm, from recruiting on campus. Police with tear gas, nightsticks, Mace, and dogs broke up the protest in and outside the building.

David Dellinger, director of the MOBE, planned Stop the Draft Week's culminating event, a march on the Pentagon in Washington. Moderates envisioned an orderly, peaceful protest, while radicals favored "free-wheeling action that would raise the political stakes." Dellinger imagined a demonstration that included nonviolent resistance and direct confrontation—it would be both "Gandhi and guerrilla." To attract young activists and to add guerrilla flavor to the Pentagon protest, Dellinger asked Rubin to help organize it.[53]

Rubin had been building his credibility among radicals and young people for the previous two years. A leader of the Vietnam Day protest in Berkeley in 1965, he had also led demonstrators in an effort to stop trains loaded with troops. After House Un-American Activities Committee subpoenaed him in Washington in 1966, Rubin mocked the proceedings, appearing in an American Revolutionary War uniform. He later ran for mayor of Berkeley and sought to organize radicals, hippies, and students. His campaign poster borrowed heavily from popular psychedelic rock art. Rubin received 22 percent of the vote on a platform that opposed the war and called for legalizing marijuana.

Rubin then moved to New York City where he teamed with Hoffman. Hoffman slowly embraced the counterculture. As late as May 1967 he thought that the counterculture was nonsense and chastised hippies for being apolitical and unreliable. Eventually he came around, dropping acid, smoking grass, and growing his hair long. Unlike many hippies, however, Hoffman never abandoned his commitment to activism and radical politics. Hoffman liked being a hippie—the drugs, sex, and hedonism—but beneath the veneer was an intellectual who read Marx, Mao, Lenin, and Marcuse. As Jonah Raskin has elucidated, Hoffman's becoming hip was part of a larger political plan. Hoffman integrated himself in the Lower East Side scene, claiming it as his own turf, while counting himself as one of the locals. Becoming a hippie "gave him an edge" in "the battle to convert hippies—the 'glassy-eyed zombies,' as he called them—to the cause of revolution." Hoffman thought that hippies could be made into almost anything he desired, so he acted as a "larger-than-life hippie role model" and began "organizing hippies." Inspired by the San Francisco Diggers, he adopted their ideas and transformed himself into one. In the summer of 1967, Hoffman and his New York Diggers planted a tree in the middle of Saint Mark's Place, threw soot on Con Edison employees to protest air pollution, organized a smoke-in, and aided a black neighborhood following the Newark riots.[54]

Hoffman and Rubin quickly became friends. In August, Hoffman, Rubin, and James Fouratt proclaimed "the death of money," showering one-dollar bills onto the floor of the New York Stock Exchange. Rubin claimed that Hoffman "revolutionized" him; Rubin grew his hair long, dropped acid regularly, shed his square clothing, donned East Village hippie garb, and started cavorting with Hoffman, Fouratt, Keith Lampe, and Ed Sanders. After going through these changes, he came to oppose the MOBE's formal tactics and advocated something newer. In late summer and early fall, Rubin and Hoffman began planning the Pentagon confrontation. They shared their thoughts about bringing hippies and activists together in a grand alliance, a coalition that promised to breathe new energy and enthusiasm into the movement. Hoffman and Rubin believed that dropouts could be an effective political force, drawn into the movement, if only theatrics, long hair, and costume became important elements of demonstrations. Rubin came up with the idea of protesting at the Pentagon instead of the US Capitol. At a press conference before the march, the two announced their intention to exorcise and levitate the Pentagon. Hoffman later declared in the *East Village Other* that lovemaking would occur on the grass near the building.[55]

More and more hippies participated in antiwar activism and some joined in the march on the Pentagon, largely as the result of Hoffman's and Rubin's efforts to infuse protest with counterculture theatrics. Longhairs dressed as witches, warlocks, sorcerers, American Indians, Sergeant Pepper's band, Martians, and Roman senators stood among the hundred thousand assembled at the Lincoln Memorial. Demonstrators high on acid marched to the Pentagon. Flower people placed daisies in the rifle barrels of soldiers and chanted, "We love you!" and "Join us!" A few MPs did, throwing down their helmets and guns. Hoffman, Ginsberg, and Sanders performed an exorcism on the Pentagon, shouting "Out, demon, out!" while others played flutes, whistles, and bells, and pounded bongos and beer cans. Later, the hippie contingent attempted to levitate the building. A communal atmosphere pervaded the grounds as demonstrators sang songs, picnicked, built campfires, and passed around joints. A few men burned their draft cards.[56]

As countercultural features became more integrated into the movement, black activists viewed the white antiwar movement as less than serious. Earlier, during the spring mobilization march to the United Nations building in New York, a Harlemite coterie of protestors including Carmichael and Floyd McKissick, according to a participant, directed their antiwhite feelings toward hippies who gave the rally a picnic-like atmosphere. The countercultural aspects of the march on the Pentagon also turned off African Americans. Omar Ahmed, a member of the Congress of Racial Equality and former associate of Malcolm X, declared that "black people are in no mood for marching to [the Pentagon] and listening to folk singing." Black radicals disliked Hoffman's and Rubin's efforts to levitate the Pentagon and doubted not only the earnestness of white peace activists but their sanity as well. "Black People are not going to go anywhere to levitate the Pentagon, okay?" said civil rights activist Gwen Patton. "We don't find that cute."[57]

EVOLVING COUNTERCULTURE VALUES

As 1968 approached, the counterculture's numbers swelled and the hippie philosophy evolved. More people meant more perspectives and the counterculture's principles multiplied, and its outlook grew broader, more nuanced, and sophisticated. Hippies still held to the basic values they had established at mid-decade, but now they exhibited and placed a greater emphasis on principles that had not been as prominent earlier.

As alienation soared, the war raged unabated, and the majority reacted with a repressive backlash, freaks put an even higher premium on dropping out, which entailed a nearly wholesale abandonment of the dominant culture and way of life, a spurning of mainstream institutions, traditions, religion, and concepts of work, status, success, power, and morality. Dropping out, of course, also included dropping into the Aquarian Age and embracing the countercultural lifestyle and values. And dropping out, hippies stressed, was an individual's only avenue to total liberation. "Reject the whole system. All of it. The system is what's making you unfree. The system is what has you in chains. The system is what's killing you. . . . Be Free. Drop out. All the way," counseled the *Communications Company*. Similarly, a hip Midwesterner contended, "Turning on to acid-rock (with or without the aid of drugs) beats playing the money-machine-don't-fuck-don't-laugh-don't-think-don't-feel game. . . . The game stinks. It steals my sex, my mind, my soul! Fuck it! I'd rather be free!" Dropping out, then, freed one physically, mentally, and emotionally. The counterculture also maintained that dropping out of the straight world facilitated personal enlightenment and the discovery of oneself.[58]

Few, however, dropped out completely. College hippies journeyed to hip communities during school breaks, yet many ultimately remained at their universities to earn degrees. Some hippies made livings ensconced in hip culture—dealing dope or as professional musicians—but few had the means to drop out totally. They worked part- or full-time, followed the laws (though not all of them), paid bills, taxes, and rent, and some used social services.

Another central value included "doing your own thing." Liberation from the dominant society and exploring and asserting one's individuality became foremost objectives. "The ultimate thing in being a hippie is being free of the society, and this involves everything: morals, so to speak; mores, economic patterns, everything," asserted a gay hippie named Randy. "Just determine your own life, live the way you want to, dress the way you want to, work the way you want to." Hippies rejected most restraints: "If it feels good, do it provided it doesn't hurt you (physically) or someone else." And because everyone did his or her thing, the counterculture remained a highly disorganized, individualistic enterprise. "Doing your own thing" involved any number of personal interests and pursuits: learning to play an instrument, writing stories, songs, or poetry, painting, meditating, yoga, investigating astrology. Most did not look to leaders for guidance or hold them in high regard. "Beware of leaders, heroes, organizers: watch that stuff. Beware of structure-freaks," a San Francisco hipster warned. "Any man who *wants* to lead you is The Man. . . . Fuck leaders." Others flatly denied that there were *any* leaders at all. And because the "revolution" was about individuals going through personal transformations, some asserted that there was no real hippie "movement."[59]

Doing one's own thing entailed an acceptance of oneself and it also led to self-discovery and searching for answers. Hippies advocated seeking. "Do your own thing. Be what you are. If you don't know what you are, find out," counseled Chester Anderson, while a Denver seeker urged others to

> blow your mind brother, that's it. Fuck up, revolt, soar to the sun, dive into hell, taste your own feces, bask in your own radiance, anything—just blow your mind. The secrets are all there. . . . Blast away the old thought patterns, tear down walls, kick open doors, and open your ever-loving eyes. . . . FREAK OUT! It's the only path to sanity. Listen to the astrologers, consult the I Ching, talk to people who claim to be from flying saucers. Now you're getting somewhere.

The counterculture broke free from what it perceived as the repressive and boring American way of life—nine-to-five at dead-end jobs, short and tidy hair, ranch homes with children in suburbia, a two-car garage, Jesus-worship at a Christian church. Hippies searched for life's meaning, the truth about themselves, and the world; seeking pulled them in a variety of directions, from isolated New England communes to the mountains of Kathmandu to the discovery of tarot and LSD.[60]

In addition, the counterculture emphasized that sex was part of being human. Sex possessed the power to revitalize a person, foster intense communication, and put one in touch with their humanity. Leah Fritz of Berkeley wrote: "As for sex—like eating, like walking in fresh air, like all human activity—it should recreate us, help us to find one another, make us real, and tangible as the earth. It should put us together again, body and soul, male and female, in harmonious intercourse."[61]

The counterculture also celebrated nudity as natural and fun. Clothing, hippies believed, acted as an impediment to total communication. Underground newspapers featured nude men and women. Cartoon characters, too, appeared in the nude and "comix" could be sexually provocative, as cartoonists strived to obliterate sexual taboos. Hippies celebrated the total body through nudity. If one repeatedly saw male and female genitalia, asserted an underground writer, then perhaps the sex organs would increasingly be seen as part of the whole body and lose their significance. "It is because they are hidden," he argued, "that they are ugly and dirty." Quite simply, hippies championed nudity as fun. It constituted evidence of a liberated individual. For LeRoy Moore Jr., hip nudity communicated, "Here I am; see me; so what is new?" Nudity was also pleasurable and completely natural: "Nudity on a beach, meadow, or forest is an experience that is very much apart from sexuality. It is a communion with all of the gods' creations. It is pure animal delight in the freedom of the body wildly playing in the elements. It is an aesthetic joy in the beauty of the human form. It is one of life's richest and most pleasurable experiences." Some hippies dissociated nudity from sexuality through skinny-dipping and shedding their clothes at rock concerts. The nude body was beautiful and nudity a means to recognize one's humanity.[62]

Although the Jesus People movement in the early 1970s would fuse the countercultural style and some of its ethics with Christianity, hippies generally dismissed or displayed hostility toward Christianity as the old, irrelevant, and "square" establishment religion. Dominant American religions, it was believed, acted as mere ciphers for establishment thought and activity. Injustice, intolerance, and hypocrisy were associated with Western religion—holy wars, inquisitions, colonial missionaries, the Ku Klux Klan, and churchmen supportive of the Vietnam War. "The Church is the enemy of youth and life," declared a hip Mississippian. "The western god is in his death thro[es], is desperate, is defiled, is depraved, has been dead for centuries." Religious institutions supported hypocrisy and narrowmindedness, boosted the establishment, maintained their wealth, and stood for the old way of doing things. Thus, longhairs found the principal faiths irrelevant and unhelpful with regard to creating the new society. Jesus had preached valuable messages, the hip thought, but the church and establishment had perverted Christ's philosophy for their own purposes. Imitating mainstream religionists, David Crosby said, "'I know what God wants! God wants this or that, and listen to me or God is going to be mad!'" They really blew it, especially the Christians. Lord help them, they really locked it, man! Lost everything."[63]

Seeking opened the way for spiritual awakenings and the exploration and embracing of various Eastern religions and mysticism. The Hare Krishna movement gained many new adherents, appealing to the counterculture with its Hindu paradises, bhakti music, and communitarian lifestyle. Its champions claimed that Krishna could get one higher than chemical drugs. Buddhism attracted new believers with its emphasis on spiritual and physical discipline and the possibility of liberation from life's troubles. Zen Buddhism, too, claimed new followers, those who strived for enlightenment by meditating and suppressing self-consciousness. Others studied Taoism and its yin-yang philosophy in an effort to attain spiritual harmony by living passively. Those who embraced Sufism searched for a "union with God," through poverty, abstinence, and repentance, while championing love. Many hip youth admired the teachings of Indian guru Meher Baba. His devotees opposed drugs, denying that they provided new insights and claimed that religion offered better revelations. The Maharishi Mahesh Yogi was better known than Baba. He popularized transcendental meditation, a form of deep relaxation aimed at awakening latent intellect and the development of a new consciousness. Hippies investigated the I Ching or Book of Changes, tossing three coins and examining its sixty-four hexagrams, hoping to acquire ancient Chinese wisdom. They also read the seven-hundred-verse Hindu poem the Bhagavad Gita. Followers of yoga believed that a combination of diet, meditation, breathing, and various exercises produced mystic euphoria and understanding. Some attempted to enhance their sexual pleasure and prolong sexual intercourse through the ancient east Indian technique of tantric yoga.[64]

Not every seeker turned to the East for answers. Time magazine struggled to define hippie religion, noting that "the hippie faith is a weird blend of superstition and spirituality that spans continents and centuries." One freak saw religion in everything, "in flowers, sex, music, sunrises, colors, sounds, touch, skin, life." Hippies delved into the occult, convinced that deep spiritual consciousness lay beyond reason. They explored occult metaphysics and the psyche through tarot card readings. Astrology and horoscopes experienced a resurgence in popularity, as hippies looked to the cosmic forces of the stars for insight. Less popular enthusiasms included palmistry, mind reading, fortune telling, Ouija boards, and numerology. Some longhairs worshipped nature; ceremonies included observing the winter and summer solstices. A few Haight-Ashbury street people practiced witchcraft and black magic.[65]

In the late 1960s especially, love was one of the counterculture's most exalted principles. Hippies prescribed it as the answer to the world's festering social and political evils. The flower people talked about love incessantly and expressed a wide range of views about its importance. They saw it in particular acts, feelings, and objects. As an author who investigated the youth revolt explained, "Love is other, love is being and letting be, love is gentle, love is giving and love is dropping out, love is turning on, love is a trip, a flower, a smile, a bell." Many hippies were thoroughly convinced that love was "the answer," that it could end war, greed, fear, suspicion, and intolerance. "All You Need Is Love," sang the Beatles, and hippies agreed wholeheartedly. Sexual intercourse was thought to be a natural expression of love, while the spiritually minded felt that God was love. Love represented the antithesis of hate and violence: "Make love, not war." Hippies also equated it with peace. "There can be no peace unless love is the weapon and the cause," maintained a female dropout. In addition, love brought people together and increased feelings of community and togetherness. Referencing Vietnam, Crosby remarked, "I don't see any other way out of it except by just helping each other and trying to learn how to love more. Because love wins. It's a true thing." Moreover, love was vital for all people. "Every human being needs love and understanding," stated an Arizonan. "No matter how ugly, how undesirable, he needs to be loved, without reservation, without qualification. A being cannot live without being loved." Finally, love, according to Lenore Kandel, meant a complete acceptance of another, flaws and all.[66]

Social philosophy on dope and drugs changed, as some hippies challenged counterculture dogma as it related to dope—the notion that LSD produced enlightenment, cosmic consciousness, and religious experiences. "Acid has no value in and of itself," contended Anderson; it "will not make you holy or good or wise or anything else except high." Some hippies recommended getting high on self-discovery and the spiritual life as dope no longer provided insights and answers. Dopers also started to worry about the possible adverse effects of LSD: did acid cause chromosome damage or lead to the birth of deformed children? Singer Pat Boone testified to the latter when he claimed, "We know that some children born to LSD users have had exposed spines, two heads, and other gruesome physical deformities." Underground newspapers frequently addressed the controversy of whether LSD ingestion resulted in chromosome damage. Eugene Schoenfeld concluded in his column "Dr. HipPocrates" that the possibility did indeed exist.[67]

In addition, hippies debated whether dope increased sexual pleasure. Leary answered in the affirmative, claiming in a Playboy interview that a woman could have "several hundred orgasms" during a carefully prepared LSD session. Many hippies, however, did not contemplate having sex while sailing on dope, as their minds were elsewhere. Those who did have intercourse under its influence had experiences that varied widely. A young man maintained that acid increased his sexual stamina, prolonging the experience amid bright colors. Others reported being frightened and having bad experiences. Because marijuana causes time distortion, some might have experienced or perceived prolonged orgasms.[68]

The drug scene underwent changes. The hippies' drugs of choice remained grass and acid. Some, however, began using amphetamines, barbiturates, morphine, cocaine, and heroin. Underground newspapers and concerned heads counseled against the use of these drugs because they were addictive, harmful, and led to early deaths. Writers elucidated the dangers associated with barbiturates and "downers" and singled out amphetamines, or "speed," for censure. "Speed kills," declared one writer. "It really does. Methedrine and amphetamine etc. can and will rot your teeth, freeze your mind and kill your body. The life expectancy of the average speed freak, from first shot to the morgue, is about five years. What a drag." Furthermore, some hippies cautioned against allowing drugs to become the center of one's existence, as there was more to living and being hip than abusing drugs.[69]

The presence of dope and drugs on college campuses increased. In 1965 only 4.2 percent of graduating seniors at Brooklyn College had smoked grass. That same year, researchers discovered that 10.7 percent of graduate students at a large urban university in southern California had tried marijuana. According to one scholar, "By 1969 the lowest reported incidence of marijuana use in high schools, in conservative Utah, was higher than the rate for graduate students in Los Angeles only four years before." The number of dopers and heads had skyrocketed. In 1968, drug arrests were up 60 percent nationwide. In California the arrest rate soared by an astonishing 324 percent. Early in the decade police arrested 5,000 grass-smokers annually in California. By 1967, they arrested 37,514 for possession. A Gallup survey of fifty-seven universities conducted in November 1969 revealed that 32 percent of students had tried marijuana. Other studies reported higher rates of usage. Stanford psychologist Richard H. Blum contended that 57 percent of students at five major California universities had smoked marijuana at least once. In another survey, 85 percent of Yale seniors admitted to having tried it. Students dropped acid, too. A 1969 study at a large eastern university revealed that over 20 percent of men and 15 percent of women had consumed LSD or other hallucinogens. The research also indicated that a small percentage of college students had started to take morphine, heroin, and cocaine.[70]

Rock and roll, like dope, remained vital to the counterculture, its lyrics making more references to dope and drugs. The Rolling Stones exclaimed, "Something Happened to Me Yesterday," the Amboy Dukes went on a "Journey to the Center of the Mind," and a "Purple Haze" swirled around Jimi Hendrix. Jefferson Airplane's "White Rabbit" spoke of "uppers" and "downers." The Velvet Underground's Lou Reed sang about putting "a spike" into his vein on "Heroin" and the Doors' Jim Morrison "couldn't get much higher" in the tune "Light My Fire." Not every rocker glorified dope, however, and some protested. Steppenwolf's John Kay damned "The Pusher" in a scathing indictment of pernicious drug dealers.

Rock lyrics also reflected hippie values—love, sex, nudity, community, flower power, alternative lifestyles, and questioning authority. I "Wasn't Born to Follow," sang the Byrds. The Grateful Dead, in "The Golden Road (To Unlimited Devotion)," referenced Haight-Ashbury and romanticized street people, inviting everyone to join an endless party. "We Can Be To-gether," proclaimed Jefferson Airplane, while they instructed their fellow counterculturalists to find "Somebody to Love." Even the bluesy Rolling Stones went through a psychedelic phase, recording "Dandelion" and "We Love You." The Youngbloods recorded the Jefferson Airplane–penned composition "Get Together," exhorting their compatriots to love one another immediately. Lyrics pertaining to sex became more explicit. In 1964 the Beatles had been content to "hold your hand;" four years later, Paul McCartney asked, "Why Don't We Do It in the Road?" Crosby's "Triad" discussed a ménage à trois, and the Stones frankly entreated, "Let's Spend the Night Together." Moby Grape recorded a tune in which the singer felt that he should be free to go "Naked, If I Want To," which highlighted authenticity and individual choice. Likewise, Jefferson Airplane's "Lather" told the story of a guy who loved to lie nude in the sand.[71]

In addition to expressing the counterculture's values and spreading its message, the music itself produced a sense of community. Hippies felt as though they shared with artists and bands a similar outlook, common goals, and the same principles. Beatle George Harrison's visit to the Hashbury during the Summer of Love is demonstrative. Dressed in flowered pants and denim jacket and sporting heart-shaped sunglasses, Harrison went to "Hippie Hill" in Golden Gate Park. A sizable crowd gathered and followed the "Quiet Beatle" as he walked back toward Haight Street, strumming a guitar. The group of hippies, who had never met Harrison, nevertheless felt a kinship with him. "How does it feel to have the *family* all together?" a hippie asked Harrison. "It's gettin' better all the time," he responded. Similarly, Ron Thelin said of the Beatles: "You feel like brothers. You feel like you meet John Lennon, you're going to know your friend. Any one of those cats, you're going to be able to talk to him, one to one; eye to eye. The vision of their feeling we can share. It's beautiful."[72]

The counterculture embodied more than a seeking, loving, "do your own thing," dope, and rock and roll philosophy, for the hippies stood against Cold War culture, opposing the majority's values and ideas. The counterculture hated the "meaningless abstractions" invoked during times of war—"nation," "country," "flag," "state," and "honor"—terms the establishment employed to appeal to those who would fight and kill. Hippies deplored what they perceived as the common emotions and behavior of the mainstream as well: greed, hate, fear, paranoia, and racial discrimination. Likewise, freaks regarded anything fake or phony with disgust, hence their reverence for authenticity. The police, justice system, war, and lying politicians figured prominently among the elements of society that longhairs abhorred.[73]

Dropouts disdained the rat race, the frantic day-to-day scramble. People worked for most of their lives at "good jobs" and the rewards, hippies argued, were few. The Mr. and Mrs. Joneses of America ended up old and tired. Hippies did not value respectability, competition, "keeping up with the Joneses," security, wealth, and material possessions, as these things did not bring contentment and fulfillment. On the contrary, freaks averred that these concepts made living difficult, miserable, and frustrating. Counterculturalists wanted to do away with the realities of mainstream daily life—schedules, routines, titles, rules, and responsibilities. Simple living was the key to true happiness.[74]

In addition, freaks took issue with the Protestant work ethic. Hippies did not oppose all work—only work that was meaningless and that led to harming people. They valued meaningful, productive, and creative exertions like playing music, acting in a theater group, writing for an underground newspaper, or aiding a friend and the community. Ideal occupations included independent crafts—such as making leather or jewelry products—or owning a hip shop. Longhairs respected play as much as work. They especially favored and enjoyed fun work. "Believe me when I say: if you enjoy it, it can still be good; it can still be 'work' (only we'll call it 'play')," Kupferberg wrote. "Play is as good as work. Work has been defined as something you dislike doing. Fuck that. Do the Beatles work? Who cares. We like what they do." Although fun work was nice, the best kind of work, hip youth thought, bettered society and made a "difference in human terms."[75]

Hippies also railed against their chief enemy: the establishment and its supporters. Politicians, military, bureaucrats, teachers, and cops forced their will on others—and hippies resisted. The establishment, its power, and the nefarious consequences of that power, represented everything the counterculture opposed: "The power structure is corrupt—the power creates sickness, the power fucks up what it was intended to heal, the power creates war, death; it tolerates poverty, arrests people, imprisons them, destroys foreign cultures physically and emotionally, turns—via the mass media—its own citizens into zombies who attack whatever is pointed out to them."[76]

HIPPIE PURISTS, HYBRID COUNTERCULTURALISTS, AND THE NEW LEFT'S COUNTERCULTURE

While opposing the establishment, the counterculture soon began a momentous and chaotic year: 1968. That year, youth arose to confront the established political and economic order in every industrialized nation on earth. Students erected barricades and grappled with police on Paris's streets, and in Czechoslovakia, democratic Communists championing "socialism with a human face" resisted invading Soviet tanks and troops. America, too, became engulfed in tumult. In January, North Vietnamese regulars and Vietcong guerrillas launched the Tet Offensive, invading every major city in South Vietnam. The attack undermined the credibility of officials in Washington who had been assuring the public that America was winning the war. In March, Lyndon Johnson shocked the nation and temporarily encouraged antiwar forces when he announced he would not seek another term as president. And the "Year of the Barricades" witnessed two assassinations: James Earl Ray gunned down Martin Luther King Jr. in April and Sirhan Sirhan did the same to Robert Kennedy in June. In the two years preceding May 1969, universities turned into battlegrounds: there were 25 bombings and 46 cases of arson, 207 campus buildings were occupied, and police arrested over 6,000 students.[77]

Defining the counterculture in the late 1960s presents a formidable task. Most scholars argue that the New Left and counterculture represented distinct phenomena. Others contest this interpretation, minimizing differences between the two camps. Because sex, dope, rock, beads, and bell-bottoms became common enthusiasms and features of radical youth culture at this time, it is difficult to discern where the New Left and counterculture overlapped, converged, or diverged, where protest ended and lifestyle began. Most scholars agree that the lines separating the two strands of the youth rebellion faded, blurred, and became murky, though the extent to which this occurred has not been deeply investigated or elucidated. Some scholars seem to conflate the New Left, Students for a Democratic Society (SDS), Yippies, movement, and counterculture, emphasizing a collective turn toward political revolution and street fighting, which was met with government repression. Robert C. Cottrell, for example, has written chapters titled "From Hippie to Yippie on the Way to Revolution" and "The Conspiracy, Street Fighting Man, and the Apocalypse." Similarly, Allen J. Matusow argues in The Unraveling of America that after 1967, "freaks abandoned the rhetoric of love for the politics of rage. They became willing cannon fodder for the increasingly violent demonstrations of the new left."[78]

The reality of this tumultuous period, however, was much more complex. A partial blending of the New Left and counterculture did indeed occur. More hippies showed up at antiwar demonstrations and more New Leftists engaged in countercultural behavior. By 1968 the counter-culture consisted of hippie purists—concerned primarily with cultural matters—and hybrid counterculturalists—who expressly mixed politics with alternative lifestyles such as the Yippies, White Panther Party, and the Motherfuckers. The New Left increasingly assumed characteristics of the counterculture, smoking dope, embracing liberated sexuality, digging rock, and growing long hair. Consequently, the New Left's countercul-ture overlapped to a considerable extent with the hippie counterculture. Yippies, hip politicos, and hippie activists became indistinguishable and joined forces at antiwar demonstrations and People's Park. Yet despite the blurring and fading of the lines that divided the New Left and countercul-ture, those lines, with some exceptions, ultimately remained intact. The divisions that set apart the two entities at mid-decade persisted, as did the animosity. All the while, hybrid counterculturalists worked to transcend these divisions, receiving contempt, skepticism, and criticism from both factions. The self-identification of members of the Boston draft resistance movement—resisters and supporters—provides insight into this convo-luted dynamic. Seventy-five percent of respondents to a 1997 survey con-sidered themselves activists and 69.1 percent a part of the New Left. On the other hand, less than half—39.7 percent—identified with the coun-terculture. A mere 7.4 percent called themselves hippies.[79]

Within SDS, the period in which one became politically active was a crucial determining factor in how one perceived the counterculture. SDS's old guard remained wary and skeptical of it. The charter generation could hardly be characterized as "hippie-dippie." Todd Gitlin doubted whether a single member of the old guard in 1967 had taken LSD and "most were leery even of marijuana." Gitlin and others felt that drugs undermined youth's commitment to the world's oppressed. He also sensed that drugs might vitiate the discipline necessary to sustain political movements.[80]

SDS's new guard—the "Prairie Power" generation—had no such con-cerns. One could maintain their radical politics, they believed, and still take part in the drug culture. The New Left and counterculture moved closer together, as the counterculture gradually influenced and penetrated the New Left. New Leftists began challenging majority social and cultural ethics. By the late 1960s the two phenomena held much in common. Many antiwar demonstrators and self-proclaimed revolutionaries embraced dope, liberated sexuality, rock music, hip clothing, and long hair.

New Left and counterculture converged at Columbia University in April, when SDS and African American radicals seized and occupied five buildings for eight days before New York authorities regained the campus. Students smoked dope, called each other brother and sister, made love, and referred to the occupied buildings as "liberated zones" and "communes." The formation of the five communes, and the agreement on a single platform by various black and white factions with divergent political and cultural impulses and interests, indicated that for a brief moment, there was—at least at the local level—unity in the movement. This was significant at a time when hippies headed back to the land, African American militants became increasingly separatist, and white students became more radicalized.[81]

Some hippies emphasized commonalities with politicos, arguing that dropping out was political. For these hippies, spurning the dominant American culture and fashioning a new culture represented a political— even revolutionary—act. As one hippie explained in the *Berkeley Barb*:

Yes, we are political; yes, we are revolutionaries; yes, we represent by the way we live a complete break with the American way of life. Yes, we stand for a new culture based on cooperation, love, and peace rather than competition, hate, and violence. . . . Yes, there is a revolution going on in the world and a fight to the death between two social orders, two ways of living and thinking.[82]

And some New Leftists contended that hippies shared their values, arguing that hippies' alternative lifestyles and rejection of the mainstream was "eminently political." They also recognized that hippies carried out ideals set forth in SDS's *Port Huron Statement*. The counterculture, in Haight-Ashbury and elsewhere, encouraged "participatory democracy" and engaged in community organizing, combating "depersonalization" and "isolation."[83]

By 1968 Carl Davidson contended that three-quarters of SDS membership could be classified as hippies. "The revolution is about our lives" became a popular slogan among political activists. As Doug Rossinow has demonstrated, New Leftists "fused their desire for individual empowerment with their dissident cultural politics." Like the counter-culture, SDSers distrusted centralized bureaucracy. Instead, they favored a looser organization, as that arrangement seemed the embodiment of participatory democracy. New Leftists also battled alienation by seeking authenticity and a better way of life, ideals and goals hippies shared. And like dropouts, they struggled to create a culture based on spontaneity, love, and community, which would constitute the foundation of a new, natural society. The "New Left's counterculture," however, differed from the hippie counterculture, because it "carried a sharper political edge." New Leftists—no matter how deeply they delved into hippiedom—always maintained their political commitments, fighting for democracy and jus-tice, while confronting the political status quo. Even some activists who tried acid and regularly used dope denied that they were a part of "the drug culture." They believed that their commitment to the antiwar move-ment precluded their membership in the counterculture by definition. For them, political activism was integral to their identity and more important than self-exploration or alternative institution building. Michael Kazin ex-plained his relationship to the counterculture this way:

> I liked rock music and I did LSD, mescaline, peyote, and lots of mari-juana, [but] I didn't feel allegiance with what seemed to be the ideol-ogy of it. I was always political . . . and I thought it was flabby thinking and people were fooling themselves about how people were going to change. You know, the old 'You have to change yourself first to change society' kind of thing. . . . I was always on the side of the politicos."[84]

Ironically, at the moment the New Left and counterculture moved closer together, sharing many of the same affinities, strains between the two poles heightened drastically, growing more intense. The under-ground press highlighted these tensions and in some instances they were laid bare in public settings.

Hippies were extremely skeptical—and in many cases, outright hos-tile—toward the concept of a political revolution and violence. Violent revolution was antithetical to the hippie ethos, as it almost certainly in-volved the possibility of killing and bloodshed. As talk of revolution among some New Leftists increased in 1968 and 1969, hippies expressed their concerns. "When you pick up a gun and learn to kill, the part of you that loved flowers and simple things will die!" a freak said to a friend. Killing for peace made no sense to the hip; radicals seemed to be advancing the same tactics and principles as the establishment. "Are you asking us to pick up our guns and fight for peace and freedom?" asked a hippie named Gemini. "That's what our government is telling us to do . . . in Vietnam."[85]

Hippies also opposed revolutions because they tended to go astray. "Tell me of one successful revolution," challenged a cynical Lennon. "Who fucked up communism-christianity-capitalism-buddhism, etc? Sick heads and nothing else." Furthermore, political radicals and revolutionaries did not offer better solutions or superior forms of government. Perhaps, dropouts thought, the revolutionaries would prove to be as bad as the establishment. "The revolutionaries even if 'successful' will only repeat the mistakes of what they oppose in new guises," explained the East Village Other. "The cycle of despair will repeat itself. And at what sacrifices!"[86]

The release of the Beatles single "Revolution" exposed a rift between politics and culture. The song's lyrics expressed Lennon's skepticism of political revolution, and explicitly put down Maoists. The song also made clear the Beatles' position on violence, as Lennon indicated that he would not participate in any movement that involved destruction. Finally, the song advocated the countercultural philosophy of turning inward, changing one's own head, and liberating oneself, rather than confronting institutions. To add confusion to the matter, Lennon sang that he could be counted "in" with regard to destruction on the White Album's version of the song.

On at least one campus, hippies and members of SDS fought over the philosophy of "Revolution." A former student at Rutgers University recalled, "I vividly remember a food fight that happened at the Ledge [a student hangout] when 'Revolution' came on the juke box right after 'Street Fighting Man' and this fight broke out between the hippies and the people in SDS. . . . We were literally throwing food at each other over whether or not a political revolution was appropriate."[87]

Radical politicos censured the song for its "clear unmistakable call for counter-revolution." A Berkeley Barb writer contended that the lyrics sounded "like the 'hawk plank'" adopted by the "National Demokratik

Death Party." The *Barb* also articulated its displeasure that the Beatles criticized Chairman Mao while neglecting to attack the American or British establishment: "They spend a verse putting down Chairman Mao. O.K. He has lots of bad points, but . . . nowhere in the song is the U.S. or British establishment attacked, or even criticized, only the people who attack or criticize the establishment." The *Barb*—inadvertently confirming that it was staffed by "closet squares"—complained that "Revolution" featured "shitty piano." The paper also called "Hey Jude" a "boring love song," before endorsing the Rolling Stones' "Street Fighting Man." Finally, the writer excoriated the Beatles for their unwillingness to contribute to the cause of revolution.[88]

An advocate of revolution penned an angry letter to John Lennon. "In order to change the world," his letter read, "we've got to understand what's wrong with the world. And then—destroy it. Ruthlessly." Lennon's reply eminently represented the position of cultural revolutionaries, who maintained that the revolution could happen one person at a time. If enough people went through personal transformations, changing their values and perspectives, politics and the world generally would change. "You're obviously on a destruction kick," Lennon retorted. "I'll tell you what's wrong with it—People—so you want to destroy them? Ruthlessly? Until you/we change your/our heads there's no chance." Counterculturalists endeavored to create new societies, not tear them down, and Lennon ended his letter conveying this idea: "(P.S. You smash it—and I'll build around it.)"

Crosby shared Lennon's outlook. Discussing Vietnam and the growing polarization among the populace, Crosby downplayed the differences between people: "The guy who shoots people in Vietnam lives in me because I have gotten mad and have hit people in my life and we're all the same person." The war, killing, and death would end, Crosby contended, if everyone attained a higher consciousness. "Somebodies got to straighten all of us out now, it's getting out of hand, man! People dying. It puts me up tight. It lives in my house and it lives in my head. You've got to start somewhere. I guess first by expanding your own consciousness and then theirs."[89]

Many hippies still believed in dope's revolutionary potential. Why engage in a violent, bloody, political revolution—or join a demonstration, for that matter—when the same end result could be achieved by taking acid? Rick Dodgson, explaining psychedelic utopianism, writes:

> Pursuing the goal of "freeing the mind" and living an "authentic" life was felt to be far more meaningful, more personal, and ultimately more revolutionary than signing on to any tired old leftist ideology or marching in yet another dreary street protest. Who needed Marxism and its conflict-driven analysis of historical change, when a single LSD trip might exorcise the "ghosts of the past" that Marx had famously said weighed down human progress[?] Forget social movements and collective action; this was a personal, individualistic revolution where everybody had the potential to "break on through to the other side," as the Doors' Jim Morrison put it.

"These drugs are potent," a head wrote. "They are changing personalities and the way people relate." And radical heads were convinced that dope had the potential to transform political realities. "After I took it [LSD], it opened my eyes," Paul McCartney told *Life*. "We only use one tenth of our brain. Just think what all we could accomplish if we could only tap that hidden part! It would mean a whole new world. If the politicians would take LSD, there wouldn't be any more war, or poverty or famine." LSD, then, went a long way toward creating the new society.[90]

Although many New Leftists had embraced hippie values, others did not, and as a result, counterculturalists continued to perceive fundamental differences between themselves and politicos. "Many of the so-called political leaders are a drag," commented Grace Slick of Jefferson Airplane. "They're not interested in our culture and its values." Furthermore, politicos bored and annoyed hippies with their long-winded speeches, rants, and announcements. "It's boring, man," continued Slick. "It's like listening to Nixon talk, only they have long hair." When the Grateful Dead played at Columbia during the siege, guitarist Bob Weir became extremely irritated by political leaders who continually interrupted the Dead's performance. Weir eventually kicked a strike leader who invaded his space. Phil Lesh became annoyed when people made a "mad rush" for the microphones. "No, man," he told them, "these microphones [are] for the music and not for politics." Lesh was called a "lame honky bastard" and a "crass bourgeois son of a bitch." The bassist hated it when politicos unleashed their political views on him. Most rockers mistrusted leftists who tried to harness their music for purposes that they themselves did not conceive of, or believe in. Few rock and rollers became part of the radical movement. "My music isn't supposed to make you riot," explained Janis Joplin. "It's supposed to make you fuck."[91]

Many New Leftists, too, continued to have misgivings about the counterculture. Marxists within the Progressive Labor faction of SDS disdained the counterculture for its escapism. They also believed that hippies sapped the strength of political movements, and alienated the working class, preventing potential student-worker alliances. Maoists and Trotskyists dressed conservatively, shunning hippie accoutrements, and maintained short hair and clean-shaven faces. Furthermore, they tried to enforce a cultural conservatism, looking down at dope smokers and occasionally ousting members who had extramarital affairs.[92]

As late as 1968 activists within the larger antiwar movement remained skeptical of the counterculture. Many young MOBE members did not look like hippies, nor did they find sex, drugs, and rock and roll particularly interesting. Conventionally dressed youth attended MOBE conferences. A *Chicago Tribune* reporter noted that MOBE members took their business seriously. Only one person, an African American man, wore beads.[93]

Prominent philosophical divisions distinguished revolutionary New Leftists from the counterculture. Revolutionaries believed that American institutions needed to be abolished so that individuals could truly be free. Liberation required a confrontation, perhaps a violent one, with the establishment. "If we want freedom, we must fight for it. It won't be handed to us. It can't be," opined the Boston underground *Old Mole*. "Human freedom has always required struggle." Furthermore, New Leftists were deeply concerned about not only their own freedom but the freedom of others as well, especially oppressed peoples in Africa, Latin America, Asia, and minorities stateside. Political revolutionaries sought to liberate these oppressed peoples, something hippies had little interest in doing: "None of us is free until we are all free."[94]

The Yippies did not believe in classifying young outlaws. On New Year's Day 1968, Hoffman and Rubin took LSD together and concocted a strategy for social change: combining political activism with hippiedom. Paul Krassner, editor of the *Realist*, suggested a name—"Yippie!"—and the

Youth International Party (YIP) was born. Yippie would be a rallying point for political hippies, a "blending of pot and politics." As hybrid counter-culturalists, Yippies welded cultural and political militancy. They were part hippie—extolling the virtues of sex, dope, rock and roll, dancing, and building the new society, and part New Left—overtly political, instigating confrontations with police, speaking of revolution, while claiming solidarity with struggling Vietnamese peasant guerrillas and blacks. Hoffman and Rubin became the most visible spokespeople for the youth movement and the most famous radical celebrities of the sixties. They sought to galvanize America's youth to action through media manipulation and by baffling the middle-class. The founders of YIP had essentially created a mythical organization and they used the media to cultivate the myth.[95]

The Yippies, as a hybrid counterculturalists and radicals, idolized black militants and sought their blessing. Yippies claimed solidarity with the Black Panthers. Hoffman demanded "immediate freedom for Huey Newton of the Black Panthers and all other black people." The Panthers and Yippies eventually made an alliance; in October 1968, Rubin and Stew Albert signed a "YIPanther" pact with Eldridge Cleaver. The Yippies also appropriated the Panthers' polarizing and vitriolic language, employing terms like "pig." Other champions of Black Power disliked hippies. Hoffman came to the defense of the counterculture when SNCC chairman H. Rap Brown sneered at "flower power" and put hippies down.[96]

The Yippies planned a massive demonstration at the Democratic National Convention (DNC) in Chicago during the last week of August. Hoffman and Rubin centered the protest on a "Festival of Life," which would serve as an alternative to the "death politics" of the convention. The Yippies enticed youth with talk of a nude grope-in, joint-rolling competition, popular rock bands, free food, guerrilla theater, and workshops on drugs. They planned to nominate a pig—Pigasus—for president and pledged to devour him after he won the election. In the months before the convention, the Yippies predicted that there would be violence, while continuing to promulgate their outrageous rhetoric: "We will burn Chicago to the ground"; "We will fuck on the beaches!"; "We demand the Politics of Ecstasy!"; "Acid for all!"; and "Abandon the Creeping Meatball!" But when the Yippies actually met to discuss the details of Chicago, they did not converse about sex, drugs, and rock and roll. Rather, they talked about party politics and political strategy. The Yippies wanted a confrontation with authorities in Chicago.[97]

The Yippies were not entirely successful at bridging the gulf between hippies and politicos, as they received harsh criticism from both. Movement people distrusted the Yippies, finding them too countercultural. Politicos at the March 22–23, 1968, Lake Villa Conference before the DNC generally tried to avoid them. Very few people felt pleased by their appearance. Eric Weinberger, the MOBE's young treasurer, worried that the Yippies were too apolitical. He also feared that they would dilute antiwar protest. Years after the conference, Dellinger criticized Hoffman and his followers for their irresponsibility and hedonism, skewering their rhetoric as "fantasies" and "bullshit" and further asserting that their culture largely mirrored the dominant culture they rejected. Lew Jones of the Marxist-Trotskyist Young Socialist Alliance (YSA) called the Yippies "regressive" and charged them with being a part of a "sick escapist milieu." The national SDS leadership, put off by the Yippies and the possibility of police violence, refused to officially endorse the DNC protest.[98]

The Yippies harbored distaste for politicos, too. They found the political left, especially Progressive Labor, boring, puritanical, and hopelessly ideological. "Act first. Analyze later," Rubin wrote. "Impulse—not theory—makes the great leaps forward." Hoffman discussed his feelings for the MOBE leadership with the Walker Study Team, which investigated the events at Chicago. "They all wear suits and ties, they sit down, they talk rationally, they use the same kind of words," Hoffman said. "I'm into emotion. I'm into symbols and gestures and I don't have a program and I don't have an ideology and I'm not a part of the Left." The Yippies, though political, hewed closer to the counterculture with their insistence on emotion and impulse and dislike for ideology and structure.[99]

The Yippies ruffled and polarized activists, but they also caused a rift within the counterculture. Although the Yippies qualified as counterculturalists and espoused cultural revolution, hippie purists opposed them. Hippie purists rejected politics entirely, even politics combined with hippie values, behavior, and rhetoric. Purists attempted to drop out of majority society—and politics—completely; for these individuals, hippiedom remained a highly individualistic experience, a personal journey. Purists strived to discover and transform themselves. The revolution, they believed, could occur in one's own mind. For purists, the counter-culture also largely remained concerned with matters of culture. They altered the way they lived, changed their values, and transformed their perspectives on life and the world around them. Most hippies continued their quests for self-liberation and focused on building the new society. While New Leftists marched, seized campuses, and grappled with cops, hippie purists meditated, attended love-ins and rock festivals, cultivated their alternative societies in cities, settled in rural communes, or hitch-hiked America, Europe, Asia, and the Middle East. Although purists sided with demonstrators against the war, they found direct political agitation largely ineffectual. "We're not that active," a dropout commented. "We say yay! [to] the pickets, and we stand and watch them and agree with 'em but we're not gonna be the ones right in there because, you know, nothing much is gonna get done, and it's just being ridiculous." A Los Angeles communard expressed the same sentiment. "Man, to me all that bullshit about peace and war and integration and all that is just part of that other plastic world, man," spat Gridley Wright of Strawberry Fields commune. "You wouldn't catch me dead at a fuckin' peace demonstration." His attitude was typical of purists throughout the late sixties.[100]

Months before the Democratic Convention, detractors came out against the Yippies and their designs for Chicago. Schoenfeld identified differences between Yippies and hippies, associating Hoffman and company with New Leftists. "All Yippies are not Hippies," he wrote. "One should distinguish pacifistic hippie from New Left groups." Many hippies did not think of themselves as "Marxist acidheads" or "psychedelic Bolsheviks," as the Yippies did—and they wanted no part of the expected confrontation. Abe Peck, a Chicago booster of the Yippies and editor of the *Seed*, issued several warnings. He argued that there could be no rock festival, which had been the primary draw for hippies. "If you're coming to Chicago, be sure to wear some armor in your hair," he cautioned, as well as, "Don't come to Chicago if you expect a five-day Festival of Life, music, and love."[101]

Hippie purists chastised the Yippies because they remained skeptical of leaders and movements. John Kois, writing for the *Milwaukee Kaleidoscope* in an article titled "The Yippee Shuck," condemned Rubin as a movement politico who thought in terms of leaders, followers, and press releases. Kois asserted that interest in political causes was waning among youth, and, consequently, the Yippies had integrated themselves into the counterculture by exploiting the "New Music" and "new lifestyle." The *Kaleidoscope* predicted that hippies—who could potentially invigorate the occasion—would not appear in Chicago. "The real danger in Chicago is that the people who might be able to make the YIP Convention a meaningful event will be absent," contended Kois. "They will be doing their thing, in their city or town or commune." In the same manner, *Rolling Stone* did not support demonstrations and confrontation, and its editor, Jann Wenner, had soured on radical politics. He denounced the Yippies, too, calling them a "self-appointed coterie of political 'radicals' without a legitimate constituency." Moreover, Wenner believed that the Yippies promoted the Festival of Life and exploited rock and roll in the hopes of luring unsuspecting hippies into senseless violence at the convention. Wenner found the Yippies and their festival "as corrupt as the political machine it hopes to disrupt." For *Rolling Stone*, music gave youth culture definition: "Rock and roll is the only way in which the vast but formless power of youth is structured."[102]

West Coast counterculturalists, too, opposed the Festival of Life. The San Francisco Diggers came out against the Yippies. They disliked Hoffman for allegedly stealing their ideas when he formed the New York Diggers. The San Francisco Diggers also abhorred the Yippies' use of the media to aggrandize themselves.[103]

The Yippies had predicted that more than forty bands and five hundred thousand young people would attend, but in the end, no more than ten thousand people came to Chicago. The rock bands did not show; MC5 was the only rock act to perform at the Festival of Life. Yippies, members of the MOBE, SDSers, radicals, and moderates backing Eugene McCarthy came to Chicago. Many hippies stayed home and avoided the bloodshed. Chicago cops chanting, "Kill, kill, kill" initiated a "police riot," clubbing and bloodying Yippies, revolutionaries, antiwar demonstrators, reporters, and innocent bystanders.

After the convention, hippies blasted Yippies. Hoffman and Rubin, skillful at using the media, had successfully taken over the hippie image in the popular press, much to the chagrin of purists who resented that hippie was becoming synonymous with politics and activism among the general public. Hippies did not preach political revolution, believe in violence, or fight with police. In Los Angeles, purists hoped to resurrect "the spirit of the first Easter love-in" and "struggle to do something real, meaningful and constructive." Some moved to distinguish themselves from Yippies in the underground press, lambasting Yippies, hippie activists, and longhaired New Leftists—the bead-wearing "phony flower children" who shouted "pig" at police:

> To someone on the outside he [may] look like one of the hip people. But the similarity is only physical. . . . he is actually just another crummy demagogue who thinks he must destroy the world in order to save it. They may seek the same goals as we but the goals aren't important. The means are what counts. Here is the real difference between us. Not whether one does or doesn't believe in an intolerant, suffocating social and political system, but whether one will use violence on other human beings in order to change things.

Purists acknowledged that New Leftists and hybrid counterculturalists sought to realize a new society like themselves. But that fact in itself was unremarkable. The method by which groups aimed to achieve the new civilization was ultimately more significant, and for purists, paths that involved violence or destruction were unacceptable, and antithetical to hippie philosophy and values.[104]

Yippies found fault with purists, too. Hoffman did not believe in dope revolution absent politics; revolution demanded action, dismantling power structures, not dropping out. "The revolution is more than digging rock or turning on," he wrote in *Woodstock Nation*. "The revolution is about coming together in a struggle for change. It is about the destruction of a system based on bosses and competition and the building of a new community based on people and cooperation."[105]

Like the Youth International Party, the White Panther Party was a hybrid counterculture organization that successfully blended revolutionary politics with dissident lifestyles. After witnessing police brutality at the DNC in Chicago, founder John Sinclair decided that the movement—including the counterculture—needed to organize politically for self-defense purposes. He also strived to politicize youth culture on a national scale. In autumn 1968, Sinclair, influenced by the Yippies and Black Panther Party, formed the White Panthers in Ann Arbor, Michigan. The Panthers believed in rock and roll's revolutionary potential and they eventually evolved into a confrontational political organization dedicated to "a total assault on the culture by any means necessary." The organization spread its revolutionary message of "rock and roll, dope and fucking in the streets" with the assistance of the politically charged band MC5, managed by Sinclair. Other aims of the party included an endorsement of the Black Panthers' ten-point platform, free food, free clothes, free drugs, and "total freedom for everybody." In addition to cultural radicalism, the White Panthers espoused revolution in political terms; member Pun Plamondon issued statements urging his brothers to "get a gun," and Sinclair communicated his "youth colony" thesis, calling on the exploited young to rise up and join forces with other colonized peoples—including urban blacks and the Vietcong—to "put the corpse of capitalism and imperialism to rest forever."[106]

Up against the Wall Motherfucker was perhaps the most outrageous hybrid counterculture group. Taking their name from a line in a poem by black nationalist Amiri Baraka and made up of artists, actors, delinquents, dropouts, and hippies, the Motherfuckers called for revolution while dedicating themselves to fighting police and trashing stores. A "street gang with analysis," this "affinity group" was inspired by European anarchism, the concept of free association, and Marxism of the Frankfurt school variety exemplified by Herbert Marcuse. The Motherfuckers were supposed to represent what the new society would look like after the revolution. Hostile to high art, they dumped garbage in a fountain at the new Lincoln Center. In addition, the group performed a street theater piece in support of Valerie Solanas, founder of Society for Cutting Up Men (SCUM) and attempted assassin of Andy Warhol. The Motherfuckers practiced martial arts and championed "Armed Love." Holding student politics in contempt, they engaged the straight left with their ideas. At an SDS convention in Lexington, Kentucky, in 1968, they waved the black flag of anarchism and distributed leaflets promoting affinity groups with drawings of men and women linked in a circle through oral sex. One member karate-chopped a brick wrapped in gold foil in half to demonstrate how they were going to smash the state and capitalism, "just like that." At an SDS national council meeting in October 1968, the Motherfuckers denounced

Progressive Labor for supporting repressive authoritarian regimes in the name of internationalism. Its adherents hated ideology and identified personal liberation as the ultimate objective: "What we're saying is that the whole thing is a struggle to live. Dig it? For survival. The fucking society won't let you smoke your dope, ball your woman, wear your hair the way you want to. All of that shit is living, dig, and we want to live, that's our thing. Action, not this bullshit rapping."[107]

Hippie purists and others inclined toward cultural and individual matters had grown weary of political revolution and militancy, rhetorical or real. "People dropped out of the straight world to seek their buried humanity," a disgruntled purist proclaimed. "They now must drop out from the 'underground,' which, thanks to the New Left, would pervert their Love to the cause of destruction."[108] In October 1968 in New York, the *East Village Other* announced the Rediscover America Be-In and criticized belligerent radicals: "We who have been hassled by the cops and militant revolutionaries who would have us kill own fathers (Oedipus-hunters), have given us all very bad vibrations and almost made us think that the world is a musky mean place when we all know it isn't."[109]

Beset by revolution-preaching New Leftists and hybrid countercultural-ists, hippie purists became even more determined to "do their own thing." Although they waned in frequency after 1967, love-ins and be-ins continued to be held. In Los Angeles on Easter Sunday 1968, between 3,500 and 4,000 young people frolicked in Elysian Park, and 5,000 attended a love-in at Tapia Park. Cultural activism continued as well. In March, roughly 200 men and women protested public nudity laws, disrobing at a "nude-in" at San Gregorio Beach in California. Hippies also attended three significant rock festivals in 1968: the Newport Pop Festival in Costa Mesa, California; the Sky River Rock Festival, an hour from Seattle; and the Miami Pop Festival.[110]

But hippies did not successfully evade the social, cultural, and political upheavals of the era. Some freaks felt as though they fought for their survival against fascist "Amerika." Writings of an apocalyptic nature emerged in the underground press. "The ship is going down," announced the *East Village Other*. "If we are not physically destroyed or imprisoned—our whole lives will become contaminated by the society—they will not become like us—we will become like them." The nation seemed to be on the precipice of a second civil war with the country's fate hanging in the balance. Hippies wondered if the representatives of the New Age would triumph over the representatives of the old order. "Are we coming now to a new age of freedom and joy or shall we first have to go through a time of civil war and chaos worse than any we have known before?" a hip Floridian wondered.[111]

THE MAINSTREAM BACKLASH

The mainstream only exacerbated the overwhelming sense of social disintegration. The social, cultural, and political movements of the decade—and the upheaval that resulted because of them—engendered a substantial backlash from the American majority, middle- and working-class citizens who valued God, family, and country. These disconcerted and angry individuals did not protest and turned against liberals whom they blamed for tolerating and even encouraging black riots. Self-proclaimed patriots fumed at liberals, moralists, pacifists, and "traitors" who opposed the Vietnam War. In the fall of 1969 a poll revealed that 69 percent of the public felt that antiwar protestors were "harmful to American life." Such citizens plastered bumper stickers on their vehicles: "America: Love It or Leave It." They demanded law and order and yearned for the country's unity. And it was hippies who shocked, threatened, and angered these mainstream citizens the most, for the counterculture represented a radical affront to the American way of life and the nation's dominant morality, values, conventions, and traditions.[112]

Many Americans distrusted or detested hippies. Restaurant owners hung signs—"Hippies not served here" and billboards along highways communicated antihippie messages—"Keep America Clean: Take a Bath," and "Keep America Clean: Get a Haircut." Most Americans made no distinction between antiwar activists and hippies, believing that those who wore long hair, beards, beads, and outrageous clothes belonged to a monolithic movement. The exploits of the Yippies at the 1968 Democratic National Convention fixed indelibly in the minds of average citizens the idea that political radicals and hippies were the same. The *Chicago Tribune*, for example, ran the headline "Cops, Hippies War in Street" the morning following the clash on Michigan Avenue. Furthermore, mainstream citizens, who identified as Christians and patriots, associated dropouts with two of the most stereotyped and despised peoples of Cold War culture: atheistic communists and gays. Members of the public penned vitriolic letters to underground newspapers. "We the decent law-abiding CHRISTIAN people of this great nation will not tolerate for long the infectious venom that is spewed from you socialist serpents," opined a woman from Brighton, New York. She went on to reference her son and his fellow marines and the fate that awaited longhairs: "What they are doing to damned [Viet] Cong will be a picnic compared to what you Kommie Kooks will get, so you better shave those beards and cut your girly hair before they do it for you. You swine."[113]

Such hatred led some to advocate murder. A New Mexico man believed hippies "should be slaughtered like pigs." So did the anonymous individual who wrote to the underground paper *Open City*: "Let me tell you that us Patriotic Americans are just waiting for the day when they declare Open Season on you Commies and beatnik Slobs! When the day comes, we'll gun down your long hair 'Pansey generation' like dogs!"[114] This hatred amounted to more than mere talk. Teenage gangs shouting, "Kill the hippies" attacked cultural activists holding a nighttime candlelight procession in Boston. The most brutal treatment of counterculturalists occurred in the most conservative regions of the country: the South, West, and Southwest. In Atlanta criminals firebombed a cooperative store. They also peppered seven youths with shotgun pellets in a drive-by and police later incarcerated six of the hospitalized hippies for disturbing the peace. In addition, snipers put twenty-seven bullet holes into Ron and Susie Jarvis's craft shop, the Leather Aardvark. "We've got a new nigger in our society," Ron told a journalist, "and the way to tell him is by his hair and his beard."[115]

Antifreak violence was even more inimical in New Mexico in 1969 and 1970. In Taos, hippies clashed with Mexican Americans, who feared that longhairs intended to take over the town. The threat was overstated; probably fewer than one thousand communards inundated the area. Nevertheless, erroneous perceptions prevailed and culture clash caused violence to flare. The residents of Taos held traditional values. Furthermore, Chicanos, most of whom were poor, resented middle-class hippies choosing poverty voluntarily. They also feared that freaks would drive away white tourists who fueled the Chicano economy. But other deeply rooted cultural issues were at play. About 25 percent of Mexican Americans were unemployed and lived on government assistance. Their poverty went back for generations and attaining the American Dream proved difficult. Most wanted to live the middle-class lifestyle that hippies had forfeited. Chicanos, too, had been told that hippies carried disease, were obsessed with sex, used drugs excessively, and harbored communist ideas. Enemies of longhairs hung a sign on a Taos building: "The only good hippie is a dead hippie. Kill." Thugs beat, stabbed, and castrated hippies, gang-raped a hippie woman, and vandalized hippie homes and free stores. Assailants dynamited a Volkswagen van and destroyed a macrobiotic restaurant. At least one youth, Michael Press, was murdered. By 1972 many of the communards had departed the area for good.[116]

The counterculture wrangled and sparred with average Americans, but the police became the hippies' greatest adversary because they were integral to the establishment and agents of the state. Freaks regularly compared cops to Nazi Germany's Gestapo. "When to call the police?" asked the *Berkeley Barb*. "Only in life emergency. If it seems someone will get killed or severely injured if you don't. Even then it's a risk."[117] Hippies held this perspective because law enforcement raided crash pads, shops, and other countercultural centers looking for runaways, narcotics, obscenity, and housing violations. Police arrested hippies for dope possession and hauled in runaways. Cops also detained dropouts for minor and trivial offenses such as loitering and jaywalking. One hippie was apprehended for placing a flower on a police car, the officer declaring, "You're under arrest for tampering with the vehicle!"[118]

Yet these encounters were inconsequential compared to the violence visited upon hippies when lawmen attacked them at their gathering places. On Memorial Day 1967, cops charged into longhairs with their nightsticks at Tompkins Square Park in New York, beating and arresting thirty-eight. Beaten bloody, handcuffed, and dragged away, a man cried, "My God, my God, where is this happening? Is this America?" On the West Coast, authorities regularly conducted street sweeps in Berkeley and San Francisco, trapping, clubbing, and arresting longhairs. Police cleared hippies from the Boston Common on a nightly basis during the summer of 1968. On one June evening, eighty-five cops with nightsticks and dogs chased off two thousand youth, making fifty arrests. A rock concert in Atlanta erupted into a small riot after a detective pulled his pistol on some hecklers. In early May 1969 police grappled with a thousand students and hippies, barraging them with exploding pepper gas canisters and breaking up a block party on Mifflin Street in Madison, Wisconsin. Fighting continued over three nights and police made over a hundred arrests.[119]

Freaks and their allies fought back. In Houston, people tired of police harassment at Allen's Landing, a public park, formed Democratic Resistance to Police Cruelty. In many cities, the American Civil Liberties Union (ACLU) defended the counterculture, intervening on behalf of youth's freedom of association, opposing harassment by authorities. Some took direct action against the police. Near the University of Washington, hip youth formed an organization—"Freedom Patrol"—to monitor local cops. The group, committed to "watching the watchers," armed with cameras, clipboards, and walkie-talkies, documented police activities.[120]

In addition to "the fuzz," hippies contended with a justice system that worked against them. In Wyoming authorities jailed hitchhikers before forcibly shaving their hair off. In Atlanta a freak was sentenced to sixty days in jail for a minor driving infraction. Other longhairs were incarcerated, placed in solitary confinement, not allowed phone calls, and held without notification of the charges. Moreover, their captors refused to tell them when they would be released. Judges set exorbitant bail and ordered compulsory haircuts.[121]

City governments attempted to contain or eradicate the perceived hippie menace. In Massachusetts, the mayor of Cambridge launched a "war on hippies," determined to drive them out of the city. In Dallas, the city council passed an ordinance limiting the sidewalk activity of hippie preachers at Stone Place and officials in Aspen, Colorado, cracked down on longhairs, enforcing vagrancy and loitering laws.[122]

The counterculture, however, survived establishment repression. In fact, the hippies' numbers continued to multiply as 1969 dawned. As the late sixties grew progressively tumultuous, the young increasingly turned away from activism and political radicalism and embraced the counterculture. *Newsweek*, assessing the mood on the nation's campuses at the end of the decade, reported that "militancy and violence are in good measure giving way to passivity and personal introspection."[123]

Multitudes of youth adopted the hippie lifestyle because alienation soared, especially as Richard Nixon moved into the White House. University students felt alienated by America's institutions and believed they required a drastic overhaul. At the end of the decade, a *Newsweek* poll conducted by the Gallup Organization revealed that only 18 percent of full-time college students gave a favorable rating to the nation's political parties. Only one-third gave organized religion a favorable rating. Less than half approved of high schools, the police, and courts; their positive ratings were 37, 40, and 46 percent, respectively.[124]

Although alienation primarily caused the counterculture's phenomenal growth, other developments fueled its expansion. The civil rights movement became increasingly militant as champions of Black Power engaged in violent confrontations with authorities. Black separatists also ousted whites from the movement (SNCC and CORE officially barred whites from membership in 1967). These white outcasts traveled to hippie enclaves in New York, Vermont, and San Francisco. The outlook on the antiwar front appeared hopeless, too, as protest failed to end American involvement in Vietnam decisively and immediately. Many weary activists began favoring cultural and individual pursuits.

BUILDING THE NEW SOCIETY ACROSS AMERICA

Many hippies believed that the world was entering a fantastic new epoch, the Age of Aquarius. The notion that humankind neared a new age gained attention in the press. In a March 1969 article, "Astrology: Fad and Phenomenon," *Time* explained that the "movement of the vernal equinox westward at the rate of about 50 seconds a year is bringing it from 2,000 years in the zodiac's sign of Pisces—characterized by skepticism and disillusionment—to the next 2,000 in Aquarius, an airy sign that will influence the world toward aspiration and faith." The highly successful Broadway musical *Hair* also celebrated the New Age: "When the moon is in the Seventh House / And Jupiter aligns with Mars / Then peace will guide the planets / And love will steer the stars. . . . This is the dawning of the Age of Aquarius."[125]

Boosted by the belief that an extraordinary new era was underway, the most ambitious and imaginative counterculturalists ventured to create a

new society, a new civilization, a new world. "We propose that the alienated, the disenchanted and the loving build their own society, within yet a
part from the fabric of present society changing it from within by refusing
to practice its values, and by love and sharing and peace and creation,"
announced *Helix*, a Seattle underground. A Yippie, according to Rubin,
was a "longhaired, bearded, crazy motherfucker whose life is theater, every moment creating the new society as he destroys the old." "We have
been cultural outsiders in this civilization," asserted Peter Berg. "We will
become the political dynamic of the new society because we are living a
new civilization." "The sixties saw a revolution among youth. . . . The
Beatles were part of the revolution," recalled Lennon. "We were all on this
ship—a ship going to discover the New World. And The Beatles were in
the crow's nest."[126]

During the Age of Aquarius the counterculture spread across the coun-
try, taking root in every corner of the nation. Hippies resided in their al-
ternative communities at 115th Street in Cleveland, Old Town in Chicago,
Pearl Street in Austin, Plum Street in Detroit, Peachtree Street in Atlanta,
West Bank in Minneapolis, Dupont Circle in Washington, DC, and Gas
Light Square in Saint Louis. Hip areas near universities included Mifflin
Street (hippies called it Miffland) in Madison and Telegraph Avenue in
Berkeley.

In the late 1960s countercultural activity remained vibrant in the Northeast. In the summer of 1968 freaks from all over the country descended
on Boston Common, where they made love, dipped in Frog Pond, and listened to bands like the Ultimate Spinach. Earlier, in January 1967, the city's
first psychedelic nightclub, the Boston Tea Party, opened at 53 Berkeley
in the South End. Willie "Loco" Alexander fronted the house band, the
Lost. Hippies called themselves the "hip community" and referred to
Boston as "BossTown." Local residents complained of happenings that
disrupted the Beacon Hill neighborhood. Street people hung out in the
store entrances of businesses on Charles Street. Beacon Hill also became
a center for the trafficking of LSD, marijuana, and cocaine. The Hip Task
Force provided free recreation and entertainment for hip youth and a free
clinic, the Medical Service, provided care to over 450 patients during the
summer of 1968. Hippies populated the local colleges—Brandeis, Boston University, Harvard, and MIT. In Boston and Cambridge, longhairs

congregated around clothing, craft, and head shops, and eateries such as Hayes-Bickford and Ye Old Beef and Shakes.[127]

In Philadelphia, longhairs read the undergrounds *Temple Free Press*, *Yarrowstalks*, and *Distant Drummer* to get the latest on books, rock concerts, films, new albums, and coffeehouse events. Hippies crowded into the Stewed Tomato, an off-campus coffeehouse, to hear speakers such as Phil Berrigan, while others attended classes on the draft at the new free university. In addition, they attended rock concerts at the Electric Factory. Students at all Philadelphia colleges challenged authority, demanded more rights, attacked in loco parentis, and called for the removal of restrictions on language, sexuality, and dress.[128]

In Seattle, the Digger-like organization Basic Needs Company offered hip youth food at love-ins and sidewalk feed-ins. Seattle, like other cities, offered crash pads for nomadic youth. Hippies tuned into KRAB-FM and went to see their favorite local bands—Magic Fern, Daily Flash, Time Machine, and Crome Syrcus—at several clubs. On March 19, 1967, Seattle's first "Trips Festival" was held at the Eagles Temple auditorium. Over six thousand crammed into the venue to see the Seeds, Daily Flash, and Emergency Exit.[129]

Portland, too, boasted a hip enclave, as between five and ten thousand hippies traveled there during the Summer of Love. The hip community established itself around Lair Hill Park. Federal agents conducted several drug raids on the neighborhood. PH Phactor Jug Band jammed for revelers at a be-in and dropouts danced to groups like the Portland Zoo and Great Pumpkin at the Pythian Building and Midtown and Crystal Ballrooms. On Sundays, freaks ate free soup distributed at Lair Hill Park and Portland State College. Hip youths looking for new threads purchased items from Phantasmagoria.[130]

Indiana's residents referred to Bloomington—home of Indiana University—as a "hippie town." Like in Madison, Wisconsin, differences between Hoosier hippies and politicos were not as pronounced as elsewhere in the nation, as the two groups shared a symbiotic relationship. Hippies augmented antiwar demonstrations, enjoying rock bands and performing guerrilla theater, and activists raised the money to pay for the fines and legal fees incurred by freaks for drug possession. On Kirkwood Avenue, longhairs bought pipes and posters at Go for Baroque, the latest records at The Other Side, items from Africa at the Black Market, and ice cream at Pill Village. Street musicians performed. Students and hippies purchased the local underground newspaper, the *Spectator*, published from 1966 to 1970. Just off Kirkwood, students and some unmarried couples lived in older houses divided into individual rooms. On warm days, the sounds of live rock music and the smell of marijuana wafted through the air.[131]

Although not as prevalent as they were on the coasts and in the Midwest, Northwest, and Northeast, hip people gradually appeared in the South and West. In Dallas, young men dressed like Confederate generals and Dracula and "Mama Cass–looking" women shocked the adults who came to listen to a symphony orchestra at Lee Park. In Austin, Shiva's Head Band entertained students and hippies, and freaks frequented the club, Vulcan Gas Company. Hundreds gathered on Sundays in New Orleans at the Mardi Gras Fountain for love-ins, while Floridians held a love-in in Tampa. In Jackson, Mississippi, the *Kudzu*, a local underground paper, invited freaks to "make new friends, draw, paint, write, eat, drink, smoke, rap, groove on trees, groove on animals, groove on whatever wants you to," at Riverside Park, where rock concerts were held on Sundays. In Reno, Nevada, 250 longhairs came to a be-in at Idlewild Park to hear the sounds of Greenfield Steamboat and Spectrum. Salt Lake City boasted a counterculture enclave as well. Utah hippies bought smoking implements, buttons, and jewelry at the Cosmic Aeroplane, and posters and paintings at the White Horse. Travelers found a place to stay at crash pads and goods at a free store. Five Fingers on My Hand performed light-shows and the Terrace Ballroom hosted popular bands such as Led Zeppelin, Steppenwolf, and Vanilla Fudge.[132]

"BACK-TO-THE-LAND" COMMUNE BUILDING

Although many hippies made their home in cities and on college campuses, just as many left urban areas, heading "back to the land" to establish rural communes. Numerous forces provoked the exodus during and following the Summer of Love. As they had earlier, hippies fled from war, racism, consumerism, materialism, and the establishment, in order to do their own thing and revel in community, but additional factors had emerged by 1967 that drove them to the countryside. First, Haight-Ashbury had taken a downward turn. A similar downturn had occurred in the East Village, though not nearly to the same extent. Hippies sought to make a new start and to escape the hassles, paranoia, greed, and dishonesty of the city environment. Second, many communalists had become alienated from radical revolutionaries, professional activists, and demonstrations. They wanted to leave behind "the movement's spiritually exhausted preoccupation with perpetual protest" as well as "the power structure" and its "predisposition to exterminate foes and dehumanize friends." The DNC protests had not paid dividends and Nixon ascended to the presidency, determined to continue the war effort. Frustrated SDS-ers founded the Weathermen, which turned to violent confrontations and eventually went underground, alienating peaceful members of the movement. Radical students won few victories on college campuses. Bucolic environs beckoned, becoming an appealing alternative. Disillusioned by politics and politicos and with no end to the war in sight, more hippies tried country living.[133]

Timothy Miller has estimated that from 1960 to 1975 there were thousands—probably tens of thousands—of communes, with hundreds of thousands, perhaps one million inhabitants. Commune building exploded in and after 1967 and did not subside until the mid-seventies.[134]

In the East, inspired by the behaviorism theories of psychologist B. F. Skinner, communards settled on a 123-acre tobacco farm near Louisa, Virginia, naming the community Twin Oaks after a double oak on the property. Eventually, around a hundred members who were committed to egalitarianism made their home there, sharing food, housing, clothing, and the costs of medical care. A 450-acre rundown farm and big house provided the site for Cold Mountain Farm near Hobart, New York, where artists, political activists, pacifists, students, poets, and anarchists lived. New England also proved a popular region for commune building. Bryn Athyn in Vermont was an eclectic commune. At one time it served as a training ground for revolutionary New Leftists, while at other times psychedelic hippies dominated it. Other well-known communes in this region included Total Loss Farm in Vermont, which Raymond Mungo wrote about in a book of the same name, and Montague Farm in Massachusetts, which Stephen Diamond wrote about in *What the Trees Said*.[135]

Communes also mushroomed in the Southwest. In Taos, New Mexico, a group of hippies founded New Buffalo and built adobe buildings for their residences. Soon, dozens of communes popped up within a twenty-five-mile radius of the city. In 1969 harassed refugees from Morning Star Ranch arrived from California, starting Morning Star East. New York and San Francisco radicals, convinced that fascists were about to take over America and destroy the nation's leftists, created Reality Construction Company. Other short-lived communes in the area included the Furry Freak Brothers, Kingdom of Heaven, and the Church of the Five Star Ranch. To the north, in southern Colorado, hippies inspired by Drop City founded Libre.[136]

According to Miller, the largest number of 1960s-era communes were probably located in the area from "San Francisco northward to the Canadian border and from the Pacific inland perhaps a hundred miles." In early 1968 the first refugees from Morning Star Ranch arrived at Bill Wheeler's property—Wheeler's Ranch—in Sonoma County, California. The commune grew to more than two hundred members. Nudity was common and the communards came together for Sunday meals, parties, sweat baths, and taking psychedelics. Olompali Ranch, located outside Novato, California, served as a retreat for the Grateful Dead. Self-reliant communards seeking total isolation settled at Black Bear Ranch, twenty-five miles from Forks of Salmon in northern California. Hippies fleeing the Haight founded Table Mountain Ranch on 120 acres in the redwoods of Mendocino County. Many countercultural values—peace, love, freedom, nature, spiritual questing, and brotherhood/sisterhood—flourished there. Other communards established communities in Oregon and Washington, including Family of the Mystic Arts, Four Winds Farm, and Family of the Three Lights.[137]

PEOPLE'S PARK, WOODSTOCK, AND THE
COUNTERCULTURE IN VIETNAM

As hippies built their communes, the New Left and counterculture merged completely for one brief moment. It happened in May 1969 in Berkeley, where radicals were hipper and hippies did not run from confrontation. The People's Park episode began when the University of California tore down some houses to make room for a soccer field or dorms. When the university left the lot vacant, hundreds of people—students, hippies, radicals, street people, young professors, and members of the neighborhood—descended on the three acres. They joyously planted vegetables and flowers, enjoyed free food, made music, danced, set up swings and slides, and installed a wading pool. Albert, a Free Speech Movement veteran and Yippie, suggested that people take the three acres from the university and transform it into "People's Park." Even Marxists and other leftists, who had earlier dismissed the park as a "hippy-dippy" endeavor, fell in love with the idea.[138]

Trouble began when Governor Ronald Reagan put pressure on Berkeley chancellor Roger Heyns to assert the university's property rights. Heyns sent police to erect an eight-foot cyclone fence around the park. Students and others decided to take the park back. On May 15—"Bloody Thursday"—deputy sheriffs fired buckshot and birdshot at the park's defenders. Demonstrators opened a fire hydrant, overturned a car, and threw bottles, rocks, and pipes. Over one hundred people were injured. James Rector, shot in the heart with buckshot, died four days later. "If there has to be a bloodbath," Reagan declared, "then let's get it over with." The governor dispatched three thousand National Guardsmen, who took over downtown Berkeley. Women danced topless in front of the guardsmen and offered them marijuana brownies. On May 21 a helicopter dumped tear gas over the entire campus and thirty thousand citizens protested the city's occupation. At People's Park, women placed flowers in the rifle barrels of guardsmen. "For a brief moment in history in People's Park, the counterculture and political activists had a magical fusion. It was a way of looking at the future. It was utopian. It was a way of saying, 'If we had control of our lives, this is what it would look like.'"[139]

Yet for the most part, hippies shied away from violent encounters, preaching love and nonviolence, while celebrating community throughout 1969. Earlier that April, four thousand strummed guitars, flew kites, built bonfires, and danced in Sheep Meadow in New York's Central Park. In August and September, Denver hippies indulged in be-ins.[140]

Rock festivals eventually overtook love-ins as the counterculture's primary gathering place. Between 1967 and 1971—the height of the outdoor rock festival era—over three million people attended more than three hundred rock festivals. 1969 became the "year of the festival," as more than one million youth trekked to concerts in every region of the country. That summer, hippies attended numerous multiday shows: the New Orleans, Texas International, Denver, Seattle, Atlanta, and Atlantic City Pop Festivals, as well as the Second Annual Sky River and Newport Jazz Festival.[141]

The Woodstock Music and Art Fair, billed as "an Aquarian Exposition," held August 15–17, was the most famous festival. Between four and five hundred thousand gathered at Max Yasgur's six hundred-acre dairy farm in Bethel, New York, for "three days of peace and music." So many tried to get to Woodstock that traffic came to a standstill on every route leading to the grounds. The promoters declared Woodstock a free festival after attendees knocked down the fences and it became impossible to collect tickets.

Music emanated from the stage, day and night. The promoters had put together a stellar billing. Among the performers were Canned Heat, Janis Joplin, the Who, the Grateful Dead, Creedence Clearwater Revival, the Band, Jefferson Airplane, Sly and the Family Stone, Santana, and Crosby, Stills, Nash and Young. Joe Cocker did a rousing cover of the Beatles song "With A Little Help from My Friends," and in front of a dwindling crowd of twenty-five thousand and garbage-strewn, muddy fields, Jimi Hendrix played a howling, psychedelic version of "The Star Spangled Banner."

For three days, Woodstock was the third largest city in the state. The crowd stayed high as an estimated 90 percent smoked marijuana. Two babies were born and two rainstorms poured down over the three days and people splashed and slid in the mud. The Hog Farm commune handed out free food flown in by the Air Force, delivered messages, and tended to people who had taken overdoses or bad acid. The festival was not without problems. Three people died, including one youth who was run over by a tractor as he slept in his sleeping bag. There were mountains of garbage and a lack of food and water, portable toilets overflowed, and phone lines came down. Yet there were no reported rapes, assaults, or robberies. Even the mainstream press pointed out the lack of violence and commended the spectators for pulling together under adverse conditions. "Overrun, strained to its limits, the system somehow, amazingly, didn't break," *Life* reported. "For three days nearly half a million people lived elbow to elbow in the most exposed, crowded, rain-drenched, uncomfortable kind of community, and there wasn't so much as a fist fight."[142]

A countercultural mood pervaded Woodstock, and with the exception of a grand sing-along to Country Joe McDonald's anti-Vietnam song, "I Feel Like I'm Fixin' to Die Rag," it was almost entirely devoid of political substance. Attendees mostly ignored the pavilion distributing political literature; salespeople had difficulty selling copies of *New Left Notes*. Trampled SDS and Women's Liberation Front leaflets were among the mountains of garbage left behind in the mud. Hoffman became involved in an embarrassing incident after he interjected politics into the festival's laidback atmosphere. As the Who rocked onstage, Hoffman grew agitated. "Oh, man, this is bullshit," he spouted to Michael Lang, one of Woodstock's producers. "I mean, we're headed in the wrong direction again, man. I gotta go up there and make a speech."

"Hey, cool it, man. Now's not the time," Lang replied.

"It's never the time as far as you hippies are concerned," a sweating, beleaguered Hoffman shot back. "No, man, I gotta go up there. I gotta tell everybody about John Sinclair, man. We gotta fight for that cat."

Hoffman was determined to make known the plight of John Sinclair, who had been sentenced to nine years' imprisonment for possession of two marijuana joints. During a break in the Who's performance, Hoffman scampered across the stage and grabbed Pete Townshend's microphone. "I think this is a pile of shit while John Sinclair rots in prison!" he screamed. An enraged Townshend hit Hoffman with his guitar, knocking him off the stage into the photographer's pit. The crowd roared its approval. The Woodstock Nation wanted little, if anything, to do with political agitation. Abbie swore at Townshend and then he ran away screaming. He did not return to the festival. Atlanta's *Great Speckled Bird* lamented this "absolutely chilling scene," calling the "split" between politics and culture, politicos and hippies, "ugly," and "self-defeating."[143]

Woodstock was, and remains, the supreme moment in the history of the counterculture. For many hippies, it represented the high point of the entire hippie phenomenon; the *Seed* called it "the definitive gathering of the tribes; a massive pilgrimage to an electrified holy land." Those in attendance felt part of a peaceful community, loving one another, sharing with one another, working together. For three halcyon days, the young smoked dope, made love, dug sublime sounds, skinny-dipped in Filippini Pond, and immersed themselves in their ideal society. Freaks had difficulty describing their experience. "It is nearly impossible to put into words what has happened here at White Lake," wrote one participant. "For the first time I feel free and we are really together. It is so peaceful and loving here that I (and many, many others) don't want to leave."¹⁴⁴

Woodstock, for many hippies, not only provided the model for a superior society but encouraged the idea that America was on the cusp of a cultural revolution. "How can I come back and do the old things?" wrote John Hilgerdt in the *East Village Other*. "This is how we should live. Can we?" Leary felt the most heartened and optimistic. "Woodstock is the great example of how it is going to be in the future," he wrote to Sinclair. "We have the numbers. The loving and the peaceful are the majority. The violent and the authoritarian are the minority. We are winning. And soon."¹⁴⁵

As the counterculture burgeoned stateside, it, too, grew overseas—in Vietnam. Some soldiers wore love beads and peace symbols and strummed guitars. GIs wrote counterculture messages on their helmets: "hippie" and "San Francisco City of Love." Musical tastes differentiated troops: drinkers favored country and heads favored rock—especially the Beatles, Rolling Stones, Jefferson Airplane, Joplin, and Hendrix. A vet named Dahlstrom offered a breakdown of base culture. "There were three groups of guys—the guys who just played cards, the hippies, and the guys who did heroin." Dahlstrom also recalled being driven around Saigon "stoned," and listening to Vietnamese rock bands: "There was music everywhere. They had a Saigon version of Woodstock. Vietnamese girls in short black skirts, Filipino and Vietnamese bands. They played a lot of Creedence and, of course, 'We Gotta Get out of This Place.'" Additionally, he told researchers about the strange things he and his fellow servicemen had done while on pot. "We used to get monkeys stoned," Dahlstrom remembered. "They'd jump off the barracks, jump down, and grab your sunglasses, so we'd blow smoke in their faces." For some GIs, listening to psychedelic music offered a way to rebel. John "Hippie" Lindquist remembered listening to Cream with his buddies, talking "about how the war was messed up." Servicemen began reading undergrounds like Detroit's *Fifth Estate* and sent letters to the paper. "This company is another 'Mash,'" wrote a soldier, "everyone gets down heavy here, even the officers, but they are young and can dig the scene. If you have any freaky posters we could really dig it for our club." A pot subculture developed among American GIs. *Newsweek* cited a study conducted by a US Army psychologist that stated 35 percent of troops smoked pot. The study also disclosed that the highest rates of use occurred in units where the men came from large cities like New York City or San Francisco. GIs obtained grass with little difficulty as cannabis grew naturally over much of the country and because Vietnamese peddlers regularly sold it to troops. According to the press, soldiers could get marijuana in Vietnam more easily than American college students at metropolitan campuses could. Despite increased busts by military police and a psychological operations program to dissuade marijuana's use, troops continued smoking. The heads in Nam, like hippies back home, championed the slogan, "Dope is hope."[146]

At least one soldier celebrated the Woodstock festival in a vicarious way. While in Vietnam, Dennis DeMarco received a cassette and a Woodstock flyer from friends back home. DeMarco marveled at Woodstock's lineup: "My God!!! I almost fell off my cot. How could a concert have every single artist and group I could possibly want to hear (except the Beatles). And I was stuck in Vietnam, nine thousand miles away. I ached with envy that my friends were going." Determined not to miss out, he devised a simple plan: "I could send some of the best marijuana I'd ever smoked to my friends, and they could take it to Woodstock. A part of me would be there for all to enjoy." DeMarco wrapped up some grass in a cassette case and sent it to Connecticut with a false name and return address on the package. His dope was a big hit with his friends. "My friend gave me credit every time he shared it with hippies from New York or Pennsylvania or Vermont," explained the vet. "I felt really happy that even though I couldn't be at Woodstock, my pot was there adding to the experience."[147]

Not everyone, however, was pleased with Woodstock and the hippie worldview. Before and after the festival, Sinclair and the White Panther Party, like the Yippies, found themselves in no-man's-land philosophically, caught between politicos on one side and hippie purists on the other. In a letter to Hoffman, Sinclair denounced most rock bands and artists as "a bunch of capitalist pigs who are wallowing in self-righteousness and hate anything 'political.'" For Sinclair, the rock industry was just a microcosm of "Amerikan capitalism" and "exaggerated beyond belief."

"LET THEM EAT CAKE is their cry," he wrote, "as they drop flowers on the people starving in the mud." In addition, he mentioned the enthusiasm for Woodstock, lamenting that people floated in the "hippy ozone." Sinclair took aim at purists and their political quietism. "I don't want any part of a Nation of imbeciles who sit around and shoot speed and listen to bogus records," he wrote. Yet vociferous New Leftists did not appeal to him, either: "The 'politicals' are just as bad too, and their culture is bogus as well. The records they listen to are even worse."[148]

Committed revolutionaries still held dropouts in contempt. For promoters of political revolution, there could be no personal revolutions or transformations as long as the system oppressed the individual. Turning on and dropping out did not constitute a real revolution. Marxism was not an irrelevant ideology, nor was Marx himself an "outdated old nineteenth-century cat" as some hippies thought. Revolutionaries believed that the oppressed needed to seize power in order to achieve self-determination. Retreating into the dope and hip scenes would not stop the establishment from tyrannizing blacks, busting young rebels at home, and napalming Vietnamese overseas. In addition, radical politicos condemned rock capitalism, arguing that hippie rock stars and music corporations enriched themselves by exploiting hip culture and ripping kids off. Jim Shoch, a member of a Marxist-Leninist group at Stanford, recalled how he felt about hippiedom: "I certainly smoked a lot of dope; that part I had no trouble with. . . . [But] I was never a hippie. You couldn't be a hippie in the Revolutionary Union. . . . We thought it was totally apolitical."[149]

The SDS leadership held similar perspectives. In June 1969, SDS had convened for its national convention in Chicago, where it splintered into three warring factions—Progressive Labor, Revolutionary Youth Movement II, and Weathermen. Each claimed to be the vanguard of the revolution. The Weathermen took their name from the Bob Dylan lyric "You don't need a weatherman to know which way the wind blows." They strived to do away with their "white-skin privilege," and wanted to assist Third World revolutionaries in overthrowing American imperialism. Calling for "armed struggle," a few hundred Weathermen determined to "bring the war home" fought with police and destroyed businesses and cars on the streets of Chicago during the "Days of Rage" in early October.

As their passion for revolution increased, Woodstock became a target. Weathermen argued that Woodstock was capitalism at work, implied that cultural rebellion was meaningless, and slammed festival revelers for their nonrevolutionary stance: "Fuck hippie capitalism. Build culture in struggle. Events like the Woodstock gentleness freakout indicate that as long as militancy isn't a threat, pig and ruling class approval is forthcoming." As the decade drew to a close, then, political revolutionaries and counterculturalists had not reconciled their differences.[150]

The New Left and counterculture, however, continued to join forces at massive antiwar demonstrations. SDS disintegrated at the same moment the antiwar movement hit its apex. President Nixon rejuvenated the antiwar movement when it became apparent that he had no intention of bringing the troops home quickly. The war seemed as if it would go on interminably, and as a result, the movement broadened significantly and gained greater legitimacy. On October 15, more than a million people nationwide, including hippies, participated in the Vietnam Moratorium Day. Vigils and demonstrations occurred in hundreds of communities across the country.

A month later, on November 15, between 600,000 and 750,000 protesters assembled and marched in Washington for Mobilization Day. Approximately 250,000 demonstrated in San Francisco. Again, many hippies participated in the antiwar movement with a diverse if uneasy coalition of the elderly, women for peace, students, antiwar veterans, blacks, politicians, trade unionists, doctors, lawyers, and working-class people. Mobilization Day in Washington, for Tom Hayden, was "the Moratorium and Woodstock." Veteran activist Louise Peck had never experienced anything like it before, describing it as "a very beautiful feeling . . . such a sense of community in that crowd . . . even alone, everyone you met was like a friend." "The city bloomed over night," observed an Illinois underground, *News from Nowhere*. "Long hair, blue jeans, freaks all over: our culture had arrived." William Hanley, who had been in charge of Woodstock's staging and sound, erected the mobilization's stage, towers, scaffolding, and sound equipment with the help of the Hog Farm commune. Folk singer Arlo Guthrie and four separate casts of the hippie musical *Hair* participated in the rally. And at one point the activists joined hands and sang Lennon's "Give Peace a Chance."[151]

ALTAMONT AND MANSON FAMILY MURDERS

The counterculture remained ebullient going into the last major concert of the year—Altamont—held on December 6 near Livermore, California. The Rolling Stones had decided to give a free concert on their tour and Altamont Speedway, a racetrack, provided the venue. The Stones hired the notorious Hell's Angels motorcycle club to handle security and the bikers received five hundred dollars' worth of beer for their services. The concert was hastily planned as the Stones put Altamont together in less than twenty-four hours.

The violence began at midday during Santana's set and continued into the afternoon when Jefferson Airplane performed. The Angels, loaded on beer and acid-spiked wine, punched and kicked spectators and beat them with chains, clubs, and sawed-off pool-cues. First-aid tents overflowed with the injured and an estimated 780 people experienced bad LSD trips. During the Airplane's show, singer Marty Balin jumped into the audience, trying to prevent the further beating of a fan. An Angel promptly knocked him out cold. Balin was one of the only people to stand up to the bikers all day.[152]

The crowd had waited for nearly ten hours by the time the Rolling Stones took the stage. Violence erupted again and again as pool-cue- and chain-wielding Angels continued to beat hippies and throw and kick people off the stage. Mick Jagger stopped the band several times to address the audience of three hundred thousand sitting or standing in the dark: "Why are we fighting? Brothers and sisters, why are we fighting?" As the band finished "Under My Thumb," commotion ensued. An eighteen-year-old African American man from Berkeley, Meredith Hunter, brandished a handgun. An Angel plunged a switchblade into his back repeatedly—four or five times—and other bikers joined the assault on Hunter, kicking and punching him. One stood on his head for a full minute. He died later that evening. The Stones, not entirely aware of what had happened, played into the night. Others died as well. A car plowed into two campers, killing them instantly, and another man drowned in an irrigation canal.[153]

Counterculturalists reacted in mixed ways to Altamont. "Pearl Harbor to the Woodstock Nation," announced one headline, and the Berkeley Tribe declared, "Stones Concert Ends: Amerika Up for Grabs." Most who attended noted the generally bad vibrations felt throughout the day: "There was no love, no joy. It wasn't just the Angels. It was everybody. In 24 hours we created all the problems of our society in one place: congestion, violence, dehumanization." Jagger was one of the most distraught and disturbed. "I thought the scene here was supposed to be so groovy," he said bitterly. "If Jesus Christ had been there, he would've been fucking crucified."[154]

Yet some expressed less disturbed and pessimistic opinions. One writer pointed out that because the violence had occurred near the stage, the people farther back in the audience had actually enjoyed themselves. Leary dismissed the concert's problems, opining that the majority of those in attendance—99 percent—were loving and peaceful, and they had vastly outnumbered the less than fifty violent individuals. And at least one underground journalist assailed the media, while defending the counterculture. "The incident is being blown out of proportion," wrote Clay Geerdes. "Violence and money are news. Must they be?. . . . Is there no way to counteract those who continue to project violence into every move that young people make toward the achievement of an alternative life pattern?" Despite these reactions, the Altamont debacle shocked, saddened, and disgusted most hippies.[155]

Altamont was not the only disconcerting news story that December. Earlier that year, on the morning of August 9, police had found the brutally butchered bodies of actress Sharon Tate and three of her friends, including the coffee fortune heiress Abigail Folger in Benedict Canyon, Los Angeles. The next evening, two more bodies were discovered, that of Leno and Rosemary LaBianca. Now, four months later, police had apprehended their suspects: Charles Manson and members of "The Family."

The mainstream press wasted no time linking Manson with the counterculture. The message was clear: hippies could be gun-toting, knife-wielding killers. Time published an article, "The Demon of Death Valley," that told of a "mystical semi-religious hippie drug-and-murder cult led by a bearded, demonic Mahdi." In another story titled "Hippies and Violence," Time quoted a doctor who confirmed the fears of many in majority society: "There has always been a potential for murder. Many hippies are socially almost dead inside. Some require massive emotions to feel anything at all. They need bizarre, intensive acts to feel alive—sexual acts, acts of violence, nudity, every kind of Dionysian thrill."[156]

During Manson's trial, the details of his life and the circumstances behind the murders became clear. He was born on November 12, 1934, to a
teenage prostitute in Cincinnati and an aunt and uncle raised him until
age eleven in Charleston, West Virginia. Manson spent his next years in
and out of juvenile schools and prisons for burglary, car theft, and cashing
stolen US Treasury checks. Upon his release from prison in March 1967,
he traveled to Haight-Ashbury wearing beads and sandals and began col-
lecting a harem of impressionable young women. Then he and his Family moved to the Spahn Ranch in western Los Angeles County where they
spent the days singing Manson's songs, dancing, taking drugs, swimming, stealing cars, and raiding garbage dumpsters, searching for food.
Manson's followers called him "Jesus" and "God." Manson had ordered
the killings in order to instigate a race war between blacks and whites, a
war he called "Helter Skelter," named after a song on the Beatles' White
Album. He hoped that the white establishment would blame "Blackie"
for the murders, igniting an apocalyptic racial conflict in which African
Americans would emerge victorious. Then, Manson thought, he and his
Family, the lone white survivors, would come out from a bottomless pit in
the desert to lord over and command the black population, as "the black
man's sole purpose on earth was to serve the white man." These were the
twisted fantasies of a madman, not a peace-loving hippie.[157]

Manson, on the surface, appeared to be a hippie—he played guitar,
enjoyed sex and orgies, took drugs, and had long hair—but all commonalities between him and the counterculture end there. Manson did
not consider himself a hippie—he loathed the very name because he associated the flower people with "pacifism" and "weakness." Manson, in
fact, was the antithesis of a hippie: he was a racist who vehemently hated
African Americans; he welcomed death and violence, persuading his followers to commit murder; he hoped to ignite a race war; and he believed
in a white "master race." Manson also felt that "Hitler was a tuned-in guy
who had leveled the karma of the Jews." Manson was not a hippie and
neither were his followers. "We never considered ourselves hippies,"
stated Family member Paul Watkins. Watkins recalled that while Manson believed "the ideas of the hippies were okay," he preached that "they
didn't have the balls or the soul to do anything for society; they hadn't
been through their changes; they hadn't seen the truth." As far as Manson

was concerned, the hippies had had their chance, but they "blew it" in Haight-Ashbury. At one point the wild-eyed leader suggested that Family members call themselves "slippies," because they slipped "beneath the awareness of people," just as Manson had slipped under the radar of the guards and prison officials earlier in his life.[158]

Members of the older generation did not know the truth about Manson. Although some freaks defended him (the *Los Angeles Free Press* in particular held him up as a martyr for the counterculture) most longhairs found him and his murderous followers horrifying. Yet hippies received the fallout for the Family's actions, especially in Los Angeles. "Did you have anything to do with the murders?" a store clerk asked a bearded man. A scared resident confronted and chased off with a shotgun a hippie couple out for a walk. "I can just see my mother reading the stories and saying, 'Oh, so that's the kind of life she's been living,'" a woman told a journalist. "They just confirm what everyone wants to believe." Some adults came to hippies' defense. "The true hippie wouldn't hurt a flea," remarked a restaurant owner who employed longhairs.[159]

Many historians argue that the counterculture had an ephemeral existence, lasting four or five years. The traditional interpretation is commonly argued, which maintains that the peaceful Woodstock festival represented the high tide of hippiedom followed by its downfall at Altamont four months later. Manson, it is said, demonstrated the dark potential of communal living and the hippie lifestyle. William L. O' Neill asserted that Manson adhered to typical hippie values because he felt "straight virtues were bad" and "free love, nature, dope, rock, and mysticism were good." He concluded, "Of course hippies were not murderers usually. But the repressed hostility, authoritarianism, perversity, and mindless paranoia that underlay much of the hippie ethic were never displayed more clearly." According to many historians and scholars, the counterculture did not survive the 1960s or faded shortly thereafter. Gerard J. DeGroot argues that Woodstock was "a false dawn," and that the "reality" of the countercultural project was "revealed in gory Technicolor four months later at a dusty racetrack called Altamont." DeGroot concludes by quoting J. Marks, who wrote of Altamont, "We knew it was all over. We were dying." Likewise, Nadya Zimmerman maintains that Altamont and the Manson murders put an end to the counterculture. Under Manson, she contends, "the countercultural sensibility had undergone a metamorphosis, becoming a philosophy that countenanced extreme excess." For Gitlin, Altamont and the Weathermen's townhouse explosion in March 1970 represented the "splattering rage of the 'death culture' lodged in the very heart of the 'life force'. . . . The revolutionary mood had been fueled by the blindingly bright illusion that human history was beginning afresh because a graced generation had willed it so. Now there wasn't enough life left to mobilize against all the death raining down."[160]

To be sure, Altamont and the Manson murders were terrible events. But they did not embody or signify the downfall of hippiedom, the end of the spirit of peace and love, a generation's lost faith, or the end of the Sixties. Most hippies did not consider Manson one of their own and few attended Altamont. In fact, Altamont quickly faded from memory when hip youth enjoyed successful, multiday rock festivals in the next decade. And, as we shall see shortly, Kent State and the backlash from the mainstream only strengthened the counterculture's resolve to create a new society. Murders and rhetorical and physical attacks by the Silent Majority, police, and military increased alienation, producing more freaks for hippiedom, while strengthening the bonds between members of the counterculture, New Left, and antiwar movement.

When the seventies dawned, the iconic counterculture with its love-ins, flower power, and acid rock passed into history. Although freaks would rarely mention the coming of the Age of Aquarius in the seventies, they did speak of, and had great faith in, the new society, the new age, and the new America they attempted to usher in. The counterculture had yet to reach its apogee.

"Upbeat" youth at the Fred C. Dobbs Café on the Sunset Strip in Los Angeles, January 1966 (Conrad Mercurio/Herald Examiner Collection/Los Angeles Public Library).

Teens protest police activity in front of Pandora's Box on the Sunset Strip in Los Angeles, November 1966 (Herald Examiner Collection/Los Angeles Public Library).

A young man, carrying a stack of papers that reads "Sun-Ray Love-In," pauses to smell a flower during the Belle Isle Love-In in Detroit, April 1967 (Walter P. Reuther Library, Archives of Labor and Urban Affairs, Wayne State University).

Hippies at a gathering in San Francisco, Summer of Love, 1967 (Dennis Maness Summer of Love Collection, San Francisco History Center, San Francisco Public Library).

Hippie woman with painted forehead at summer festival in San Francisco, 1967 (Dennis Maness Summer of Love Collection, San Francisco History Center, San Francisco Public Library).

Hippie women dancing at summer music festival in San Francisco, 1967 (Dennis Maness Summer of Love Collection, San Francisco History Center, San Francisco Public Library).

Beatle George Harrison pays a surprise visit to San Francisco's Haight-Ashbury, August 1967 (Associated Press).

Students gather on the Texas Union patio for a love-in at the University of Texas at Austin, 1968 (UT Office of Public Affairs Records, e_utopa_00066, Dolph Briscoe Center for American History, University of Texas at Austin).

Activists stand in front of a row of National Guard soldiers at the Democratic National Convention in Chicago, August 1968 (U.S. News & World Report Magazine Photograph Collection, Prints and Photos Division, Library of Congress, LC-DIG-ppmsca-40810).

Yippies in a tree protest at President Nixon's inauguration, January 1969 (U.S. News & World Report Magazine Photograph Collection, Prints and Photos Division, Library of Congress, LC-DIG-ppmsca-56668).

Hippies in an apartment, March 1969 (U.S. News & World Report Magazine Photograph Collection, Prints and Photos Division, Library of Congress, LC-DIG-ppmsca-56682).

Hippies walking in downtown Atlanta, 1970 (By Doy Gorton, White South Project Archive, e_wsp_0254, Dolph Briscoe Center for American History, University of Texas at Austin).

Antipollution teach-in at Wayne State University in Detroit on Earth Day, April 1970 (Walter P. Reuther Library, Archives of Labor and Urban Affairs, Wayne State University).

A gay-in in Central Park, New York City, 1970 (Photo by Diana Davies, Manuscripts and Archives Division, New York Public Library).

John Lennon and Yoko Ono perform at the John Sinclair Freedom Rally at the University of Michigan, 1971 (BL014432, Michiganensian vol. 76 [1972], 208, Bentley Historical Library, University of Michigan).

Demonstrators at the US Capitol in Washington, DC, May 1971 (U.S. News & World Report Magazine Photograph Collection, Prints and Photos Division, Library of Congress, LC-DIG-ppmsca-50431).

Communards in front of a tipi at Morning Star Ranch near Occidental, California, 1971
(Eddie Adams Photographic Archive, e_ea_0254, Dolph Briscoe Center for American History,
University of Texas at Austin).

Disabled Vietnam veteran Bill Henshaw attends a Vietnam Veterans Against the War (VVAW)
demonstration during President Nixon's second inauguration, January 1973 (WHI-49679,
Wisconsin Historical Society).

A woman and two men behind beer taps at Armadillo World Headquarters in Austin, 1973 (Coke Dilworth Photographic Archive, di_05824, Dolph Briscoe Center for American History, University of Texas at Austin).

Mifflin Street Community Co-op in Madison, Wisconsin, 1974 (WHI-40213, Wisconsin Historical Society).

4

In 1971, *Time* proclaimed, "Too many hippies. We can only afford so many people alienated from society."[1] The counterculture reached its apogee in 1971, as it grew to epic proportions and projected its greatest influence. It had undergone a drastic transformation since its inception, hardly resembling the counterculture of 1968, even less so the counterculture of 1965. Gone, for the most part, were Edwardian suits, frills, cravats, lace cuffs, psychedelic sounds, pulsating liquid light shows, happenings, flower power, body paint, and the conviction that LSD could transform the world. Gone, too, were the distinct philosophies that characterized—and divided—hippies and activists. Freaks no longer grooved at love-ins. Now they jetted into Amsterdam, explored Afghanistan, hitchhiked America, backpacked and camped in secluded wildernesses, consumed organic food, farmed in Tennessee, opened hip clothing stores and co-ops, converted to vegetarianism, and removed refuse from creeks.

A number of changes made the counterculture of the early 1970s distinct from previous incarnations. First, and most significantly, following the tragic killing of four students at Kent State, nearly all the aspects differentiating the New Left and counterculture disappeared as young, mostly white people—demonstrators, activists, politicos, communards, Jesus Freaks, dropouts, drifters, runaways, hippies, Yippies, cultural feminists, and select gays, Vietnam veterans, and

environmentalists—became a more common and integrated countersociety dedicated to creating the new America, while standing against the
Vietnam War, Richard Nixon, the Silent Majority, and the establishment.
Second, the counterculture's values grew in number and diversity and
some took on greater importance than others. While nudity, sex, and rock
music remained somewhat significant, new principles and enthusiasms
disproportionately commanded the counterculture's interest, including
environmentalism, overseas trailing, natural living, and commune building. Third, although some counterculturalists initially felt uncomfortable
with and resisted open displays of homosexuality and radical feminism,
the counterculture as a whole, near the end of its tenure, advocated for
both gay liberation and women's rights. In fact, numerous gays and cultural feminists themselves took part in the counterculture. Fourth, hippiedom continued to expand. Freaks suffused America, making appearances
in Idaho, Mississippi, and South Dakota. Finally, cultural activism exploded. Hippies and political activists combined their energies, founding myriad alternative institutions and services in many cities and college
towns, furthering the project of creating a new society.

COUNTERCULTURE ENVIRONMENTALISM
AND EARTH DAY

As the seventies began, the counterculture discovered a new cause for its
efforts: environmentalism. To be sure, environmentalism had long predated the counterculture and hippies were not responsible for the rise of
the modern environmental movement, nor were they its leading proponents. Environmentalism, however, became a major concern for freaks
and communards in the early 1970s.

Environmentalists had been active earlier, but it was not until the 1960s
that the modern environmental movement gained momentum. In 1962
Rachel Carson published her influential *Silent Spring*. Carson, a marine
biologist, pointed out the dangers inherent in agribusiness's use of pesticides like DDT. Toxic chemicals, she elucidated, found their way into human fat, breast milk, and water. Pesticides also built up in the food chain,
killing birds and other creatures, and threatened people. Carson advanced
an ecological outlook, arguing that people and nature were interconnected

and that humans needed to cease engaging in activities that harmed eco-logical systems. A public debate about pesticides that Carson had helped to instigate continued throughout the 1960s. The twelve most toxic sub-stances she had listed in the book were eventually banned or restricted.[2]

Ecological disasters alerted the public to environmental problems. Some wildlife disappeared; Louisiana's state bird, the brown pelican, no longer inhabited the state's shores. Noise pollution harassed cities, as jet, subway train, and truck sounds exceeding 85 decibels threatened to damage hearing and noises that reached 165 decibels could kill small ani-mals like cats. Pollution plagued the nation's waters, too. Human waste, industrial discharge, soap, and fertilizer flowed into lakes and rivers. In 1965 a study showed that only one river in the entire country, the Saint Croix, between Wisconsin and Minnesota, remained unpolluted. In Janu-ary 1969 an oil well off of Santa Barbara caught fire and exploded, sending 235,000 gallons of petroleum into the Pacific Ocean, and a slick gradually spread over two hundred miles of coastline. So much oil and chemical pollution flowed into Cleveland's Cuyahoga River that it caught fire sev-eral times and burned two railroad trestles. Meanwhile, companies and municipalities polluted Lake Erie with chlorides and sulfates. Authorities warned that the lake was "almost dead." *Newsweek* reported that its waters no longer supported life, except for sludge worms and mutated carp. Air pollution concerned citizens as well. Automobiles produced ninety-five million tons of air waste per year and harmful smog floated over the na-tion's cities, especially Los Angeles. Smog's deleterious effects included crippled livestock, discolored house and car paint, dead pine trees, and human respiratory ailments.[3]

Environmentalism became a popular aim and conviction on college campuses in 1969. Hippies and New Leftists who had struggled to main-tain control of People's Park in Berkeley were part of the burgeoning ecol-ogy movement. "The People's Park and all parks like it," declared Active Conservation Tactics, "are part of the attempt by people to beautify, save, or newly create even the smallest portion of our dehumanized land." In November 1969 the *New York Times* reported a story with the headline "En-vironment May Eclipse Vietnam as College Issue." After the massive an-tiwar marches that fall, the paper noted that Vietnam seemed "physically remote," and that many students felt that the war issue offered a "limited scope for student action." Alienated activists seized on environmentalism as a new cause. "A lot of people are becoming disenchanted with the anti-war movement," observed a young man at Boston University. "People who are frustrated and disillusioned are starting to turn to ecology."[4]

Like war and racism, youth saw the degradation of the environment as another symptom of a sick establishment. Activists perceived environmentalism and the war as intertwined. Vietnam's critics saw the war as a huge ecological disaster. Students demonstrated against Dow Chemical, a company that made napalm. Herbicides such as Agent Orange not only burned away jungle canopy, vegetation, and crops but also harmed American troops who came into contact with it.[5]

The number of people involved in the environmental movement soared. In 1960, 124,000 people claimed membership in the top twelve environmental groups; by 1972, that number had climbed almost ten times, to over 1.1 million. Membership jumped by 38 percent between 1969 and 1972, when 300,000 new environmentalists joined organizations. In a January 1970 article titled "The Ravaged Environment," Newsweek declared that "the general public has been seized with such anger and alarm as to goad political leaders into proclaiming conservation of the environment the chief task of this decade—and perhaps of the rest of the century."[6]

Earth Day—the largest demonstration of the sixties era—clearly indicated that the degradation of the environment worried Americans. On April 22, 1970, an estimated twenty million people and four thousand ecology groups celebrated the first Earth Day. Wisconsin senator Gaylord Nelson had suggested the idea, recommending a teach-in on the dangers of pollution. Denis Hayes, a Harvard law student, acted as national coordinator. Teachers and students participated in ecological happenings and teach-ins at 1,500 colleges and 10,000 high schools. Police closed in Fifth Avenue in New York, allowing 100,000 people to parade up and down the street. In Washington, 10,000 people reveled around the Washington Monument for twelve hours. From Boston to Sacramento, schoolchildren walked along roads and vacant lots picking up discarded tires and beer and soda cans. At the University of Wisconsin, one could attend any of fifty-eight different environmental programs. At Florida Technological University, students put a car on trial for polluting the air before destroying it. At least 1,000 Cleveland State University students collected litter around the city, while 1,200 students in Letcher County, Kentucky, symbolically interred a casket filled with garbage. President Nixon did not partake in the day's activities, but an aide relayed his approval. Businesses responded by announcing new environmentally friendly programs and products.[7]

"Earth Day may be a turning point in American history," Senator Nelson announced in front of a crowd of four thousand in Denver. "It may be the birth date of a new American ethic that rejects the frontier philosophy that the continent was put here for our plunder, and accepts the idea that even urbanized, affluent, mobile societies are interdependent with the fragile, life-sustaining systems of the air, the water, the land." Hippies praised Earth Day, too. The *Free Press of Louisville* called it "a groovy spring thing" and a "real funk festival," while acknowledging the "the message was pretty heavy": the "Earth is dying."[8]

Environmentalism became one of the hippies' foremost ethics and it grew after Earth Day. Freaks believed that environmental problems were among the most crucial issues confronting humanity and called for decisive and immediate efforts to confront those problems. "Ecology evolution is a fight for life," argued a New Mexico underground, *Astral Projection*, "and if action is not taken soon, the fight will be quickly lost." For environmental counterculturalists, humankind and nature were one—not separate—and individuals had an obligation to take care of and preserve the land, wildlife, and environment—not conquer it. Being in harmony with nature was tantamount to preserving humanity. By taking care of the environment, hippies argued, people ultimately looked after themselves and one another. Many longhairs assumed that human preservation hung in the balance: "We are cheapening this life, defiling our world, and headed fast towards an extinction of our species."[9]

Hippies advocated adopting environmentally conscious lifestyles. To combat air pollution, they endorsed walking, riding a bike, hitchhiking, carpooling, or utilizing mass transit instead of driving a car. Undergrounds advised people who did drive a car to keep the engine tuned and to get the pollution control devices checked regularly. Activists recommended initiating lawsuits as an effective means to fight air polluters. To conserve water, hippies urged people to refrain from bathing every day and to use as little water as possible when washing clothes. They promoted recycling and favored nonpolluting energy sources. Undergrounds also recommended the use of various environmentally friendly substances—potato slices, vinegar, and linseed oil for polishing wood furniture, salt to eliminate food stains, and baking soda in place of toothpaste.[10]

Ecology organizations proliferated at universities and in cities. Students on campuses from Maine to Hawaii expressed concerns over a variety of environmental crises ranging from global overpopulation, water pollution, to preservation of natural areas. At the University of Minnesota, students disturbed by the effects of air pollution buried a gasoline engine in a mock funeral. Student activists conducted campaigns to save San Francisco Bay and northern California's redwood forests, and attempted to stop the building of new dams in the Colorado River. Students for Environmental Control at the University of Illinois removed six tons of refuse from a nearby creek, a University of Texas student founded a state environmental newsletter, and at the University of Washington, students prepared an eighty-page document detailing the environmental problems of Puget Sound. Hundreds of students, many of them bearded and wearing hippie clothing, blocked access to the Santa Barbara Wharf to protest oil operations and oil pollution. Northwestern Students for a Better Environment proposed a statewide ban on laundry detergent and other phosphate-containing substances in Illinois. Crisis Biology at Indiana University fought the university's coal-burning power plants, a source of smoke pollution. At Michigan State, student government leaders and ecology clubs protested a proposal to build a highway across campus. In Seattle, the Institute for Ecological Studies held workshops on water resources, noise and air pollution, and population; and in Austin, Ecology Action urged people to start mini recycling centers in their apartment complexes and neighborhoods. Other environmentalists opposed the building of oil pipelines.[11]

Environmentalists, environmentalism, and Earth Day became targets for movement radicals and New Leftists who found Earth Day "trivial" and a "diversion" from more important and crucial developments like the war, racism, imperialism, poverty, and police repression. Some politicos suggested that the Nixon administration created enthusiasm for environmentalism in order to split the movement into internecine factions.

Radicals cited as evidence establishment participation and approval, especially among mainstream politicians and members of Nixon's cabinet. Some New Leftists also saw environmentalism as a moderate phenomenon concerned with lifestyle issues rather than the egregious effects of capitalism.[12]

To be sure, the counterculture and New Left never merged entirely. Some politicos remained hostile toward those who turned their energies away from the war. Political radicals perceived hippies dwelling in rural communes as "escapists" hiding from pressing issues and real problems. And some self-described revolutionaries felt as much disdain for hippie purists as they did for the establishment. "These people whose perverse idea [it] is to remain uninvolved and apathetic," a Kentucky underground contended, "are to be blamed for the shameful condition this country is in as much as the Fascist oppressors." Other politicos blamed purists for their enervating effects on political activism. In late summer 1970, for example, the People's Army Jamboree marched on the city of Portland, but, according to one of the participants, its strength "had been greatly diminished, or rather siphoned off, by two simultaneous rock festivals." The People's Army consisted of only 1,500 "dedicated revolutionaries," a militant lamented, because "the peaceniks and flower children" had defected.[13]

Some hippie purists also endured, refusing to participate in demonstrations, and worked at building the new society in secluded rural communes. And purists continued to vehemently oppose violent radicals. "Here I am, your past follower in the virtues of 'Peace' and 'Love,' wanting only to smoke my pot and exchange caresses with my girlfriend; and you persons have taken to writing of guns and grenades," a hippie wrote to Houston's *Space City!* "Whatever happened to the old values?" Purists opposed violent political revolution as a viable avenue for change, advocating cultural revolution or ill-defined rock revolution in its place. "I confess, by the way, that my most subversive, 'violent-overthrow' thought is to build a huge, towering and terrifying amplification system . . . and hook in Jefferson Airplane during the dead of night," admitted a hippie. "Then, I'd hammer and rock the city right into the river—not angrily, but happily, to be sure."[14]

INVASION OF CAMBODIA AND KENT STATE

Purists and revolutionaries disliked President Nixon. His Vietnam policy infuriated students, the antiwar movement, and hippies. Nixon planned to withdraw American troops gradually. He also intended to renew bombing, go head-to-head with Hanoi in negotiations, and shift responsibility for South Vietnam's security to Vietnamese combat soldiers—"Vietnamization." Nixon had plans for Cambodia, too. A year earlier, American troops had made a secret incursion into Cambodia to sabotage communist supply routes. The president had kept these actions under wraps for fear of inciting the wrath of the press and antiwar movement. In April 1970, Nixon ordered bombing and troop raids of Cambodia in an attempt to destroy communist supply depots and sanctuaries. Other military and diplomatic goals motivated the invasion. Nixon wanted Hanoi to know that America was not backing down. Moreover, the United States could protect the American-friendly Lon Nol government in Cambodia from the communists. By destroying supply sanctuaries, Nixon hoped to deny the North Vietnamese badly needed materials in the South.

Youth felt betrayed. Nixon had promised to "wind down" the war—then, suddenly, he expanded it into Cambodia. Protest erupted: hundreds of thousands of students at over seven hundred colleges demonstrated. A national strike unfolded on a wide range of campuses, from hotbeds of activism in Berkeley and Madison to religious schools, community colleges, and southern institutions where little protest activity had existed previously. At two universities, demonstrations turned deadly. At Kent State University in Ohio, the governor called out the National Guard after rioters firebombed a Reserve Officers' Training Corps building. On May 4, troops opened fire on students, killing four—two men and two women—and wounding eleven others. Tragedy struck again the following week when state police killed two African Americans at Jackson State University in Mississippi. The week after Kent State, four million students contributed to demonstrations that engulfed over 50 percent of the nation's campuses. Some hundred thousand marched on the White House. Sixteen states activated the National Guard to quell rioting on twenty campuses and police and students clashed at over twenty universities. Five hundred campuses closed down, and fifty-one did not reopen that semester.[15]

Nixon showed no sympathy for the slain students; rather, he announced to the shocked country that "when dissent turns to violence it invites tragedy." The Silent Majority also showed little sympathy. The country was profoundly divided. Polls indicated that a majority supported Nixon's invasion of Cambodia and blamed the students rather than the National Guard for the shooting. In Kent, Ohio, there were "few regrets expressed by the townspeople over the deaths of the four students, and those few are usually prefaces to baffled outrage over the smashing of store windows, the burning of the Army R.O.T.C. building and the prevalence of long hair." In the days after the tragedy, townspeople wrote to local newspapers to express their anger. One suggested "a very simple compound with barbed wire and a minimum of conveniences" to put an end to student unrest. Few people in Kent and the neighboring communities blamed the guardsmen—many adults felt that the troops "should have shot more of them." Some even voiced their contempt for the dead. "They were dirty and they had long hair," an older woman commented. "The newspapers printed their high school pictures so people would think they were nice kids, but they weren't."[16]

NEW LEFT-COUNTERCULTURE FUSION AND THE RISE OF THE COUNTERSOCIETY

In the early seventies, the counterculture and New Left, for the most part, merged into a cohesive and inclusive countersociety that stood in opposition to Nixon, Vietnam, the Silent Majority, and the establishment. Several factors account for this unification. In the wake of Kent State, determined white radical youth of all persuasions resisted the Nixon administration, the seemingly interminable and widening war in Vietnam, and Nixon's straitlaced supporters. Hippies and freaks flooded the movement, putting aside their reservations about activism, and activists and politicos became thoroughly countercultural. A pervasive sense of commonality, inclusivity, and unity arose among youth who felt part of a cohesive "society" and "nation." Philosophical and ideological disputes lessened in intensity and barriers between the cultural and political spheres atrophied, as more and more youth combined political and cultural radicalism. Counterculturalists and New Leftists essentially became the same kinds of people. The countersociety, then, had a common core of adherents with the same objectives: an end to the war in Vietnam, opposition to Nixon, support for and furthering of egalitarian and cultural liberation movements, and building the new society complete with co-ops, free stores, free clinics, free universities, community switchboards, and head shops, among other alternative institutions. At the same time, massive segments of youth culture grew tired with the antiwar movement, and increasingly pursued individual and personal matters, putting their values into action, resolving to "live the revolution." Furthermore, following the implosion of SDS and violent incidents, few people remained within the movement that hippie purists opposed. And purists themselves diminished. Champions of rock and dope revolution and those who expressed hostility toward political engagement nearly disappeared.

For youth, Kent State was a "massacre" and "slaughter" and signaled the establishment's "declaration of war" on the antiwar movement and noncompliant kids. "William Schroeder, Allison Krause, Jeffrey Miller, Sandy Scheuer. Four brothers and sisters were murdered by the Ohio National Guard," wrote Liberation News Service's Jeff Gerth. "Their murder had all the efficiency of a cold blooded killing." The shooting forced the young to choose sides. "Prior to the Kent State tragedy," wrote a rock commentator, "the majority of youth could remain sympathetic to the alternative cause but they didn't need to be activists. Now, most observers say that most have made personal decisions. You either do something about changing the bull-like rush of the Establishment, or you become part of the Establishment. No longer is there any middle ground."[17]

In this polarized atmosphere it had become Us versus Them, Left versus Right, Longhairs versus Straights, the peaceful versus the bellicose and intolerant. In the aftermath of Kent, few hippies raised objections to demonstrators and politicos, and activists generally refrained from criticizing hippies. Young people began to think of themselves as a singular "counterculture," "tribe," and "people." They commonly used phrases like "our society" and "our nation." Some conceived of and discussed an expansive counterculture composed of disparate individuals opposed to the establishment—black snipers, dopers, peace marchers, student radicals, and draft resisters. Likewise, the Revolutionary People's Constitutional Convention, which met in Philadelphia in September, proclaimed its dedication to empowering "the people": women, denizens of the Third World, GIs, college students, workers, lesbians, gays, welfare recipients, and hippies. Of course, the countersociety was never as all-embracing as some people believed; nevertheless, youth sensed a certain cohesion and solidarity among one another when they faced down the establishment. "We are a people, we recognize each other as brothers and sisters united in a common struggle for our freedom, for our survival, and we recognize each other because we share a common culture," asserted John Sinclair. "We do the same things, we live the same way, we listen to the same music, smoke the same sacraments, we are united by our age, our common values, our common vision of the future." Similarly, the *Madison Kaleidoscope* articulated lucidly the pervasive feeling held by radicals of all persuasions—including hip Marxists—that they were part of a common and inclusive youth culture pitted against the mainstream and majority society:

> The youth culture is spreading like a plague over diseased Amerika, killing capitalist minds and stealing a whole generation away from their parents. The kids exult in their dropping out of PIG culture by growing their hair long, blowing the capitalist smog out of their minds with illegal drugs, living Woodstock, and, by committing the ultimate anti-social act—having fun. Kids from Boise, New York, and Berkeley live on communes, smoke dope, fuck, create, and because they are the country's most wanted criminals, must fight pigs together.[18]

And fight together they did. Hippies and politicos put aside their differences, for their shared opposition to the war and Nixon proved more important than their opposing approaches to social change. Dope dealers and political heavies hung out at a local bar in Lawrence, where the University of Kansas is located. The two groups vocally sparred over who had more influence on students. After Nixon's escalation of the war into Cambodia, however, the groups came together, organizing the university's most militant protests.[19]

Most youth believed that the new society would come about when the young worked together. "Alternatives to the Amerikan culture are being found and experimented with as a new culture, a new society is being built. We cannot define the new culture, we can only work it out as we live it. It will involve struggle; continuous, collective struggle," asserted the Joplin, Missouri, underground, *Cahoots!* From the perspective of hippies and politicos alike, youth needed to immerse themselves in the new culture, while collectively attempting to create the new society. And most of the new society builders no longer made distinctions between political and cultural radicalism. Contributors to *Cahoots!* made clear that the paper would report on music, art, lifestyles, and the war in Vietnam, "for there is no separation between culture and politics."[20]

More and more youth combined political and cultural radicalism—few perceived a barrier between the two. As Blake Slonecker has shown, the Liberation News Service contingent that became communards in Vermont and Massachusetts believed that "rural communalism and New Left politics represented two sides of the same activist coin." In fact, the denizens of Montague Farm maintained that moving to the countryside "was the most revolutionary thing LNS has done." For the communalists, political and cultural radicalism did not represent separate impulses. Neither was rural living an abandonment of the movement. Activists and hippies alike turned inward and strived for personal awakenings and self-realization. Politicos and New Leftists recognized that they had neglected to focus on personal matters. Now they were poised to make that transition. "In the past few years we have talked a lot about working for political change," announced the underground *Tiohero*. "Now we are becoming increasingly aware of our need to radically change ourselves, simultaneously realizing that in our relating to people politically and otherwise we cannot continue to mirror this society." Riot, demonstration, and strike participants determined to "make the revolution," also struggled "intensely on a personal level." Values such as love became universal among the politicos and hip. In Berkeley, for example, a member of the Youth Coalition for Self-Defense made reference to getting high "on the love which sustains our politics."[21]

Hippies and activists became indistinguishable—they were often the same people. This was not the case only a few years earlier. The counterculture had dominated love-ins and be-ins, while the antiwar movement and New Left had dominated demonstrations. In the early 1970s protests resembled counterculture gatherings and radiated an ambiance similar to the rock festivals and love-ins of the late 1960s. In Louisville, Kentucky, for instance, youth gathered for a "picnic for peace" in the city's Central

Park. The University of Louisville Committee for Survival, an organization active in both the antidraft and ecology movements, sponsored the event. Conception and Milk Sea provided music for nearly one thousand people who basked lazily in the sun. Picnic revelers wearing flowers in their hair shared cookies, fruit, sandwiches, water, and marijuana—and then they became demonstrators. About six hundred people marched to the post office led by a "couple of freaks" carrying a banner: "Out of Vietnam, Laos, Cambodia." At their destination, the protesters chanted, "What do we want? Peace! When do we want it? Now!"[22]

A countercultural atmosphere pervaded demonstrations. Activists considered themselves "movement freaks," part of Woodstock Nation, and they spoke of "building a new America." At the White House, young people splashed around naked in a fountain. Guerrilla theater actors and actresses soaked in animal blood held out animal organs to spectators and shouted, "This is the blood of the victims of the war!" Protestors sold and smoked marijuana joints. In 1971 at least fifteen thousand people stayed the night near the Washington Monument huddled in sleeping bags as rock bands played into the early morning hours. Jesus Freaks walked around urging the crowds to "get right with God," entertainers sang, "Freak out, freak out, freak out now," and people danced happily in the mud. At a demonstration in New York, an estimated twenty thousand sat on the grass in Central Park listening to speeches and music. Blue jeans and army fatigues became popular clothing items.[23]

New Left–counterculture fusion also occurred because nearly all rebellious youth pursued cultural radicalism. Fewer students protested the war. As Nixon wound the war down, the antiwar movement faded. April 24, 1971, marked the last major national demonstration. Indeed, a 1971 study of college students revealed that only 11 percent identified with the New Left, while the other 89 percent "pressed forward in their search for a cultural revolution while taking a step backwards from political revolution." After agitating politically for years, many activists sought to repair their psyches and put their lives back together. Politicos, like hippies, headed back to the land for solace and reflection and waged personal revolutions. A sociological study of the residents of 120 communes, for instance, revealed that 57 percent were former antiwar demonstrators, 33 percent had participated in civil rights demonstrations, 22 percent had rioted, and 30 percent had been arrested. Ex-activists dedicated to "renewing the social order" and changing their daily thought and life patterns, bought 280 acres, a house, and a barn in Oregon, establishing Alpha Farm. Similarly, political radicals and psychedelic dropouts set up Mayday Farm in Vermont. Tom Hayden joined a Berkeley commune, the Red Family. Carl Oglesby, a former president of SDS, decided "that it was time to burn out and, really, it was a great burnout." Oglesby ended up on a farm in Vermont, where he enjoyed "lots of parties, great reefer, good acid," and lovely friends. "It was the best part of the struggle," he recalled. "The best part of the struggle was the surrender."²⁴

The diminishment of hippie purists facilitated the New Left–counterculture merger as well, for purists had often voiced objections to activism and confrontation, and been at odds philosophically with politicos. Confronted with the realization that rock music was big business and integral to corporate capitalism, individuals espousing rock revolution, for the most part, faded away. In addition, most freaks no longer believed that cultural revolution would arrive by way of dope and drugs; in fact, the deaths of superstars Janis Joplin, Jim Morrison, and Jimi Hendrix belied that fanciful notion. Moreover, fewer hippies believed that transforming their individual outlooks and values—personal revolutions—were sufficient to bring about lasting social and cultural change. Something more tangible, more immediate, had to be done. Purists grew weary waiting for the revolution. Rather, they strived to make it happen. In 1968 John Lennon had exemplified the purist position in the song "Revolution" when he advocated "changing heads" and "freeing minds" as the best path to social change. By 1971, however, he supported direct involvement, singing in "Power to the People": "Say we want a revolution / We better get it on right away / Well you get on your feet / And out on the street." Rolling Stone, apolitical for its first few years of publication, felt compelled to enter the political fray after Kent State, declaring, "Either Nixon must be forced into resignation or he must be impeached." The brief column exhorted readers to "do something." And on top of these new currents, cultural activism burgeoned. The aperture between hippies and New Leftists closed, as they created alternative institutions together.²⁵

Violent actions committed by political revolutionaries also facilitated the merging of New Left and counterculture. In the early morning hours of August 24, 1970, a militant group known as the New Year's Gang, led by Karl Armstrong, detonated a bomb at the Army Mathematics Research Center at the University of Wisconsin. Armstrong had previously been a Eugene McCarthy supporter and became a radical following the Democratic National Convention. Opponents of Army Math contended that its researchers aided the American military in Vietnam. The facility became a target—Armstrong intended to "bring the war home." The New Year's Gang loaded a stolen van full of explosives, parked it next to Sterling Hall—the building that housed Army Math—and lit the fuse. The bomb destroyed Sterling Hall, damaged twenty-six adjacent buildings, and shattered windows over a six-block area. The explosion blew people who lived near the site out of bed. The blast, which killed one and wounded three others, woke the city and could be heard for thirty miles.

The incident stunned the Wisconsin campus and Madison residents. Students almost universally regretted the death of Robert Fassnacht, a thirty-three-year-old postdoctoral researcher in physics and father of three, who had been killed by the explosion. Ironically, Fassnacht had opposed the war. Most students found the bombing revolting and condemned it. "What the hell, they didn't accomplish anything except hurt the university," expressed a twenty-three-year-old political science major. "The Army can build 10 more research centers, but the bombing has turned hostility toward the wrong persons—the students." A young female student felt "disgusted" and asserted, "I don't see how the university can go on. The bombing typifies the atmosphere that pervades this campus, an atmosphere of violence, intolerance and irrationalities."[26]

The bombing's impact extended far beyond the Wisconsin campus. After the incident, the antiwar movement generally retreated from violence and activists worked within the system to effect change. The New Year's Gang's deed did not kill the movement, but altered it. The Army Math bombing demonstrated that the use of violence to hasten social change could produce tragic results. Armstrong's actions did not give rise to revolution. Instead, as author Tom Bates has argued, "they had brought about a renewal of the peace movement's original commitment to nonviolence."[27]

As political violence receded, antiwar activists, hippies, and the New Left became more unified. In 1971 a survey of college students revealed that a mere 10 percent categorized themselves as politically radical. Almost 70 percent did not believe that a mass revolutionary party should be created, and 87 percent thought that radicals of the left threatened individual rights as much as the radical right. Violent revolutionaries no longer figured prominently in the movement; thus, few people remained with whom hippie purists differed philosophically. Three Weathermen blew themselves and their townhouse to smithereens in Greenwich Village in March 1970 after one man accidentally touched off a nail bomb. The Weathermen—extreme, isolated, and few in number—went underground. Although the newly named Weather Underground came to praise the youth and drug culture in December 1970, some of its members were never entirely comfortable with hippiedom. Moreover, the organization did not withdraw from violence despite their newfound love of the counterculture. During the same period, a bomb killed two members of the Student Nonviolent Coordinating Committee (SNCC) who were attending the arson trial of H. Rap Brown. These explosions, including the Sterling Hall bombing, shattered the romantic image of revolutionaries. Meanwhile, the Black Panthers faced their ruin under government surveillance and repression. In 1969 alone, police killed an estimated twenty-eight Panthers and incarcerated hundreds of others. Released from prison in 1970, Panther cofounder Huey Newton became a cocaine addict and megalomaniac. SNCC's Stokely Carmichael went into exile.[28]

ROCK FESTIVALS AND ROCK REVOLUTIONARIES

A united countersociety attended rock festivals. Most hippies, rock enthusiasts, and promoters had forgotten about the tragedy at Altamont or dismissed it as the new decade began. Majority society and law enforcement officials, however, had not. For them, counterculture gatherings promoted drug abuse, social chaos, and moral decline, and they sought to prevent further rock events from taking place. To stop them, antifestival forces used two effective techniques: court injunctions and health and sanitary regulations. Court injunctions were difficult to obtain, but even the threat of one often dissuaded organizers from attempting to establish an event in a contested locale. Health regulations, too, worked to the advantage of antifestival citizens, as promoters refused to deal with the hassle of abiding by such rules, taking their festival plans elsewhere. A court injunction derailed the Powder Ridge Festival in Connecticut, but hippies attended other successful festivals. At the Atlanta Pop Festival over the July 4 weekend in 1970, two hundred thousand enjoyed music by the Allman Brothers, Procol Harum, Rare Earth, Cactus, Poco, and Johnny Winter. Thirty thousand freaks also loved New York's Randall Island Festival held July 17–19, 1970, which featured Grand Funk Railroad, Jethro Tull, Steppenwolf, and Ten Years After.[29]

Rock's most fervent devotees considered it an instrument of revolution. "MUSIC IS REVOLUTION," proclaimed John Sinclair. "Rock and roll music is one of the most vital forces in the West—it blows people all the way back to their senses and makes them feel good, like they're alive again in the middle of this monstrous funeral parlor of western civilization." The revolution involved establishing "a situation on this planet where all people can feel good all the time." Sinclair praised rock as a "weapon of cultural revolution" and "model of the revolutionary future" because it was "immediate, total, fast-changing and on-going." The music, Sinclair believed, worked "to free people on all levels." Rock also produced a sense of community. Rock bands and "tribes," like communes, were "totally interdependent and totally committed to the same end." Franklin Bach, minister of the White Panther Party, exalted rock in a similar fashion, ascribing great power to it. For Bach and other hippies, rock furthered individuals' personal development, and enhanced their strength, while liberating them. "Our rock and roll is the baddest music of all time," he proclaimed in the *Madison Kaleidoscope*, "It's the nitty-gritty, the most open, out front statement of how we feel and think and move and love one another there is. Rock has given us strength, kept us growing, set us free."[30]

Warner Brothers' release of the three-hour, color film *Woodstock* dealt a death blow to proponents of rock revolution. The Woodstock festival was, from the beginning, a business venture. The four promoters wanted at least fifty thousand people to come to the festival and they began advertising in undergrounds across the country and on hip radio stations. When the festival ended, it seemed as though the enterprise had failed. The promoters claimed they had lost over a million dollars. They did not stay in the red for long. The *Woodstock* film, released in March 1970, set box office records in New York, Washington, DC, Boston, Dallas, and Los Angeles, and eventually grossed some $17 million. Tickets sold for five dollars, a higher price of admission compared to other features. The White Panthers and other radical organizations organized a boycott of the film, calling it a culture ripoff. The *Woodstock* soundtrack on LP also sold well, pushing over 500,000 units by July. The film, a critical success and embraced by the mainstream, won the Academy Award for best documentary feature.[31]

Rock festivals, too, became big business, another reality that undermined hippies' faith in rock revolution. Promoters capitalized on the popularity of festivals, hoping to accumulate large profits. In 1970 entrepreneurs touted their events as "another Woodstock." Abbie Hoffman and others attacked festival promoters as vanguard capitalists only interested in profits and accused them of atrophying the festivals' social significance. Hoffman and the Yippies demanded an end to these capitalist ventures and went on an "offensive," demanding half of the profits of a planned New York festival. Festivals made rock artists wealthy. In 1969, the highest-paid entertainers made around $15,000 for their performances. In 1970, Led Zeppelin and Crosby, Stills, Nash, and Young demanded and received as much as $50,000 for a single show.[32]

While hippies enjoyed festivals, the movement fragmented, splintering into several autonomous movements made up of gays, American Indians, Chicanos, women, and blacks seeking individual empowerment. The counterculture interacted and contended with several of these social and political movements.

THE COUNTERCULTURE AND WOMEN'S LIBERATION

The counterculture's relationship to women's liberation changed over time. From the mid-1960s up to approximately 1972, many male and female counterculturalists were skeptical of, if not resistant toward, feminism. Hip men found some feminist critiques, especially the notion that underground papers sexually exploited women, puritanical. Hippie women believed that women were essentially different from men and assumed traditional and normative gender roles. However, by 1972, if not before, men and women within the counterculture became more amenable to feminist ideas and objectives, and eventually supported the women's movement. Hippie women became cultural feminists, making difference-based, women-identified claims to power. Male longhairs attended lectures by feminists detailing how men fit into women's struggle for freedom and equality. Counterculture icons like Hoffman and Jerry Rubin called for male supremacy to be smashed or excised from the movement. And John Lennon urged his male counterparts to reevaluate their relationships with women.

The antecedents of the women's movement dated back to 1963 when Betty Friedan published *The Feminine Mystique*, which aided feminism's resurgence. The book exposed "the Problem That Has No Name": many American women—especially those with college degrees—lived unfulfilled lives, experiencing depression, illness, and suicidal thoughts, because society had foisted the feminine mystique and role of housewife and mother upon them. Friedan encouraged women to break free from this mold by pursuing higher education and careers. In addition, she called for the government to offer financial assistance to women like it had for men. Friedan argued that for women to reach their full potential, traditional marriage roles had to be redefined and husbands needed to assist their wives with nurturing children.

The modern women's movement also had its roots in the New Left and civil rights. Within the movement, women experienced male sexism and domination. At a conference in the fall of 1964, Casey Hayden and Mary King of SNCC anonymously circulated a position paper that broached the issue. Women, the authors showed, had been relegated to clerical work and barred from decision-making processes and leadership positions because of "the assumption of male superiority." SNCC president Carmichael answered their memo by stating famously that a woman's place in the organization was "prone." The following year, Hayden and King produced "a sort of memo," which argued that movement women were members of a sex-caste system and were exploited. Other women felt the same way. In 1966 and 1967 women in SDS organized women's caucuses and workshops. Soon, independent women's liberation groups formed throughout the nation, including Chicago and New York.[33]

Meanwhile, another arm of the nascent feminist movement materialized. Women displeased with the results of the Kennedy Commission and Johnson's Equal Employment Opportunity Commission (EEOC) and its reluctance to enforce Title VII of the 1964 Civil Rights Act, which outlawed sex discrimination in employment, formed the National Organization for Women (NOW) in 1966. Friedan was among the founding members. NOW stated its commitment to a "fully equal partnership of the sexes" and its intention to "bring women into full participation in the mainstream of American society."[34]

Many younger feminists, however, viewed NOW as a moderate political organization with a legalistic approach that moved too slowly. "Radical Women" and "Women's Liberationists" called for full gender equality and they wanted it more quickly. Capitalism and patriarchy constituted the two systems responsible for oppressing women. Groups like the Redstockings focused on women's immediate private lives. They called for an "assault on marriage and the family," recommended that children be raised communally, and argued that freedom would encompass getting "child-rearing off their backs." New York Radical Women simply stated, "We take the women's side in everything."[35]

In 1970, the women's movement came to fruition. On August 26, women's groups from NOW to radical feminists to lesbians to moderate businesswomen staged the Women's Strike for Equality, demanding childcare centers, abortion on demand, equal pay, equal educational opportunities, and the passage of the Equal Rights Amendment. Tens of thousands of women marched in New York, San Francisco, Los Angeles, Washington, DC, Seattle, Denver, Boston, and Baltimore. The feminist impulse spread widely. In most cities and on most campuses, feminists established "consciousness-raising" groups and their own newspapers, coffeehouses, women's shelters, health clinics, and bookstores. In 1973 a group of activists, the Boston Women's Health Collective, published the book *Our Bodies, Ourselves*, which spread across the country—and eventually the globe. Containing medical, sexual, reproductive, and contraceptive information, it helped create a feminist health movement.

Many radical women actively opposed the counterculture. The counterculture predated women's liberation, and like the mainstream culture surrounding it, the male-dominated counterculture was, initially, sexist and hierarchical. During the 1960s many male hippies—while radical in most respects—held traditional ideas about women and girls, femininity, and gender roles.

Men dominated rock and roll and their lyrics communicated sexist messages. Some of the Rolling Stones' most popular songs—"Stupid Girl," "Under My Thumb," "Honky-Tonk Women," and "Brown Sugar"—either put down or sexually objectified women. In the 1965 Beatles song "Run for Your Life," Lennon indicated that he would rather see "his" woman dead than with someone else. Women played limited roles in rock, as go-go dancers or groupies. In rock culture, it was believed that women were not strong enough to play drums or aggressive enough to play hard-driving rock. Women typically played acoustic, not electric guitars, and all-female rock bands were extremely rare—Ace of Cups out of San Francisco was an exception. Women in rock steadily lost stature as hit-makers as well. Women "declined on the year-end singles charts from an all-time high of 32 percent in 1963 to six percent in 1969."[36]

The underground press sexually exploited women. Naked nymphs appeared all over the pages of underground newspapers and so did graphic sex ads, demonstrating male hippies' belief in liberation from prevailing sexual and moral conventions. Women appeared as wide-eyed innocents or sexually experienced seductresses. Both images appealed to male fantasy. The *East Village Other* presented hip pinup girls in largely the same vein, as virgins or vamps. In either case, the women depicted sought to elicit male lust. Other images that originated from the minds of men included the beautiful cosmic love goddess and nurturing earth mother. Men elevated these female forms, less overtly sexual, to unattainable status. All of these personifications—virgin, vamp, goddess, and earth mother—failed to capture the essence of real hippie women and their experiences. Underground comix portrayed women in even more demeaning ways. Male cartoonists, letting their fantasies run wild, created ready and willing hippie "chicks" engaged in group sex, gang rape, and sex with animals. Men propositioned women—"groovy chicks who like to smoke weed and ball"—in the personal classified sections. Pornographic papers originated in the underground press. *Screw* was one of the most popular, originally published out of the office of the *New York Free Press* in a scheme to make additional money.[37]

For many feminists and radical women, the sexual revolution was a sham, a "dirty joke" that advanced men's sexual proclivities and interests. Sexual liberation became a cover for promiscuity. Men capitalized on women's new sexual availability and expected to sleep with as many women as possible, regardless of women's needs. Movement men used sex as currency. In her piece "The Grand Coolie Damn," Marge Piercy took movement men to task. She condemned the fact that "a man can bring a woman into an organization by sleeping with her and remove her by ceasing to do so." She also excoriated men for "purging" women for "no other reason than that he has tired of her, knocked her up, or is after someone else." Within the counterculture, some men labeled women who did not "put out" as "frigid" or "hung up." Movement women, and some movement men, found the White Panthers' manifesto revolting. It urged men to "fuck your woman so hard till she can't stand up." Men exerted significant pressure on women to have sex. "Guys just refused to take NO for an answer," remembered a baby boomer woman, "so you gave in because you got tired of hassling and giving reasons not to." Unrestrained male libidos had dire consequences for women such as rape, unwanted pregnancy, and abandonment. And penetration of the vagina, followed by male orgasm and ejaculation, largely defined sex for hippie men. Before the rise of feminism, many male freaks were not particularly concerned whether a woman reached climax or not. Hippie women certainly experienced a newer, freer, atmosphere in which sex took place in many and varied settings. Yet sex in the counterculture, though liberating in some respects, did not always result in greater sexual satisfaction for women.[38]

Radical women found it increasingly difficult to distinguish male hippies' treatment of women from the establishment's. A cartoon that appeared in undergrounds depicted two men discussing their lives. A straight man, holding a briefcase and dressed in suit and tie says, "When I come home from the office, beat, my wife gives me something good to eat. She takes good care of my kids all day and to be frank, she's a terrific lay." The longhaired hippie wearing a peace medallion responds, "My old lady's outasite. Made brown rice and fish last nite. She's soft and quiet and good for my head. Her sign is Virgo, and she's good in bed." In short, hippie men, like their straight brethren, confined women to domesticity, expected them to perform domestic tasks and childrearing, and be skilled sexually as well. From the feminist perspective, the counterculture, like majority society, oppressed women and stifled their full potential.[39]

In her essay "Goodbye to All That," which appeared in the underground Rat in February 1970, Robin Morgan took aim at the "counterfeit male-dominated Left." After censuring the New Left, she concentrated her broadsides on the counterculture: "Goodbye to Hip Culture and the so-called Sexual Revolution, which has functioned toward women's freedom as did Reconstruction toward former slaves—reinstituted oppression by another name." Morgan criticized several male counterculturalists, including Hugh Romney—Wavy Gravy of the Hog Farm. Morgan pointed out that Romney considered himself a part of the "cultural revolution," and yet he had boasted that Hog Farm's women made the commune's clothing. She proceeded to compare Hoffman to a "movie star" before admonishing him for ditching "the first wife and kids" as soon as he was "Making It." Morgan said goodbye to Paul Krassner, Yippie and editor of the Realist, for bragging about sleeping with a number of women in the movement and for being a "sexist oppressor." She also called Sinclair a "counterfeit Christ." Finally, "Goodbye to All That" criticized the ecology movement—and by extension the back-to-the-land movement—for its downgrading of women as "earth mothers" and "frontier chicks." Morgan argued that leadership of the movement should be ceded to women as they did not pollute and their bodies were "locked in" to humanity and the biosphere.[40]

The Rat staff also focused on sexism in the world of rock. A former female hippie turned women's liberationist elucidated how hippie men expected their women to conform to a specific—and limited—role:

> Women are required at rock events to pay homage to the rock world. . . . And what is that woman supposed to be like? Well it's not enough to be just a plain old cunt—we have to be beautiful and even that's not enough—we've got to be groovy—you know, not uptight, not demanding, not jealous or clinging or strong or smart or anything but loving in a way that never cuts back on a man's freedom. And so women remain the last legitimate form of property that the brothers can share in a communal world. Can't have a tribal gathering without music and dope and beautiful groovy chicks.

Most radical feminists advised women to abandon what they saw as an oppressive counterculture. "In culture after culture men have destroyed our minds and fucked over our bodies," asserted *Rat*. "There is no reason for us to go back into the alienation and isolation of Woodstock Nation."[41]

Feminists criticized female communards. The women who came out of the New Left had liberated themselves from discrimination and sexual objectification. They cast "feminine" characteristics as a social construct. Women grappled with men in the movement over strategy, theory, and tactics. As such, they denied inherent differences between the sexes, in an attempt to prevent movement men from employing those supposed differences to rationalize and bolster their subordination of women. Hippie women puzzled and angered radical feminists because they seemed content with essentialist gender roles—cooking and childrearing—in the counterculture. Valerie Solanas, in the Society for Cutting Up Men (SCUM) manifesto, proclaimed that communes violated "females' rights, privacy and sanity." In a letter to the *Berkeley Barb*, "Queen of the Gypsies"—a pseudonym intended to disparage hippie women—asserted, "On the street, on the road, in tribes, families and communes—the female is much in evidence. She's the cow—the little mother—the breadwinner—the vagina, and most of all, she's available." Hippie women, this "militant sister" believed, had been exploited and reduced to their reproductive and sexual functions.[42]

Other feminists, however, took part in the counterculture. As Gretchen Lemke-Santangelo has persuasively argued, hippie women were cultural feminists. Hip women rebelled against mainstream class and gender norms while rejecting and evading suburban domesticity. In rural communes, they resuscitated an older, agrarian ideal that placed a greater value on women's labor and productivity. Hippie women abandoned the nuclear family norm, engaging in a communal lifestyle that allowed them to share chores, advice, and knowledge with other women. They found their work varied and challenging. Performed in the service of the larger countercultural project, women assigned political significance to their exertions. Women played an integral role in the counterculture. Men often made "transitory contributions" in communes, so women's efforts sustained hippiedom. Their sense of importance was enhanced because women were believed to "naturally" possess characteristics essential to the hippie way of life—cooperation, reciprocity, expressiveness, closeness to nature, egalitarianism, and nonaggression. And sexual liberation benefited many hippie women; it, in effect, "ultimately translated into a wider range of options, including lesbian partnerships." "Slowly but surely," writes Lemke-Santangelo, female hippies "began to articulate a feminist vision that emphasized the dignity, if not superiority, of traditional 'feminine' values and labor."[43]

Many hip men initially resisted feminism, especially its radical variant. Male counterculturalists had great difficulty adjusting to the women's movement and changing their sexual values, which celebrated heterosexuality, often centered around a man's desires, needs, pleasure, and satisfaction. Male freaks found it difficult to alter their values, for their sexual ethics had been firmly entrenched since the mid-1960s, before the ascent of feminism. Hippie women also believed in essential differences between men and women. Women were thought to be more intuitive, nonaggressive, and emotional, particularly suited to be mothers and caregivers. Some hip men's responses to women's liberation bordered on hostile, focusing predominantly on sexual issues. "Are we all really the male chauvinist pigs that the more extreme wing of Fem Lib contends we are?" asked Norman Spinrad in the *Los Angeles Free Press*. "The more extreme elements of the Fem Lib movement," he continued, "exhibit a pathological female chauvinism that puts to shame even the most rabid male supremacist." For some hip men, certain aims of the feminist movement were antithetical to counterculture values. Hippies championed open sexual expression and free speech, principles feminists seemed to be attacking. Spinrad accused feminists of "re-establishing Victorian sexual shackles for men." He then condemned the feminist attack on sexually explicit materials, writing, "Unless we are prepared to accept the hoary puritan notion that all sexual feelings are evil, there is nothing inherently wrong with pornography." Instead of assailing male-oriented skin flicks, Spinrad suggested that women demand or produce pornography that appealed to women. He went on to accuse women of being partially responsible for the proliferation of pornography because they put men through hoops just "to get a little." Consequently, men had no other choice but to consume pornography as "a substitute for you, baby." The columnist then turned to what he called the "Cult of the Vibrator," lamenting that the use of such devices denied "not merely the humanity of sex but the community of life." Spinrad acknowledged that many men treated women badly and as a result, the women's movement attracted "lesbians, confused asexual man-haters, or enraged neo-puritan neurotics." These kinds of women, he maintained, gave men, who would otherwise be sympathetic to "legitimate" and "reasonable" feminist movement objectives "bad vibes." For Spinrad, the women's movement had reached a critical juncture. "Women's Liberation will eventually have to make some cold, hard decisions," he wrote. "As things now stand, the movement is on its way to alienating the male population with its overtones of puritanism, anti-sexuality, psychopathology, and female chauvinism."[44]

Male counterculturalists did eventually become sympathetic and responsive to feminism. The underground press, by the early 1970s, frequently published articles and editorials pertaining to women's liberation and lesbianism. Communes battled sexism and championed egalitarianism. The Movement for a New Society sought to eliminate sexism and abolish rigid gender roles. At Twin Oaks, residents did not distinguish between "men's work" and "women's work"—the community allowed and encouraged women to try their hand at every kind of labor. Women learned carpentry, became auto mechanics, drove tractors, and shoveled manure, while men learned cooking, knitting, and sewing, and washed dishes. Men did not expect women to wear makeup or follow the latest fashion trends. By the fall of 1970 Hoffman had come to support feminism, at least rhetorically. He acknowledged that women's liberation, "more than any other movement to emerge during the last two years, forces us to examine our style of living." In order to "have revolution in our lifetime," Hoffman argued in an interview, "male supremacy must be smashed." The songs of Lennon and Yoko Ono represented the counterculture's growing sensitivity toward and acceptance of feminism. Lennon's solo career became more political, a departure from his earlier work with the Beatles. In 1971, he called for "Power to the People." The lyrics asked men to take a critical look at how they treated women. Likewise, 1972's "Woman Is the Nigger of the World," on the album *Sometime in New York City*, excoriated male politicos for excluding or relegating women to subservient positions within the movement.[45]

THE COUNTERCULTURE AND GAY LIBERATION

The dominant culture and society ridiculed and demonized gays. Every state in the union had made homosexual activity illegal and most Americans called their behavior "deviant." In the 1950s, researcher Alfred Kinsey reported on homosexual behavior in the general population, yet many chose to deny its existence. Those who acknowledged homosexuality often went on the attack; heterosexual people menaced gays with taunts like "queer," "fag," and "homo." Mental health professionals and doctors deemed homosexuality an illness, subjecting gays to a wide variety of "treatments" like electroshock, hypnotism, and large drug doses. Gays lived a harried existence. Police looked the other way as toughs beat them. The military dishonorably discharged gays, local communities harassed them, and government employers frequently fired them.

Gay liberationists arose to challenge the social structures that kept them underground and hidden. Unlike other movements, gay liberation's origins can be traced a single spontaneous event: the Stonewall riot. On June 27, 1969, Manhattan police attempted to close the Stonewall Inn, a Greenwich Village bar and gay hangout. Police had routinely raided gay bars throughout the 1960s, but nothing went according to plan this time. Lawmen brought patrons out of the Stonewall Inn and put them into police vans. A crowd assembled outside and taunted the officers. Inside, a lesbian began putting up a fight, igniting a violent scene. Gays hurled bottles and coins at the police and someone set the inn alight. Officers clashed with rioting homosexual crowds late into the night. Graffiti proclaiming "Gay Power" appeared on the walls and sidewalks of Greenwich Village the next day. The riots, which occurred over an entire weekend, indicated that a major social movement had arrived.[46]

Gay liberation evolved into a powerful movement. Gay radicals demonstrated against businesses that discriminated against homosexuals and established their own newspapers, *Gay Power* and *Come Out!* Others staged street dances in New York, Chicago, and Berkeley, and on the first anniversary of Stonewall in June 1970, ten thousand activists proudly marched down New York's Sixth Avenue. Nearly eight hundred gay and lesbian groups had formed by 1973. They established gay-friendly bars, churches, medical clinics, restaurants, newspapers, law offices, travel agencies, community centers, and many other businesses. At least ten cities passed gay rights ordinances, a success for activists.[47]

From the mid-1960s to the early 1970s, some within the counterculture were not entirely comfortable with the gay community. The counterculture predated the opening salvo of gay liberation by four years and hippies were overwhelmingly heterosexual. Although most counterculturalists tolerated gays, some were, or bordered on, homophobic. Timothy Leary touted acid as a cure for homosexuality. On the street and in underground newspapers, hippies commonly threw around the term "fag" or "faggot" as an insult. When hip capitalists took over an establishment and opened it up as a rock ballroom in the Haight, they named it the Straight Theater to ward off gays accustomed to watching pornography films there. The *East Village Other*'s founder Walter Bowart refused to put out a story on Andy Warhol's film *Chelsea Girls* because he disliked the scene surrounding the artist. "The blatant displays of homosexuality were not pleasing to me," Bowart recalled. While recording "Baby, You're A Rich Man" for the *Magical Mystery Tour* album, Lennon took a shot at the Beatles' gay manager, Brian Epstein. Surrounded by a lively group of people, including Brian Jones and Mick Jagger of the Stones, Lennon, "grinning like a jackal," sang, "Baby, you're a rich fag Jew." Although many communes accepted gay members, many did not always fit in comfortably among their mostly heterosexual peers. They were reluctant to acknowledge their sexuality even in such sympathetic environments.[48]

Yet most counterculturalists supported gay liberation by 1972 if not before. In the early seventies, undergrounds provided abundant coverage and support of gay liberation and rights. Hip journalists contended that homosexuality was natural and good, that people should not have to keep their sexuality hidden, and that all sexual activity that occurred between consenting adults should be legal. Moreover, undergrounds decried discrimination against gays and affirmed the right to choose one's sexual partners—whatever their gender. The *New York City Star* carried a story on a gay and lesbian switchboard that referred callers to "gay doctors, lawyers, therapists, carpenters, movers, travel agencies, and astrologers." In addition, it provided information on gay happenings and organizations. Most importantly, callers could talk to another gay person "about anything that's on his mind: feeling unsure about coming out, feeling angry at the oppressive bullshit gay people have to deal with every day, feeling lonely or down or confused or whatever." Jefferson Poland, who founded the Sexual Freedom League (SFL), considered himself bisexual and the SFL championed the gay cause. Ron Thelin claimed that "no prejudice" existed toward homosexuals in Haight-Ashbury. And gay men testified to the good treatment they received from the hip. "I feel so free among them, being older, since they accept all ages and treat all as humans," remarked one gay man. "They are broadminded toward us, although 99 percent [are] heterosexual, as I see so many with their arms around girls." Other gay men felt a kinship with hippies as police and majority society harassed and persecuted both groups. Some took inspiration from the hip. "We should tell off the Establishment as do the hippies," commented one. "As minorities, we have enough in common to support them." Another gay man asserted, "We should fight for the hippies' rights as if they were our own."[49]

Even before gays and lesbians came to terms with their sexuality, the movement—civil rights, women's liberation, New Left, and counterculture—helped to demarcate them from the rest of society. As Martha Shelley, president of the New York City Daughters of Bilitis, explained:

> There was a whole movement that was supporting my not fitting in. The civil rights movement gave me a deep underpinning. The women's movement questioned sexual roles. The yippies and the left-wing movements of the sixties questioned the politics I grew up with, questioned the economic and social underpinnings of the whole society. Then the drugs, LSD, and writers and philosophers caused me to really question everything and to say, "The whole perception of reality I was raised with is fucked up, totally crazy, certifiably insane."

The movement, for many gays, undercut and then obliterated their understanding of society and how it was supposed to function.[50]

Many gays and lesbians found the counterculture liberating. The spirit of nonconformity that hippies promoted allowed people to discuss and express forms of sexuality that deviated from the norm. Male hippies cast off traditional masculine appearance and behavior, which became associated with aggression, war, and constrictive nine-to-five jobs. Even gays who did not live communally or dress like hippies found inspiration in the counterculture's emphasis on sexual liberation and antiauthoritari-anism. Gay men, too, discovered and adopted the androgynous clothing styles that became pervasive at antiwar demonstrations and on campuses. The prospect of being killed in Vietnam stimulated men emotionally and resulted in a questioning of longstanding beliefs. Many disregarded the idea that men should suppress their feelings. The sexual experimentation that the counterculture encouraged caused gays and lesbians to come out sooner than they might have in a more repressive environment. Likewise, "doing one's own thing," and "marching to a different drummer," both central to the counterculture creed, facilitated the frank recognition of one's sexuality. A gay man interviewed in the late 1960s proclaimed, "It was the hippie scene, in a way, that gave me my final freedom."[51]

Many homosexuals became hippies, adopting the counterculture's styles, values, and practices. "Make way for the new homosexual of the Seventies," wrote Tom Burke in *Esquire*, "an unfettered, guiltless male child of the new morality in a Zapata moustache and an outlaw hat, who couldn't care less for Establishment approval, would as soon sleep with boys as girls, and thinks that 'Over the Rainbow' is a place to fly on 200 micrograms of lysergic acid diethylamide." Gays and bisexuals immersed themselves in the counterculture in New York City and Los Angeles; they read *Steppenwolf* and tarot cards, smoked marijuana, dropped acid, applied body paint, wore American Indian headbands, necklaces, and military surplus, and spoke of love and peace.[52]

Some gays also became communalists. Robert McRuer maintains that the "burgeoning gay movement made possible the formation of new identities, individual and collective, and because of this, communal liv-ing could indeed be seen as a natural part of some people's coming-out process in the early 1970s." Openly acknowledging one's homosexual-ity and taking part in a collective "marked a refusal to live according to those terms set by straight society." Straight society in this case meant not only straight people but the dominant society as well, which many gays, like the counterculture, considered "gray and lifeless." Gays em-ployed the same language as the counterculture in opposing the main-stream. Analyzing *Out of the Closets*, a collection of essays written by gays and published in 1972, McRuer writes, "The refusal to conform in dress and behavior, the rhetoric of revolution through love, and the idea that love can bring different kinds of people together in unexpected ways were all signs that these 'voices of gay liberation' were simultaneously voices of the counterculture."[53]

The 95th Street Collective in New York City was the first gay male collective in the United States. The five inhabitants experimented sexually, worked out arrangements related to money, meals, and chores, held group discussions to mediate conflicts, and helped organize the gay movement, as the collective functioned as a meeting place for the Gay Liberation Front (GLF). The first night that John Knoebel stayed at the two-bedroom apartment, he and the others got stoned and listened to music. Knoebel and the other members understood that "the personal is political," that they needed to "struggle" to enact change, and that they had to examine their experiences together in order to better understand their oppression by heterosexual society. The collective became their own "small world" that they could shape. The members had to reach consensus before they made any decision. Every member was required to say their piece. The communards shared expenses equally and took evening walks in Riverside Park—all holding hands. "We were a tight group," wrote Knoebel.[54]

Lesbians, too, built their own communes. Some women, encouraged by the sexual liberation ethic of the counterculture, expressed their lesbian, bisexual, and transgender identities. Female communards embraced a model of feminism that celebrated women's differences. At Lime Saddle commune near Oroville, California, women who began to identify as bisexual and lesbian became receptive to feminist causes and writings. The men at Lime Saddle—threatened by the women's new claims to power and the coming out of lesbians—eventually left the commune. More and more hippie women discovered that they didn't need men for sexual fulfillment. They joined lesbian and bisexual women who had recently departed from the radical women's movement to create communes and separatist institutions.[55]

While select gays and lesbians became part of the counterculture, hippies—who never had strong ties to African American militants to begin with—parted ways with Black Power. After a falling out with Leary in Algeria in the 1971, Eldridge Cleaver no longer found hippies constructive to the cause of black people: "It was very useful some years ago when people

rebelled against the straitjacket rules and regulations of Babylonian society . . . by shattering to smithereens those values, by getting high, freak-
ing out, whatever term you want to apply. . . . It is no longer useful to our
struggle and it has to be stopped." The Panther did not consider hippies
revolutionary. Neither were the Yippies. Cleaver denounced them and
"the whole silly psychedelic drug culture quasi-political movement" at the
end of 1970. Cleaver wanted people to "gather their wits," "sober up" and
"get down to the serious business of destroying the Babylonian empire,"
and endorsed "sober, stone cold revolutionaries . . . men and women who
fit the description given by Comrade Che Guevara, 'Cold, calculating killing machines.'" As the antiwar movement became more countercultural,
African American activists treated it with disdain and saw it as less than
serious. Black activists voiced their concerns at an antiwar conference in
January 1971, arguing against staging "another series of middle class—
white-nude-be-in or psychedelic 'cultural experiences.'" Those furthering
the interests of people suffering from police terror, poverty, and hunger
found such expressions to lack resolve.[56]

In the early seventies, millions of young people felt a part of hippiedom
and participated in it. The counterculture peaked in 1971. "It Just Won't
Go Away," announced *Commonweal* in October. "The counter-culture is
alive and growing." Ten Years After, in the song "I'd Love to Change the
World," made mention of the ubiquitous counterculture, singing, "Everywhere is freaks and harries." It is no coincidence that in 1971, Liberation
News Service distributed 895 packets—its peak year. Many of the forty
million Americans aged fifteen to twenty-five partook in—or, at a minimum, sympathized with—some aspect of the counterculture, whether
it be growing longer hair, wearing bell-bottoms, using dope and drugs,
seeking to discover oneself, holding a lenient attitude about sex, tolerating dissenting politics and lifestyles, questioning authority, opposing
war, digging rock, or building the new society.[57]

The counterculture welcomed Vietnam veterans to its ranks. Alienated
veterans returning to "the world" experienced discrimination when they
converted to the counterculture. "I tried to get a job after I was discharged
from the marines," one man divulged to an underground paper. But his
prospective employer told him, "Your hair's too long, you can't work here.
You must be one of those communist hippies who hate this country."

"I'll tell you something," parried the veteran, "I love this country more than you think. I just hate most of the people in it."[58]

Vietnam Veterans Against the War (VVAW) believed the war was morally reprehensible. Nixon's "Vietnamization" strategy did little to mollify them, as many still had friends fighting overseas. VVAW wanted to end the war quickly. During Operation Rapid American Withdrawal (RAW), on September 4–7, 1970, the organization's "gritty style of protest" had merged "countercultural fashions with military attire," and it planned to continue in this vein. By the end of Sunday, April 18, 1971, nearly nine hundred veterans had arrived at Potomac Park in Washington, DC, setting up tents and flying banners. Thousands of veterans began to arrive from all over the country in caravans, and by train and plane. Vets from Ohio christened themselves the Buckeye Liberation Army. A bus reminiscent of Ken Kesey and the Merry Pranksters' vehicle, "Furthur," arrived with Texan Jon Floyd at the wheel, singing veterans behind him. Mostly from blue-collar backgrounds and single, over 70 percent considered themselves "radical" or "extremely radical." During the first two days of Operation Dewey Canyon III, VVAW engaged in guerrilla theater. In front of Capitol Hill, veterans performed "search-and-destroy missions" for tourists and the press. The "Buckeye Recon" and "Philadelphia Quaker Troupe" fired their rifles at actresses wearing straw coolie hats before destroying their toy M-16s on the Capitol steps in front of a shocked audience. On the evening of April 21, the vets celebrated Nixon's decision to not evict them from the park. The cast of Hair performed. The vets sang "Age of Aquarius," and two Lennon songs—"Power to the People," and "Give Peace a Chance." "The scene now evoked was less that of a firebase than, perhaps, an Aquarian version of the American Legion," noted the Washington Post. On April 23, thousands of members of VVAW marched to the Capitol, where they threw their medals and ribbons over a fence to protest the war machine. Veterans—some in wheelchairs, others missing a limb—wept or raged against US policy. VVAW included men who looked like hippies; they grew long hair, sideburns, and mustaches, wore old tattered army fatigues, and used marijuana. "It is a war and we are soldiers again, as tight as we have ever been, a whole lost generation of dope-smoking kids in worn jungle boots coming from all over the country to tell Nixon a thing or two," wrote veteran Ron Kovic.[59]

GROWING ALIENATION AND THE
PEAK OF THE COUNTERCULTURE

In 1971, the last major national antiwar demonstrations occurred. On April 24 in Washington, five hundred thousand protestors—hippies, students, adults, blacks, gays and lesbians, trade unionists, religious groups, and Vietnam vets—paraded down Pennsylvania Avenue toward the Capitol steps to demand an end to the war: "ENOUGH—OUT NOW!" In San Francisco, 150,000 demonstrators led by active-duty servicemen marched seven miles to a rally in Golden Gate Park. May Day protests in Washington followed. The activists engaged in mass nonviolent civil disobedience and intended to shut down the nation's capital. On May 3, police arrested and incarcerated over 7,200 people.

But on October 25 and 26, demonstrations in Washington organized by the People's Coalition for Peace and Justice (PCPJ) and May Day Tribe attracted no more than 1,000 people. More turned out for November 6 protests—40,000 in San Francisco, 15,000 in Denver, 30,000 in New York, and 10,000 in Boston—but not the numbers of previous years. The antiwar movement's energy dissipated because Nixon began to wind the war down. In 1971 draft calls declined from 17,000 per month at the beginning of the year to 10,000 in the fall. American casualty rates plummeted as well, from 200 per week in May 1970 to 35 a year later. Moreover, Nixon was bringing the troops home. By the end of June 150,000 had returned. By the end of 1971, only 157,000 troops remained in Vietnam.

As the antiwar movement ebbed, the counterculture's numbers soared. "Students Are Turning Away from Protest to Seek Own Goals," declared a headline in the *New York Times*. After the Kent State shooting, massive protests had raged; now, students seemed "by and large, to be concentrating on the small, the individual and the personal." The new mood, according to Yale president Kingman Brewster Jr., was one of "eerie tranquility." Weary of tear gas, nightsticks, and mass demonstrations, more and more students declared their independence, focusing on individual matters. Large numbers of activists became demoralized because they believed that their efforts had little effect on Washington. Few students wore Mao buttons and even fewer heeded calls to shut down universities. At Oberlin College, a senior who had recently worked sixteen-hour days as head of the campus resistance movement remarked, "I'm tired, I'm beaten and I guess I just don't care."[60]

The counterculture, too, peaked because alienation remained widespread. A survey of college students discovered that over 80 percent believed, either strongly or partially, that America was a racist nation. More than 60 percent thought that "things are going badly in the country" and a majority who held an opinion agreed with the statement "we are a sick society." Nearly 70 percent concluded that society, to some degree, was "characterized by 'injustice, insensibility, lack of candor, and inhumanity.'" Moreover, over a quarter of students had little faith in Democrats and Republicans; a Harris poll indicated that 26 percent would refrain from voting or refuse to cast their ballot for a candidate of the major political parties.[61]

EVOLVING COUNTERCULTURE VALUES

In the 1970s, the counterculture's values continued to evolve, multiplying in number and growing in diversity. Hippies' sexual relationships and sexual morals developed to the point where they challenged the institution of marriage. The Harrad Experiment, by Robert Rimmer, greatly influenced sexual liberationists. A 1967 novel about a sexually free college in New England, The Harrad Experiment communicated a clear thesis: jealousy, monogamy, and shame would disappear if only people adopted a rational perspective on sex. Monogamy was grounded in the concept of women as property, a barbaric idea, and, therefore, it should be abolished in an enlightened world. Group marriages, the book contended, could be happy and satisfying without the consequences of jealousy, secrecy, adultery, and divorce. Liberated couples treated The Harrad Experiment as a guide for a more fulfilling life. Some couples who formed relationships in the 1960s and 1970s carried on nonmonogamous, open relationships for multiple years or decades. In Berkeley, Harrad Experiment acolytes founded Harrad West. These individuals hoped to marry six, eight, or even a dozen people. Rimmer received so many letters from individuals in group marriages that he published the correspondence in two volumes. Group marriage became such a phenomenon that the New York Times estimated that at least two thousand group marriages had occurred in the United States.[62]

Hippies still took dope—plenty of it—and its use grew extensive. A Gallup poll revealed that over 40 percent of college students had tried pot, while a College poll estimated a higher number, at 60 percent. Marijuana and LSD also pushed into the Great Plains and Mountain West. At the University of Kansas, a sample of 219 students indicated that 69 percent had smoked grass and 92 percent revealed that their friends smoked it.[63]

The older generation found rising drug use rates among college students alarming, but the prevalence of dope and drugs at high schools distressed them even more. Educators, researchers, students, and federal health and law enforcement authorities noted that more and more high schoolers across the nation smoked marijuana. Though less common, LSD, speed, heroin, and cocaine filtered into high schools as well. "Now that sophomores in my high school are taking dope and acid, I know that the scene has spread all over the country," a girl from a town of four thousand in Idaho told a researcher.[64]

Like dope, rock music remained an integral element of hippiedom—although it did not hold nearly as much significance as it had a few years earlier. The new crop of musicians, for most hippies, did not generate the same level of enthusiasm, excitement, or reverence as earlier acts. The most famous and admired band of the 1960s—the Beatles—split up in 1970. Underground papers no longer provided the same amount of coverage to music as they had earlier. Since 1967, Juicy Lucy wrote in the *Great Speckled Bird*, "rock has ridden a downhill train . . . Where is the sense of discovery that was there when we first saw Hendrix or Joplin or the Stones or Cream?"[65]

Crosby, Stills, Nash, and Young proved an exception. Hippies loved the band's chart-topping album *Déjà Vu*. David Crosby sang "Almost Cut My Hair," upholding long hair as a symbol of rebellion against straight society. The tune also popularized the phrase "let my freak flag fly." In addition, the band recorded Joni Mitchell's "Woodstock," a paean to the famous festival, communal values, and the hippie lifestyle. Following Kent State, the group released Neil Young's single "Ohio," which ultimately charged President Nixon with the murders, as the National Guardsmen were merely "tin soldiers." The song had an "us versus them" feel to it. "Soldiers are cutting us down," sang Young as he exhorted the antiwar movement to confront the establishment.[66]

The 1970s, too, witnessed the ascent in popularity of the singer-song-writer. Musicians like James Taylor, Mitchell, Carly Simon, Paul Simon, Carole King, and Harry Chapin exemplified the inward-turning character-istics of the counterculture as they wrote and performed deeply personal and introspective songs. The apolitical nature of the singer-songwriter genre represented a retreat from radical politics as well. The recordings of singer-songwriters often featured acoustic guitar or piano and rarely em-ployed studio effects. King recorded *Tapestry* at the height of the women's movement, and although the album lacked political content, it seemed to capture the feminist currents of the time. King was one of the first female musicians to be taken seriously for her instrumental, vocal, and compo-sitional talents.[67]

Back-to-the-land commune building coincided with hippies' new in-terest in country rock, a genre that fused country with rock and roll and that glorified simple living and rural traditions. Rock musicians recorded music that incorporated country themes, vocal styles, and instrumenta-tion—pedal-steel guitar in particular. The rising popularity of country rock, *Time* contended, was "a symptom of a general cultural reaction to the most unsettling decade the U.S. has yet endured. The yen to escape the corrupt present by returning to the virtuous past—real or imagined—has haunted Americans, never more so than today." Groups and artists such as Gram Parsons, the Byrds, Flying Burrito Brothers, New Riders of the Purple Sage, the Band, Poco, Eagles, Creedence Clearwater Revival, and Bob Dylan recorded and performed country rock. These musicians showed hippies that country music was not solely the preserve of right-wing audiences and musicians. The success of Crosby, Stills, Nash, and Young indicated that many youths had embraced country-styled music. Graham Nash's country-influenced "Teach Your Children"—which showcased the Grateful Dead's Jerry Garcia on pedal steel—went to num-ber sixteen on the Billboard pop chart.[68]

Rock festivals continued to proliferate and the greatest calamity since Altamont occurred in June 1971: the Celebration of Life. Held on the banks of Louisiana's Atchafalaya River near the small town of McCrea, the Cel-ebration of Life was billed by promoters as "the resurrection of the rock festival." It was not to be. The Celebration of Life turned into a lamenta-tion of death. The festival's location changed three times in a week and it was announced several times that the festival was canceled. It lasted only four days, though it had been scheduled for eight. Four people drowned in the river, swept away by strong currents, while another overdosed. The Galloping Gooses, a Louisiana motorcycle gang, acted as snipers, shooting at people along the water's edge from treetops. A biker told a reporter that "it was a bitch man, watchin' the chicks scatter when they heard the shots. It was cool seein' their boobies bounce as they ran for cover, ya' know what I mean?" Nearly a dozen rapes were reported. The Gooses, tired of playing security, beat and robbed dope dealers, taking both their money and stashes. In a scuffle between police and festivalgoers, someone discharged a gun, the bullet striking a man in the thigh. When the Celebration of Life ended, five people were dead, hundreds were in jail, and many were tending to injuries sustained by the violent motorcycle gangs.[69]

Former Beatle George Harrison's Concert for Bangladesh was much more successful and became the blueprint for channeling the popularity of rock and roll and star power toward moral causes. Conflict between Pakistan and East Bengal, and the subsequent declaration of the state of Bangladesh, combined with natural disasters, resulted in massacres, displacement, and starvation. After being approached by his musical mentor and friend Ravi Shankar, whose father was born in Bengal, Harrison decided to help alleviate the suffering, drafting an array of talent—Ringo Starr, Leon Russell, Eric Clapton, members of Badfinger, and Dylan—for two benefit concerts at Madison Square Garden on August 1, 1971. Rock journalists speculated whether the concert would bring the Beatles back together. Harrison did in fact ask Lennon to join the bill, but stopped discussing the possibility when Lennon insisted that Ono accompany him. The concert did, however, mark the first time that two Beatles shared the stage since 1966 after Starr agreed to play. In the end, the performances at Madison Square Garden boosted the fame of the artists and focused attention on the suffering people of Bangladesh, although the British and American governments siphoned off in taxes much of the monies intended to help those people. Yet the shows made Harrison one of the biggest solo stars in the world and elevated rock music to become more than entertainment: it could be steered to aid the world's hungry and deprived.[70]

But sex, drugs, and rock and roll never constituted the core of the counterculture, nor its primary objective. To be sure, when hippies first came into existence, these values figured prominently in their pantheon of principles. In the counterculture's final years, however, these values assumed a small degree of importance in comparison to hippies' emerging beliefs. Youth formed a different counterculture now, one made up, in part, by the younger brothers and sisters of the original hippies who constituted the iconic counterculture of the late sixties. The countersociety had different priorities, cherishing environmentalism, the organic, the outdoors, vegetarianism, back-to-the-land commune building, mobility, travel, and creating alternative institutions.

Closely related to environmentalism was the counterculture's newfound love of the outdoors. The press reported that the "backpacking boom" had "practically revolutionized American outdoor life." One survey estimated that twenty million Americans had tried backpacking and most of them fell between ages eighteen and thirty-four. Longhairs carrying backpacks with enough food, water, and clothing to last weeks, walked trails and penetrated deep into the isolated wilderness. Like their communard counterparts, they endeavored to escape society, daily hassles, and urban life, and to find peace of mind. Three Berkeley street people searching for "better vibrations," for example, gathered their resources, bought packs, sleeping bags, and eighty pounds of brown rice, and went up into the Rocky Mountains, where they built and lived in a lean-to. "Up there with the trees for four months I learned my head," remarked one of the men. Hippies felt free in the secluded wilderness, sleeping in meadows and sitting under waterfalls. Furthermore, the backpack itself became a symbol of significance for the counterculture; in contrast to the suitcase, which usually marked a temporary traveler with a permanent home, the backpack represented "transience and unfettered spirit."[71]

Nature-loving hippies enjoyed camping as well. Freaks invaded national parks. In California, Yosemite proved a popular location for recreation. On peak weekends during the summer, fifty-five thousand people came to the Yosemite Valley, one-third of them under the age of twenty-five, according to estimates by park officials. Even in pastoral environments, the hip confronted the establishment, authorities, and "square" society. Yosemite became the site of the first riot in national park history in July 1970 when the National Park Service attempted to break up a party in Stoneman Meadow. Rangers wielding rope, chemical Mace, and nightsticks battled over 400 young people, resulting in over 130 arrests and 30 hospitalizations. The *Berkeley Tribe* described the eastern region of the Yosemite Valley as an "occupied zone" for youth, while another writer urged a "freak army" to recapture the area. Hippies camped at other national parks, too. In Yellowstone, Grand Teton, and Sequoia parks, longhairs disrobed, blared rock music, pounded bongos, smoked dope, and grappled with older campers. The Park Service established roving riot squads to quell disturbances, and at Point Reyes, north of San Francisco, rangers monitored backwoods sites where youth used dope and drugs.[72]

Backpackers and campers infatuated with the wilderness frequently used the words "natural" and "green," as hippies became obsessed with the "organic." They valued organically grown food that sprang from uncontaminated natural soil, free of pesticides and fertilizers. In addition, longhairs purchased organic food because they eschewed highly refined, chemicalized, and processed goods. Hippies concerned with their health argued that organic food tasted better and was more nutritious. Natural food without chemicals, they contended, made people happier and healthier. Traditional prepared and processed foodstuffs, on the other hand, could be harmful. But organic food tended to be expensive; therefore, some hippies pooled their resources to buy in bulk directly from growers, which drove prices down. Freaks also planted and cultivated their own organic gardens and opened natural foods restaurants. And they prized natural whole grains from which a wide variety of foods—pudding, bread, noodles, soups, coffee, tea, cereals, and pancakes—could be made.[73]

Natural Life Styles, a periodical introduced in 1971, capitalized on and appealed to the counterculture's growing interest in the organic and natural living. Each edition disseminated information intended to bring people closer to each other and nature and facilitate self-discovery. *Natural Life Styles* proclaimed, "REAL FOOD for the body and soul is our chief concern." Hippies read about natural childbirth, mushroom hunting, government environmental policies, herbal body care, and how to start a co-op. Other articles appeared on organic gardening, stone house building, and whether people should eat meat. Recipes for organic cooking appeared regularly as well.[74]

Advocates of the organic employed natural remedies for common ailments such as cold, fever, and flu. The Minneapolis underground *Hundred*

Flowers, for example, recommended treating colds with catnip, sage, peppermint, bayberry bark, ginseng, Indian hemp, and a host of other substances. For fevers, the paper vouched for sweet balm, shepherd's purse, wintergreen, and dandelion, and, for the flu, white pine and poplar.[75]

Some hippies became vegetarians, which appealed to them on several grounds. First, it was inexpensive. Second, DDT and other chemicals infiltrated meat, contaminants they hoped to avoid. Third, Eastern religions influenced hippies—yoga stressed a balanced diet that included natural foods, and Hindus emphasized the importance of all living things, including animals. Hippies, too, believed that vegetarianism aided meditation and facilitated reaching higher awareness. Fruitarians scrapped meat and vegetables altogether, eating fruit exclusively. Zen Buddhists adopted a macrobiotic diet, a yin-and-yang balancing of the food world, consisting of brown rice, fish, and vegetables. Macrobiotic enthusiasts insisted that their diets made them less aggressive and more spiritual. Furthermore, many hippies adopted yoga and macrobiotic diets as a substitute for drugs.[76]

Counterculturalists published books and catalogs celebrating nature, the natural, and simple living. Alicia Bay Laurel's *Living on the Earth*, a large paperback printed in a handwritten lettering style, contained "storm warnings, formulas, recipes, rumors, & country dances." Laurel instructed her readers on how to make tents, soap, wine, baskets, candles, herbal tea, musical instruments, and sandals out of old tires. *Living on the Earth* taught additional skills as well: how to smoke fish, build an outhouse, deliver one's own baby, even cremate a deceased loved one in the forest. In addition, the book recommended the *I Ching* and hatha yoga and identified stores where one could buy natural foods and backpacking equipment.[77]

More popular was Stewart Brand's *The Whole Earth Catalog*, which also appealed to cultural dissidents seeking to live the simple life. It proved useful to communards learning to live off the land. A counterculture Sears and Roebuck, the *Whole Earth Catalog* contained an enormous range of information and objects that defied categorization. One could find information on Danish earth shoes, high lama prayer wheels, and Australian wind generators. Furthermore, Brand's catalog featured books on cosmic energy, carpentry, and plumbing. One could also purchase volumes on goat husbandry and sources on how to build fireplaces, domes, tipis, log

228 | CHAPTER FOUR

and earth houses, and concrete boats. Andrew J. Kirk has elucidated how Brand sought to "create a service that would blend the liberal social values and technological enthusiasm of the counterculture" with his and others' "emerging ecological worldview." Brand endeavored to connect likeminded but widely dispersed peoples by providing them with access to the technologies and information necessary to realize their individual and ecological visions. He hoped to enable individuals in local communities to adopt small-scale technology that, when multiplied across the nation, would result in a sustainable economy. Despite the objections of some environmentalists who elevated nature over the individual, the *Whole Earth Catalog* appealed to technoecological readers.[78]

Hippies treasured living naturally and they also valued mobility: thousands hit the road hitchhiking. The quest to see the country and to experience freedom and adventure impelled many to take to the highway. "Freedom is mobility of one kind or another, and mobility is the essence of a free life—particularly geographic mobility," asserted an underground writer. And, like rock festivals and the earlier be-ins, hitchhiking fostered community. "It's the brotherhood of the road," said one hiker. "It's the only place people are accepted for what they are. You don't know anything about their past." Youth from the East, Midwest, and Great Plains hitchhiked across the country to California. Once they arrived, they usually moved up and down California 1—sometimes referred to as "hippie highway"—which ran along the Pacific Coast from Los Angeles to San Francisco. "Far out," reported *Newsweek*. "Hundreds of hitchhiking freaks with beards, back packs, guitars, flutes, wild hair and dogs—the Panzer troops of the Age of Aquarius—in steady motion along California 1." Near on-ramps, especially in bustling cities, as many as fifty hitchhikers waited to be picked up by fellow freaks or anyone else willing to give them a lift. Some spent a year on the road, sleeping in ditches, woods, churchyards, and on sandy beaches, or camping at Big Sur. Young hippie women were especially vulnerable to sexual assault by the men who picked them up. Hitchhiking became so central to the Los Angeles scene that three hundred hippies invaded City Hall to protest a proposal outlawing hitchhiking by juveniles.[79]

Other counterculturalists did not limit their travels to America. In the late 1960s and continuing into the early 1970s, freaks toured the world.

Many attempted to escape the frantic pace and degenerate values of the West. Cheap and abundant dope provided another incentive, while others endeavored to live a simple life and to find themselves. Living cheaply appealed to hippies' antimaterialism. Overseas trailing is perhaps the only counterculture activity that did not change significantly between 1967 and 1974.

Dropouts roamed Europe. American "knapsack nomads" joined millions of their European counterparts in "wandering far and wide from Hammerfest to Gibralter—and points even farther out." "Maybe I'll go to Switzerland. Or maybe Spain. Anyplace with lots of young people. Just follow the crowds," a twenty-three-year-old seeker told *Time*. Young Vietnam veterans traveled the world, enjoying the good life, while trying to discover themselves. "When I was in the jungle, I vowed that if I ever got out alive, I'd spend a long time in Europe—drinking the local brand and making it with all the chicks until I got my fill. Then I'd return home and do something constructive," a vet confessed. "I still haven't any notion of what I should do back home, or even who I really am." Hippies traveling Europe lived cheaply, taking free meals from friendly adults or eating at university cafeterias, staying at inexpensive youth hostels, hitchhiking, and traveling second-class on trains. The British Student Travel Center and other youth organizations offered especially affordable plane tickets to full-time college and high school students.[80]

Thousands flew into Amsterdam—"the hippie capital of the world." Police rarely, if ever, enforced drug laws, and nightclubs sold low-grade hashish. Freaks "did their own thing" in private booths. Seekers in Rome hung out on the Spanish Steps, eating stale bread, strumming guitars, and smoking pot. In Copenhagen, longhairs enjoyed open-air theater productions, orchestra recitals, and free rock concerts. Dropouts stayed at hostels and "youth cities," which consisted of cots and army tents. American seekers also made their way to Paris, London, Bonn, and Zurich.[81]

Beyond Europe, seekers journeyed to India. In 1969, over ten thousand Americans and Europeans lived there, mostly in Bombay. Some traveled to the foothills of the Himalayas, some moved into the hinterlands to live among the peasantry, while others frolicked in the surf and sand on the beaches of Goa, or studied meditation with a guru. At least one hippie trailer experienced a religious epiphany after taking LSD in Goa. "It had an incredible effect," explained a man named William. "I was never going to be the same again." William became a serious Buddhist, more introspective, and digested Buddhist texts and works by Carl Jung. In contrast, a man named Widdicombe, after hearing Harrison's song "My Sweet Lord," and reading the Bhagavad Gita, traveled to India where his interest in dope became increasingly muted. "I went to India because I wanted to find a way of getting high without taking drugs," he explained. Some longhairs devised harebrained schemes to make money. Harvey Meyers, stuck in Calcutta in 1968, sent a marijuana-laden sitar to the United States with a returning friend who was instructed to sell the dope at high prices. Unfortunately for Meyers, his friend disappeared with the grass and instrument.[82]

Thousands traveled to the Kathmandu Valley in Nepal, high up in the Himalayas. Cheap, legal, and abundant dope attracted many, but so did the beautiful scenery and solace from frantic daily life in America. "Here we breathe freely, away from the poisonous air of modern materialistic civilization which has made a mess of life in the West," a hip woman told a newsperson. Hippies loved simple living in Nepal, passing the days relaxing, meditating, smoking dope, painting, writing poems, and reading. They also found its abundant shops, cafes, and lodging houses appealing. Most of Kathmandu's hip population stayed at the Quo Vadis Hotel. The hotel's owner let hippies stay for free, as he made his money in the legal drug trade. The premises were filthy and dark. Patrons stayed in rooms with dirt floors. There were no beds and no toilets—just a running tap in the laundry.[83]

Freaks found Southeast Asia particularly attractive. International hitchhikers settled in Thailand and Vientiane, the capital of Laos, where they lived in cheap hotels, basked in the sun, swam in the Mekong River, and easily purchased marijuana, hashish, and opium. Hip visitors also came to journey's end in Indonesia and Malaysia.[84]

Seekers also visited or lived in the Middle East and Africa. Hundreds found Kabul, Afghanistan, with its legal, high-quality, and cheap hashish, enticing. Hippies paid little for housing and food—another draw. "Vincent" happily recalls the time he spent in Herat, indulging himself with walnuts, oranges, grass, and opium. Furthermore, seekers found Afghanis friendly, even welcoming. Trailers, on the other hand, found

neighboring Pakistan crowded, unwelcoming, and generally uninterest-
ing. Longhairs traveled to Iran, Lebanon, Turkey, Morocco, and the bush
country of Kenya as well. A female seeker named Lola fondly remembers
purchasing a large ball of dope in Morocco, sitting on a Land Rover,
smoking, and being amazed while gazing at the stars. In Istanbul, hippie
trailers made sure they stopped at the Pudding Shop, which tailored spe-
cifically to such clientele. From there, trailers usually made an attempt to
visit the Blue Mosque. Journeying through eastern Turkey was a different
matter entirely: hippies encountered stone throwing and women experienced sexual harassment. Longhairs found Iran more civilized. Although
Iranians proved less antagonistic, women travelers again experienced harassment.[85] Closer to home, freaks journeyed to Mexico. Hippies loved its
picturesque beaches, bright sun, bustling cities, open roads, and small
villages. Thousands of men and women crossed the border, hitchhiking
around the country with everything they owned on their backs.[86]

Although reports and stories suggested that life on the "hippie trail"
was an endless party and bacchanal, the reality was quite different. Sharif
Gemie and Brian Ireland interviewed and gathered information from
eighty former travelers. They found "few signs of a sexual revolution thriving on the trail." Many trailers went long stretches without sexual encounters. Some felt frustrated, others were not surprised, and some welcomed
the situation. Some women became sexually liberated along the trail.
Cleo Odzer—a "Goa Freak" and former model—had many sex partners,
had sex with men in order to procure drugs or lodging, and used sex to
elicit favors while in an Indian prison. Odzer disdained expected paths for
women, including marriage and childrearing. Yet other women treated
the trail as an adventure unencumbered by sex. While a few men experienced sexual harassment from other men, every woman who participated
in Gemie and Ireland's study told stories of stares from men, barricading
themselves in their rooms to keep men outside, and unwelcome physical
contact like groping, pinching, and grasping. In the East in particular,
women had their passports taken by police who demanded sexual favors
in exchange for their documents. Some men acknowledged losing their
virginity to prostitutes. Other trailers fell in love along the journey and
got married.[87] Like freaks elsewhere, hippie trailers reproduced dominant gender paradigms, including a gendered division of labor. Women

cooked and washed clothes. Men drove the vehicles and acted as guides. Women did not participate in the repair of coaches, cars, or vans, and men often blamed women for misfortunes encountered during travels.[88]

Foreign officials treated hippie invaders harshly. Mexican authorities deported or jailed them. They also confiscated their vehicles and shaved their hair and beards. Many were arrested on marijuana charges. College students spent months in jails sleeping on cold cement floors. Kenyan officials threatened to turn back Americans, Canadians, and Britons with "long, shaggy, unkempt hair." General Prapas Charusathien, Thailand's interior minister, "asked the foreign office to instruct its embassies to refuse visas to the flower children." Malaysian government officials instructed Malaysia-Singapore Airlines to deny service to anyone with "Beatle-type hairdos or hippie clothes." Many of the native Nepalese disliked hippies, especially restaurant and hotel owners who lost money when indigents could not afford to pay for meals and lodging. Indian police and civic officials charged hippies with exerting a bad influence on Indian youths and conservative and religious Indians found nude and seminude hippies repulsive. By 1972 the number of dropouts in the country shrank to four thousand when the Indian government issued fewer new visas and extended fewer older ones. In 1971 over seven hundred Americans sat in jails overseas for drug possession and drug dealing.[89]

CULTURAL ACTIVISM AND BUILDING THE NEW SOCIETY

At the same time hippies traversed the world, crisscrossed the country hitchhiking, and marched in the last major antiwar demonstrations, the desire to build their own society reached its pinnacle. In the early 1970s the counterculture's audacious social experiment of constructing a new society never came closer to being fully realized. The counterculture was a genuine counter to Cold War culture, producing its own values, music, art, literature, language, and clothing, but, in the early 1970s, it also became a countersociety. Cultural activism exploded as activists, former activists, and hippies—together—channeled their efforts into constructive action, creating counterinstitutions. As the countersociety spoke of the New Age and the New America, it established co-ops, hip businesses, head shops, free stores, free universities, free clinics, legal services, "churches," underground newspapers, radio stations, community switchboards, and shelters for street people and runaways, in unprecedented numbers. Longhairs, immersed in hippie enclaves, completely evaded majority society. Indeed, when freaks resided in a bustling hip community, they "almost lived in another country, an alternative America, filled with people of similar commitments and affinities." "People are goal oriented now," observed Max Scherr, publisher of the *Berkeley Barb*. "They are trying to make a structured society of their own. They came here looking for a revolution and now they've found one—they don't have to go out on the street anymore." Sinclair, jailed in 1969 and released in 1971, testified to the countersociety's unparalleled growth while he sat in prison. He found the exceptional surge in cultural activism astonishing:

> Everything looks so beautiful out here—freaks are everywhere! I've never seen so many freaks before in my life!. . . . for me it's like coming out into a whole different world from the one I left in 1969, a world where all the stuff we were talking about and trying to bring about has all come true and now there are thousands and thousands of brothers and sisters sitting around waiting for something to happen . . . ready to support any kind of programs and projects that are brought forth to deal with the people's needs. There's so many of us that we can do goddamn near anything we set out to do now, and it's really blowing my mind![90]

Longhairs opened co-ops to boost the sense of community, distribute healthy food, and undercut big business. They first appeared around 1970 and freaks initially called them "food conspiracies." Over the next decade, according to the Cooperative League of the USA (CLUSA), counterculturalists established between five and ten thousand co-ops. By the late seventies, such stores sold more than a half billion dollars' worth of food per year. Co-ops served the common good and "the people" owned and operated them. "The concept of the cooperative is really together," asserted the *Big Muddy Gazette*, an Illinois underground. "It means what the title says—co-operation, community, coming together to meet our needs, being sure that the basic needs of our brothers and sisters are met. It's just a beginning." Furthermore, hippies disliked giving their money to corporate grocery stores and enriching stockholders, so co-ops appealed to their antimaterialist, anti-big-business sensibilities: "We feel that food is a basic right and that it shouldn't be sold for profit." Co-ops cut prices as well. Individuals pooled their often scarce resources together to purchase goods in bulk directly from distributors, farmers, or wholesalers at a cheaper cost than that of well-established chain stores. Moreover, co-ops functioned as meeting places for hip communities. Finally, co-ops stocked the shelves with products hippies desired—wholesome, nutritious goods—not highly processed, synthetic foods. Co-ops proliferated in hippie enclaves all over the country "from Louisville to New York City, from Chicago to rural Maine, from Austin to the Puget Sound." The counterculture operated Dallas Food Co-Op in Texas; North Country Co-Op in the Twin Cities; Common Market in Denver; Aquarius Food in New York City; Bethesda Community Food Store near Washington, DC; New Haven Co-op in Connecticut; Our Store in Fresno, California; People's Food in Lincoln, Nebraska; Common Market Food Conspiracy in Madison, Wisconsin; and Serve the People in Saint Louis.[91]

Similarly, activist entrepreneurs founded natural foods stores to further the movement, enhance health, and improve the lives and environments of the hip community. Although they reaped sizable profits, the owners of such establishments were often just as interested in causes that animated the movement and counterculture, including peace and environmentalism. In addition, hip store owners sought to undermine large corporate supermarkets, mainstream diets tantamount to "food pollution," exploitive labor practices, and environmental degradation, while promoting health, harmony, and spiritual rejuvenation. Moreover, natural foods stores' management implemented democratized business practices such as open records, consensus decision-making, and hiring by vote. Austin, Texas, boasted several natural foods stores. The first, the Good Food Store, opened in 1971. Five years later, five branch stores had opened in Texas, employing nearly eighty people. Around the University of Texas, at least a dozen independent natural food stores opened their doors. By the mid-1970s the capital of the Lone Star state had "four natural foods co-ops, ten co-op houses, three co-op farms, and a variety of worker collectives that included a bakery and a vegetarian restaurant." Close to a thousand people belonged to the Austin Community Project, an umbrella organization for co-ops.[92]

The counterculture established non-food-related co-ops to build community and enhance purchasing power. In Atlanta, hippies organized the Laundromat, a crafts cooperative. In Jackson, Mississippi, amateur and professional photographers set up the Pearl River Photography Cooperative. The organization did developing and printing at reduced rates and pooled their resources together to purchase equipment. They also planned to share a cooperative dark room. Counterculturalists also established clothing co-ops in several cities.[93]

Hip businesses multiplied, supplying the community with clothing, art, and handcrafts. Youths purchased numerous items: shirts, bell-bottoms, military surplus, belts, tie dye, leather products, jewelry, candles, posters, and incense. Hip entrepreneurs, too, opened record shops and bookstores, and craft shops that sold handmade goods and art. Dropouts clogged the checkout lines of non-hippie businesses as well, especially secondhand clothing shops like the Salvation Army and Goodwill Industries. Hippies patronized the General Store in Omaha, Nebraska; the Strawberry Patch in New Brunswick, New Jersey; Heart Shop in Wausau, Wisconsin; and the Thread Shed in Rapid City, South Dakota.[94]

Hippies opened head shops, which flourished in the early 1970s, and became some of the most successful counterculture businesses. Longhairs purchased incense, beads, posters, underground newspapers, and bongs, pipes, and rolling papers for marijuana and hashish. According to one estimate, over thirty thousand head shops were open for business by 1979. Dopers browsed the Flower Factory and the Third Eye in Los Angeles; the Entrepreneur and Headland in Chicago; Pipefitter in Madison; the Trance in Columbia, Missouri; the Head Shed in Worcester, Massachusetts; and Strawberry Fields in Lawrence, Kansas.

"Activist entrepreneurs," argues Joshua Clark Davis, were not merely interested in selling psychedelic merchandise. They sought to furnish an alternative to plastic, mainstream consumerism, while providing a public space for the hip community, free from the harassment of its many detractors and enemies. Head shops functioned as community centers, too; musicians looking for new bandmates or hippies who simply needed a place to stay could browse message boards or converse with other customers. Head shop owners intended to transport their customers "psychologically, to delight their senses, to take them on a proverbial trip."

Amid incense, loud rock music, and psychedelic lights, patrons of these psychedelic establishments "could search for spiritual freedom and enlightenment." In addition, hip entrepreneurs championed the transformative nature of mind-expanding substances, determined to facilitate a cultural—and even societal—revolution. Head shop owners, like other countercultural entrepreneurs, aspired to "right livelihoods," striving for self-sufficiency, performing meaningful work that improved the hip community. Activist entrepreneurs elevated enlightenment and community above rigid business practices and high profit margins, seeking only to live comfortably. "Yesterday I gave away more than I sold," admitted an owner in Eugene, Oregon. "I just want to make enough money to pay the rent, and to eat." In the late 1960s and after, law enforcement and mainstream Americans targeted head shops because they were countercultural centers. Police monitored and raided them, and private citizens picketed and even physically attacked them.[95]

Head shops—though thoroughly countercultural institutions—aided political causes as well. Activist entrepreneurs, Davis contends, "forces us to rethink the widespread idea that the work of social movements and political dissent is by definition antithetical to all business and marketplace activity." Young people could purchase New Left newspapers and pick up free antiwar information at head shops. And some activist entrepreneurs involved themselves in antiwar protests, including Doug Brown of Oat Willie's in Austin. Moreover, head shops backed efforts to reform and eradicate restrictive drug laws. In addition to disseminating information on drug reform, activist entrepreneurs helped bankroll organizations agitating for the decriminalization of marijuana—Amorphia and the National Organization for the Reform of Marijuana Laws (NORML)—by selling their paraphernalia on consignment. By the late-1970s, however, after coming under fire by lawmakers and antidrug warriors, head shops moderated their tone, recasting themselves as conventional businesses, not advocates of social and political reform like the original countercultural shops.[96]

Hip entrepreneurs affixed their social values to T-shirts, buttons, and posters, marketing and selling them. Hippies bought "Fuck the Draft" posters and buttons that read "Peace Now" and "Majority for A Silent Agnew." Jesus Freaks especially liked Day-Glo buttons with religious messages—"Truckin' with Jesus," and "No 'Jive' Jesus is Alive."[97]

Most hip enclaves organized switchboards—a direct-help telephone line and communications hub, or walk-in service—which aided local communities, locating housing, crash pads, communes, food for transients, and finding rides for travelers. Switchboards depended on volunteers to offer their homes as temporary quarters for people passing through. In addition, these community services notified runaways if their parents had left messages for them. Drifters and dropouts benefited from switchboards in Berkeley, San Francisco, Austin, Houston, Eugene, Oregon, and Washington, DC.[98]

Free clinics mushroomed, as freaks believed vehemently that health care was a basic human right. In 1972 more than 340 were in operation. Counterculturalists valued free clinics because they served the health care needs of the community and provided services free of charge, a major benefit to hippies lacking money. Supporters of free clinics felt that all humans had a right to health care at all times. Moreover, health professionals and patients—the community—controlled such institutions, an arrangement the counterculture cherished. Doctors and other professionals staffed these nonprofit establishments and treated a wide variety of ailments: bad drug trips, addiction, hepatitis, sexually transmitted diseases, and malnutrition. Likewise, some clinics provided free medication, while others offered counseling on birth control, pregnancy, and venereal disease. Free clinics were vulnerable, as they depended on outside resources for drugs, equipment, and access to hospitals. And because free clinics treated social pariahs, they often avoided social workers, police, and organized medicine. Dropouts took advantage of free clinics in Berkeley, Nashville, Austin, Carbondale, Illinois, and hundreds of other locations.[99]

Free stores and free food services spread as well, embodiments of the counterculture's antiacquisitive and anticorporate values. Such establishments relied on donations and dropouts acquired various items at them—shirts, trousers, shoes, blankets, and furniture. Free stores opened in New York City, Seattle, Detroit, and Madison. In addition to free stores, some communities benefited from free food programs. The University Lutheran Chapel in Berkeley fed two hundred people a night. Legal aid services for the hip also proliferated in Illinois and Massachusetts.[100]

Hard drugs became such a pressing problem in the early seventies that some hippies actively campaigned against them. In Nashville, Bill

Dawson, coordinator of the Human Improvement Project (HIP) and thirty-
six others, many of them former addicts, spoke out against hard drug use
and dangerous narcotics. The organization did not attempt to dissuade
marijuana use, as it did not consider grass a drug. HIP set up centers and
a twenty-four-hour hotline for drug users and runaways in Atlanta and
Memphis. Hip activists called out heroin and pills for censure. Not only
did these drugs kill people, they stifled social movements, too, claiming
the lives of would-be activists. "Heroin, downs, ups, and assorted other
garbage are killers," asserted the *Paper* in Stamford, Connecticut. "They
not only kill people but they kill movements. Pigs aren't going to worry
about some freak sitting in a park or closet on the nod. . . . wake the hell
up, and think a little; besides killing yourself, you are killing your brothers
and sisters."[101]

Detroit's Open City consolidated several institutions into one community service organization. Open City helped tens of thousands—perhaps
hundreds of thousands of people—throughout its existence. It operated
a twenty-four-hour switchboard that handled five thousand calls per
month, providing entertainment information and assisting suicidal callers and victims of disastrous drug trips. In addition, Open City ran a free
store, a free clinic that aided thousands, a food co-op, and counseling service. Crossroads in Rapid City, South Dakota, served a similar purpose,
assisting people who had taken bad doses of LSD, offering a referral service for legal aid and birth control, and furnishing food and crash pads.[102]

The counterculture continued to establish free universities, which informed members of the movement and furthered a vision of the new society. Hippies and college radicals could attend classes at a "free U" in most
major and mid-sized cities and scores of college towns. Fifty thousand
people attended classes annually. The average alternative university offered instruction in political and cultural radicalism; doctoral candidates
and radical faculty members usually taught the courses. Most of these
schools had an ephemeral existence, typically lasting a year or two. Students received no credit, but this did not matter as increasing one's knowledge, not getting a degree, constituted the objective. Free universities
represented more than a counterinstitution, as they were dedicated to a
larger and weightier enterprise. The Mid-Peninsula Free University in Palo
Alto, California, for example, proclaimed that its goal was to "implement

a vision of cultural revolution in which a new society might develop within the shell of the old." At the Free University of Seattle, rebellious students enrolled in such classes as "The Art of Sexual Love," "Fundamentals of Astrology," "Compulsory Military Service and the Draft Act," and "Neo-Colonialism and Revolution in Asia, Africa, and Latin America," while at the Free University of New York, interested youth took the "Sexual Revolution," and "Hallucinogenic Drugs."[103]

In addition to free universities, hippies formed "churches," usually to worship sex or dope. In 1965, Art Kleps—Chief Boo-Hoo—had founded the Neo-American Church, which employed LSD as a religious sacrament. Jefferson Poland, cofounder of the Sexual Freedom League, organized a similar institution in Berkeley: the Psychedelic Venus Church. Like other psychedelic churches, the Venus church resolved to legitimize dope smoking as a religious sacrament and experience. Such rituals affirmed the right to use dope and were an affront to authorities that might interfere. The church engaged in a ritual that involved marijuana, massage, and group sex. A typical "evening of worship and fellowship" proceeded in four stages—"blind meditation and touch," followed by "nude group sensitivity encounter," "cannabis communion with OM chanting," and "church social." Church members worshipped Aphrodite as a "symbol of hedonic pleasure" and believed that the goddess watched over their orgies. The organization also planned a "nude rock dance" as well as "an experiment in sadomasochism." Some hippies raised objections to psychedelic religionists, contending that they took themselves and their sacraments too seriously, as there was nothing wrong with dope smoking for secular purposes.[104]

Other counterculture-friendly churches were founded in California. Two young ministers, Richard L. York and John Pairman "Jock" Brown, had established the Berkeley Free Church in 1967 and it thrived into the early 1970s. The ministers preached against the war in Vietnam and the church's motto was "Celebrate life—off the world pig!" The church aided the street community. Up to one hundred teenagers slept in York's home nightly during the Summer of Love and he always left his door unlocked. York and Brown adapted "Episcopalian practices to hippie needs," staging outdoor communions complete with incense, candles, incantations, body paint, and rock music. The two ministers founded a free dining room, too. Despite being devoted to liberation theology, the church was concerned more with form than with doctrinaire Christianity. In Los Angeles, hippies gathered at the Oracle-Cosmic Joy Fellowship. The prelates, known as "coordinators," led services in which worshippers sat cross-legged, held hands, and chanted "Om," amid incense, Indian print cloths, votive candles, and statues of Buddha. "Om," a Hindu word, signified "the ultimate religion."[105]

Portland's hip community emerged in the late sixties and continued to expand in the early seventies. Local hippies benefited from many counterinstitutions. At the Psychedelic Supermarket, heads acquired pipes, black velvet posters, incense, belt buckles, art, and buttons. Customers made free sandwiches and scanned a bulletin board carrying information about crash pads and rides. Dropouts and hippie college kids loved to sit in the wading pool at Neighborhood House. Other longhairs, runaways, and high school dropouts attended classes at Willamette Learning Center, where one could earn a special certificate if they passed the General Educational Development exams, lived communally, and completed an independent project. Outside In, "a Socio-Medical Aid Station," which opened in June 1968, provided "medical attention for alienated youth or for anyone who drifts in." Portland's hip also read the local underground *Willamette Bridge* and tuned into the radio station KBOO, which aired college lectures, community concerts, and the pontifications of Scientologists, Christians, and Hare Krishnas. Among the city's artistic contingent was the Storefront Theatre. The troupe, made up of musicians, artists, and actors, put on a production of *Lysistrata* in June 1970 that featured huge phalluses and a naked woman holding a dove.[106]

Madison's counterculture thrived as well. At the University of Wisconsin, according to Matthew Levin, most students experienced the New Left and counterculture "as one seamless movement." In April 1967, the first of a series of be-ins were held, and in October of that year, the San Francisco Mime Troupe led demonstrators up Bascom Hill to the Dow Protest. By the late 1960s, campus newspapers highlighted and analyzed dope and drugs and university administrators became concerned about the spread of LSD and heroin on campus. After the Stonewall Riots in New York, a gay rights movement emerged. The Gay Liberation Front and Gay Madison Sisters provided gay students with a community and voice. Many students championed environmentalism. The *Daily Cardinal* carried stories about pollution, population control, nuclear energy, and the state of local lakes. The center of counterculture activity was on Mifflin Street, where many graduate students lived. They bought food at the Mifflin Street Co-op, attended productions at the experimental Broom Street Theater, and took classes at the free university.[107]

Atlanta was home to one of the most vibrant countercultural scenes in the South. The section of the city near Peachtree Street and 10th Street was the center of hippie activity. Hippies populated an area that became known as "the Strip" or "the Neighborhood," bordered by Piedmont Park on the east, 14th Street on the north, Spring Street on the west, and 7th Street on the south. An estimated five thousand hippies made the Neighborhood their permanent residence by the summer of 1970. On any given day, the sidewalks teemed with so many people that one had to push their way down the street. Freaks easily obtained marijuana, LSD, mescaline, and the *Great Speckled Bird* from street dealers. The hip community browsed boutiques and craft shops and saw performances at art theaters. Atlanta hippies also experienced numerous activities and events: art and pop festivals, love parades, peace marches, and women's liberation demonstrations. Dropouts congregated around the Wall on the corner of Peachtree and 10th, a windowless brick building with a giant Jesus mural painted on the side. Popular rock bands included the Bag, Traveling Freak Show, Hampton Grease Band, and Dr. Espina's Banana Boat Blues Band. In addition, longhairs benefited from free health clinics and drug rehabilitation centers.[108]

"LIVING THE REVOLUTION" AND BUILDING THE NEW SOCIETY IN RURAL COMMUNES

While urban counterculturalists struggled to create the new society in cities, hippie communards did the same in the countryside. The early 1970s marked an extraordinary increase in the number of rural and urban communes. The surge in commune building during this era "dwarfed what had gone before."[109] Communards articulated their desire to build the new society. "Our purpose is to set up and maintain a society aimed at and operated for the benefit of its citizens," stated Twin Oaks, "to create a culture which produces happy and useful people, who cooperate with one another for the general good and who deal with problems in a peaceful and rational way." Bruce Taub of the Earthworks commune in Franklin, Vermont, aspired "to help create a society that would provide an alternative to the despair and destruction we were experiencing in our culture, our country and our environment." Fashioning a new society, in fact, was such a general intention, that one network of communes took the name Movement for a New Society.[110]

Furthermore, rural communards took an active role in hastening the "revolution." The residents of Twin Oaks, for instance, "lived as though the revolution were over" and urged others to "go ahead and start building revolutionary societies." While some political radicals spoke of overthrowing America and its imperialism, Twin Oaks' members advocated "building small-scale alternatives now" instead of "trying to tear down the present power structure." Thelin, a former Haight-Ashbury luminary who resided in a commune in Northern California in 1971, communicated the same sentiment: "We have won the revolution—and it continues."[111]

Constructing the new society and precipitating or living the revolution, of course, represented hippies' grandest ideals. More practically, communards initiated their experiments because they rejected the dominant order, idealized rural surroundings, advocated open land, and sought to put the principles of egalitarianism, warm community, and environmentalism into action.[112]

The Farm, probably more than any other single commune, exemplified the spirit of back-to-the-land living. The idea for the Farm originated in Haight-Ashbury. Ego-denying hippies dedicated to egalitarianism founded the commune near Summertown, Tennessee, in 1971, and by September 1973 six hundred people lived there on 1,750 acres. The Farm's members called themselves a "church," and they sought "to live a spiritual life." The commune's faith pulled from all the world's major religious traditions. Although few of them had had any experience as farmers, the residents endeavored to attain self-sufficiency, growing most of what they ate. Countercultural attributes abounded at the commune. Many members practiced vegetarianism. The Tennessee hippies also aided thousands of dropouts who turned up at the gates. They lived in poverty voluntarily, while dedicating themselves to helping the Third World's poor. Rock and roll was the Farm's "church music," and the Farm Band toured the country, playing forty-one cities for free. The communards used psychedelics and smoked marijuana, as they considered getting high an "essential implement in their spiritual toolbox." A medical staff rendered first aid services and teachers led classes at the Farm school. Midwives delivered babies "all natural." Births, like marriage, represented a "sacrament." Couples on the Farm practiced tantric sex. Men made a point of holding back so that women could achieve orgasm, which unleashed the female energy necessary for counterbalancing the male's ego, facilitating his spiritual progress. In contrast to the prevailing sexual practices of the West that elevated male pleasure, women controlled sex at the Farm.[113]

Many communities consisted of a few houses, a barn, and a communal house. Communes pooled their resources in service of the common good, sharing everything—money, food, labor, expenses, shelter—and members felt responsible for the needs of the entire community. Some provided on-site medical care and education and reared children communally. Income came from a variety of sources. The Farm sent farming and construction crews out to work for pay. Others performed odd jobs or accepted money from friends or relatives. Many communities operated their own businesses. Hammock industries, for example, largely sustained Twin Oaks and East Wind, a commune in Tecumseh, Missouri. Some communards took government benefits such as food stamps and welfare. Although this practice was broadcast in the establishment press, it was highly controversial in the counterculture, since many loathed the idea of entanglement with the corrupt government.[114]

Hippies put their values—self-discovery, freedom, love, community, and environmentalism—into practice in most communes. Finding oneself, attaining "self-actualization, fulfillment and wholeness of identity in all facets of existence" constituted a fundamental objective. Two premier values included love and community; the Aquarians in rural southern Illinois exemplified these sentiments with their motto, "Find love in yourselves then share it with others." Like the Aquarians, the Farm's residents made a point of practicing "loving kindness and brotherhood." The Farm's founder, Stephen Gaskin, wrote in a newsletter, "I really love you and I really love God and I really love this universe." Gaskin glorified freedom, too, calling "free will" a "God-like thing." Springtree commune, in

Virginia, valued natural foods, free schooling, and permissive childrearing. Because communards took environmentalism seriously, they tried to live harmoniously with nature and viewed the environment as a precious resource worthy of protection and preservation. Noncompetition and nonviolence were among common values. Communards also held egalitarianism in the highest regard. East Wind called itself "an egalitarian society." By "egalitarian," the commune's members meant "equal opportunity for people to develop skills, speak their mind, and grow in desired directions." Some communes sought to purge possessiveness and self-centeredness.[115]

When not working, communards indulged in a variety of activities. Many did yoga, studied astrology, and meditated, while others made pottery. Many back-to-the-land hippies played guitar and led community singalongs.[116]

JESUS PEOPLE, RUNAWAYS, AND DRIFTERS

The advent of the Jesus Freaks, or street Christians, as many preferred to be called, marked another addition to, and significant development within, the counterculture. The Jesus People movement, which traced its origins to Haight-Ashbury in San Francisco during the Summer of Love, combined conservative religion with rebellious counterculture. Ted Wise, one of the first converts during the Jesus Freaks' gestational period in San Francisco, struggled with his lack of character. He read the New Testament and became fascinated by Jesus, his claims to divinity, and Paul's emphasis on responding to Jesus's invitation to be born again. Wise recalled, "I found it necessary to cry out to God to save my life in every sense of the word. Jesus knocked me off my metaphysical ass. I could choose Him or literally suffer a fate worse than death." Wise publicly proclaimed his newfound faith at a party in Berkeley in early 1965. He and his wife dropped acid and Wise announced, "Jesus is my Lord," which confused the other partygoers.

Jim Doop was another early convert. A member of the Berkeley Sexual Freedom League, he discovered that "God is my Father and I am His child," one night after smoking marijuana. Doop found that Jesus's words increased his love for God and humankind and began telling his friends,

"I was dropping LSD, smoking marijuana, and that Jesus Christ was my Lord. . . . I had turned on, tuned in, and Christ was leading me out." Near the end of the Summer of Love, Wise and others founded the Living Room on Page Street to start evangelizing hippies. At one point, Charles Manson dropped by and proclaimed that he was God. Wise laughed and expressed his disappointment.[117]

In 1968, hippieized Christian activity exploded in southern California, from Santa Barbara to San Diego. Jesus Houses proliferated, as hippies abandoned the drug culture to live communally with other devout Christians. Jesus Freaks simultaneously established coffeehouses like the Lost Coin in San Diego, where guitar-slinging Christian singers performed. Jesus bands—Agape, Mustard Seed Faith, and J.C. Power Outlet—jammed in public parks, gyms, and churches to attract potential converts for Christ, while entertaining the faithful. Jesus People publicized and promoted their cause with a fervor equal to that of the other movements of the Sixties, distributing underground papers, buttons, posters, and bumper stickers. Southern California was the nexus from which the Jesus movement was galvanized and encouraged. Before 1970 came to an end, its advocates emerged in places like Boise, Idaho, and Waterloo, Iowa. Jesus infiltrated youth culture, evidenced by spiritually themed pop music racing up the charts and the popularity of rock opera *Jesus Christ Superstar*. The mainstream press seized on the story, too. *Time, Life*, and the *Wall Street Journal* published articles on the Jesus movement and it became one of the top ten news stories of 1971. By the late 1970s, however, the movement had run its course. Former Jesus Freaks settled into their jobs, married, raised families, and attended local churches. Most were subsumed into the rising evangelical subculture, which, by that time, was becoming increasingly political and projecting a national presence.[118]

The new converts had forsaken dope and drugs—acid, heroin, mescaline, and speed—to become dedicated evangelical Christians preaching their "love for Jesus." Others had originally investigated Eastern religions before wandering back to Christianity. "Lots of youths are freaked out on drugs or meditation or Zen," one Jesus Person told a journalist. "We've been through that and found it wasn't satisfying. Now we're freaked out on Jesus." Some found the image of Jesus the rebel, the martyr for peace and brotherhood, attractive, yet most sought an intense, personal relationship with Christ, whom they worshipped as the ultimate savior, judge, and ruler of their destinies.[119]

The Jesus People movement attracted many counterculturalists. According to a survey of 812 former participants conducted by Larry Eskridge, 42 percent considered themselves liberal before their conversion experience. Likewise, 39 percent self-identified as hippies, 30 percent regularly used marijuana, 10.5 percent regularly took acid, another 16 percent used it occasionally, and 78 percent regularly listened to rock music. Over 14 percent answered affirmatively that drugs had contributed to their becoming Jesus Freaks. Jesus People abandoned drugs and forbade sex outside of marriage, although these practices could not be entirely contained in youthful religious communes. Yet in other respects, they remained hippies through and through. When not communicating about Christ, most talked hip lingo. They donned secondhand clothes, granny dresses, blue jeans, army surplus clothes, sandals, and sported long hair. Like their more secular counterparts, hippieized Christians took aim at establishment practices, criticizing the straight churches for their rigidity, emphasis on doctrine, even racism—at the expense of authenticity. Many discarded formal jobs, preferring to work on the street, evangelizing hippies and others. On the Sunset Strip in Los Angeles, police had difficulty distinguishing the "pushers from the priests." Jesus Freaks shared with early Christians the belief that Doomsday might arrive at any time and sought to save souls. "If you ain't saved by the blood of Jesus, man, forget it. You're damned to the pits of hell," said one bearded street Christian to a passerby. "You don't need no pills," proselytized Arthur Blessitt, "Jes' drop a little Matthew, Mark, Luke, and John. Christ is the ultimate, eternal trip."[120]

Like other hippies, Jesus Freaks established their own communes— Jesus Houses. Jesus People lived communally for several reasons. First, they believed that according to scripture, first-century Christians had lived communally, sharing everything in common. Accordingly, Jesus Freaks sought to duplicate such living arrangements, expressing their commitment to authenticity. Second, the new converts lacked funds, as many teenage runaways and hippies became converts. Third, in a communal environment elders could monitor the new followers of Christ to ensure that they did not relapse into drug taking and addiction. Jesus Freaks founded more than two hundred Jesus Houses in California alone, while others were located in the Pacific Northwest, Chicago, Detroit, and other cities. Jesus People started their own underground papers, too; *Right On!* in Berkeley and the *Hollywood Free Paper* boasted some of the largest circulations. Famous musicians converted to the Jesus movement, including Johnny Cash, Eric Clapton, and Paul Stookey of Peter, Paul, and Mary. Jeremy Spencer of Fleetwood Mac joined the Children of God.[121]

In addition to Jesus People, the counterculture added to its ranks an estimated half million runaway teens. Alienated kids ran away from "hassles"—parents, cops, and school. Hundreds of counterculture counseling services sprouted up across the country for the purpose of supporting runways with drug addictions and family and personal problems. Alternative agencies "situated themselves between the hip and the straight worlds, acting as a kind of bridge between the two for adolescents." They represented a significant departure from the state child welfare and juvenile justice systems as well. Whereas state institutions assumed a protective role that did not allow youth to make their own decisions, alternative services allowed autonomy. "At the very heart of their work was respect for youthful autonomy and an emphasis on the centrality of youth decision-making," writes Karen M. Staller. "Thus the values of the alternative agencies were deeply rooted in the youth rights movement and consistent with the counterculture discourse on power, autonomy, and freedom." Runaways contacted services of their own free will. The state did not place them there. Houses offered legal advice, medical care, personal and group therapy to alienated teens, and a telephone so that they could contact their parents. The agencies refused to turn their clients over to the police, nor did they force them to return home. Some runways and street people used the houses for extended stays, while others treated them like crash pads, spending one night before moving on to another city. Project Place in Boston offered assistance and advice to forty or fifty runaways a month. Similar establishments included Huckleberry House in San Francisco; Ozone House in Ann Arbor, Michigan; The Bridge in Atlanta; Looking Glass in Chicago; and Runaway House in Washington, DC.[122]

In addition to teenage runaways, drifters augmented the counterculture's numbers. Thousands of young people—mostly nonstudents—migrated to universities all over the country to escape straight society and live cheaply. To be sure, there had been street communities before—two to four thousand dropouts had made their homes in Berkeley and Cambridge, Massachusetts. By 1971, however, drifters populated the University of Kansas in Lawrence and Isla Vista, a "youth ghetto" near the University of California, Santa Barbara. On the outskirts of campuses—Telegraph Avenue in Berkeley, Mifflin Street in Madison, Putnam Square near Harvard, and Morningside Heights in New York City—longhairs clad in beads, boots, headbands, tie-dyed shirts, and jeans hung around and utilized alternative institutions—crash pads, free clinics, and head shops. Young dropouts lived for the moment, wandering from campus to campus, selling underground newspapers and doing odd jobs, dealing dope, panhandling, and sleeping in dorm rooms. Universities furnished environments—concerts, libraries, lectures, and arty shops—that attracted alienated ex-students and nonstudents.[123]

Hippiedom had grown to epic proportions in the early 1970s. The countersociety, made up of disparate factions, movements, and individuals, diligently constructed the new society with its alternative institutions in cities and college towns across the nation. Within a few years, however, multiple factors combined to ensure the counterculture's decline.

5

In January 1972, Yippie Jerry Rubin looked forward to the year ahead, urging the rejuvenation of the movement and creation of an alternative culture. "This year is the year for everyone to come back and start again, to come together again, in new ways, to build our culture without male chauvinism, bad drugs and crazy freakouts. We should try to build our culture once more, only this time with more self-awareness and self-control. We need more public events, even a huge political Woodstock at the Republican National Convention next August." Rubin's exhortations represented the new direction of the counterculture. The aging Yippie sought not only to galvanize the movement but to alter the counterculture in particular into something different, to promote more demonstrations; excise harmful drugs, male supremacy, and chauvinism; and most importantly, to steer its energies into the political arena.[1]

The counterculture's forms and participants in its closing phase differed considerably from those in its early years. Fewer hippies with their strange dress, flowers, utopian aspirations inspired by LSD, and emphasis on peace and love made their presence felt. And fewer people discussed the merits or possibility of cultural revolution. Yet the broader counterculture carried on, exhibiting a conspicuous political bent. Thoroughly countercultural individuals, whose values and interests included dope and sexual liberation, meditation, yoga, art, organic food, alternative services, and rock festivals, became politically active, supporting various egalitarian and cultural liberation movements and reformist electoral politics. To be sure, cultural activists still agitated for dope legalization and built counterinstitutions. And some counterculture types of the purist persuasion refused to partake in activism. But many others resolved to effect lasting transformations in their lives and worlds through demonstrations and protest. This impulse manifested itself in efforts to elect George McGovern in the 1972 presidential contest, oust Richard Nixon after the Watergate revelations, and protest against the continuing—though deescalating—war in Vietnam. Others championed the women's movement, gay liberation, and the American Indian Movement. An upsurge in local activism coincided with the counterculture's growing politicization, as activists engaged in lettuce boycotts in support of farm workers, supported workers' strikes and rights, demonstrated against nuclear power, and attempted to prevent naval vessels from taking munitions onboard.

The counterculture, then, had undergone a profound transformation: it was nearly diametrically different in its approach from when it first began, advancing change in the political sphere rather than in the cultural realm. By 1974 most activists and freaks had hung up their alternative lifestyles after America withdrew from Vietnam, the draft ended, the economy stagnated, and the mainstream began to co-opt their values and styles. However, the counterculture's influence was immense and longlasting, leaving a different America in its wake.

RURAL COMMUNARDS STRUGGLE TO "LIVE THE REVOLUTION"

Rural counterculturalists continued to create the new society, find right livelihoods and economic sustainability, and "live the revolution." Tom Fels's memoir of communal life in Massachusetts, *Buying the Farm*, sheds light on these struggles. Principles and action often needed clarification. Typical questions revolved around work outside the community, monetary contributions, household chores, and retention of particular members. After their initial arrival, Fels and others worked to "regain the meager comforts we had renounced." Keeping warm in cold climates could be trying; so could keeping running water available, as pipes froze. Vehicle maintenance was challenging. Many communards had little knowledge of mechanical matters and service stations were miles away. What few clothes people had grew tattered, and they welcomed new threads from family members and mined thrift stores like the Salvation Army.[2]

Yet such challenges provided opportunities and avenues for ingenuity and new practices, ultimately facilitating new lived experiences. Communards spent significant time gathering, splitting, and sawing wood for wood stoves. Kerosene lamps replaced electricity for light. They reached out to more mechanically talented friends to help with their vehicles. The communalists discovered furniture at dumps adjacent to affluent towns, car parts at junkyards, and "treasures" at thrift shops. They spent their days cooking meals, shoveling snow, repairing the house, and mending clothes and furniture. Communal living also provided ample time for individual, intellectual, and communal activities. As Fels put it, "People talked to each other, learning more about who we really were. We meditated, thought, observed, and reflected. Cathy would do her bookbinding, Susan found time to paint. Writers would write, potters would pot, musicians would practice." Of course, "forays into the mind-altering substances much explored at the time" occupied members as well. A form of "collective emotion" emerged, as members got to know each other, solved problems, and shared their small world. They began to "think and act as one" to a considerable extent and enjoyed small tasks like fixing a vehicle, baking a pie, or cutting wood. And even though it sometimes posed problems, the residents reveled in their closeness to nature.[3]

Montague Farm's members had other experiences that formed the contours of a new, invented life. Their neighbors to the north at Packer Corners, who had more experience, offered instructive and valuable advice. Neighbors and friends proved instrumental in introducing maple syrup and honey to their diets, replacing sugar. Whole grains, granola, salads, fresh eggs, and dairy products became food staples. The women made a vital contribution by introducing organic farming, considered "fringe" at the time. This practice squared well with the communards' environmentalism, as it involved fewer chemicals, more recycling and composting, and companion planting. The turn to organic farming was significant for several reasons. Not only did it confirm the ability of Montague's inhabitants to make a decision and work together but it also represented the growing impact of the women's movement. Men treated women as equals and valued their contributions. And women had shown their potential as leaders. Because the commune depended on the land, its members came to see themselves as its stewards, protecting and honoring it. Their relationship to the land was reciprocal—what it produced hinged on how they treated it. Making peace with the land required work. The garden and cucumber patch had to be planted and tilled, and once the growing began, the members weeded, watered, and pruned the plants by hand. Crops that were not eaten were canned, frozen, dried, and stored. Other vegetables were brought to market. Ultimately, the denizens at Montague Farm found this labor-intensive life satisfying.[4] Communards, especially, lived environmentally friendly lifestyles. Some communes attempted to be as energy efficient as possible. Urban collectives in the Minneapolis area, for example, consumed natural gas "at a rate 40 percent below that for an average Minneapolis house of 900 square feet occupied by 2.6 people, electric power at a rate 82 percent below the Minneapolis average, and gasoline at a rate 36 percent below the national average." Other communes pioneered the use of nontraditional forms of energy. The Farm in Tennessee, for example, utilized solar power and other alternative energies.[5]

PROTESTING THE WAR

Eminently countercultural activists protested the dwindling Vietnam War and demonstrations contained countercultural elements. In late March 1972 hundreds of protestors gathered at the state capitol of Pennsylvania for Holy Week, a series of workshops, rallies, and liturgies. Ten thousand people appeared at a demonstration in support of the Harrisburg Seven the following week, on April 1, 1972. These seven alleged conspirators, including Reverend Philip Berrigan, were put on trial for planning to kidnap Henry Kissinger, among other offenses. At the demonstration, Bread and Puppet Theater presented "Mr. Bigman," a "giant Uncle Sam who 'eats the children of the world.'"[6]

On April 6, Nixon ordered the resumption of bombing in North Vietnam and on April 15, fighter-bombers and B-52s began striking Hanoi and Haiphong. These were the first attacks on the two cities since Johnson had halted the bombing in March 1968. The administration made it clear that no military targets in the north were off limits. Nixon provoked the nation's campuses, which had been considerably dormant since the Kent State shooting, into action. The National Student Association, affiliated with 515 campuses, set a date of April 21 for a strike. When the day came, most demonstrations occurred without incident. But others turned violent. Students at Princeton, Columbia, the University of Michigan, and Boston University seized or attacked buildings, while students at Stanford and the University of Maryland blocked highways.

National Peace Action Coalition (NPAC) coordinated Peace Action Day, which took place on April 22. People in Washington, Madison, Gainesville, San Francisco, and Los Angeles headed into the streets; myriad protests happened in scores of other locales, the result of local initiative. About fifty thousand marched in New York. A group called the Rhinestones performed John Lennon's "Give Peace a Chance." Members of Vietnam Veterans Against the War attended as well. Some demonstrators carried black balloons; others held signs: "Drop Nixon in Haiphong."

Protests occurred throughout the next month. On May 9, students from the University of California, Santa Barbara, impeded Highway 101 and demonstrators staged a "die-in" at Nixon's campaign headquarters in Los Angeles. Veteran Ron Kovic, wounded in Vietnam and paralyzed from the waist down, participated, lying on the sidewalk. "I'm opposed to the insanity of President Nixon's putting the whole world in jeopardy with his lies, his deceit and the continuing policy of genocide against the people of Vietnam," Kovic told a reporter. "Nixon speaks of honor. The most honorable thing Nixon can do is let the Vietnamese alone. Let them choose their own destiny." But after Nixon's "Christmas bombing" commenced in December, fewer people protested.[7]

"THE NEW POLITICS," GEORGE MCGOVERN, AND THE ADVENT OF THE ZIPPIES

Counterculturalists began to advocate electoral politics and liberal reform as avenues for change. The countercultural lifestyle, typically, though not always, went hand in hand with political liberalism, left-libertarianism and anarchism, and left-wing politics—even in the mid-to-late 1960s. In a survey of 1,005 members of the "Sixties Generation" conducted in 1977 and 1978—which included many activists and drug users—37 percent characterized their political stance in the 1960s as liberal. Even more, 43 percent, considered themselves radical. Only four percent called themselves conservative. Among drug users, 37 percent held liberal political views in the 1970s, another 27 percent remained radical, and only 2 percent were conservative. Respondents cited pollution, limitation of nuclear weapons, marijuana decriminalization, corporate power, and passage of the Equal Rights Amendment as the issues of most concern in the 1970s. In the early seventies those who became vegetarians, used dope and drugs, opposed the war and draft, dug rock festivals, built counterinstitutions and businesses, and lived in urban communes favored liberal or radical political causes, and if they voted at the national level, they likely cast their ballots for the Democratic Party.[8]

In 1972, antiwar activists, hippies, gays, people of color, feminists, and environmentalists—champions of the "new politics"—lined up behind Democratic presidential candidate George McGovern, a senator for South Dakota who, at one point, promised to end the war and bring the troops home in ninety days or less. Since the 1968 convention, women and minority delegates tripled and the number of delegates under the age of thirty increased tenfold. The movement had captured the Democratic Party. Increasingly thereafter, radical liberals ran for, and won, offices at the local, state, and national levels, almost invariably as Democrats. Cold War liberalism vanished.[9]

In the leadup to the election, the counterculture rallied to McGovern's side. In December 1971 Lennon performed at the John Sinclair Freedom Rally at the University of Michigan before an audience of fifteen thousand. His friendships and associations with radical activists like Sinclair, Rubin, Abbie Hoffman, and Bobby Seale troubled the government. The Nixon administration feared that Lennon might galvanize young voters against the president, and the Justice Department started deportation proceedings as a result. Hoffman and Rubin supported McGovern after he pledged to withdraw troops from Vietnam. Rubin viewed him as the "left-wing candidate" challenging the political establishment. Actors Warren Beatty and Shirley MacLaine organized a series of fundraising shows for the South Dakota senator. Numerous artists performed, including Simon and Garfunkel, Chicago, and Country Joe McDonald. On their 1972 tour,

Chicago wholeheartedly promoted McGovern's candidacy. People could register to vote and collect Democratic Party literature at the venues where they performed. The stage was so festooned with McGovern banners and propaganda, in fact, that members of the audience had difficulty seeing the performers. Bruce Barthol, former bassist of Country Joe and the Fish, wrote pro-McGovern songs for a theater company that featured actors from the San Francisco Mime Troupe. Neil Young and Graham Nash released a single, "War Song," to boost "a man [who] says he can put an end to the war," while opposing sinister forces that would "burn that jungle down and kill those Vietnamese."[10]

Hippies appeared in the headlines less in 1972. However, the Zippies— a breakaway faction of the Yippies led by Tom Forcade that considered Hoffman and Rubin old and irrelevant—organized political counterculture activities. In a leaflet, they claimed to have disrupted Democratic presidential candidate Ed Muskie in Wisconsin, released rats at the National Republican Women's Dinner in New York City, demonstrated at ABC in Chicago, demanding equal time for their candidate, "the Rock," and held free concerts in Tampa and Austin. The Zippies staged smoke-ins in New York City, Madison, Milwaukee, and Boulder as well. The organization planned a voter registration drive "to put a freek in office today," and a "spring plant-in" to grow marijuana. In addition, Zippies announced their simple, one-point program: "Unconditional surrender of the U.S. government. U.S. out of America now."[11]

In the summer, the counterculture descended on the Republican National Convention to protest the war, promote various causes, and confront the delegates. Unlike the 1968 Democratic Convention in Chicago, where few counterculturalists beyond Yippies had shown up, the disparate groups and individuals that constituted the countersociety—hippies, Zippies, Yippies, all-female guerrilla theater groups, Jesus Freaks, veterans, gays, environmentalists, pacifists, anarchists, and Maoists—arrived in Miami Beach, camping out in Flamingo Park. Some three thousand people eventually congregated there. Counterculturalists smoked pot, took speed, listened to rock bands, and disrobed freely. A few men found themselves socially ostracized after being caught staring intently at bare-breasted women who tried to stay cool in the sweltering heat. The Coconut Co-op and a local "Green Power" group distributed free food.

Women's Song Theater out of Atlanta performed skits condemning sexism, racism, and imperialism as interrelated social problems. Another women's theater group dressed as Vietnamese held disemboweled dolls. A preacher proclaimed, "Christ is coming," and Jesus People worked diligently to make converts. Even the rock bands showed a "great deal of political awareness." Gook, for example, played a show with the songs divided by themes: sexism and racism; war and imperialism; and "religion and bullshit." The Silent Majority attended as well. One man wrenched down an upside-down American flag so aggressively that he put a gash in his friend's forehead with the pole. The Zippies planned several events: a "piss-in," a flag burning, and a free marijuana rally complete with twenty-foot joint. Demonstrators put up a "vomitorium" tent where visitors could "throw up periodically to demonstrate the depth of their feelings toward President Nixon." Demonstrators executed a series of marches on the convention hall. Vietnam Veterans Against the War led one march; Zippies led another. Over a hundred Zippies raised a Vietcong flag at a local high school and declared the National Guard under arrest. A few guardsmen raised a clenched fist or waved a peace sign. On August 23, police arrested over a thousand protestors who tried to stop Republican delegates from entering the convention hall.[12]

While the countersociety met in Miami, freaks in Texas and the Southwest adopted an American Western style, wearing buckskin, leather boots, American Indian moccasins and beads, bandanas, and slouched leather and felt hats. "The cultural populism of hip white youth in the early 1970s," writes Doug Rossinow, "emphasized a rehabilitation of the cowboy figure and even of 'rednecks,' converting these distinctly male and, in the conventional liberal or leftist view, politically retrograde personae into countercultural heroes." Michael Martin Murphy, a club performer in Austin, Texas, wrote "Cosmic Cowboy," a song that fused cowboy culture with hippiedom. The Nitty Gritty Dirt Band later recorded the tune live and their version became the better-known of the two. In the song, the cosmic cowboy seeks to put his "little pony in over-drive" to "head out West" and yearns for "skinny dippin' and Lone Star [beer] sippin' and steel guitars."[13]

Austin, a relatively liberal university city, became the center of the progressive country music and hippie cowboy scene. An alternative social, cultural, and musical environment developed around a warehouse-turned-music-venue on Barton Springs Road, the Armadillo World Headquarters. Longhairs and progressive country musicians made the music hall their own. Opened in 1970 by hip entrepreneur Ed Wilson, Armadillo World Headquarters featured various kinds of music, from Muddy Waters and Howlin' Wolf to traditional country musicians and psychedelic acts like Vanilla Fudge. Progressive country musicians tended to be liberal pot smokers and closet rock and rollers who played loud and whose lyrics were considered taboo in establishment country music circles, pertaining to such topics as despair and drugs, and even homosexuality. Willie Nelson, a regular performer at the venue, epitomized the merging of country-western music with the hippie style. Nelson had long, braided hair and used pot recreationally. He brought hippies and rednecks of different cultures, politics, and classes together over music and beer.[14]

Oklahoma college students retreated to pastoral environments and communal living, seeking authenticity while reimaging certain traditions to carve out new lives. Tired of protesting the war and repression of free speech, and aware of the dangers posed by law enforcement and FBI, students and former activists transitioned to cultural retreat. Oklahoma's "prairie hippies," small in number, became targets for conservatives disturbed by their appearance, drug taking, and the jobs they took up. Conservative families disowned or booted their hippie sons and daughters, denouncing them as communists for their commitments to peace and racial harmony. Evangelical ministers, too, condemned counterculture types as communists when they diverged from "old-fashioned" Americanism. Yet the religion that prairie hippies professed blended the Bible, I Ching, and indigenous peyote practices. On the whole, it was informed by evangelicalism, working within a larger framework of Western Christianity.

One of the first counterculture events in Oklahoma occurred on Easter Sunday, April 6, 1969, along the banks of the South Canadian River. The gathering, which began the night before, culminated in a sunrise service led by Ray Eppler, recently ordained in the Universal Life Church. Local bands jammed, as freaks sat around bonfires, using marijuana and mescaline. Other hippies retreated to "the farm," east of Norman, to get away from it all. However, their urban counterparts remained dedicated activists. Oklahoma undergrounds *Home Cookin'* and the *Jones Family's Grandchildren* ran articles on women's liberation, gay rights, and the American Indian Movement (AIM). Counterculturalists, when not directly involved in these movements, followed them avidly in underground newssheets. *Home Cookin'* carried the *Oklahoma Gaily* as an insert for several months before the *Gaily* moved to independent publishing. A former student, Terry Allen, called the University of Oklahoma a "liberal oasis." Allen viewed the various movements of the early 1970s—civil rights, gay rights, women's rights, and AIM—as "all kind of the same thing."[15]

"THINK GLOBAL, ACT LOCAL"

In Austin, Norman, and elsewhere, activists focused less on national issues, pivoting to problems that affected their local communities. Demonstrators believed that they might make a significant impact on the world if they started confronting issues in their immediate surroundings; "Think Global, Act Local," became a widely shared sentiment. Activists struggled to further various causes—workers', women's, and prisoners' rights, police reform, gay liberation, nuclear disarmament, environmental activism, and AIM—at the local and state level. None of these causes were themselves inherently countercultural. Nevertheless, they commanded the attention and energies of quintessentially countercultural individuals, many of whom had resisted and demonstrated against the draft and Vietnam War.[16]

Underground newspapers solicited donations in the form of food, money, and letters, for workers on strike. Atlanta's *Great Speckled Bird* celebrated increased pay for members of the newly formed Mississippi Poultry Workers Union. The *Bird* also supported unionized construction workers striking against Georgia Power, and Black Steelworkers from American Cast Iron Pipe Company, which demonstrated against job discrimination and police brutality in Alabama. Furthermore, activists lobbied to protect workers from asbestos and corporate exploitation. Counterculturalists supported the United Farm Workers of America and lettuce growers' strikes. They championed fair wages, protection from lethal pesticides, an end to child labor, and decent living and working conditions. Longhairs lamented that fruit and vegetable pickers worked under "primitive conditions: no toilet facilities, limited drinking water, long hours, low piece-rate pay scales, no grievance procedures and no job security." Freaks lead local lettuce boycotts and secondary boycotts of stores such as Safeway. In East Lansing, Michigan, an underground urged its readers to boycott the local McDonald's. It condemned the franchise for its exploitation of high school workers, low wages, unhealthy food, and the mandate that male employees maintain short hair. Moreover, activists in Chicago and elsewhere backed efforts at police reform, combating systemic racism, corruption, civilian shootings, and police brutality.[17]

Advocates of liberal reform defended electoral politics, arguing that "marching around" and "do-nothing discussion groups" were as "bullshit" as voting and participation in the political system. Young voters supported liberal politicians knowing that their legislative efforts and successes would have a lasting impact on their communities. Liberal reformers backed increased welfare payments to families with dependent children, corporate taxes, daycare centers, lower consumer taxes, family planning, and unionization. Electoral politics affected issues that were of "crucial importance to THE PEOPLE"—the same people whom "bourgeois quasi-radicals constantly talk about serving." Defenders of liberal reform asked, "WOULDN'T LIBERAL RESPONSES BE A DAMN SIGHT BETTER THAN FASCIST REPRESSION?" Activists hoped that newly appointed judges would be sympathetic to the movement, that thoughtful people would be placed on the Board of Regents of universities, and that environmentally conscious people would ascend to important government posts. Others speculated that liberal judges might grant amnesty or pardons to political prisoners, draft resisters, and draft evaders. As the prospect of revolution seemed increasingly remote, electoral politics offered a promising avenue to promote needed changes. Yet reformers denied that they had become part of the liberal establishment; rather, they proclaimed, "We are revolutionaries, even at the ballot box."[18]

A self-described member of the counterculture urged others to see that politics and the world in which they lived were inescapable. "We cannot escape politics," wrote David Larry in the Eugene, Oregon, underground Augur. "There aren't any worlds apart." Politics did make a difference, he argued, especially at the local level. He chastised dropouts and those who called politics uncool and unhip. "If something is happening that you don't like and you do nothing to change it, then you have no right to complain. When you drop out of the process, you volunteer for the casualty count, you become a non-operative. And the only people who are glad to see that are those who see your vote as a threat." For Larry, politics and local elections presented an opportunity for effectual change and the improvement of lives.[19]

John Sinclair tempered his revolutionary rhetoric and zeal, becoming involved in local politics in Ann Arbor. "Young voters are going to take the power," he proclaimed in January 1972, "and we're gonna use it." Sinclair's Rainbow People's Party threw its weight behind the Human Rights Party in its April campaign. The Human Rights Party supported an end to the war, legalizing marijuana, eradicating racism and sexism, and greater oversight of the police by the community. Sinclair placed his faith in reform politics, believing elections could bear formidable results, making democracy a reality rather than an illusion. "There are more than 30,000 students and maybe 10,000 freaks in the city," he declared, "and we're gonna elect us some city officials who are gonna be responsive to the people's needs. We're gonna bring rock 'n' roll politics to this town, man, and we're gonna change things and make them work." The party's exertions proved successful, as Ann Arbor elected two members of the party to the city council.[20]

Others supported prisoners locked behind bars "under the fascist rule of the state." By 1970 prisons had become centers for a radical movement. Incarcerated Black Panthers and other African Americans came under the tutelage of those who had digested the writings of Frantz Fanon, Ho Chi Minh, Eldridge Cleaver, Malcolm X, and Che Guevara. In September 1971 more than a thousand prisoners at Attica Correctional Facility in New York engaged in an uprising, taking guards hostage and demanding improved prison conditions. Governor Nelson Rockefeller sent state police and the National Guard to retake the prison. The uprising ended with the deaths of twenty-nine prisoners and ten guards. In November, Lennon played a benefit concert for Attica prisoners at the Apollo Theater in New York City under the influence of Rubin. The following year, the former Beatle expressed his solidarity with the prisoners and blamed Governor Rockefeller for their deaths in the song "Attica State," a cut from his latest album.

Underground newspapers urged readers to send money for the defense of inmates involved in the uprising. Journalists hoped that the funds would thwart attempts by authorities to isolate "politically conscious" convicts from the rest of the prison population. For many movement activists, Attica represented state violence directed at oppressed minorities. "It's clear that the spirit of freedom is infectious and that the rebellious spirit of Attica will spread rather than be contained," proclaimed the *Seed* in Chicago. It was not to be, as the uprising disappeared from public memory within a few years. Other counterculturalists attacked the prison system. In 1973, Timothy Leary called for the closing of all California prisons. Leary and Political Reform Organization for Better Education (PROBE) brought a federal class action lawsuit against the California penal system on the grounds that prisons violated the civil rights of Leary and others.[21]

Underground papers carried stories supporting abortion rights. Even before women's liberation materialized, activists pushed for abortion reform throughout the sixties. They included male doctors and lawyers as well as welfare rights groups and champions of population control. Little progress was made until groups such as the National Organization for Women and the National Association for the Repeal of Abortion Laws organized, agitated, and rallied against criminalized abortion. At "abortion speakouts" in New York and elsewhere, women discussed the risky and illegal circumstances under which they had sought and undergone abortions. Eleven states passed liberalized abortion laws by the early 1970s; however, women remained hemmed in by hospitals and medical professionals. Doctors in California subjected a woman to two psychiatric evaluations that deemed her unfit for motherhood before the abortion could proceed. Feminists rejected the "reform" approach and called for the repeal of all laws limiting abortion rights. Activists testified before the New York legislature. They distributed blank sheets of paper representing their preferred abortion law. Female columnists in undergrounds emphasized a woman's right to choose and autonomy over their bodies. "What we are trying to tell you doctors, lawyers, husbands, judges and boyfriends, is that no one has more right to control our bodies than we do, and we will do what we have to to win back the legal rights to that control," declared Maralee in the *Seed*. "Our bodies, our lives, our right to decide!" On

January 22, 1973, the Supreme Court rendered its decision in *Roe v. Wade*, decriminalizing abortion based on the constitutional right to privacy.[22]

AMERICAN INDIAN MOVEMENT

Counterculturalists supported American Indian rights. After centuries of oppression, Indians formed a movement of their own. Inspired by African Americans' advocacy of Black Power, thousands of Native Americans demanded "Red Power" in an effort to secure their basic civil rights. Activists founded the American Indian Movement in 1968, organizing protests and engaging in civil disobedience. Dennis Banks, Russell Means, and Leonard Peltier became the movement's most militant figures.

Counterculturalists were among Red Power's earliest allies. Sherry L. Smith persuasively argues that from the early 1960s fish-ins in Washington state through AIM's occupation of Wounded Knee, "counterculture and other non-Indians enthusiastically applauded and actively supported Indian demands for radical change regarding their place and power in America." Hippies and New Leftists seeking authenticity witnessed Native American Church ceremonies and traveled to Indian reservations. Activists supported native treaty rights, cultural revivals, and tribal sovereignty. Although hippies formed some alliances with reservation leaders, they forged most of their connections with American Indian communities and organizations in cities such as San Francisco, Seattle, Denver, and Minneapolis, and on college campuses. Underground newspapers like the *Berkeley Barb* carried articles publicizing the Indian struggle for autonomy. While some Indians opposed hippie interest in Native Americans—folk singer Buffy Sainte-Marie declared, "They'll never be Indians"—others, including Sun Bear, remarked, "More power to them. I feel that this is the start of something, that if people can come together and help each other to survive and improve things on this basis, then perhaps we are getting somewhere."[23]

In November 1969, members of AIM and six hundred Indians seized Alcatraz Island in San Francisco Bay. The occupiers fended off the federal government for over a year. They argued that they should be allowed to keep the island, as the federal prison there had been closed since 1963. AIM intended to establish an Indian university, cultural center, and museum.

CHANGING THE WORLD | 263

President Nixon sent federal marshals and the FBI to evict the activists in June 1971 without meeting their demands. AIM did succeed, however, in bringing national attention to the terrible conditions that Indians faced.

Counterculturalists rallied behind the occupation. Peter Bowen and Brookes Townes—two young antiestablishment-types who opposed the Vietnam War and sought to usher in a "dream" that included communal living and free love—ferried ninety Indians to the island under cover of darkness. Over the next nine days, Townes transported hundreds more Indian activists to Alcatraz. The Sausalito hippie houseboat community circumvented a coast guard blockade, delivering food and water to the occupiers. A headline in the *Berkeley Tribe* proclaimed, "Americans Recover the Rock" and its office collected items—clothes, firewood, blankets, food, and toilet paper—to sustain the activists. Rock group Creedence Clearwater Revival contributed $10,000, some of which bought an additional boat.[24]

A year after being ousted from Alcatraz, AIM fomented more activism. Hundreds of Indian protestors drove in a caravan to Washington, DC, right before the 1972 election. They called the planned march the "Trail of Broken Treaties." But politicians refused to meet with them. In response, AIM and other Indian organizations seized the Bureau of Indian Affairs. They issued a statement of twenty demands. The proclamation insisted that the federal government restore 110 million acres to the Indians, honor all treaties, restore civil rights, and relinquish control of all Indian affairs. The occupiers destroyed artwork, furniture, and papers, and fought police. Counterculturalists rallied to the cause when Wavy Gravy and the Hog Farmers arrived to support the occupiers.[25]

In February 1973, approximately three hundred members of AIM took over Wounded Knee, South Dakota, taking eleven hostages and barricading a church. The militants made several demands, calling for the immediate improvement of conditions on reservations, sovereignty over their own affairs, and government recognition of independent Indian nations. For seven weeks, the siege continued, with shots fired on occasion. The *New York City Star* argued that, whatever happened at Wounded Knee, it represented the "greatest spiritual revival among Native Americans since the Ghost Dance." *Breakdown*, in Klamath Falls, Oregon, publicized the siege, asking its readers to provide money, food, and medical supplies for the resistance movement. "Our first Americans have been largely neglected, exploited, and lied to," proclaimed *Caravan* in Sarasota, Florida. "Treaties supposedly protecting their rights haven't been worth the paper they have been written on." On March 9, 1973, students at the University of California held a "U.S. Hands Off Wounded Knee!" rally in Sproul Plaza. The Allman Brothers, Alice Cooper, the Band, and the Grateful Dead organized a committee to raise money for the occupiers. Eventually, the Nixon administration would meet many of AIM's demands, including Indian self-rule. In 1975, Congress passed the Indian Self-Determination and Education Act.[26]

While American Indians channeled the counterculture's interest in Native American culture into constructive activism, Philip Deloria argues that young people in the 1960s and 1970s "played Indian" in an effort to "find meaningful identities in a world seemingly out of control." "Playing Indian" allowed "counterculturalists to have their cake and to eat it." Communalists symbolically embraced Indianness, but rarely engaged with Indian communities. When the two parties did connect, both came away largely dissatisfied. Communards were surprised by the social restrictiveness of Indian reservations, and native people grew tired of setting hippies straight with regard to their culture. Hippies, who valued "Indian Otherness and its assorted meanings," busily erected tipis and wore buckskins, yet most were uninterested in learning anything about social order or individualism from real natives. The antiwar movement also likened itself to Indian resistance of the nineteenth century. Mitchell Goodman asserted that youth were a "primitive tribe." Playing Indian, then, allowed young demonstrators to "become vicariously a victim of United States imperialism" as they faced down the military in the streets. Appropriating an Indian persona, Deloria contends, "had as much to do with individual expression and fashion as it did with social change." While this behavior warrants scrutiny and perhaps criticism—even scorn—the counterculture, on the whole, as Smith has convincingly shown, readily supported the American Indian Movement.[27]

Counterculturalists fixated on presidential politics when Nixon became embroiled in a series of scandals—Watergate. Five of Nixon's "plumbers" had been arrested after they attempted to break into the Democratic National Committee's headquarters at the Watergate office complex in Washington. Nixon ordered a coverup of the incident. Among other abuses of power, Nixon had directed the IRS and Justice Department to punish his foes and used counterintelligence operations against domestic dissidents. Freaks raged against Nixon, identifying his attacks on freedom of the press, usurpation of the powers of Congress, and the transformation of grand juries into instruments of political surveillance, as causes for concern. "The President must be impeached," declared the Memphis underground *Head Lines*. "He intends to function above the law. Our Bill of Rights is seriously threatened. . . . If allowed to go unchecked by the American people, Nixon and other future presidents can seriously, perhaps even totally, deprive the American people of their civil liberties." For activists and freaks alike, the president's power needed to be blunted (and he ultimately needed to be removed from office) so that citizens' liberties would endure. Moreover, Nixon might set a dangerous precedent for his successors. [28]

"MAY DAZE," YIPPIE ACTIVITY, WILLIE NELSON'S PICNIC, AND WATKINS GLEN

Despite the discomfiting news from Washington, the counterculture continued to revel at events strikingly similar to the be-ins of the late 1960s. In April 1973 contributors to the East Lansing, Michigan, underground *Joint Issue* announced May Daze, a gathering to "celebrate the coming of spring, life, and all people all over the world." Like the iconic be-ins before, little was planned or coordinated. The objective was to have fun, create an instant community, and celebrate togetherness. May Daze had "no organizing committee, no group sponsors," and "no real leadership." The promoters stressed that they strived for "no authority or main focus," which allowed "the people in the park to construct the atmosphere necessary for all to laugh and sing, dance and play, or simply talk and be together." In contrast to earlier be-ins, however, these gatherings encouraged the integration of politics and culture, hippies and New Leftists— a testament to the growth of a unified countersociety. *Joint Issue* invited political groups to set up information booths to provide opportunities to "get involved." Yet the paper emphasized that politics constituted only part of the celebration, encouraging craftspeople and artisans to display their work, and musicians and bands to perform. May Daze "did not want to leave anyone out."[29]

On May 4, the Yippies released a press statement boasting about the organization's latest activities. The Yippies continued to engage in cultural activism, agitating for an end to unjust dope laws. Although authorities denied it, 900 people had recently smoked pot in Central Park in Boulder, Colorado. In Iowa City, 350 gathered at the old state capitol to smoke and be entertained by "Reefer Man," who wore red tights and ran around with a big R embroidered on his shirt. Cops busted one of the smoke-in's organizers, who sat in a local jail for promoting the event. Elsewhere, a mini riot allegedly occurred in Lafayette, Indiana, when police tried to arrest two fifty-year-old women for lighting up. In Columbus, Cleveland, Hartford, and Atlanta, the "hairy hordes" demanded "freedom for all Prisoners of Weed (P.O.W.'s)" and spread word of the impending "July 4th Impeach-Nixon March."[30]

Like the Yippies, other activists entered the political arena with their efforts to legalize marijuana. They pointed to studies showing that marijuana was not addictive, and that its use did not lead to harder drugs like heroin, or cause crime. Activists bemoaned severe penalties for possession. In Alabama and Minnesota, the first conviction for marijuana use carried a prison sentence of up to twenty years. The hip also decried the fact that a judge had sentenced a young civil rights activist, Lee Otis Johnson, to thirty years in prison for giving marijuana joints to an undercover agent. "It seems to us that people smoking dope should be left alone in the privacy of their own home unless they're a clear and present danger to the public," editorialized the Saint Louis New Times. The Times reminded the reader that the Fourth Amendment right to privacy was gained through a violent revolution—the American Revolution. The paper's writers did not want to "fight for the right to tell everybody what to do," but rather "fight for our right to NOT be told what to do."[31]

On July 4 more than a thousand Yippies and their supporters held an all-day smoke-in on the National Mall in Washington. As a rock band played, Yippies distributed hundreds of joints, which were smoked openly. Police made no arrests. More than five hundred people high on marijuana marched on the capitol and demanded the legalization of pot and impeachment of President Nixon. For activists, Nixon's egregious transgressions made dope smoking seem inconsequential. "Pot law violations are not as destructive as some of the violations of law in the White House since Watergate," commented organizer Mike Chance. At the capitol, longhairs played in an ornamental pool, while others dismembered a Nixon mannequin.[32]

At the same time, freaks mingled with rednecks at Nelson's Fourth of July Picnic in Dripping Springs, Texas. Nelson chose to host a gathering where progressive country music fans could hear, in a safe environment, the latest sounds emanating from Austin. He hoped to capitalize on progressive country's growing commercial potential as well. Approximately twenty-five thousand fans and partygoers came to the show. The picnic elicited a Woodstock-like feel, as cars sat in a massive traffic jam outside the grounds and festivalgoers had to walk the last few miles. Many of the best-known progressive country artists performed: Nelson, Waylon Jennings, Kris Kristofferson, Billy Joe Shaver, and John Prine. Cosmic cowboys and cowgirls openly smoked pot and pot-bellied sheriffs gazed at scantily dressed women.[33]

The counterculture's last major outdoor festival unfolded on August 4, 1973. The Watkins Glen Summer Jam, held on a single day in New York, surpassed Woodstock's attendance: six hundred thousand youth from across the nation came to hear three bands—the Grateful Dead, the Band, and the Allman Brothers. Cars jammed the two-lane highways leading to the festival grounds and some people had to walk twenty miles to get to the site. The festival's promoters had planned well; the crowds enjoyed plenty of food, water, and portable toilets. Bathers swam in local ponds and both men and women strolled the grounds naked. Few people required medical evacuations. Festivalgoers talked of peace and love, flashed the peace sign, and imbibed booze, beer, and quaaludes in addition to marijuana. Campers named wooded areas "Hippie Highway" and "Big Pink."[34] Some saw the festival as an indication of the counterculture's rejuvenation. "It's a return to Woodstock Nation," commented Bill Graham's West Coast publicist. "This country is turning around. Look at Watergate. Look at Watkins Glen. The hippies are once again winning."[35]

The festival, however, was not a return to Woodstock Nation but a mass pilgrimage to find it and feel part of it once again. The Summer Jam, *Time*

reported, "seemed somehow an atavism, more a class reunion than a happening, a nostalgic spectacle of youth in search of its youth." The Jam's
participants were mostly the younger brothers and sisters of the people
who had been at Woodstock. Despite the comparisons, the Summer Jam
was not like the mythologized festival at Max Yasgur's farm four years
earlier. Although Woodstock had contained little overt political activity,
it had effectively *symbolized* the youth culture's opposition to Vietnam and
represented a challenge to the establishment. Conversely, Watkins Glen
"was positively somnolent," according to one attendee. "It lacked political overtones. It possessed little countercultural vitality." "So, what does
it Really All Mean?" asked the *New York Times*. "Not much, this time. The
social significance, I think, was left behind 160 miles to the east at the
1969 Woodstock festival. This time the kids just came to have fun, a great
big stoned celebration in the world's largest outdoor singles' bar."[36]

THE COUNTERCULTURE, FEMINISM, AND GAY LIBERATION

Meanwhile, freaks championed the women's movement. The *Los Angeles
Weekly News*, launched by the staff and journalists of the *Los Angeles Free
Press*, promoted a "Women's Culture celebration" that unfolded at Ran-
cho Park on August 26, 1973, the fifty-third anniversary of the passage of
the Nineteenth Amendment, which granted women suffrage. Columnist
Mary Harper drew readers' attention to the "Great Guts Awards Presen-
tation," which honored women who had voted in 1920 as well as those
who reported sex discrimination to the Equal Employment Opportunity
Commission (EEOC) in 1973. Others nominated for awards included
singer Helen Reddy, tennis star Billie Jean King, deceased lesbian author
Radclyffe Hall, and Vietnamese Women Against the War. Hundreds of
Los Angeles feminists planned numerous activities: theater presenta-
tions, feminist press displays, art shows, and a workshop on self-defense.
The Feminist Women's Health Center put together a slide show and ex-
hibits on women's health care.[37]

Feminists exerted greater influence on the counterculture. Max Scherr,
publisher of the *Berkeley Barb*, announced in August 1973 that his paper

would no longer accept sex ads, a major reversal for the newssheet. The *Barb* stressed that sexualized ads reduced people to mere things. In a two-thousand-word statement, the paper declared that it would "no longer allow its advertising to demean or degrade any human being or to suggest that any person is an object." In part, Scherr arrived at his decision as "a matter of conscience." His friends had been critical of the paper's reliance on sex ads. Although he maintained that his original decision to include the ads was indeed correct—striking a blow against censors and opponents of press freedoms—he acknowledged that "times have changed," and that the ads had become "lucidly repulsive" and exploitive. In the end, however, the sex-oriented advertising continued for another five years. In July 1980 the *Barb* folded for good.[38]

Male freaks and activists became receptive to both gay and women's liberation and ultimately supported both movements. Men at Michigan State University founded the Male Role Workshop to discuss men's issues—and how men related to feminism—in a rapidly changing society. The group held "rap sessions" and engaged in activism. The Male Role Workshop urged men with "varied experiences and differing philosophies to meet" in order to "explore each other's common concerns." Some feminists criticized profeminist men's consciousness-raising groups for equating women's oppression at the hands of the patriarchy with men's "oppression." Nevertheless, a series of workshops and sessions organized by the group highlighted how the changing culture applied to and affected men. One workshop titled "A Dialogue between Men and Women" examined "points of conflict" in the "battle of the sexes" and aimed to "achieve greater mutual understanding" between men and women. The staff of the East Lansing Women's Center led another discussion titled "Men and the Women's Movement," in which they presented the feminist perspective on men's roles within society and women's struggle for equality. Yet another seminar focused on systemic sexism in the military, economy, and government. Finally, members of the gay liberation movement addressed the "homosexual taboo," and the ways in which "fear of homosexuality limits and distorts men's everyday behavior." Thoroughly countercultural rock bands and artists supported gay rights as well. Pink Floyd headlined a benefit concert for the Gay Liberation Front in April 1971, and David Bowie did the same in October of that year.[39]

COMMUNAL ACTIVISM

Some back-to-the-land communards, like their countercultural peers in the cities, increasingly turned to political activism. In the case of Montague Farm in Massachusetts, the impending construction of twin nuclear reactors near the farm galvanized former members of Liberation News Service to reconnect with their political activism, which had gone dormant. Sam Lovejoy rose to prominence in the mid-1970s antinuclear movement, which became one of the foremost grassroots endeavors of radicalized liberals in the post-Vietnam era. The antinuclear movement revived nonviolent civil disobedience tactics, the likes of which had not been seen since the early 1960s. Not only did Montague Farm assume the vanguard in opposing the multibillion-dollar nuclear industry, it took the lead in advancing energy alternatives such as solar power as well. In keeping with the currents of the times, Montague Farm stressed that local organizations should drive the fight against nuclear power in their communities. The collective succeeded in uniting forces from across the political spectrum.[40]

Northeast Utilities announced in December 1973 that Montague would be home to a new nuclear power station. Lovejoy opposed its construction on the grounds that it posed dangers to the public health. Moreover, he decried corporations' and governments' prizing profits over the well-being and autonomy of the community. Montague Farm and other local communes formed Nuclear Objectors for a Pure Environment and Franklin County Alternative Energy Coalition to rally the community and against Northeast Utilities. The communards employed a film, *Lovejoy's Nuclear War*, as an organizing tool. After a protracted struggle, the power station was never built.[41]

Lovejoy, Harvey Wasserman, and Charles Light continued their antinuclear activism, which culminated in a concert series by Musicians United for Safe Energy at Madison Square Garden in 1979. Over five days, September 19–23, more than ninety thousand fans watched performances by Jackson Browne, James Taylor, Graham Nash, and Tom Petty and the Heartbreakers. Bruce Springsteen headlined the event. Hoffman referred to the shows as "the most significant cultural/political event since Woodstock."[42]

Another commune, Movement for a New Society (MNS), became involved in political protest. Made up largely by Quakers and centered in Philadelphia, MNS was founded in 1971. Eventually, additional intentional communities with the same name appeared in Minneapolis, Ann Arbor, Madison, Denver, Eugene, Seattle, and Durango, Colorado. Communards debated whether MNS could best be characterized as decentralized socialism or communitarian anarchism. Whatever its nature, its central objective was clear: "We believe in taking charge of our own lives and starting to *live the revolution now*, creating new institutions alongside the old, developing new forms of human relationships." MNS's social activism focused on a broad range of issues ranging from feminism, gay liberation, ecology, war, and neighborhood organizing to nuclear power and world militarism. Members moved from house to house depending on their interests and the emphasis of the individual collective. MNS engaged in nonviolent direct action. In July 1971 activists in canoes and kayaks attempted to prevent the docking of a Pakistani ship, which was picking up military supplies, in Baltimore harbor. The coast guard defeated the small armada and its members were thrown in jail. MNS wanted to prevent the authoritarian Pakistani military government from suppressing political adversaries in East Pakistan. Likewise, in April 1972, with the assistance of Vietnam Veterans Against the War, MNS tried to block the USS Nitro from taking on munitions. The ship was to sail for the Gulf of Tonkin. Again, authorities successfully thwarted MNS's endeavor. Five sailors on the Nitro, however, defected from their command and tried to join MNS on its canoes. In March 1973 MNS mobilized to assist the American Indian Movement at Wounded Knee. Members from collectives in Madison, Minneapolis, Milwaukee, Des Moines, Denver, Portland, and Philadelphia drove to the South Dakota site and positioned themselves between AIM and authorities, before the government ousted them. Years later, MNS organized protests against nuclear power after the disaster at Three Mile Island in 1979.[43]

The environmental activists who formed Greenpeace assailed nuclear power as well. In the early 1970s, American peace activists and draft evaders coalesced with Canadian counterculturalists in Vancouver. Among them was journalist Bob Hunter, who enjoyed chain-smoking, dropping acid, and reading the I Ching. These hip expatriates and their Canadian comrades formed the Don't Make a Wave Committee (DMWC) after learning of the US military's plan to explode a nuclear bomb on Amchitka, a small island in the North Pacific. The activists believed that the nuclear testing could result in an ecological catastrophe. Accordingly, in 1971, they boarded an aging halibut seiner, the *Greenpeace*, and headed for Amchitka to protest, but never reached their destination. Nevertheless, an environmental organization that would eventually have an international reach was born in 1972 when DMWC changed its name to the Greenpeace Foundation. In the ensuing years, Greenpeace marshaled its direct action protests against Japanese and Soviet whaling and French nuclear testing in the South Pacific.[44]

THE COUNTERCULTURE'S DECLINE

Despite its continuing activism and alternative institution building, the counterculture was fading. "Kids still come to Haight Street," reported the *New York Times*. "Usually broke, carrying their meager belongings in dusty knapsacks, dressed in patchwork clothes, they seem like the last stragglers of a retreating army as they search for what is left of the free and easy street life." Gregg Kilday of the *Los Angeles Times* speculated as to why the counterculture lost momentum: "The kids turned on now in grade school. Dope was cool. Sex was easy. Rock no longer threatened. No one was marching anymore."[45]

The commercialization of the counterculture facilitated its collapse: as it was subsumed into mass consumer culture, it ceased to be counter. Ultimately, capitalism could withstand and absorb cultural revolution, as it was so easily marketable. Mainstream and big businesses capitalized on the counterculture successfully. Pepsi ran a psychedelic advertisement featuring a flashing strobe light and a woman with a fluorescent flower painted on her face dancing to a rock band. AT&T used the slogan "The Times, They Are A-Changin'," a car company proclaimed the "Dodge Rebellion," and a Columbia Records advertisement featured the line, "If you won't listen to your parents, the Man, or the establishment, why should you listen to us?"[46]

The counterculture also entered the mainstream through film and theater. *Hair: The American Tribal Love Rock Musical*, sold $20 million worth of tickets. A critic called *Hair* "the youth culture Disneyfied, freaks with little white gloves." It went mainstream on Broadway. On stage, actors and actresses appeared in the nude. The performers took off their clothes in *Oh! Calcutta!* as well, which accumulated big profits. The counterculture, too, began to dominate the movies. A series of expensive films performed poorly at the box office, while low-budget films did well. Peter Fonda made *Easy Rider* for half a million dollars, yet the film grossed many times that amount. Fonda's film celebrated the countercultural lifestyle and values—dope, sex, physical mobility, brotherhood, freedom, and communal living—although at the end of the film the bikers are murdered by bigoted rednecks. *The Graduate* and *Bonnie and Clyde* also became huge box office smashes with countercultural themes. In *The Graduate*, Benjamin Braddock, played by Dustin Hoffman, is an alienated middle-class youth seeking to escape the artificiality of suburban life and a boring career—especially one in "plastics." *Bonnie and Clyde* pitted two rebellious nonconformists against greedy, selfish, manipulative lawmen and bankers.[47]

Rock capitalists co-opted the counterculture's language and marketed the counterculture back to youth. "The grown-ups are having the last laugh," opined *Ramparts*. "Rock and roll is a lovely playground, and within it kids have more power than they have anywhere else in society, but the playground's walls are carefully maintained and guarded by the corporate elite that set it up in the first place." Rock had been a commercial enterprise from the beginning, an "American creation on the level of the hamburger or the billboard." Record companies started capitalizing on antiestablishment fervor in the late sixties. CBS promoted some of its artists as "The Revolutionaries" as early as 1968. A Columbia advertisement featured the slogan "THE MAN CAN'T BUST OUR MUSIC." The car company Opel promised that their new cars could "light your fire!," a reference to the Doors song, and Jefferson Airplane performed radio commercials boosting white Levi's jeans.[48]

By 1973, rock had become big business. It raked in $2 billion a year—about the same amount that the sports and film industries made combined. Corporate rock made huge sales overseas, too, grossing over $500 million in Japan, $450 million in West Germany, and over $440 million in the Soviet Union. And rock stars were awash in cash. *Forbes* estimated that at least fifty artists earned between $2 million and $6 million per year.

The music industry became a solid investment for Wall Street. Large music companies took over smaller ones. Huge nonmusic conglomerates bought properties in the music business. The industry became concentrated in a few companies. The top four record corporations sold over half of all records and tapes. Nearly 40 percent of the sales belonged to two companies alone, Warner Communications and CBS.[49]

The rock press, like rock and roll itself, became big business. Many counterculturalists denounced *Rolling Stone* as a capitalist scam, but Jann Wenner, the magazine's founder, did not waver. By 1971 he had fully embraced the term "capitalist." *Rolling Stone*'s Third Street office cost $7,000 a month to rent. In 1972 *Rolling Stone* covered the McGovern-Nixon race, not radical politics. For Wenner, a solid economic footing for the magazine was more important than the political and cultural scene surrounding the music he loved. "As long as there are bills to pay, writers who want to earn a living by their craft, people who pay for their groceries, want to raise children and have their own homes," he wrote in an editorial, "*Rolling Stone* will be a capitalistic operation."[50]

Mainstream Americans increasingly adopted the counterculture's style and values and the more mainstream the counterculture became, the less counter it was. Businessmen smoked dope, suburbanites engaged in "swinging" and "wife swapping" and called it sexual revolution, and truckers and police grew long hair and sideburns. Marijuana use became especially widespread. Jim Conklin, a former marine and Vietnam veteran, joined Nixon's war on drugs in the early 1970s, working for the Bureau of Narcotics and Dangerous Drugs (BNDD) in New York City. "It was an unusual time," he recalled. "When I came on with BNDD it was a time when drugs were used by everybody, all the common people, all my friends from New York, the guys I knew in college. You'd go to a party in New York City, everybody would be using drugs." Adults and mainstream youth wore casual and hippie-like clothing and buttons sporting messages. Older, straight Americans began questioning government policy and participating in demonstrations and some considered adopting new values. Hoffman and Andy Warhol became household names and chains of hip clothing stores materialized and flourished. As early as 1972, an observer noted:

All sorts of people suddenly appeared as other than they were: stock-brokers dressed as if for an African safari; sociologists came as greas-ers, motorcycle dropouts; English professors looked like stevedores; businessmen like circus trainers; accountants like Jesse James; grand-mothers were in pants suits, young girls in granny dresses. Others came disguised as farmers, housepainters, telephone linesmen, American In-dians, Gypsies, Pancho Villa gunmen, or people from old photographs. Who was giving the masquerade, where was the costume party?[51]

Many of the counterculture's sexual ethics, at one time novel—even radical—went mainstream, progressively adopted by younger and older Americans alike. In the 1970s sex outside marriage became commonplace. The divorce rate rose. So did the number of couples cohabiting. Moreover, the belief in sex's centrality to one's individual happiness gained ascen-dance. Adolescents understood that unmarried people had sex and they did the same when they grew older. Sex permeated the culture—it seemed to be everywhere—and Americans discussed it more openly than they had in the past. And they eagerly consumed sexualized materials. Books like *The Joy of Sex*, the *Hite Report* on female sexuality, and *Everything You Always Wanted to Know about Sex* climbed the best-seller lists. Pornography and eroticism proliferated in public places like Times Square in New York. Born-again Christian Jimmy Carter divulged to *Playboy*, "I've committed adultery in my heart many times." When the 1980s dawned, advice colum-nists like Ann Landers fielded and answered questions pertaining to sex in a forthright manner.[52]

Many young people did not commit to living the hippie lifestyle for any prolonged period. Although some recreational and weekend hippies had existed from the beginning, their numbers soared exponentially in the mid-1970s. These individuals—many of whom possessed ample eco-nomic means—could, and did, fade back into the mainstream whenever they wanted. "A $200 round-trip ticket to London lets you be a part-time dropout," commented a Cornell teaching assistant. "You can go on the bum for the summer and still be back in time for classes. You can live a counterculture life-style and not really mean it at all. It's like they say, 'Scratch a hippie and you'll find a Porsche.'"[53]

The counterculture became, for more and more young people, a fashion statement and a fad—long hair, bell-bottoms, dope and drugs, easy sex. These individuals did not adhere to authentic hippie values, but went in search of a good time, a big party, another Woodstock. They eroded hippiedom, for the counterculture always entailed more than a style, more than long hair, dope, free love, and three-day rock festivals. "You can't find God in a stained-glass window, or buy 'hip-ness' in a head shop," a New Jersey hippie admonished his "brothers and sisters." "Woodstock is not a place; it's a state of mind, a frame of reference, and most importantly, an attitude. It is not composed of things, or even people so much as the way those people treat each other. The more we tell ourselves that we can recreate it at the drop of a joint, the more it is going to stay hidden in the woods in which we try to find it. You don't find it in the hills, you bring it there." By 1974, fewer hip youth agreed.[54]

Communes deteriorated and came apart. Noncontributing individuals overran communities with an open-door policy, overwhelming hardworking idealists. Vandals and thieves caused communes to crumble despite attempts by veterans to keep them afloat. Internal conflicts resulted in failures. Some people never adjusted to living in close quarters among others. Character flaws, large and small, disrupted harmonious living and brought communities down. Sometimes these social experiments failed to withstand the departure of a single leader or that leader singlehandedly closed the commune. In some cases, once-devout followers rejected the founder or charismatic guru; in others, members left one by one until communes disintegrated. Many found themselves evicted from rented premises, and in some cases outside pressure from authorities caused communities to fold.[55]

American involvement in Vietnam ended. On January 27, 1973, North Vietnam and the United States signed a truce. The North Vietnamese agreed to release all prisoners of war; in return, America arranged to pull its troops out of South Vietnam within sixty days. By spring the war was over. The conflict that many kids saw as obscene, brutal, and immoral no longer disillusioned them. Furthermore, an all-volunteer military replaced the draft, which had hung ominously over the heads of baby boomer men and boys. Two central alienating issues responsible for the counterculture's existence and expansion, then, no longer harried America's youth.

Unprecedented postwar prosperity and economic expansion came to an end. Astronomical military spending caused deficits, which weakened the dollar and led to inflation rates of 4.5 percent in 1971. Nixon imposed wage and price controls in an effort to slow rising inflation. When the president removed these measures, inflation skyrocketed to an unprecedented 8 percent, rising to nearly 10 percent by the end of 1973. After the Yom Kippur War the Organization of the Petroleum Exporting Countries (OPEC) enacted an oil embargo, cutting oil production by 25 percent, which amounted to a 10 percent cut in the world's oil supply. Cars waited in long lines at gas stations as motorists feared running out of fuel. In addition to the embargo, OPEC raised oil prices markedly. Gas prices almost doubled and home heating fuel prices shot up by as much as 33 percent. America experienced its worst economic downturn since the Great Depression. Industrial productivity stagnated, real income fell, and the standard of living dropped. Under these circumstances, it became more difficult to live on society's margins. Baby boomers searched for jobs at a time when rent rates, the cost of goods, and unemployment were rising. Moreover, the sixties generation was aging. Many hip people decided to settle down, marry, attain stable jobs, raise families, and put away money for retirement.

An underground writer in Lincoln, Nebraska, recognized and lamented the movement's loss of momentum. He acknowledged that many youths seemed to be abandoning the revolution and the creation of a new, better world. Former counterculturalists and activists grasped for security rather than continue the struggle. The social structures they had once rebelled against now provided aging hippies with definition and a sense of self:

Now is the time for people to continue on with this revolution. A time to build anew our relationships using all the creativeness and wisdom we can put forth. . . . Somehow this momentum of change has greatly decreased in the last couple of years. At a time when there is a need for even greater energy and courage . . . to create a new and more livable world, we have lost heart and do not continue forward. It is as if people who once chafed against the roles and patterns of society now have not the strength and courage to go on without these patterns to stand on for security and identity.[56]

The counterculture, though on the decline, would have enormous consequences. What began as an isolated phenomenon limited to the coasts and large universities involving tens of thousands of cultural rebels in 1965 had evolved into a massive countersociety of millions in the 1970s. In 1968, the Beatles had declared, "We all want to change the world," and many freaks had strived to do just that. Hippies and other cultural insurgents failed to replace the dominant society with a new one. Yet, in the final analysis, the counterculture had bequeathed a powerful legacy—it transformed America.

Who won the uncivil wars of the Sixties? Conservatives won the political battle, while liberals triumphed on the cultural front. No one won the wars. In fact, Americans are still fighting those uncivil wars today. The Sixties, and the counterculture, have cast a long shadow over the nation's politics. Liberals generally see the 1960s as a good decade, a time of high idealism, optimism, and promise. They admire the Great Society for its attempts at combating poverty, improving health care, and providing educational opportunities for everyone. Moreover, they applaud the most crucial liberal achievement of the decade and the zenith of social justice in the twentieth century: civil rights. Furthermore, liberals have a favorable opinion of the antiwar, women's, and environmental movements. Finally, most liberals are pleased with the loosening of traditional social and cultural restraints that the era wrought.[1]

Conservatives, on the other hand, generally perceive the 1960s as a bad decade, a time when American values—self-reliance and discipline, personal responsibility, patriotism, and local communities—began to decline. While conservatives today praise John F. Kennedy's presidency, they generally criticize the mid-to-late 1960s, assailing Lyndon Johnson's costly war on poverty, the federal government's intervention into state affairs on behalf of racial minorities, and spoiled New Leftists who cost America victory in Vietnam. In addition, conservatives regret other consequences they ascribe to the Sixties: drug abuse, crime, teen pregnancy, poverty, multiculturalism, abortion, and homosexuality. Roger Kimball's critical appraisal is representative. In 1997, he wrote in *New Criterion*:

> Make no mistake: the radical, emancipationist demands of the Sixties have not receded. They have—to an extent that is astonishing to contemplate—triumphed throughout society. They have insinuated themselves, disastrously, into the curricula of our schools and colleges; they have dramatically altered the texture of sexual relations and family life; they have played havoc with the authority of churches and other repositories of moral wisdom; they have undermined the claims of civic virtue and our national self-understanding; they have degraded the media

and the entertainment industry, and subverted museums and other institutions entrusted with preserving and transmitting high culture. They have even, most poignantly, addled our hearts and innermost assumptions about what counts as the good life.[2]

Conservatives have been more successful than liberals in electoral politics and policymaking. As the unprecedented economic growth of the postwar era seemingly came to an end in the mid-1970s, a new cohort of economists rose to prominence stressing the superiority of unrestricted markets in allocating resources and producing affluence, while casting doubt on the federal government's ability to manage the economy. Ordinary citizens, too, embraced the market as the best and most efficient means to distribute goods and services and renew prosperity. Fewer people welcomed government regulation. Supply and demand, consumers believed, would deliver the items they wanted. Friedrich von Hayek, whose book *The Road to Serfdom* (1944) skewered socialism as a path to slavery, was awarded the Nobel Prize in economics in 1974, which represented a profound change within the profession, shifting emphasis away from Keynesianism. Milton Friedman, a proponent of unfettered markets as a liberating force, won the Nobel Prize for economics in 1976. By the end of the decade Friedman was the most influential economist in the world.[3]

While the left lost energy and its numbers dissipated, conservatives assembled the best-financed and largest grassroots movement in the country by the late 1970s. Evangelical Protestants, businesspeople, and others helped boost Ronald Reagan, George Bush Sr., and George W. Bush to the presidency. Blamed for the upheavals of the 1960s, liberals found it exceedingly difficult to regain their momentum. The word "liberal" itself became a liability, used by conservatives to undercut their opponents with the electorate. Indeed, most Democrats refused to embrace the term at the dawn of the twenty-first century. Democrat Bill Clinton eradicated deficits and ended guaranteed welfare payments to single mothers with dependent children—objectives long supported by conservatives. Although most Americans value the centerpieces of the New Deal, Great Society, and support other liberal causes—social security, Medicare, Medicaid, federal aid to education, and environmentalism—the right has dominated the social and economic debate. It has become conventional wisdom in American politics that "antipoverty programs do not help the poor; taxes should always be lowered; 'preferential treatment' for minorities is wrong; business is overregulated; and the size of government ought to be reduced."[4]

Conservatives, however, have lost the culture. The counterculture transformed American culture—and thus America—and this is its legacy. The aesthetic and stylistic changes of the Sixties have had a lasting impact. Personal liberty has increased as individuals have greater freedom to dress as they please and socialize with whom they want. Longer hair for men has generally become acceptable, including in the workplace. Most Americans wear informal clothing. Rock and roll is popular and mainstream. Even conservative politicians campaign in blue jeans. President George W. Bush spoke to the press in a windbreaker and Reagan played Bruce Springsteen's "Born in the U.S.A." on the campaign trail, which horrified the rocker. In the aftermath of the Vietnam War, more people, especially the young, elevated the individual over country.[5]

Sexual mores have become more relaxed and Americans have become more sensitive to women's issues. Frank public discussions and depictions of sex occur regularly in movies, literature, art, and television. Popular music since the 1960s has contained greater sexual expression and profanity. Millions of couples live together before marrying. Interracial relationships and marriages have become more acceptable and people commonly marry across ethnic and religious lines. Most Americans back a woman's right to choose in the abortion debate. Many are more attuned to other issues affecting women: sexual harassment, rape, and domestic abuse. Although it still exists, the double standard with regard to sexuality has diminished. Birth control and a growing general permissiveness in the sexual attitudes of the larger culture allow women—and men—to enjoy more sexual freedom. A large majority believe premarital sex is socially acceptable; even 69 percent of those who attend church "nearly weekly" hold this view.[6]

Americans are more tolerant of gay lifestyles. Millions of gays are open about their sexual identities. The government furthered their rights when the Supreme Court struck down a Texas antisodomy law in *Lawrence v. Texas* in 2003 and the Defense of Marriage Act in 2013. A Democratic Congress also repealed "Don't Ask, Don't Tell" in 2010, allowing gays to serve openly in the military. In 2011 nearly two-thirds of Americans, according to Gallup, believed that same-sex relations between consenting adults should be legal, 56 percent found same-sex relationships to be "morally acceptable," and 53 percent supported gay marriage. In June 2015 the Supreme Court decided the case *Obergefell v. Hodges*, which legalized gay marriage based on the due process and equal protection clauses of the Fourteenth Amendment.[7]

Attitudes toward marijuana have loosened considerably and grassroots activists have made great strides to legalize it. A 2002 *Time/CNN* poll revealed that 80 percent were accepting of medical marijuana use, while 72 percent felt that people caught for marijuana possession should get off lightly with a fine. Nearly half of all Americans—47 percent—had tried marijuana at least once. Today, eleven states and the District of Columbia have legalized weed for recreational use. Ailing people in thirty-three states can use medical marijuana legally. A 2013 Pew Research Center study revealed that 52 percent support marijuana's legalization.[8] Still, most conservatives see drug use as corrupting. Since the Nixon years, the federal government has waged a war on drugs. During the Reagan and Bush presidencies, drug users and dealers faced mandatory minimum sentences, asset forfeiture, and withholding of welfare benefits. Mounting public concern about drug abuse led many businesses to administer urine tests to employees and prospective employees.

Questioning authority is another legacy. Americans became more skeptical and suspicious of the government, political leaders, and military. People no longer accepted the word of authorities at face value. They asked questions and demanded explanations, especially when it came to issues such as war and peace, the environment, corruption, and individual rights. The press, too, asked questions it never would have prior to the sixties. After the Vietnam debacle, many Americans became skeptical and cynical of the nation's foreign policy. Most were reluctant to commit troops to overseas military engagements—the "Vietnam syndrome." Questioning authority, however, diminished during the runup to the Iraq War in 2003. Most Americans did not pay attention, wanted revenge for 9/11, and believed the Bush administration's claims regarding Saddam Hussein and weapons of mass destruction. And the press failed to demand explanations, repeating the administration's talking points. A veteran reporter found that between September 2002 and the beginning of the war, only six of over four hundred articles raised questions about the necessity of going to war.[9]

Political and cultural dissenters curbed the power of government and bureaucracies. Following the sixties, the police, National Guard, military, IRS, and FBI, intrude less into individuals' daily lives. These agencies became more integrated and diverse as well, hiring racial minorities and women. Moreover, students exercised greater rights at and played a greater role in governing the university.

Environmentalism continues to thrive. Enthusiasm for environmental causes reached a crescendo in 1970 and resulted in the passage of several significant environmental measures. President Nixon cared little about environmental issues, but refrained from contesting reformers, and signed several bills passed by bipartisan majorities. In January 1970 he approved the National Environmental Policy Act, which established the Environmental Protection Agency (EPA). The EPA was tasked with enforcing environmental laws. It also required government agencies—and later, most nongovernment entities—to submit environmental impact statements for various projects. In the early 1970s Congress passed, and Nixon signed, several other important laws designed to protect the environment, including a Clean Air Act (1970), a Federal Water Pollution Control Act (1972), and in 1973, an Endangered Species Act. President George H. W. Bush signed another Clean Air Act into law in 1990. In more recent times, the threat of global warming has galvanized environmentalists to action. Other environmental movement legacies include an interest in recycling and renewable energy.

The natural foods movement is prospering. Health-conscious consumers hoping to avoid pesticides and antibiotics in meat and milk buy organic. Whole Foods has enjoyed great success; in 2002, over 130 stores were in operation. The chain made $2.3 billion and its profits surged 20 percent in 2001. The share price of its stock rose 125 percent between 2000 and 2002 and more than 750 percent between 1992, when Whole Foods was founded, and 2002. Individual stores that had been established for at least six years experienced a 6 percent growth rate compared to 1.5 percent for a typical chain. Natural and organic foods sales throughout the country grew at the rate of 18 percent per year, and in 2002, analysts expected total sales to exceed $17 billion. In addition to eating organic foods, many practice organic gardening and composting, buy produce at farmers' markets, and use holistic medicine.[10]

Millions of Americans do yoga, from stars and athletes to judges on the highest courts. In 2001, some 15 million people included yoga in their exercise regimen, double the number that did in 1996. Most health clubs—75 percent—offer yoga lessons. Others have adopted practices previously associated with the counterculture like sensitivity training, meditation, body awareness, and Erhard Seminars Training aimed at enhancing personal growth.[11]

Counterculturalists contributed to the creation of the personal computer and internet. Not every counterculturalist opposed the technological and intellectual output of the American research culture and military-industrial complex. Fred Turner has demonstrated how the "New Communalists" envisioned the potential for world harmony through the "cybernetic notion of the globe as a single, interlinked pattern of information." Stewart Brand, creator of the *Whole Earth Catalog*, channeled his scientific background into new creative and imaginative enterprises. Like other counterculturalists, he distrusted large corporations like IBM that had a monopoly on giant mainframe computers and might use them for nefarious ends. As the cost of making computers dropped, Brand endeavored to allow individuals to harness their power. He coined the term "personal computer" and announced in 1974, "Ready or not, computers are coming to the people." He and others hoped to put knowledge in the hands of individuals, while simultaneously undercutting the power and wealth of huge corporations, which had no interest in developing the PC. In short, the PC "was the high-tech version of an idealized hippie world." Young white middle-class PC hobbyists loved rock music and technology, and they founded the first PC club in Menlo Park, California, in 1966: the People's Computer Company. The company's building was not very far from where Jerry Garcia had formed the Grateful Dead. Steve Jobs was one of these suburban hobbyists. As a young man in California, Jobs wore a beard, grew his hair long, adopted vegetarianism, dropped LSD, smoked dope, and dug rock music. When he graduated high school, he and his girlfriend moved into a cabin in the hills. After spending a semester at Reed College in Portland before dropping out, Jobs traveled to India in

1974 and became immersed in mediation and Zen Buddhism. He returned to the states a changed man. After connecting with technical genius Steve Wozniak, the two founded Apple in 1976. By 2015 over two billion people used computers worldwide.[12]

Rock music from the 1960s remains well-loved and corporations have capitalized on its popularity. Nike used the Beatles song "Revolution" in a television ad in the 1980s. In 1998, Sprint used the Rolling Stones' "Time Is on My Side" to sell a calling plan, AT&T used Sly and the Family Stone's "I Want to Take You Higher" to show, ironically, how its products aided job promotion, and Pontiac used Jimi Hendrix's "Fire" to advertise its Sunfire model.

The Beatles continue to be immensely popular. Three generations of Beatles fans love them and eagerly purchase their products. The Beatles album 1, a collection of twenty-seven chart-topping British and American hits, released in 2000, sold 7 million copies and spent eight weeks at number one. Observers pointed out that kids under twelve contributed greatly to the album's sales. In September 2009 *The Beatles: Rock Band*, a video game, was unveiled, and Apple Corps/Capitol reissued all thirteen of the band's albums, digitally remastered. Beatlemaniacs could also buy a box set that contained every Beatles song in mono for nearly $300.[13]

The Beatles' rivals, the Rolling Stones, still record and perform. The Stones released a new album in 2005, *A Bigger Bang*. The band followed the album's release with "A Bigger Bang" tour that fall, which grossed $437 million worldwide, a new record. In 2008 director Martin Scorsese produced a Stones concert film, *Shine a Light*. Ticket prices for their 2013 tour ranged from $150 to more than $2,000. In December 2016, the group released *Blue and Lonesome*, which debuted at number four on the Billboard chart and became their record-setting thirty-seventh top ten album.[14]

Business is booming for the Grateful Dead, too. The band ranked among the top revenue-grossing rock acts until the untimely death of frontman Garcia in August 1995. From 1990 to 1995, the Dead racked up $285 million on tour. Nearly eight million people—devoted fans dubbed "Deadheads"—attended 530 shows. After the celebrated band's demise, jam band followers flocked to the shows of Phish and the String Cheese Incident, groups similar to the Dead. Today, various products—luggage, video games, ceramic mugs, a version of Monopoly, even a red wine—display the Dead's logo. The band still commands an enormous fan base: 1.8 million people follow its Facebook page.[15]

Countercultural outposts survived into the 1980s and beyond. In 1984 some twenty-five thousand hippies journeyed to the Modoc National Forest of California for a "Rainbow Family" reunion. They erected tents, tipis, and yurts, and openly smoked dope and dropped acid. Other festivities took place as well. Children marched in a parade with painted faces, carrying banners and balloons, and on top of a mountain, five thousand participated in a silent prayer. Hundreds of communes founded in the Sixties still exist, including Hog Farm, the Farm, and Twin Oaks.[16]

Countercultural trends endured into the 1990s. Early in the decade, fans of "alternative" music bucked the mainstream, and by decade's end, various subcultural groups with alternative identities—goths, Rastafarians, and ravers—surfaced. With the advent of the internet, youth visited conspiracy theory sites and posted about dope on psychedelic bulletin boards. Hundreds of thousands of kids attended rock festivals like Lollapalooza, HORDE, and Lilith Fair.[17]

Woodstock became a political issue in the leadup to the 2008 presidential election. At a debate in October 2007, John McCain, a Republican presidential candidate, remarked, "A few days ago, Senator [Hillary] Clinton tried to spend one million on the Woodstock concert museum. Now, my friends, I wasn't there. I'm sure it was a cultural and pharmaceutical event. I was tied up at the time. No one can be president of the United States that supports projects such as these." In 1969, when Woodstock took place, McCain was being held prisoner by the North Vietnamese. He used the "tied up" line to be humorous, but the implications of his statement went much deeper. A political commercial that McCain ran in New Hampshire aired the remarks he made above, while presenting a series of images. One was of a young woman dancing "trance-like" at Woodstock; the other was McCain lying on his back, smoking a cigarette as a prisoner of war. McCain used Woodstock as a symbol to polarize the electorate, dredging up divisive issues of the past—and, as it turned out, the present. The counterculture still divides Americans today, and McCain employed Woodstock to draw distinctions, in his mind and the minds of many others, between God-fearing, responsible, patriotic, conservatives who answered their country's call to arms, and those who attended Woodstock—draft-dodging, drug-abusing, anti-American liberals.[18]

Some on the right have noted growing alienation among conservatives and posit that conservatism itself is the new counterculture. Yuval Levin, writing in *Modern Age* following the election of Donald Trump in 2016, contends that the voters who cast ballots for the real estate mogul are alienated from America's dominant culture, politics, and economy. Trump voters believe that the nation's social order and its institutions are insane and fraudulent, and the Republican candidate deftly articulated their frustrations with the FBI, IRS, media, electoral process, judiciary, and political parties. Trump galvanized a constituency that had become apathetic or hostile toward elite politicians and policy debates over marginal income tax rates. Many conservatives held Trump up as the last chance to save the country from certain "death" and the triumph of progressivism. Greg Jones, writing for the *Federalist*, acknowledges the forceful legacy of the movement and the Sixties, arguing that "authoritarian liberalism" pervades the culture. For Jones, progressivism is the establishment, as former activists and hippies zealously infiltrated the nation's institutions—especially academia—and fanatical leftists dominate Silicon Valley and the entertainment industry. "The movement," he writes, "has grown old, ornery, and hell-bent on maintaining its twisted orthodoxy, so much that it is openly abandoning its most basic ideals, such as individual liberty and skepticism of authority. Yet these ideals are still meaningful to modern-day conservatives and libertarians." According to Jones, the "real rebels" are conservatives, those who have "tuned in" to the opinions of people like Ben Shapiro and Jordan Peterson. The hippies of yesteryear, he maintains, share similarities with today's conservatives who value freedom of expression, individual autonomy, and distrust government.[19]

While the counterculture's legacy is clear, evaluating the counterculture is ultimately an exercise in subjectivity. No scholar can prove definitively whether it succeeded or failed. Moreover, being a part of the counterculture was almost entirely an individual experience. Thus, no historian can conclude objectively whether a person's personal journey was meaningful or worthwhile or misguided or anything else.

There is much to question and criticize. A dope revolution did not come to pass—in fact, the idea that LSD and other drugs could change the world turned out to be a hopeless delusion. Drugs and alcohol claimed the lives of untold rank-and-file counterculturalists and numerous celebrity hipsters: Jim Morrison, Brian Jones, Jimi Hendrix, Janis Joplin, Keith Moon, Gram Parsons of the Byrds and Flying Burrito Brothers, Dennis Wilson of the Beach Boys, John Bonham of Led Zeppelin, Danny Whitten of Crazy Horse, Pigpen of the Grateful Dead, and Alan Wilson and Bob "The Bear" Hite of Canned Heat. Many who wandered the Haight during the Summer of Love did not take cultural radicalism seriously or seek to better themselves or society. For some individuals, being a hippie meant little more than getting laid and stoned. "The air was so thick with bullshit you could cut it with a knife," recalled cartoonist Robert Crumb. "Guys were running around saying, 'I'm you and you are me and everything is beautiful, so get down and suck my dick.' These young, middle-class kids were just too dumb about it. It was just too silly." An unfortunate result of the counterculture's uninhibited sexuality was the spread of sexually transmitted diseases. Reported cases of gonorrhea among teenagers between fifteen and nineteen nearly tripled between 1956 and 1969. Other hippies lived like bums and engaged in self-destructive behavior, sleeping, stealing, and begging on the street, strung out on every kind of drug imaginable—weed, hash, mescaline, cocaine, heroin, and pills of all sorts. In Afghanistan, freaks went to extraordinary lengths to get a drug fix, selling themselves or their girlfriends into prostitution. And some hippies—especially men—had sex with doped-up adolescents. "A lot of us slept with underage girls," recalled a member of the Brotherhood of Eternal Love. "We knew they were young but these runaways were pouring into the canyon and all they wanted to do was get high and sleep with us. We were only eighteen years old ourselves, but I think we really screwed a lot of people up."[20]

But many, if not most, former counterculturalists look back fondly at their experiences. Nearly all of the hundreds of people contacted by the 60s Communes Project, for instance, believed that their time as communards "was a high point in American history as well as in their own lives." Although most remembered the intensity of communal living, they all found it exhilarating. Don McCoy called his time at Olompali Ranch a "life-changing experience and a change for the better and the most colorful time in my life." Most believe that their communes were successes. The simple fact that they had attempted communal living at all and had new and learning experiences was reason enough to deem it a success, even if their collective had fallen apart. "I often describe Drop City as the best years of my life," remarked Clark Richert. "It was a period of freedom and the feeling of unlimited possibilities." Despite being portrayed as vamps, groupies, and hangers-on to the male-dominated counterculture, hippie women summoned the courage to break free from the mainstream and helped build an alternative society. They, too, speak positively about their experiences and roles within hippiedom. As Kathleen Taylor explains:

> It took a lot of courage to move against the tide, to forge deeper, more intimate relationships with our partners and children, to seek meaningful work or right livelihood, to live simply and within ecological boundaries and constraints. It wasn't about sex, drugs and rock and roll, it wasn't some woo-woo spiritual fantasy, it was real women creating and sustaining viable alternatives to the unimaginative, militarist, consumption-oriented status quo.[21]

Finally, many former freaks are completely unapologetic for the Sixties and their part in the counterculture, for they believe it altered America for the better. "Our victories occurred in the deep waters of culture and not the frothy white water of current events, so they rarely surface in the media," wrote Peter Coyote in his memoir, *Sleeping Where I Fall*. "The way people view health issues, the environment, human rights, spirituality, agriculture, women, and consciousness itself has been redefined by my generation. These changes are as ubiquitous and invisible as the atmosphere." David Crosby, speaking to *Time* in 2006, remarked, "I think we were right about everything except the drugs. We were right about civil rights; we were right about human rights; we were right about peace being better than war. Most of the causes we espoused then were correct." And Paul Kantner of Jefferson Airplane spoke for many when he stated, "For like two weeks in the middle of 1967 . . . it was perfect."[22]

NOTES

INTRODUCTION

1. Peter Braunstein and Michael William Doyle, "Introduction: Historicizing the American Counterculture of the 1960s and '70s," in *Imagine Nation: The American Counterculture of the 1960s and '70s*, ed. Peter Braunstein and Michael William Doyle (New York: Routledge, 2002), 7–8. For the traditional interpretation see Nadya Zimmerman, *Counterculture Kaleidoscope: Musical and Cultural Perspectives on Late Sixties San Francisco* (Ann Arbor: University of Michigan Press, 2008); William L. O'Neill, *Coming Apart: An Informal History of America in the 1960s* (Chicago: Quadrangle, 1971); Allen J. Matusow, *The Unraveling of America: A History of Liberalism in the 1960s* (New York: Harper & Row, 1984); John Anthony Moretta, *The Hippies: A 1960s History* (Jefferson, NC: McFarland, 2017); Todd Gitlin, *The Sixties: Years of Hope, Days of Rage* (New York: Bantam, 1987); David Steigerwald, *The Sixties and the End of Modern America* (New York: Bedford/St. Martin's, 1995); Klaus P. Fischer, *America in White, Black, and Gray: The Stormy 1960s* (New York: Continuum, 2006); Edward P. Morgan, *The 60s Experience: Hard Lessons about Modern America* (Philadelphia: Temple University Press, 1991); Godfrey Hodgson, *America in Our Time: From World War II to Nixon—What Happened and Why* (New York: Doubleday, 1976); David Chalmers, *And the Crooked Places Made Straight: The Struggle for Social Change in the 1960s* (Baltimore: Johns Hopkins University Press, 1991). Timothy Miller concludes his *The Hippies and American Values* (Knoxville: University of Tennessee Press, 1991) in 1970, as does Moretta in *Hippies*; W. J. Rorabaugh's *American Hippies* (New York: Cambridge University Press, 2015) does cover the early 1970s, but focuses largely on communes during that period; Robert C. Cottrell, *Sex, Drugs, and Rock 'n' Roll: The Rise of America's 1960s Counterculture* (Lanham, MD: Rowman and Littlefield, 2015) ends in 1971.

2. For single-chapter histories of the counterculture within a larger volume on the 1960s see O'Neill, *Coming Apart*; Matusow, *Unraveling of America*; Hodgson, *America in Our Time*; Chalmers, *And the Crooked Places Made Straight*; Gitlin, *Sixties*; William E. Leuchtenburg, *A Troubled Feast: American Society since 1945* (Boston: Little, Brown, 1979); David Burner, *Making Peace with the 60s* (Princeton, NJ: Princeton University Press, 1996); Mark Hamilton Lytle, *America's Uncivil Wars: The Sixties Era from Elvis to the Fall of Richard Nixon* (New York: Oxford University Press, 2006); Gerard J. DeGroot, *The Sixties Unplugged: A Kaleidoscopic History of a Disorderly Decade* (Cambridge, MA: Harvard University Press, 2008); Terry H. Anderson, *The Movement and the Sixties* (New York: Oxford University Press, 1995); Irwin Unger, *The Sixties* (New York: Pearson, 2011); David Farber, *The Age of Great Dreams: America in the 1960s* (New York: Hill and Wang, 1994); W. J. Rorabaugh, *Berkeley at War: The 1960s* (New York: Oxford University Press, 1989). For an early appraisal see Theodore Roszak, *The Making of a Counter Culture: Reflections on the Technocratic Society and Its Youthful Opposition* (Garden City, NY: Doubleday, 1969). For single location or element see Charles Perry, *The Haight-Ashbury: A History* (New York: Random House, 1984); Zimmerman, *Counterculture Kaleidoscope*; David McBride, "Death City Radicals: The Counterculture in Los Angeles," in *The New Left Revisited*, ed. John McMillian and Paul Buhle (Philadelphia: Temple University Press, 2003); Rick Dodgson, *It's All a Kind of Magic: The Young Ken Kesey* (Madison: University of Wisconsin Press, 2013); Robert Greenfield, *Timothy Leary: A Biography* (New York: Harcourt, 2006); Martin A. Lee and Bruce Shlain, *Acid Dreams: The Complete Social History of LSD: The CIA, the Sixties, and Beyond*

(New York: Grove, 1985); Emily Dufton, *Grass Roots: The Rise and Fall and Rise of Marijuana in America* (New York: Basic Books, 2017); Miller, *Hippies and American Values*; Timothy Miller, *The 60s Communes: Hippies and Beyond* (Syracuse: Syracuse University Press, 1999); Abe Peck, *Uncovering the Sixties: The Life and Times of the Underground Press* (New York: Pantheon, 1985); John McMillian, *Smoking Typewriters: The Sixties Underground Press and the Rise of Alternative Media in America* (New York: Oxford University Press, 2011); Blake Slonecker, *A New Dawn for the New Left: Liberation News Service, Montague Farm, and the Long Sixties* (New York: Palgrave Macmillan, 2012); Larry Eskridge, *God's Forever Family: The Jesus People Movement in America* (New York: Oxford University Press, 2013); Preston Shires, *Hippies of the Religious Right* (Waco, TX: Baylor University Press, 2007); Joshua Clark Davis, *From Head Shops to Whole Foods: The Rise and Fall of Activist Entrepreneurs* (New York: Columbia University Press, 2017); Sharif Gemie and Brian Ireland, *The Hippie Trail: A History, 1957–78* (Manchester: Manchester University Press, 2017); Gretchen Lemke-Santangelo, *Daughters of Aquarius: Women of the Sixties Counterculture* (Lawrence: University Press of Kansas, 2009); Tim Hodgdon, *Manhood in the Age of Aquarius: Masculinity in Two Countercultural Communities, 1965–83* (New York: Columbia University Press, 2008); Andrew G. Kirk, *Counterculture Green: The Whole Earth Catalog and American Environmentalism* (Lawrence: University Press of Kansas, 2007); Frank Zelko, *Make It a Green Peace!: The Rise of Countercultural Environmentalism* (New York: Oxford University Press, 2013); Sherry L. Smith, *Hippies, Indians, and the Fight for Red Power* (New York: Oxford University Press, 2012); Travis D. Stimeling, *Cosmic Cowboys and New Hicks: The Countercultural Sounds of Austin's Progressive Country Music Scene* (New York: Oxford University Press, 2011); Michael J. Kramer, *The Republic of Rock: Music and Citizenship in the Sixties Counterculture* (New York: Oxford University Press, 2013); Braunstein and Doyle, *Imagine Nation*.

3. Etan Ben-Ami, interview with Peter Coyote, January 12, 1989, www.petercoyote.com; Melton quoted in James J. Farrell, *The Spirit of the Sixties: The Making of Postwar Radicalism* (New York: Routledge, 1997), 203; Grateful Dead in Peter Richardson, *No Simple Highway: A Cultural History of the Grateful Dead* (New York: St. Martin's, 2014), 90.

4. Catherine O' Sullivan Shorr, *Andy Warhol's Factory People* (Scotts Valley, CA: CreateSpace Independent Publishing, 2014); Howard Sounes, *Down the Highway: The Life of Bob Dylan* (New York: Grove, 2001), 249–250.

5. White and black radicals on parallel tracks in John McMillian, "'You Didn't Have to Be There': Revisiting the New Left Consensus," in McMillian and Buhle, *New Left Revisited*, 6; Robin Morgan in Ruth Rosen, *The World Split Open: How the Modern Women's Movement Changed America* (New York: Penguin, 2000), 136. Theodore Roszak found common ground and a shared language between African American militants, New Leftists, and hippies; see Roszak, *Making of a Counter Culture*, 44, 56–66. For interpretations that underscore a New Left–counterculture convergence see McBride, "Death City Radicals"; Alice Echols, "Nothing Distant about It: Women's Liberation and Sixties Radicalism," in *The Sixties: From Memory to History*, ed. David Farber (Chapel Hill: University of North Carolina Press, 1994); Doug Rossinow, *The Politics of Authenticity: Liberalism, Christianity, and the New Left in America* (New York: Columbia University Press, 1998); Julie Stephens, *Anti-disciplinary Protest: Sixties Radicalism and Post-Modernism* (New York: Cambridge University Press, 1998); McMillian, *Smoking Typewriters*, 11–12; Davis, *From Head Shops to Whole Foods*. Several scholars make the case for an expansive counterculture. Thomas Frank's definition in *The Conquest of Cool* (1997) is all-encompassing: it included anyone who assumed a flamboyant youth style and championed unrestrained personal expression. In 2002 Debra Michals argued for a counterculture made up of any entity

with utopian visions aimed at altering and replacing prevailing economic, cultural, and political models. Likewise, Jeremi Suri, in a 2009 *American Historical Review* article, incorporated virtually anyone who protested or felt a discontent with the societal status quo, from corporate employees, civil rights marchers, college students, and the Weather Underground to Betty Friedan. Robert C. Cottrell includes the Berrigan brothers, radical feminists like Robin Morgan, and "radical chic" supporters of the New York Panther 21—Leonard Bernstein among them—in his narrative; see Debra Michals, "From 'Consciousness Expansion' to 'Consciousness Raising,'" in Braunstein and Doyle, *Imagine Nation*, 45; Jeremi Suri, "The Rise and Fall of an International Counterculture, 1960–1975," *American Historical Review* 114, no. 1 (February 2009): 45–68; Thomas Frank, *The Conquest of Cool: Business Culture, Counterculture, and the Rise of Hip Consumerism* (Chicago: University of Chicago Press, 1997); Cottrell, *Sex, Drugs, and Rock 'n' Roll*, 319–326.

6. A. James Speyer, "Hippies Are," Seed (Chicago), vol. 1, no. 7 (1967).

7. John Manning, "Letters," Rebirth (Phoenix), vol. 1. no. 2 (1969).

8. "The Group W Bench," Kudzu (Jackson, MS), January 14, 1969.

9. "Spotlight on 'Hippies': A First-Hand Report," U.S. News & World Report, May 8, 1967, 61.

10. Embree quoted in Slonecker, *New Dawn for the New Left*, 2; McMillian, *Smoking Typewriters*, 4, 6, 11, 80.

11. Leonard Wolf and Deborah Wolf, eds., *Voices from the Love Generation* (Boston: Little, Brown, 1968), 221.

CHAPTER 1. IMPRISONED IN THE AMERICAN DREAM

1. Burton H. Wolfe, *The Hippies* (New York: Signet, 1968), 9–14.

2. Theodore Roszak, *The Making of a Counter Culture: Reflections on the Technocratic Society and Its Youthful Opposition* (Garden City, NY: Doubleday, 1969), 8, 50–51.

3. For direct influence of Beats see Godfrey Hodgson, *America in Our Time: From World War II to Nixon—What Happened and Why* (New York: Doubleday, 1976), 324–325. David Farber argues that hippies looked to Beats "for inspiration and guidance." He also contends that the Beats taught young people the virtues of drug trips; see Farber, *The Age of Great Dreams: America in the 1960s* (New York: Hill and Wang, 1994), 172. For direct outgrowth see John C. McWilliams, *The 1960s Cultural Revolution* (Westport, CT: Greenwood, 2000), 65. Larry Eskridge also argues that the counterculture "had its origins" in the Beat movement; see Eskridge, *God's Forever Family: The Jesus People Movement in America* (New York: Oxford University Press, 2013), 11. For the argument that LSD was the crucial element that facilitated a "transformation" from Beat to hippie see Allen J. Matusow, *The Unraveling of America: A History of Liberalism in the 1960s* (New York: Harper & Row, 1984), 287; and Irwin Unger, *The Sixties* (New York: Pearson, 2011), 146. "Set the stage" in Robert C. Cottrell, *Sex, Drugs, and Rock 'n' Roll: The Rise of America's 1960s Counterculture* (Lanham, MD: Rowman and Littlefield, 2015), 7; numbers in W. J. Rorabaugh, *American Hippies* (New York: Cambridge University Press, 2015), 4.

4. William L. O'Neill, *Coming Apart: An Informal History of America in the 1960s* (Chicago: Quadrangle, 1971), 234–243; William E. Leuchtenburg, *A Troubled Feast: American Society since 1945* (Boston: Little, Brown, 1979), 179; Rorabaugh, *American Hippies*, 2; Hodgson, *America in Our Time*, 311–312, 315–316; Matusow, *Unraveling of America*, 277–287, 306; Roszak, *Making of a Counter Culture*, 30–32; Timothy Miller, *The 60s Communes: Hippies and Beyond* (Syracuse, NY: Syracuse University Press, 1999), 4–6; Klaus Fischer, *America in White, Black, and Gray: The Stormy 1960s* (New York: Continuum,

2006), 300–302; Edward Morgan, *The 60s Experience: Hard Lessons about Modern America* (Philadelphia: Temple University Press, 1991), 172–178; David Chalmers, *And the Crooked Places Made Straight: The Struggle for Social Change in the 1960s* (Baltimore: Johns Hopkins University Press, 1991), 95–97. Pioneers in Matusow, *Unraveling of America*, 280. Single satisfactory explanation in David Burner, *Making Peace with the 60s* (Princeton, NJ: Princeton University Press, 1996), 128.

5. G. Petrovic, "Alienation," in *Encyclopedia of Philosophy*, 2nd ed., ed. Donald M. Borchert (Farmington Hills, MI: Thomson Gale, 2006), 120–121.

6. Emmanuel Hansen, *Frantz Fanon: Social and Political Thought* (Columbus: Ohio State University Press, 1977), 73–76, quote on 76; Robert Nisbet, *The Quest For Community: A Study in the Ethics of Order and Freedom* (Wilmington, DE: ISI Books, 2010), xxiii; Gwynn Nettler, "A Measure of Alienation," *American Sociological Review* 22 (1957): 672.

7. Art Johnson, "'What Have You Got?'" *Fifth Estate* (Detroit), November 15–30, 1966; Richard Pine, "The Diggers' Creative Society," *Digger News* (Los Angeles), June 1967, in Jerry Hopkins, ed., *The Hippie Papers: Trip-Taking, Mind-Quaking, Scene-Making Word from Where It's At* (New York: New American Library, 1968), 27.

8. Abbie Hoffman, *Woodstock Nation: A Talk-Rock Album* (New York: Vintage Books, 1969), 15; Michael Brand, "And You Don't Know What It Is, Do You, Mr. Jones?," *Bauls* (West Lafayette, IN), January 6, 1969–February 2, 1969.

9. Churchill quoted in Joseph C. Goulden, *The Best Years, 1945–1950* (New York: Atheneum, 1976), 257.

10. Truman quoted in Alonzo L. Hamby, *Man of the People: A Life of Harry S. Truman* (New York: Oxford University Press, 1995), 387.

11. H. W. Brands, *The Devil We Knew: Americans and the Cold War* (New York: Oxford University Press, 1993), 22, 31.

12. William E. Leuchtenburg, *The American President: From Teddy Roosevelt to Bill Clinton* (New York: Oxford University Press, 2015), 331.

13. Richard Fried, *Nightmare in Red: The McCarthy Era in Perspective* (New York: Oxford University Press, 1990); and Douglas T. Miller and Marion Nowak, *The Fifties: The Way We Really Were* (Garden City, NY: Doubleday, 1975), 23–24.

14. Miller and Nowak, *Fifties*, 26; Fried, *Nightmare in Red*, 66–70.

15. Fried, *Nightmare in Red*, 70–72; David Caute, *The Great Fear: The Anti-Communist Purge under Truman and Eisenhower* (New York: Simon and Schuster, 1978), 275, 280–281.

16. McCarthy quoted in David M. Oshinsky, *A Conspiracy So Immense: The World of Joe McCarthy* (New York: Oxford University Press, 1983), 197; and J. Ronald Oakley, *God's Country: America in the Fifties* (New York: Barricade Books, 1990), 61–62.

17. McGrath quoted in Lawrence S. Wittner, *Cold War America: From Hiroshima to Watergate* (New York: Praeger, 1974), 86–87.

18. Fried, *Nightmare in Red*, 34, 98, 161; Eric F. Goldman, *The Crucial Decade and After: America, 1945–1960* (New York: Vintage Books, 1960), 258; Oakley, *God's Country*, 73–74.

19. Peter Doggett, *There's a Riot Going On: Revolutionaries, Rock Stars, and the Rise and Fall of the '60s* (Edinburgh: Canongate, 2007), 22–23; Ron Chepesiuk, *Sixties Radicals, Then and Now: Candid Conversations with Those Who Shaped an Era* (Jefferson, NC: McFarland, 1995), 242; Connell Persico, "Live and Let Live," in *To Make a Difference: A Student Look at America: Its Values, Its Society and Its Systems of Education*, ed. Otto Butz (New York: Joanna Cotler Books, 1967), 113–114; Hopkins, *Hippie Papers*, 100–101.

20. *Woman's Guide* quoted in John Patrick Diggins, *The Proud Decades: America in War and Peace, 1941–1960* (New York: W. W. Norton, 1988), 212.

21. John Keats, *The Crack in the Picture Window* (Boston: Houghton Mifflin, 1956), xi.

22. Lewis Mumford, *The City in History: Its Origins, Its Transformation, and Its Prospects* (New York: Penguin, 1961), 486.

23. James T. Carey, *The College Drug Scene* (Englewood Cliffs, NJ: Prentice Hall, 1968), 50.

24. Adlai Stevenson, "Commencement Address," in *America in the Sixties—Right, Left, and Center: A Documentary History*, ed. Peter B. Levy (Westport, CT: Praeger, 1998), 15.

25. Oakley, *God's Country*, 314–315.

26. Chester Linderman, "A Lemon in Orange County," *Indian Head* (Santa Ana, CA), November 17, 1967; John Curl, *Memories of Drop City: The First Hippie Commune of the 1960's and the Summer of Love* (Lincoln, NE: iUniverse, 2007), 10.

27. Oakley, *God's Country*, 302–303.

28. Jerry Rubin, *Do It! Scenarios of the Revolution* (New York: Simon and Schuster, 1970), 18; "Bringing It All Back Home," *Tiohero* (Ithaca, NY), March 1971.

29. Stephanie Coontz, *The Way We Never Were: American Families and the Nostalgia Trap* (New York: Basic Books, 1992), 24–25; Oakley, *God's Country*, 228–229.

30. Liza Williams, "Which Way to the Exit?" *Los Angeles Free Press*, January 6, 1967.

31. Franklin Bach, "Our Music against the Pig," box 17, folder 21, John and Leni Sinclair Papers, Bentley Historical Library, University of Michigan, Ann Arbor; John Raymond, "M. Mouse Dies at 65," *Berkeley Citizen*, December 23, 1966.

32. Gretchen Lemke-Santangelo, *Daughters of Aquarius: Women of the Sixties Counterculture* (Lawrence: University Press of Kansas, 2009), 35–58; Lauren Kessler, *After All These Years: Sixties Ideals in a Different World* (New York: Thunder's Mouth Press, 1990), 184.

33. Lewis Yablonsky, *The Hippie Trip* (New York: Pegasus, 1968), 160–161; Harrison Pope Jr., *Voices from the Drug Culture* (Boston: Beacon Press, 1971), 11.

34. Lillian Roxon, *Rock Encyclopedia* (New York: Grosset & Dunlap, 1978), 241.

35. Carl Belz, *The Story of Rock* (New York: Oxford University Press, 1972), 31; Rubin, *Do It*, 18.

36. Robert Palmer, *Rock and Roll: An Unruly History* (New York: Harmony, 1995), 51–52.

37. Grace Elizabeth Hale, *A Nation of Outsiders: How the White Middle Class Fell in Love with Rebellion in Postwar America* (New York: Oxford University Press, 2011), 49, 52–60.

38. Hale, 51, 61–62, 72.

39. John Sinclair, *Guitar Army: Street Writings/Prison Writings* (New York: Douglas Book, 1972), 13; Hoffman, *Woodstock Nation*, 22, 24; Leonard Wolf and Deborah Wolf, eds., *Voices from the Love Generation* (Boston: Little, Brown, 1968), 251–252.

40. Allen Ginsberg, *Collected Poems, 1947–1980* (New York: Harper & Row, 1988), 126–132.

41. Stephen L. Tanner, *Ken Kesey* (Boston: Twayne, 1983), 18.

42. Wolf and Wolf, *Voices from the Love Generation*, 154; Tom Jarrell, "Confessions of a Two-Time Draft Card Burner," *Avatar* (Boston), February 2–15, 1968.

43. John Sinclair interview in Allen Katzman, ed., *Our Time: An Anthology of Interviews from the East Village Other* (New York: Dial, 1972), 190; Wolf and Wolf, *Voices from the Love Generation*, 41–45, 123, 217, 250.

44. Mitchell Goodman, ed., *The Movement toward a New America: The Beginnings of a Long Revolution (A Collage)—A What?* (New York: Alfred A. Knopf, 1970), 522–523.

45. Wolf and Wolf, *Voices from the Love Generation*, xxi; "Moriarty Lives!," *Open City Press* (San Francisco), December 6–12, 1964; "End of the Road," *Los Angeles Free Press*,

February 16–22, 1968; Toni del Renzio, *The Flower Children* (London: Solstice Productions, 1969), 86.

46. Charles Perry, *The Haight-Ashbury: A History* (New York: Random House, 1984), 5; Leary quoted in Rorabaugh, *American Hippies*, 41.

47. Katzman, *Our Time*, 115–116; Wolf and Wolf, *Voices from the Love Generation*, 120.

48. Gene Anthony, *Magic of the Sixties* (Layton, UT: Gibbs Smith, 2004), 134; Nicholas von Hoffman, *We Are the People Our Parents Warned Us Against* (Chicago: Quadrangle, 1968), 22; Chepesiuk, *Sixties Radicals, Then and Now*, 258–259.

49. Nicholas von Hoffman, "A New Drug Culture is Burgeoning," *Washington Post*, August 21, 1966, E1.

50. Joel Williamson, *A Rage for Order: Black-White Relations in the American South since Emancipation* (New York: Oxford University Press, 1986), 85; C. Vann Woodward, *The Strange Career of Jim Crow* (New York: Oxford University Press, 1955), 97–109; Harvard Sitkoff, *The Struggle for Black Equality, 1954–1992* (New York: Hill and Wang, 1993), 3–36.

51. Frank H. Joyce, "The United States: A Country That's Lost Its Way," *Fifth Estate* (Detroit), May 1, 1967; Dave Lee, "Editorial—Who Will Lead?" *Berkeley Barb*, August 20, 1965; Peter Richardson, *No Simple Highway: A Cultural History of the Grateful Dead* (New York: St. Martin's, 2015), 45–46.

52. Chepesiuk, *Sixties Radicals, Then and Now*, 125.

53. Robert Shelton, *No Direction Home: The Life and Music of Bob Dylan* (New York: William Morrow, 1986), 149, 170, 179; David Allyn, *Make Love, Not War: The Sexual Revolution: An Unfettered History* (Boston: Little, Brown, 2000), 44; Chepesiuk, *Sixties Radicals, Then and Now*, 244; Dave McBride, "Counterculture," in *A Companion to Los Angeles*, ed. William Deverell and Greg Hise (Oxford: Wiley-Blackwell, 2010), 329.

54. Stephen J. Whitfield, *The Culture of the Cold War* (Baltimore: Johns Hopkins University Press, 1991), 5–7.

55. Sanders quoted in Abe Peck, *Uncovering the Sixties: The Life and Times of the Underground Press* (New York: Pantheon, 1985), 15.

56. "Age of Insanity," *Sanity* (Madison, WI), Winter 1962; Curl, *Memories of Drop City*, 11; "Survival: How to Exist after World War III," *Paper* (Mendocino, CA), June 1966.

57. Hal Draper, "The Mind of Clark Kerr," *Los Angeles Free Press*, November 5, 1964; "Comments on Berkeley," *Free Student News* (New York), n.d., 1965; Savio in Hal Draper, *Berkeley: The New Student Revolt* (New York: Grove, 1965), 98.

58. Martin A. Lee and Bruce Shlain, *Acid Dreams: The Complete Social History of LSD: The CIA, the Sixties, and Beyond* (New York: Grove, 1985), 127–129; Hunter S. Thompson, *The Great Shark Hunt: Strange Tales from a Strange Time* (New York: Summit, 1979), 403; Goodman, *Movement toward a New America*, 637; Richardson, *No Simple Highway*, 53–54.

59. Quoted in Thompson, *Great Shark Hunt*, 402.

60. Barry Miles, *Hippie* (New York: Sterling, 2004), 60; Wolfe, *Hippies*, 91–93; Michael Hicks, *Sixties Rock: Garage, Psychedelic, and Other Satisfactions* (Urbana: University of Illinois Press, 1999), 59.

61. Jack Bruce, "Rappin'," *Rebirth* (Phoenix), vol. 1, no. 2 (1969).

CHAPTER 2. SOMETHING HAPPENING

1. Leonard Wolf and Deborah Wolf, eds., *Voices from the Love Generation* (Boston: Little, Brown, 1968), 28.

2. Gulf of Tonkin Resolution quoted in George C. Herring, *America's Longest War: The United States and Vietnam, 1950–1975* (New York: Alfred A. Knopf, 1986), 122.

3. Lawrence Lipton, "The Wasp," *Los Angeles Free Press*, January 21, 1966.

4. Bertram Garskof, "A Way Out of the Next Few Wars," *Paper* (East Lansing, MI), May 16, 1967.

5. Haight-Ashbury quoted in Michael J. Kramer, *The Republic of Rock: Music and Citizenship in the Sixties Counterculture* (New York: Oxford University Press, 2013), 4; Ray Mungo, *Famous Long Ago: My Life and Hard Times with Liberation News Service* (Boston: Beacon, 1970), 3.

6. "The Great Underground Freeway," *Helix* (Seattle), April 13, 1967; resister quoted in Mitchell Goodman, ed., *The Movement toward a New America: (A Collage)—A What?* (New York: Alfred A. Knopf, 1970), 19.

7. Beth Bailey, *Sex in the Heartland* (Cambridge, MA: Harvard University Press, 1999), 78–79; "Ideologue: Who Owns the University?" *Free Student News* (New York), 1965; "Students: Moods & Mores," *Time*, November 18, 1966, 95–96.

8. Todd Gitlin, *The Sixties: Years of Hope, Days of Rage* (New York: Bantam, 1987), 20–21; *Time* quoted in Joseph C. Goulden, *The Best Years, 1945–1950* (New York: Atheneum, 1976), 265; Landon Y. Jones, *Great Expectations: America and the Baby Boom Generation* (New York: Coward, McCann and Geoghegan, 1980), 82–83.

9. Mark Matthews, *Droppers: America's First Hippie Commune, Drop City* (Norman: University of Oklahoma Press, 2010), 28, 31; Rikki Houston, "UWM Free University," *Kaleidoscope* (Milwaukee), October 6–19, 1967; Robert M. Gerfy, "Freshmen Ferment," *Western Activist* (Kalamazoo, MI), October 20, 1966; Char Jolles, "A Word to Freshmen," *Paper* (East Lansing, MI), September 29, 1966; Farber in Jerry Hopkins, ed., *The Hippie Papers: Trip-Taking, Mind-Quaking, Scene-Making Word from Where It's At* (New York: New American Library, 1968), 160–168; "Letters to the Editor," *Open City Press* (San Francisco), January 6–13, 1965; Garcia quoted in Peter Richardson, *No Simple Highway: A Cultural History of the Grateful Dead* (New York: St. Martin's, 2015), 90–91.

10. "Letter to the Editor," *Los Angeles Free Press*, July 16, 1965; William Estes, "Building Officials Aid Drive on Gang, Beatnik Hangouts," *Los Angeles Times*, August 26, 1965, SF1; "FBI Dogs Anti-draft Organizer," *Berkeley Barb*, October 22, 1965; "Cops Crack Down, But is it Curfew?" *Berkeley Barb*, January 14, 1966.

11. Doc Stanley, "Policemanship: A Guide," *Los Angeles Free Press*, February 18, 1966.

12. David Smothers, "Mopheads Refuse the Brush-Off," *Boston Globe*, September 26, 1965, 28.

13. Hopkins, *Hippie Papers*, 25–26.

14. John McMillian, *Smoking Typewriters: The Sixties Underground Press and the Rise of Alternative Media in America* (New York: Oxford University Press, 2011), 4–5; Louis Menand, "It Took A Village: How the *Voice* Changed Journalism," *New Yorker*, January 5, 2008, 44.

15. Abe Peck, *Uncovering the Sixties: The Life and Times of the Underground Press* (New York: Pantheon, 1985), 29–36.

16. Timothy Miller, *The Hippies and American Values* (Knoxville: University of Tennessee Press, 1991), 103.

17. Paul J. Robbins, "The Strip Is a Bummer?" *Los Angeles Free Press*, January 14, 1966; John Sinclair, "The Coatpuller," *Fifth Estate* (Detroit), December 15–31, 1966; Mungo, *Famous Long Ago*, 116; Miller, *Hippies and American Values*, 88–90.

18. Paul J. Robbins, "Bob Dylan as Bob Dylan," *Fifth Estate* (Detroit), July 30, 1966; Sinclair, "Coatpuller"; W. J. Rorabaugh, *American Hippies* (New York: Cambridge University Press, 2015), 112; Roy Ald, *The Youth Communes* (New York: Tower, 1970), 140.

19. "'Getting Used to It,'" *Fifth Estate* (Detroit), July 30, 1966.

20. Beth Bailey, "Sexual Revolution(s)," in *The Sixties: From Memory to History*, ed. David Farber (Chapel Hill: University of North Carolina Press, 1994), 235–258.

21. Lawrence Lipton, "The Wasp," *Los Angeles Free Press*, February 12 and November 26, 1965; Richard Thorne, "A Step toward Sexual Freedom in Berkeley," *Berkeley Barb*, September 4, 1965; Rorabaugh, *American Hippies*, 114–115; Miller, *Hippies and American Values*, 65–66.

22. Burton H. Wolfe, *The Hippies* (New York: Signet, 1968), 69; Lewis Yablonsky, *The Hippie Trip* (New York: Pegasus, 1968), 121.

23. David Allyn, *Make Love, Not War: The Sexual Revolution: An Unfettered History* (Boston: Little, Brown, 2000), 42–44.

24. Allyn, 46.

25. Allyn, 46–47.

26. Allyn, 41, 42, 49.

27. Bernard Gavzer, "New Kicks on the College Campus?" *Baltimore Sun*, June 5, 1966, FC1; Leonard Downie Jr., "Drug-Taking Spreads on Nation's Campuses," *Washington Post*, September 9, 1965, A1; "An Epidemic of Acid Heads," *Time*, March 11, 1966; Harry Nelson, "Educated Youths Face Danger from Marijuana," *Los Angeles Times*, April 3, 1966, B1.

28. Martin A. Lee and Bruce Shlain, *Acid Dreams: The Complete Social History of LSD: The CIA, the Sixties, and Beyond* (New York: Grove, 1985), 150; Cohen quoted in "An Epidemic of Acid Heads"; "Essay: LSD," *Time*, June 17, 1966; Harry Nelson, "Psychosis Peril Seen in Marijuana," *Los Angeles Times*, February 11, 1966, 4; Nelson, "Educated Youths Face Danger," B1.

29. Miller, *Hippies and American Values*, 25; Tom Coffin, "Dope," *Great Speckled Bird* (Atlanta), October 16, 1969.

30. Miller, *Hippies and American Values*, 26–29; David Farber, "The Intoxicated State/ Illegal Nation: Drugs in the Sixties Counterculture," in *Imagine Nation: The American Counterculture of the 1960s and '70s*, ed. Peter Braunstein and Michael William Doyle (New York: Routledge, 2002), 34.

31. John Wilcock, "The Village Square," *Los Angeles Free Press*, August 6, 1965; Richard Neff, "Marihuana—A Key Issue," *Distant Drummer* (Philadelphia), May 2–9, 1969; "Referendum Would Remove Marijuana Prohibition," *Los Angeles Free Press*, January 21, 1966.

32. Albert Hofmann, *LSD: My Problem Child* (New York: McGraw-Hill, 1980), 19.

33. Matthew Oram, *The Trials of Psychedelic Therapy: LSD Psychotherapy in America* (Baltimore: Johns Hopkins University Press, 2018), 3–5.

34. Paul Perry, *On the Bus: The Complete Guide to the Legendary Trip of Ken Kesey and the Merry Pranksters and the Birth of the Counterculture* (New York: Thunder's Mouth, 1990), 4, 7–9; Lee and Shlain, *Acid Dreams*, 3–43.

35. Perry, *On the Bus*, 4–7; Lee and Shlain, *Acid Dreams*, 44–53.

36. Lee and Shlain, *Acid Dreams*, 71–113.

37. Timothy Leary, *Flashbacks: An Autobiography* (New York: G. Putnam, 1990), 49–50, 253.

38. Charles Perry, *The Haight-Ashbury: A History* (New York: Random House, 1984), 107–108; Garcia quoted in David Pichaske, *A Generation in Motion: Popular Music and Culture in the Sixties* (New York: Schirmer Books, 1979), 126.

39. Peter Edler, "The Human Element in LSD," *Open City Press* (San Francisco), March 17–23, 1965; "LSD—The Way to God," *Modern Utopian* (San Francisco), May

1966; Miller, *Hippies and American Values*, 35–36; James T. Carey, ed., *The College Drug Scene* (Englewood Cliffs, NJ: Prentice Hall, 1968), 63.

40. Miller, *Hippies and American Values*, 35; Will Albert, "Who Is Mary Jane?" *Notes from the Underground* (Dallas), August 15–31, 1967; student quoted in Nicholas von Hoffman, "A New Drug Culture is Burgeoning," *Washington Post*, August 21, 1966, E1.

41. Nicholas Schou, *Orange Sunshine: The Brotherhood of Eternal Love and Its Quest to Spread Peace, Love, and Acid to the World* (New York: Thomas Dunne Books, 2010), 1–96, 123–124, 167–173, 215–242.

42. Peter Maguire and Mike Ritter, *Thai Stick: Surfers, Scammers, and the Untold Story of the Marijuana Trade* (New York: Columbia University Press, 2014), 1–9, quote on 2.

43. Wolfe, *Hippies*, 26.

44. Wolfe, 25.

45. Joan Morrison and Robert K. Morrison, *From Camelot to Kent State: The Sixties Experience in the Words of Those Who Lived It* (New York: Oxford University Press, 2001), 205, 213.

46. Miller, *Hippies and American Values*, 33; "The New Gurus," *Oracle of Southern California*, December 1967; "LSD—The Way to God."

47. "LSD—The Way to God."

48. Gitlin, *Sixties*, 197–198.

49. Anthony Scaduto, *Bob Dylan* (New York: Grosset & Dunlap, 1971), 175.

50. Robbins, "Bob Dylan as Bob Dylan;" Scaduto, *Bob Dylan*, 176; Goodman, *Movement toward a New America*, 378–379.

51. Goodman, *Movement toward A New America*, 379–380; Andrew Grant Jackson, *1965: The Most Revolutionary Year in Music* (New York: Thomas Dunne Books, 2015), 110–111.

52. David Szatmary, *Rockin' in Time: A Social History of Rock and Roll* (Upper Saddle River, NJ: Prentice Hall, 1996), 98–101; Nicholas Schaffner, *The Beatles Forever* (New York: McGraw-Hill, 1978), 25, 31, 33.

53. Carl Belz, *The Story of Rock* (New York: Oxford University Press, 1972), 124, 128.

54. Fred Haines, "The Beatles Are Fun," *Los Angeles Free Press*, 1964; David A. Noebel, *Communism, Hypnotism and the Beatles: An Analysis of the Communist Use of Music, The Communist Master Music Plan* (Tulsa, OK: Christian Crusade, 1965), 10–15; Rex Weiner and Deanne Stillman, *Woodstock Census: The Nationwide Survey of the Sixties Generation* (New York: Viking, 1979), 80.

55. Peter Doggett, *There's a Riot Going On: Revolutionaries, Rock Stars, and the Rise and Fall of the '60s* (Edinburgh: Canongate, 2007), 13; Schaffner, *Beatles Forever*, 49, 54–58.

56. Schaffner, *Beatles Forever*, 49–50.

57. Schaffner, *Beatles Forever*, 62–64; Pichaske, *Generation in Motion*, 187.

58. Reebee Garofalo, *Rockin' Out: Popular Music in the U.S.A.* (Upper Saddle River, NJ: Prentice Hall, 2008), 185–187; Charlie Gillett, *The Sound of the City: The Rise of Rock and Roll* (New York: Outerbridge & Dienstfrey, 1970), 316–317.

59. Doggett, *There's a Riot Going On*, 62–63; Belz, *Story of Rock*, 168–170.

60. Michael Hicks, *Sixties Rock: Garage, Psychedelic, and Other Satisfactions* (Urbana: University of Illinois Press, 1999), 60–62, liner notes quoted on 61; Pichaske, *Generation in Motion*, 119.

61. Wolf and Wolf, *Voices from the Love Generation*, 86; Weiner and Stillman, *Woodstock Census*, 81.

62. Kramer, *Republic of Rock*, 5, 8, 11–12.

63. Stewart Albert, "Should Free University Be Grateful to Hearst?" *Berkeley Barb*, September 4, 1965; Brad Lang, "FUEL: The Torch is Passed," *Paper* (East Lansing, MI), April 7, 1966.

64. Matthews, *Droppers*, 49.

65. Timothy Miller, *The 60s Communes: Hippies and Beyond* (Syracuse, NY: Syracuse University Press, 1999), 20–22.

66. Miller, 23–26, woman quoted on 25.

67. Miller, 31–37, quote on 31.

68. Perry, *Haight-Ashbury*, 7–11; Jackson, 1965, 243.

69. Duncan quoted in Jackson, 1965, 245–246.

70. Lee and Shlain, *Acid Dreams*, 146–147.

71. Rorabaugh, *American Hippies*, 34; John Wilcock, "The Village Square," *Open City Press* (San Francisco), February 3–9, 1965.

72. Bob Spitz, *The Beatles: The Biography* (New York: Back Bay Books, 2005), 745–747, quote on 747.

73. Doc Stanley, "Poetry and Music Thing at Bowman-Mann Gallery," and Paul Earls, "First Draco Concert," *Los Angeles Free Press*, August 13, 1965; "Total Theatre on Dec. 27," *Los Angeles Free Press*, December 24, 1965.

74. James Wojack, "A Pseudo-Psychedelic Eve in the 'God Box,'" *Open City Press* (San Francisco), February 3–9, 1965; "Symphony at Laughing Stock is a Bit Hard on the Nerves," *Open City Press* (San Francisco), January 13–19, 1965.

75. John Wilcock, "The Village Square," *Open City Press* (San Francisco), February 3–9, 1965; "Incense and Bass: LSD Show is S.R.O.," *New York Times*, April 11, 1965, 58.

76. Perry, *Haight-Ashbury*, 27–29; Kelley quoted in Richardson, *No Simple Highway*, 53.

77. Barry Miles, *Hippie* (New York: Sterling, 2004), 99–100.

78. Perry, *Haight-Ashbury*, 30–31.

79. Miles, *Hippie*, 99–100.

80. Robert C. Cottrell, *Sex, Drugs, and Rock 'n' Roll: The Rise of America's 1960s Counterculture* (Lanham, MD: Rowman and Littlefield, 2015), 142.

81. James Henke and Parke Puterbaugh, eds., *I Want to Take You Higher: The Psychedelic Era, 1965–1969* (San Francisco: Chronicle Books, 1997), 91–96; Franklin Bach, "Bach on Rock," *Fifth Estate* (Detroit), October 16–31, 1966; John Sinclair, "The Coatpuller," *Fifth Estate* (Detroit), November 15–30, 1966.

82. Richardson, *No Simple Highway*, 64.

83. Ralph Young, *Dissent: The History of an American Idea* (New York: New York University Press, 2015), 456–457.

84. Lee and Shlain, *Acid Dreams*, 133–134, Dylan quoted on 134; Tom Wolfe, *The Electric Kool-Aid Acid Test* (New York: Farrar, Straus and Giroux, 1968), 221–224.

85. Rebecca Klatch, *A Generation Divided: The New Left, the New Right, and the 1960s* (Berkeley: University of California Press, 1999), 136–137; Shea Were, "Seeing with the Other Eye: Cool and Uncool," *Berkeley Barb*, January 28, 1966.

86. McGuinn quoted in Tom Nolan, "The Frenzied Frontier of Pop Music," *Los Angeles Times*, November 27, 1966, W36; "Hate War? Stay at Home on 1st 'Gentle Thursday,'" *Open City Press* (San Francisco), March 17–23, 1965; GS, "We All Want to Change the World," *Aquarian Herald* (Nyack, NY), November 30, 1969.

87. Klatch, *Generation Divided*, 137.

88. Klatch, *Generation Divided*, 137; David Farber, "The Counterculture and the Antiwar Movement," in *Give Peace a Chance: Exploring the Vietnam Antiwar Movement*, ed. Melvin Small and William D. Hoover (Syracuse, NY: Syracuse University Press, 1992), 12.

89. Lee and Shlain, *Acid Dreams*, 119–120; Rick Dodgson, *It's All a Kind of Magic: The Young Ken Kesey* (Madison: University of Wisconsin Press, 2013), 145; Ken Kesey, *Kesey's Garage Sale* (New York: Viking, 1973), 175.

90. Lee and Shlain, *Acid Dreams*, 121–123, Kesey quoted on 121.

91. Lee and Shlain, *Acid Dreams*, 123–124; Dodgson, *It's All a Kind of Magic*, 145.

92. Press release quoted in Gene Anthony, *The Summer of Love: Haight-Ashbury at its Highest* (Milbrae, CA: Celestial Arts, 1980), 103.

93. Paul Jay Robbins, "Lysergic A Go-Go as It Went," *Los Angeles Free Press*, November 26, 1965.

94. Perry, *On the Bus*, 151; Miles, *Hippie*, 54, 96; Kesey quoted in Martin Torgoff, *Can't Find My Way Home: America in the Great Stoned Age, 1945–2000* (New York: Simon and Schuster, 2004), 119.

95. Kesey and Garcia quoted in Lee and Shlain, *Acid Dreams*, 143–144; Perry, *Haight-Ashbury*, 99–100.

96. Peck, *Uncovering the Sixties*, 37–40, 58–59, Allen Katzman quoted on 39.

97. Miller, *60s Communes*, 41–43.

98. Miller, 46–51, woman quoted on 48–49.

99. Miller, *60s Communes*, 44–46; Jay Stephens, *Storming Heaven: LSD and the American Dream* (New York: Atlantic Monthly Press, 1987), 305.

100. Art Buchwald, "Rub-a-Dub-Dub: All Those Demonstrators Oughta Be Dunked in a Tub," *Washington Post*, April 25, 1965, E7; Eisenhower quoted in Joseph Dinneen Jr., "Across the City Desk: Ike So Right on Beatniks," *Boston Globe*, October 17, 1965, 78; Louis Harris, "Public Registers Strong Disapproval of Nonconformity," *Washington Post*, September 27, 1965, A2; professor quoted in Gavzer, "New Kicks on the College Campus?" FC1; truck driver quoted in J. L. Simmons and Barry Winograd, *It's Happening: A Portrait of the Youth Scene Today* (Santa Barbara, CA: Marc-Laird, 1966), 76.

101. Laurence Leamer, *The Paper Revolutionaries: The Rise of the Underground Press* (New York: Simon and Schuster, 1972), 40.

102. Jerry Hopkins, "Making It on the Strip," *Los Angeles Free Press*, December 24, 1965; Miles, *Hippie*, 62, 65, 136–137; Richard Goldstein, "On Sunset Strip," *Boston Globe*, July 18, 1966, 8.

103. Miles, *Hippie*, 129.

104. Jackson, 1965, 66, 133, quotes on 133.

105. Miles, *Hippie*, 132.

106. Christopher Mele, *Selling the Lower East Side: Culture, Real Estate, and Resistance in New York City* (Minneapolis: University of Minnesota Press, 2000), 153–166.

107. Mele, *Selling the Lower East Side*, 62; Young, *Dissent*, 466–467; Miles, *Hippie*, 148–152.

108. Arthur Marwick, *The Sixties: Cultural Revolution in Britain, France, Italy, and the United States* (Oxford: Oxford University Press, 1998), 342–343.

109. James Roose-Evans, *Experimental Theatre: From Stanislavsky to Peter Brook* (New York: Universe Books, 1989), 105; Judith Malina quoted in Marwick, *Sixties*, 343.

110. Miles, *Hippie*, 156–158; Doggett, *There's a Riot Going On*, 21–22, Sanders quoted on 22; Sanders quoted in Peck, *Uncovering the Sixties*, 16.

111. Walt Crowley, *Rites of Passage: A Memoir of the Sixties in Seattle* (Seattle: University of Washington Press, 1995), 48–64.

112. Jeff Hale, "The White Panthers' 'Total Assault on the Culture,'" in Braunstein and Doyle, *Imagine Nation*, 127.

113. Hale, 127, 129–130.

114. "Festival for People," *Fifth Estate* (Detroit), July 30, 1966; Gary Grimshaw, "Detroit Freaks Out with First Participatory Zoo Dance," *Fifth Estate* (Detroit), October 16–31, 1966.

115. Matthew Levin, *Cold War University: Madison and the New Left in the Sixties* (Madison: University of Wisconsin Press, 2013), 141–142; "Essay: LSD," *Time*, June 17, 1966.

116. Doug Rossinow, *The Politics of Authenticity: Liberalism, Christianity, and the New Left in America* (New York: Columbia University Press, 1998), 256–262; advertisement in *Rag* (Austin), October 31, 1966.

117. "Students: The Free-Sex Movement," *Time*, March 11, 1966, 66; Gary Chason, "Sexual Freedom League: The Naked Truth," *Rag* (Austin), August 17, 1966.

118. Perry, *Haight-Ashbury*, 21.

119. Rorabaugh, *American Hippies*, 139–140; Lee and Shlain, *Acid Dreams*, 170–175.

120. Cohen quoted in Gene Anthony, *Magic of the Sixties* (Layton, UT: Gibbs Smith, 2004), 169; leaflet in Perry, *Haight-Ashbury*, 92–93; Lee and Shlain, *Acid Dreams*, 149; Don McNeill, *Moving through Here* (New York: Alfred A. Knopf, 1970), 23.

121. Miles, *Hippie*, 140–145; "Youths Again Rally along Sunset Blvd.," *Los Angeles Times*, November 16, 1966, 3; Pete Johnson, "400 Youths on Strip Hold 'Brutality' Protest," *Los Angeles Times*, November 19, 1966, 19; "Youth: Sunset along the Strip," *Time*, December 2, 1966, 69; Wilcock quoted in Doggett, *There's a Riot Going On*, 66–67.

122. Perry, *Haight-Ashbury*, 110–111.

123. Cottrell, *Sex, Drugs, and Rock 'n' Roll*, 140–141; Warren Hinckle, "The Social History of the Hippies," *Ramparts*, March 1967, 25.

124. Gretchen Lemke-Santangelo, *Daughters of Aquarius: Women of the Sixties Counterculture* (Lawrence: University Press of Kansas, 2009), 96; Crescent Dragonwagon, *The Commune Cookbook* (New York: Simon and Schuster, 1972), 154, 156.

CHAPTER 3. VIBRATIONS ACROSS THE NATION

1. Lang quoted in Bruce J. Schulman, *The Seventies: The Great Shift in American Culture, Society, and Politics* (New York: Free Press, 2001), 18.

2. Hippie numbers in Terry H. Anderson, *The Sixties*, 4th ed. (New York: Pearson, 2012), 117.

3. Martin A. Lee and Bruce Shlain, *Acid Dreams: The Complete Social History of LSD: The CIA, the Sixties, and Beyond* (New York: Grove, 1985), 159–160; "Tune In/Turn Out/Be-In," *Berkeley Barb*, January 13, 1967; Steve Levine, "The First American Mehla," *San Francisco Oracle*, February 1967.

4. "Dropouts with a Mission," *Newsweek*, February 6, 1967, 92; Gene Anthony, *The Summer of Love: Haight-Ashbury at Its Highest* (Milbrae, CA: Celestial Arts, 1980), 7.

5. Lee and Shlain, *Acid Dreams*, 164–167; Leary in John Bryan, *Whatever Happened to Timothy Leary?* (San Francisco: Renaissance, 1980), 96; and Jesse Kornbluth, ed., *Notes from the New Underground: An Anthology* (New York: Viking, 1968), 123.

6. "Human Be-In: Tribes Assemble on North Beach Avenue," *Seed* (Chicago), May–June 1967.

7. Bernard Weinraub, "10,000 Chant 'L-O-V-E,'" *New York Times*, March 27, 1967, 1.

8. Dave Larsen, "Hippies Fill Glen with Splendors of Love and Miniskirts," Los Angeles Times, March 27, 1967, 3; "It's Love, Love, Love!," Ebony, July 1967, 100.

9. "Letters," East Village Other (New York), July 1–15, 1967; "Love is Great, I Love It," Berkeley Barb, January 20, 1967; Warren Hinckle, "A Social History of the Hippies," in The American Experience: A Radical Reader, ed. Harold Jaffe and John Tytell (New York: Harper & Row, 1970), 284.

10. Sheila Ryan, "Out of the Ashes, a Phoenix," Washington Free Press, April 2, 1967.

11. Douglas Robinson, "100,000 Rally at U.N. against Vietnam War," New York Times, April 16, 1967, 1–2; Don McNeill, Moving through Here (New York: Alfred A. Knopf, 1970), 11.

12. Robert J. Anglin, "Seven Thousand Attend Blissful 'Be-in' at Franklin Park Zoo," Boston Globe, April 23, 1967, 1, 14.

13. "Houston Love-In," Rag (Austin), May 8, 1967.

14. Shell Salasnek, "Love-In," Fifth Estate (Detroit), May 15–31, 1967; Jeff A. Hale, "The White Panthers' 'Total Assault on the Culture,'" in Imagine Nation: The American Counterculture of the 1960s and '70s, ed. Peter Braunstein and Michael William Doyle (New York: Routledge, 2002), 130–134.

15. Walt Crowley, Rites of Passage: A Memoir of the Sixties in Seattle (Seattle: University of Washington Press, 1995), 60, 74; Alan J. Stein, "Be-In Is Held at Seattle's Volunteer Park on April 30, 1967," History Link, June 20, 2007, https://www.historylink.org/file/8189.

16. "Human Be-In," Seed.

17. "30 Seized in Philadelphia as 2,500 Stage a 'Be-In,'" New York Times, May 15, 1967, 14.

18. Abe Peck, Uncovering the Sixties: The Life and Times of the Underground Press (New York: Pantheon, 1985), xv, 43–133.

19. Alex Apostolides, "It's Tough When You Don't Want to Kill People," Los Angeles Free Press, September 29–October 5, 1967.

20. "To the Students," Buffalo Insighter (Buffalo, NY), September 25, 1967; Farrel Broslawsky, "'Legitimate' Protest Sustains Institutions," Los Angeles Free Press, November 10–17, 1967.

21. "Letters," East Village Other (New York), May 1–15, 1967; "Letters," Extra! (Providence), May 27–July 1, 1969.

22. Jolm Raymond, "Yes, Virginia, There's a $anta," Berkeley Citizen, December 23, 1966; "Joe Pyne Interviews Jesus Christ," F.T.E.! (Los Angeles), March 1967.

23. John Sieler, "What is Obscene?" Asterisk (Omaha), January 8, 1969.

24. "Editorial: Pray for Cleveland," Buddhist Third Class Junkmail Oracle (Cleveland) vol. 1, no. 5 (1967); Don Peterson, "Smile at Narcs?" Kaleidoscope (Milwaukee), October 6–19, 1967; "Heads Busted on 25st," Washington Free Press, May 5–11, 1967; Jack Newfield, "One Cheer for the Hippies," Nation, June 26, 1967, 809; "1,500 in Florida Hold the State's First Love-In," Baltimore Sun, June 12, 1967, A4; "Hippie Love-in Draws 10,000 in Seal Beach," Los Angeles Times, June 26, 1967, OC8; "New Orleans Has Love-in," Boston Globe, July 10, 1967, 16; "Be-in Bugged by Brusque Burlesque," Spokane Natural vol. 1, no. 11 (1967).

25. Peck, Uncovering the Sixties, 45.

26. Horace Sutton, "Hip Ideas on How to Visit Hippieland in the Bay Area," Los Angeles Times, July 2, 1967, G7; Jeff Jassen, "What Price Love?" Berkeley Barb, May 5–11, 1967.

27. Lewis Yablonsky, *The Hippie Trip* (New York: Pegasus, 1968), 26.

28. Jerry Rosenfield, "To No More Call a Man a Spade," *Berkeley Barb*, March 10, 1967; Chester Anderson, "Two Page Racial Rap," *Communications Company* (San Francisco), February 9, 1967, and Chester Anderson, "Freedom Now," *Communications Company*, n.d., box 1, folder 6, Hippies Collection, San Francisco Public Library; Martin Arnold, "Organized Hippies Emerge on Coast," *New York Times*, May 5, 1967, 40; "Negroes Angered by Coast Hippies," *New York Times*, September 24, 1967, 30.

29. Larsen, "Hippies Fill Glen with Splendors of Love and Miniskirts," 3.

30. Anderson, "Two Page Racial Rap" and Anderson, "Freedom Now;" Tuli Kupferberg, "The Hip and the Square: The Hippie Generation," *Berkeley Barb*, August 4, 1967.

31. Dave McBride, "Counterculture," in *A Companion to Los Angeles*, ed. William Deverell and Greg Hise (Oxford: Wiley-Blackwell, 2010), 331–332.

32. Jim Solono, "Love-In That Made Mostly Enemies," *Open City* (Los Angeles), September 7–13, 1967.

33. Jonah Raskin, *For the Hell of It: The Life and Times of Abbie Hoffman* (Berkeley: University of California Press, 1996), 107–108; "Hippies Stage a Be-In in Newark Negro Area," *New York Times*, July 23, 1967, 18.

34. Stephen A. O. Golden, "Police Look on as Hippies Stage a Park Smoke-In," *New York Times*, July 31, 1967, 23; "Hippies 'Integrate' with Puerto Ricans," *New York Times*, August 16, 1967, 36.

35. Eldridge Cleaver, *Soul on Ice* (New York: Dell, 1968), 75; Leary quoted in Robert Greenfield, *Timothy Leary: A Biography* (New York: Harcourt, 2006), 414; and Robert C. Cottrell, *Sex, Drugs, and Rock 'n' Roll: The Rise of America's 1960s Counterculture* (Lanham, MD: Rowman and Littlefield, 2015), 335.

36. Tim Hodgdon, *Manhood in the Age of Aquarius: Masculinity in Two Countercultural Communities, 1965–83* (New York: Columbia University Press, 2008), 44–46; "Warning to So-Called 'Paper Panthers,'" *Black Panther* (Oakland), September 14, 1968.

37. Philip Norman, *Shout! The Beatles in Their Generation* (New York: Simon and Schuster, 1981), 288–291.

38. Norman, 289, 293.

39. Norman, *Shout!*, 292–293; Leary in Nicholas Schaffner, *The Beatles Forever* (New York: McGraw-Hill, 1978), 71.

40. Robert Santelli, *Aquarius Rising: The Rock Festival Years* (New York: Dell, 1980), 21–59.

41. "Death of Hippie—Birth of Free," *Seed* (Chicago), October 14–November 3, 1967; Lee and Shlain, *Acid Dreams*, 175–179.

42. "Uncle Tim's Children," *Communications Company* (San Francisco), April 16, 1967, box 1, folder 4, Chester Anderson Papers, BANC MSS 92/839 c, Bancroft Library, University of California, Berkeley; John Luce, "Haight-Ashbury Today: A Case of Terminal Euphoria," *Esquire*, July 1969, 68.

43. "Death of Hippie—Birth of Free"; "Hippie Movement Has Lost 'Spirit,'" *Dallas Morning News*, October 6, 1967, 2; "Hippies: Where Have All the Flowers Gone?" *Time*, October 13, 1967, 30–31.

44. Emanuel Perlmutter, "Girl, Youth Slain in 'Village' Cellar," *New York Times*, October 9, 1967, 1.

45. "Trouble in Hippieland," *Newsweek*, October 30, 1967, 84; "Hippies—A Passing Fad?" *U.S. News & World Report*, October 23, 1967, 42; "Hippie Movement Has Lost

'Spirit,'" 2; "Hippies: Where Have All the Flowers Gone?" 30–31; Earl Shorris, "Love Is Dead," *New York Times Magazine*, October 29, 1967, 27.

46. Jack Jenkins, "A Positive Hip Philosophy," *Open City* (Los Angeles), January 5–11, 1968.

47. McBride, "Counterculture," 330–332; Michael Walker, *Laurel Canyon: The Inside Story of Rock-and-Roll's Legendary Neighborhood* (New York: Farrar, Straus and Giroux, 2006), xiii–xiv.

48. Christopher Mele, *Selling the Lower East Side: Culture, Real Estate, and Resistance in New York City* (Minneapolis: University of Minnesota Press, 2000), 153–179.

49. "Human Be-In," *Solid Muldoon* (Denver), September 27, 1967; "He Falls Asleep," *Solid Muldoon* (Denver), November 10, 1967; and "Interview: Communal Living," *Solid Muldoon* (Denver), December 1, 1967; Charles Perry, *The Haight-Ashbury: A History* (New York: Random House, 1984), 227.

50. "'Pot' Arrests Spark Protest by Hippies," *Washington Post*, August 22, 1967, A12; "500 Hippies Stage a Protest March," *New York Times*, August 23, 1967, 19.

51. Golden, "Police Look on as Hippies Stage a Park Smoke-In," 23; "Smoke-In Held at Cambridge," *Boston Globe*, October 9, 1967, 4; "Heat Cool at Boston Pot-In," *Los Angeles Free Press*, October 20–26, 1967; "Saturday Smoke-In," *Berkeley Barb*, September 1–7, 1967.

52. Robert Rothman, "Bigot Boy vs. the Hippies," *Kaleidoscope* (Milwaukee), October 6–19, 1967; Mary Ann Wynkoop, *Dissent in the Heartland: The Sixties at Indiana University* (Bloomington: Indiana University Press, 2002), 51.

53. Raskin, *For the Hell of It*, 117.

54. Raskin, *For the Hell of It*, 90, 97–108, quote on 97. "Organizing hippies" comes from the subtitle of chapter 4 in Marty Jezer, *Abbie Hoffman: American Rebel* (New Brunswick, NJ: Rutgers University Press, 1992).

55. Raskin, *For the Hell of It*, 117–120; Lee and Shlain, *Acid Dreams*, 203.

56. Lee and Shlain, *Acid Dreams*, 203–204; Jezer, *Abbie Hoffman*, 117–119; Paul Cooper, "Washington," *Notes from the Underground* (Dallas), November 1967.

57. Simon Hall, *Peace and Freedom: The Civil Rights and Antiwar Movements in the 1960s* (Philadelphia: University of Pennsylvania Press, 2005), 109, 124–125.

58. "Invitation to the Psychedelic Community," *Communications Company* (San Francisco), January 28, 1967, box 1, folder 6, Hippies Collection, San Francisco Public Library; Michael Brand, "And You Don't Know What It Is, Do You, Mr. Jones?," *Bauls* (West Lafayette, IN), January 6–February 2, 1969.

59. Henry Gross, *The Flower People* (New York: Ballantine Books, 1968), 56; Joseph Berke, ed., *Counter Culture* (London: Peter Owen, 1969), 85; Jerry Hopkins, ed., *The Hippie Papers: Trip-Taking, Mind-Quaking, Scene-Making Word from Where It's At* (New York: New American Library, 1968), 17–18; John Sinclair, "Coatpuller," *Fifth Estate* (Detroit), May 15–31, 1967.

60. Hopkins, *Hippie Papers*, 18; "Denver seeker" in *Solid Muldoon* (Denver), October 27, 1967.

61. Timothy Miller, *The Hippies and American Values* (Knoxville: University of Tennessee Press, 1991), 54; Leah Fritz, "Female Sexuality and the Liberated Orgasm," *Berkeley Tribe*, October 16–23, 1970.

62. Miller, *Hippies and American Values*, 59–61; "Beast and the Beauty," *Helix* (Seattle), July 18, 1968; LeRoy Moore Jr., "From Profane to Sacred America: Religion and the Cultural Revolution in the United States," *Journal of the American Academy of Religion* 39,

no. 3 (September 1971): 333; Gina Shepard, "If It's Their Thing Just Let 'em Leer," *Berkeley Barb*, July 7–13, 1967.

63. Bro. Sartoris Snopes, "Aquarian Trip," *Kudzu* (Jackson, MS), October 3, 1968; Miller, *Hippies and American Values*, 18; "David Crosby of the Byrds," *Oracle of Southern California* (Los Angeles), October 1967.

64. Robert S. Ellwood, *The Sixties Spiritual Awakening: American Religion Moving from Modern to Postmodern* (New Brunswick, NJ: Rutgers University Press, 1994), 143–144.

65. Snopes, "Aquarian Trip"; John Bassett McCleary, *The Hippie Dictionary: A Cultural Encyclopedia (and Phraseicon) of the 1960s and 1970s* (Berkeley, CA: Ten Speed, 2002), 34; "Doctrines of the Dropouts," *Time*, January 5, 1968, 62.

66. Toni del Renzio, *The Flower Children* (London: Solstice Productions, 1969), 59; "The Hippies of Hashberry," *Ebony*, August 1967, 118; "David Crosby of the Byrds"; Mike Clevenger, "Memoirs of the Living Dead," *Rebirth* (Phoenix) vol. 1, no. 6 (1969); Leonard Wolf and Deborah Wolf, eds., *Voices from the Love Generation* (Boston: Little, Brown, 1968), 36.

67. Hopkins, *Hippie Papers*, 68; "Get High," *Rebirth* (Phoenix) vol. 1, no. 6 (1969); Pat Boone, *A New Song* (Carol Stream, IL: Creation House, 1970), 181; Eugene Schoenfeld, "Dr. HipPocrates," *Los Angeles Free Press*, August 18–24, 1967.

68. Timothy Leary, *The Politics of Ecstasy* (New York: Putnam, 1968), 129; Ray Nelson, "Sex under LSD," *Intercourse: A Journal of Sexual Freedom* (Berkeley), n.d.; Miller, *Hippies and American Values*, 40–41.

69. "Downers," *Der Zeitgeist* (Phoenix), n.d.; Hopkins, *Hippie Papers*, 68–72.

70. Godfrey Hodgson, *America in Our Time: From World War II to Nixon—What Happened and Why* (New York: Doubleday, 1976), 330; Peter Maguire and Mike Ritter, *Thai Stick: Surfers, Scammers, and the Untold Story of the Marijuana Trade* (New York: Columbia University Press, 2014), 23; Emily Dufton, *Grass Roots: The Rise and Fall and Rise of Marijuana in America* (New York: Basic Books, 2017), 7; "The New Mood on Campus," *Newsweek*, December 29, 1969, 42, 44; "The Drug Generation: Growing Younger," *Newsweek*, April 21, 1969, 107; Harrison Pope Jr., *Voices from the Drug Culture* (Boston: Beacon, 1971), 7–8.

71. David Pichaske, *A Generation in Motion: Popular Music and Culture in the Sixties* (New York: Schirmer Books, 1979), 109, 113; W. J. Rorabaugh, *American Hippies* (New York: Cambridge University Press, 2015), 92.

72. David Swanston, "A Beatle Does His Thing," *San Francisco Chronicle*, August 8, 1967, 3; Wolf and Wolf, *Voices from the Love Generation*, 218.

73. Kornbluth, *Notes from the New Underground*, 206.

74. Guy Strait, "What Is a Hippie?" *Haight-Ashbury Maverick* (San Francisco), April 1967; Miller, *Hippies and American Values*, 112.

75. Berke, *Counter Culture*, 85; "Roving Rat Fink," *Berkeley Barb*, July 4–10, 1969.

76. Tuli Kupferberg, "The Politics of Love," *East Village Other* (New York), May 1–15, 1967.

77. Campus statistics in John Morton Blum, *Years of Discord: American Politics and Society, 1961–1974* (New York: W. W. Norton, 1991), 357.

78. For New Left and counterculture as distinct and separate phenomena see Rorabaugh, *American Hippies*; Miller, *Hippies and American Values*; David Caute, *Year of the Barricades: A Journey through 1968* (New York: Harper & Row, 1988); Thomas Frank, *The Conquest of Cool: Business Culture, Counterculture, and the Rise of Hip Consumerism* (Chicago: University of Chicago Press, 1997); Stewart Burns, *Social Movements of the 1960s: Searching*

for Democracy (Boston: Twayne, 1990); Jack Whalen and Richard Flacks, *Beyond the Barricades: The Sixties Generation Grows Up* (Philadelphia: Temple University Press, 1989); Todd Gitlin, *The Sixties: Years of Hope, Days of Rage* (New York: Bantam, 1987). For those who contest the traditional interpretation see David McBride, "Death City Radicals: The Counterculture in Los Angeles," in *The New Left Revisited*, ed. John McMillian and Paul Buhle (Philadelphia: Temple University Press, 2003); Richard Candida-Smith, *Utopia and Dissent: Art, Poetry, and Politics in California* (Berkeley: University of California Press, 1995); Julie Stephens, *Anti-disciplinary Protest: Sixties Radicalism and Post-modernism* (New York: Cambridge University Press, 1998); Joshua Clark Davis, *From Head Shops to Whole Foods: The Rise and Fall of Activist Entrepreneurs* (New York: Columbia University Press, 2017). For the turn to violence see Cottrell, *Sex, Drugs, and Rock 'n' Roll*, chapters 14–17; and Allen J. Matusow, *The Unraveling of America: A History of Liberalism in the 1960s* (New York: Harper & Row, 1984), 303.

79. Michael S. Foley, *Confronting the War Machine: Draft Resistance during the Vietnam War* (Chapel Hill: University of North Carolina Press, 2003), 356.

80. Gitlin, *Sixties*, 212, 225.

81. Blake Slonecker, "The Columbia Coalition: African Americans, New Leftists, and Counterculture at the Columbia University Protest of 1968," *Journal of Social History* 41, no. 4 (Summer 2008): 967–996.

82. Kornbluth, *Notes from the New Underground*, 284.

83. Dennis Jarrett, "Blood Sugar," *Great Speckled Bird* (Atlanta), August 2–15, 1968; see also Theodore Roszak, *The Making of a Counter Culture: Reflections on the Technocratic Society and Its Youthful Opposition* (Garden City, NY: Doubleday, 1969), 56–59.

84. Jarrett, "Blood Sugar"; Doug Rossinow, "'The Revolution Is about Our Lives': The New Left's Counterculture," in Braunstein and Doyle, *Imagine Nation*, 99–121; David Farber, "The Counterculture and the Antiwar Movement," in *Give Peace a Chance: Exploring the Vietnam Antiwar Movement*, ed. Melvin Small and William D. Hoover (Syracuse, NY: Syracuse University Press, 1992), 14; Rebecca Klatch, *A Generation Divided: The New Left, the New Right, and the 1960s* (Berkeley: University of California Press, 1999), 142–143.

85. Mike Wheelock, "Is Love Dead?" *Los Angeles Free Press*, November 22, 1968; "Letters," *Fifth Estate* (Detroit), November 28–December 11, 1968.

86. Ethel Grodzins Romm, *The Open Conspiracy: What America's Angry Generation Is Saying* (New York: Giniger, 1970), 108; Kupferberg, "Politics of Love."

87. Farber, "Counterculture and the Antiwar Movement," 14.

88. "Beatles Revolution: Two Views," *Seed* (Chicago), vol. 2, no. 13 (1968); Peck, *Uncovering the Sixties*, 168.

89. Romm, *Open Conspiracy*, 108; "David Crosby of the Byrds."

90. Rick Dodgson, *It's All a Kind of Magic: The Young Ken Kesey* (Madison: University of Wisconsin Press, 2013), 146–147; "Acid Rock and Revolution," *Seed* (Chicago) vol. 2, no. 10 (1968); Thomas Thompson, "The New Far-Out Beatles," *Life*, June 16, 1967, 105.

91. Allen Katzman, ed., *Our Time: An Anthology of Interviews From the East Village Other* (New York: Dial, 1972), 203–204; Dennis McNally, *A Long Strange Trip: The Inside History of the Grateful Dead* (New York: Broadway Books, 2002), 261; Lesh quoted in Peter Richardson, *No Simple Highway: A Cultural History of the Grateful Dead* (New York: St. Martin's, 2014), 164–165; Maurice Isserman and Michael Kazin, *America Divided: The Civil War of the 1960s*, 5th ed. (New York: Oxford University Press, 2015), 155.

92. Rossinow, "'Revolution Is about Our Lives,'" 101.

93. David Farber, *Chicago '68* (Chicago: University of Chicago Press, 1988), 89.

94. Jon Supek, "The Hip Radical—What's Ahead?" *Old Mole* (Boston), September 13, 1968; Melody Kilian, "All You Need Is Love," *Space City News* (Houston), June 5, 1969.

95. Lee and Shlain, *Acid Dreams*, 206–208; Abbie Hoffman, *Revolution for the Hell of It* (New York: Dial, 1968), 102.

96. Raskin, *For the Hell of It*, 109–110, 155; Jezer, *Abbie Hoffman*, 177–178.

97. Lee and Shlain, *Acid Dreams*, 214–215; Raskin, *For the Hell of It*, 132–133.

98. Farber, *Chicago '68*, 89.

99. Jerry Rubin, *Do It! Scenarios of the Revolution* (New York: Simon and Schuster, 1970), 116; Hoffman quoted in Raskin, *For the Hell of It*, 136.

100. James T. Carey, *The College Drug Scene* (Englewood Cliffs, NJ: Prentice Hall, 1968), 17; Yablonsky, *Hippie Trip*, 72–73.

101. Eugene Schoenfeld, "All Yippies, NOT Hippies," *Los Angeles Free Press*, June 21–27, 1968; Abe Peck, "Yippies," *Distant Drummer* (Philadelphia) vol. 1, no. 11 (1968); "Don't Come to Chicago!" *Avatar* (Boston), August 16–29, 1968.

102. John Kois, "The Yippee Shuck," *Kaleidoscope* (Milwaukee), May 10–23, 1968; Jann Wenner, "Musicians Reject New Political Exploiters," *Rolling Stone*, May 11, 1968, 1, 22.

103. "The New Order," *Los Angeles Free Press*, September 6, 1968; Raskin, *For the Hell of It*, 128.

104. "More Letters," *Los Angeles Free Press*, November 15, 1968.

105. Abbie Hoffman, *Woodstock Nation: A Talk-Rock Album* (New York: Vintage Books, 1969), 77.

106. Jeff A. Hale, "The White Panthers' 'Total Assault on the Culture,'" in Braunstein and Doyle, *Imagine Nation*, 125–151; "White Panther Manifesto," *San Francisco Express Times*, November 13, 1968; "Ideology of the White Panther Party (Draft)," box 17, folder 23, John and Leni Sinclair Papers, Bentley Historical Library, University of Michigan, Ann Arbor.

107. Gitlin, *Sixties*, 238–241; William L. O'Neill, *Coming Apart: An Informal History of America in the 1960s* (Chicago: Quadrangle, 1971), 292.

108. "More Letters".

109. "Be-In!" *East Village Other* (New York), October 4, 1968.

110. William Drummond, "Police Arrest 76 Hippies at Easter Love-In Festivities," *Los Angeles Times*, April 15, 1968, 3; "San Gregorio Nude-In Cool," *Berkeley Barb*, March 29–April 4, 1968.

111. Kupferberg, "Politics of Love"; "What's Happening Here?" *Aquarian* (Tampa Bay), October 30, 1969.

112. Farber, *Age of Great Dreams*, 167–168.

113. "Cops, Hippies War in Street," *Chicago Tribune*, August 29, 1968, 1; "Other Voices," *Los Angeles Free Press*, October 27–November 2, 1967.

114. James S. Kunen, "There's an Exterminator in Santa Fe," *Boston Globe*, July 27, 1969, A7; "Letters," *Open City* (Los Angeles), June 23–29, 1967.

115. "Is Nothing Sacred?" *Newsweek*, August 5, 1968, 26; "The Great Hippie Hunt," *Time*, October 10, 1969, 22–23; "Paradise Rocked," *Time*, June 20, 1969, 55.

116. Timothy Miller, *The 60s Communes: Hippies and Beyond* (Syracuse, NY: Syracuse University Press, 1999), 222–224; Jon Stewart, "Communes in Taos," in *Conversations with the New Reality: Readings in the Cultural Revolution*, ed. Editors of Ramparts (San Francisco: Canfield, 1971), 209–210; Kunen, "There's an Exterminator in Santa Fe," A7.

117. Tuli Kupferberg, "How to Think about the Police," *Berkeley Barb*, December 22–28, 1967.

118. Michael E. Brown, "Condemnation and Persecution of Hippies," *Trans-action*, September 1969, 36; JAS, "Flower Power," *Berkeley Barb*, April 7, 1967.

119. Brown, "Condemnation and Persecution of Hippies," 36–38; Sylvan Fox, "9 Hurt, 38 Arrested as Hippies Clash with Police," *New York Times*, May 31, 1967, 1; William A. Davis, "Police Rout 2000 off Common," *Boston Globe*, June 30, 1968, 2; "The Great Hippie Hunt," 22–23; "Madison Police Rout 1,000 Students," *New York Times*, May 5, 1969, 26.

120. Thorne Dreyer, "At Love St. Ugly Cops," *Rag* (Austin), August 21, 1967; "ACLU," *Helix* (Seattle), April 13, 1967; "Watching the Watchers," *Helix* (Seattle), August 16, 1967.

121. Brown, "Condemnation and Persecution of Hippies," 36–38; "Great Hippie Hunt," 22–23.

122. "Smoke-In Held at Cambridge," 4; "City Council Lays Down Law on Stone Place," *Dallas Morning News*, August 8, 1967, 1; "Aspen Hippies Sue, Demanding Police Halt 'Harassment,'" *New York Times*, August 18, 1968, 53.

123. "The New Mood on Campus," *Newsweek*, December 29, 1969, 42.

124. "New Mood on Campus," 43.

125. "Astrology: Fad and Phenomenon," *Time*, March 21, 1969, 47.

126. "A Proposal," *Helix* (Seattle), August 16, 1967; Rubin, *Do It!*, 82; Berg in Wolf and Wolf, *Voices from the Love Generation*, 262; Beatles, *The Beatles Anthology* (San Francisco: Chronicle Books, 2000), dustjacket flap.

127. "Love-In in BossTown," *Time*, July 12, 1968; Moying Li-Marcus, *Beacon Hill: The Life and Times of a Neighborhood* (Boston: Northeastern University Press, 2002), 125–130.

128. Paul Lyons, *The People of This Generation: The Rise and Fall of the New Left in Philadelphia* (Philadelphia: University of Pennsylvania Press, 2003), 193–202.

129. "A Free People," *Helix* (Seattle), August 16, 1967; Crowley, *Rites of Passage*, 60–69.

130. "Nirvana on the Willamette," *Willamette Bridge* (Portland), June 7–20, 1968; Polina Olsen, *Portland in the 1960s: Stories from the Counterculture* (Charleston, SC: History Press, 2012), 15–26, 63–91.

131. Wynkoop, *Dissent in the Heartland*, 153–155.

132. Maryln Schwartz, "Thousands Jam Lee Park for Concert," *Dallas Morning News*, April 15, 1968, 1; *In Arcane Logos* (New Orleans), July 3, 1969; "High Culture in Tampa," *Aquarian* (Tampa), May 31, 1969; Rev. Heavy Hog, "The Coming of a New Age Maybe," *Kudzu* (Jackson, MS), May 13, 1969; "Idlewild Park?" *Love* (Reno, NV), November 1–14, 1968; *Electric News* (Salt Lake City) vol. 1, issue 4 (1968).

133. "Letters," *Avatar* (Boston), July 7–20, 1967; F. Salstrem, "A Future in Post-urban Communal Living," *Los Angeles Free Press*, August 1, 1969; Miller, *60s Communes*, 68.

134. Miller, *60s Communes*, xviii.

135. Miller, 56–63, 86–88.

136. Miller, 63–65, 78–83.

137. Miller, 53–56, 69–77.

138. Gitlin, *Sixties*, 353–356.

139. Rob Kirkpatrick, *1969: The Year Everything Changed* (New York: Skyhorse, 2009), 100–102, Reagan quoted on 100 and "fusion" quote on 102.

140. "Kites, Fists Fly at 'Love-In, Be-In,'" *New York Times*, April 7, 1969, 25; see *Chinook* (Denver), September 4, 1969.

141. Santelli, *Aquarius Rising*, 2, 87–119.

142. "The Big Woodstock Rock Trip," *Life*, August 29, 1969, 14B, 20.

143. Frank, *Conquest of Cool*, 246n21; Sharon Brinkman, "Woodstock: First and Last," *Heterodoxical Voice* (Newark, DE), September 1969; Robert Stephen Spitz, *Barefoot in Babylon: The Creation of the Woodstock Music Festival, 1969* (New York: Viking, 1979), 463; Miller Francis Jr., "Woodstock," *Great Speckled Bird* (Atlanta), September 1, 1969.

144. "Electric Mud," *Seed* (Chicago) vol. 4, no. 4 (1969); John Hilgerdt, "That Aquarian Exposition," *East Village Other* (New York), August 20, 1969.

145. Hilgerdt, "That Aquarian Exposition"; letter from Timothy Leary to John Sinclair, December 9, 1969, box 3, folder 7, John and Leni Sinclair Papers, Bentley Historical Library, University of Michigan, Ann Arbor.

146. Michael J. Kramer, *The Republic of Rock: Music and Citizenship in the Sixties Counterculture* (New York: Oxford University Press, 2013), 5; Doug Bradley and Craig Werner, *We Gotta Get Out of This Place: The Soundtrack of the Vietnam War* (Amherst: University of Massachusetts Press, 2015), 50, 110, 112; "Letters," *Fifth Estate* (Detroit), December 10–23, 1970; "In Vietnam: Mama-San Pushers vs. Psyops," *Newsweek*, April 21, 1969, 108.

147. Bradley and Werner, *We Gotta Get Out of This Place*, 77–78.

148. Letter from John Sinclair to Abbie Hoffman, September 22, 1969, box 2, folder 40, John and Leni Sinclair Papers, Bentley Historical Library, University of Michigan, Ann Arbor.

149. Kilian, "All You Need Is Love"; Klatch, *Generation Divided*, 144.

150. Weathermen quoted in Nancy Zaroulis and Gerald Sullivan, *Who Spoke Up? American Protest against the War in Vietnam, 1963–1975* (Garden City, NY: Doubleday, 1984), 261.

151. Peter Briggs, "Moratorium: Washington," *News from Nowhere* (Dekalb, IL), December 1969; Zaroulis and Sullivan, *Who Spoke Up?*, 289–290.

152. Santelli, *Aquarius Rising*, 172–178.

153. Santelli, 155–161, 178–182.

154. Jonathan Eisen, ed., *Altamont: Death of Innocence in the Woodstock Nation* (New York: Avon Books, 1970), 215; Jagger quoted in Stephen Davis, *Old Gods Almost Dead: The 40-Year Odyssey of the Rolling Stones* (New York: Broadway Books, 2001), 323, 324.

155. Eisen, *Altamont*, 239; Miller, *Hippies and American Values*, 84; Clay Geerdes, "Stones' Satisfaction," *Kaleidoscope* (Milwaukee), December 19, 1969–January 2, 1970.

156. "The Demon of Death Valley," *Time*, December 12, 1969, 22, 25; "Hippies and Violence," *Time*, December 12, 1969, 25.

157. Paul O'Neil, "The Wreck of a Monstrous Family," *Life*, December 19, 1969, 20–31; Vincent Bugliosi, *Helter Skelter: The True Story of the Manson Murders*, with Curt Gentry (New York: W. W. Norton, 1994), 294, 303, 330.

158. Bugliosi, *Helter Skelter*, 298, 302, 316; Paul Watkins, *My Life with Charles Manson*, with Guillermo Soledad (New York: Bantam Books, 1979), 64.

159. Quotes in Steven V. Roberts, "The Hippie Mystique," *New York Times*, December 15, 1969, 1.

160. O'Neill, *Coming Apart*, 263–264; Gerard J. DeGroot, *The Sixties Unplugged: A Kaleidoscopic History of a Disorderly Decade* (Cambridge, MA: Harvard University Press, 2008), 411; quote in J. Marks, "The Dream Is Over," in *The Eloquence of Protest: Voices of the 70's*, ed. Harrison E. Salisbury (Boston: Houghton Mifflin, 1972), 230; Nadya Zimmerman, *Counterculture Kaleidoscope: Musical and Cultural Perspectives on Late Sixties San Francisco* (Ann Arbor: University of Michigan Press, 2008), 174; Gitlin, *Sixties*, 408.

CHAPTER 4. FREAKS AND HARRIES EVERYWHERE

1. Timothy Tyler, "The Cooling of America: Out of Tune and Lost in the Counter-culture," *Time*, February 22, 1971, 15.

2. John McCormick, *Reclaiming Paradise: The Global Environmental Movement* (Bloomington: Indiana University Press, 1989), 56.

3. "The Ravaged Environment," *Newsweek*, January 26, 1970, 31–40.

4. Bulletin, Active Conservation Tactics, Social Protest Collection, BANC MSS 86/157 c; BANC FILM 2757, reel 88, Bancroft Library, University of California, Berkeley; Gladwin Hill, "Environment May Eclipse Vietnam as College Issue," *New York Times*, November 30, 1969, 1, 51.

5. McCormick, *Reclaiming Paradise*, 64; Mark Hamilton Lytle, *America's Uncivil Wars: The Sixties Era from Elvis to the Fall of Richard Nixon* (New York: Oxford University Press, 2006), 328–329.

6. "Ravaged Environment," 31.

7. "A Memento Mori to the Earth," *Time*, May 4, 1970, 16.

8. "Memento Mori to the Earth," 16; Chuck Worth, "Earth Rap," *Free Press of Louisville*, May 14, 1970.

9. "Planet Homework," *Astral Projection* (Albuquerque), June 18, 1970; Worth, "Earth Rap."

10. Phillip Winslow, "Garbage," *Helix* (Seattle) vol. 11, no. 13 (March 26, 1970); Bob, "The Air Is Everywhere," *Augur* (Eugene, OR), July 2, 1971; Day Chalurohdi, "A Proposal," and "Air Pollution Action" in *Astral Projection* (Albuquerque), December 15, 1971; Gail Seward and Brandi, "How You Can Improve the Environment," *Caravan* (Sarasota, FL) vol. 1, no. 6 (1973).

11. Hill, "Environment May Eclipse Vietnam," 1, 51; "200 Block a Wharf at Santa Barbara in Pollution Protest," *New York Times*, January 30, 1970, 23; Robert Nolte, "Students Turn Off War Protests, Turn to Issues Closer to Home," *Chicago Tribune*, November 23, 1971, 2; "Ecology," *Helix* (Seattle) vol. 11, no. 13 (March 26, 1970); "Mini Recycling Centers," *Rag* (Austin), October 4, 1971; Mary Kay Becker, "An Oil Report," *Northwest Passage* (Bellingham, WA), December 20, 1971.

12. Uncle Rollo, "Earth Day—A Diversion Developed by Our Leaders?" *Free Press of Louisville*, May 14, 1970.

13. Booklet, *Journal of a Walden Two Commune: The Collected Leaves of Twin Oaks*, vol. 1 (Yellow Springs, OH, 1972), 39, David L. Rice Library, University of Southern Indiana, Evansville; Uncle Rollo, "Earth Day"; Leslie Zador, "Rock Festivals Drain Strength," *Los Angeles Free Press*, September 11–17, 1970.

14. "Filigree Seduced," *Space City!* (Houston), September 19–October 3, 1970; "Drug Abuse," *Free Press of Louisville*, September 14–21, 1970.

15. Nancy Zaroulis and Gerald Sullivan, *Who Spoke Up? American Protest against the War in Vietnam, 1963–1975* (Garden City, NY: Doubleday, 1984), 320.

16. Nixon quoted in Lytle, *America's Uncivil Wars*, 355; John Kifner, "Regrets Are Few in Kent, Ohio," *New York Times*, June 13, 1970, 23.

17. Jeff Gerth, "Slaughter at Kent State," *Omaha Kaleidoscope* vol. 1, no. 6 (1970); rock commentator quoted in Peter Doggett, *There's a Riot Going On: Revolutionaries, Rock Stars, and the Rise and Fall of the '60s* (Edinburgh: Canongate, 2007), 358.

18. Dennis Junot, "Peace Picnic," *Free Press of Louisville*, May 14, 1970; "Food Co-op," *Big Muddy Gazette* (Carbondale, IL), 1970; Pat Boyle, "Cultural Revolution Rooted in Depression," *Liberator* (Morgantown, WV), February 1970; Donald Freed, "Huey

Newton—The People Must Burn the Pig Constitution," *Los Angeles Free Press*, September 11–17, 1970; John Sinclair, *Guitar Army: Street Writings/Prison Writings* (New York: Douglas Book, 1972), 207; "Youth Culture," *Madison Kaleidoscope*, May 5, 1970.

19. David Farber, "The Counterculture and the Antiwar Movement," in *Give Peace a Chance: Exploring the Vietnam Antiwar Movement*, ed. Melvin Small and William D. Hoover (Syracuse, NY: Syracuse University Press, 1992), 14–15.

20. "Celebrate! Celebrate! Dance to the Music," *Cahoots!* (Joplin, MO), June 1971.

21. Blake Slonecker, *A New Dawn for the New Left: Liberation News Service, Montague Farm, and the Long Sixties* (New York: Palgrave Macmillan, 2012), 41–42; "About This Issue," *Tiohero* (Ithaca, NY), March 1971; TNW, "Youth Coalition," *Berkeley Tribe*, September 11–18, 1970.

22. Junot, "Peace Picnic."

23. John Herbers, "Big Capital Rally Asks U.S. Pullout in Southeast Asia," *New York Times*, May 10, 1970, 1, 24; "All Sides Applaud Peaceful Protest in Washington," *New York Times*, April 26, 1971, 31; Lee James, "Joplin's People's Coalition for Peace Demonstrate," *Cahoots!* (Joplin, MO), June 1971; Joseph Lelyveld, "Status of the Movement: The 'Energy Levels' Are Low," *New York Times*, November 7, 1971; Martin Gansberg, "Thousands Join in War Protest," *New York Times*, November 7, 1971, 81.

24. Daniel Yankelovich, *The Changing Values on Campus: Political and Personal Attitudes of Today's College Students* (New York: Washington Square, 1972), 7; Timothy Miller, *The 60s Communes: Hippies and Beyond* (Syracuse, NY: Syracuse University Press, 1999), 75–76, 88; Joan Morrison and Robert K. Morrison, *From Camelot to Kent State: The Sixties Experience in the Words of Those Who Lived It* (New York: Oxford University Press, 2001), 307; Benjamin David Zablocki, *Alienation and Charisma: A Study of Contemporary American Communes* (New York: Free Press, 1980), 115.

25. "Random Notes," *Rolling Stone*, May 28, 1970, 4.

26. "Madison, Wis., Is Tense after Blast," *New York Times*, August 30, 1970, 40.

27. Tom Bates, *Rads: The 1970 Bombing of the Army Math Research Center at the University of Wisconsin and Its Aftermath* (New York: HarperCollins, 1992), 55, 443–444.

28. Yankelovich, *Changing Values on Campus*, 59, 64.

29. Robert Santelli, *Aquarius Rising: The Rock Festival Years* (New York: Dell, 1980), 187–188, 215–228.

30. Sinclair, *Guitar Army*, 113–119; Franklin Bach, "Getting Off Our Rock," *Madison Kaleidoscope*, May 5, 1970.

31. Joan Holden, "The Woodstock Movie: A $4 Revolution," *Ramparts*, October 1970, 60–62, 64; Santelli, *Aquarius Rising*, 149–150.

32. Santelli, *Aquarius Rising*, 189–190.

33. Sara Evans, *Personal Politics: The Roots of Women's Liberation in the Civil Rights Movement and the New Left* (New York: Vintage, 1979), 84–88.

34. John Robert Greene, *America in the Sixties* (Syracuse, NY: Syracuse University Press, 2010), 114.

35. Redstockings and New York Radical Women quoted in Greene, 115.

36. "Cock Rock: Men Always Seem to End Up on Top," *Rat* (New York), October 15–November 18, 1970; Reebee Garofalo, *Rockin' Out: Popular Music in the U.S.A.* (Upper Saddle River, NJ: Prentice Hall, 2008), 210.

37. Gretchen Lemke-Santangelo, *Daughters of Aquarius: Women of the Sixties Counterculture* (Lawrence: University Press of Kansas, 2009), 24–26; Terry H. Anderson, *The*

Movement and the Sixties (New York: Oxford University Press, 1995), 261; Sandra Levinson, "Sexploitation in the Underground Press," *Ramparts*, August 1969, 66–70.

38. Ruth Rosen, *The World Split Open: How the Modern Women's Movement Changed America* (New York: Penguin, 2000), 144–148; Robin Morgan, ed., *Sisterhood Is Powerful: An Anthology of Writings from the Women's Liberation Movement* (New York: Random House, 1970), 430; baby boomer woman in Rex Weiner and Deanne Stillman, *Woodstock Census: The Nationwide Survey of the Sixties Generation* (New York: Viking, 1979), 176; Lemke-Santangelo, *Daughters of Aquarius*, 65.

39. "Up from under Women Unite," *Sunshine Aura* (Erie, PA) vol. 2, no. 6 (1972).

40. Robin Morgan, "Goodbye to All That," *Rat* (New York), February 6, 1970.

41. "Cock Rock."

42. Lemke-Santangelo, *Daughters of Aquarius*, 22, 160, Solanis quoted on 22; Queen of the Gypsies, "Ego Trips," *Berkeley Barb*, August 7–13, 1970.

43. Lemke-Santangelo, *Daughters of Aquarius*, 2, 4.

44. Lemke-Santangelo, *Daughters of Aquarius*, 59; Norman Spinrad, "You've Come a Long Way Baby," *Los Angeles Free Press*, September 11–17, 1970.

45. "We Can Envision a New Society," flyer; "Moving toward a New Society," brochure; and "Leaves of Twin Oaks," newsletter, all April 1972, David L. Rice Library, University of Southern Indiana, Evansville; Hoffman quoted in Marty Jezer, *Abbie Hoffman: American Rebel* (New Brunswick, NJ: Rutgers University Press, 1992), 222.

46. John D'Emilio and Estelle B. Freedman, *Intimate Matters: A History of Sexuality in America* (Chicago: University of Chicago Press, 1997), 318–319.

47. Anderson, *Movement and the Sixties*, 318–319, 405; D'Emilio and Freedman, *Intimate Matters*, 323.

48. Leary and Straight Theater in Alice Echols, *Shaky Ground: The '60s and Its Aftershocks* (New York: Columbia University Press, 2002), 33–34, 148; Bowart quoted in Abe Peck, *Uncovering the Sixties: The Life and Times of the Underground Press* (New York: Pantheon, 1985), 33; Lennon in Bob Spitz, *The Beatles: The Biography* (New York: Back Bay Books, 2005), 685–686; Miller, *60s Communes*, 138; Slonecker, *New Dawn for the New Left*, 67–68.

49. Timothy Miller, *The Hippies and American Values* (Knoxville: University of Tennessee Press, 1991), 57–58; "Gay Switchboard," *New York City Star*, June 1, 1973; David Allyn, *Make Love, Not War: The Sexual Revolution: An Unfettered History* (Boston: Little, Brown, 2000), 162; Merla Zellerbach, "The Gay Community Views the Hippies," *San Francisco Chronicle*, July 31, 1967, 37.

50. Eric Marcus, *Making Gay History: The Half-Century Fight for Lesbian and Gay Equal Rights* (New York: Perennial, 2002), 124.

51. Margaret Cruikshank, *The Gay and Lesbian Liberation Movement* (New York: Routledge, 1992), 37, 61–62; man quoted in Henry Gross, *The Flower People* (New York: Ballantine Books, 1968), 56.

52. Tom Burke, "The New Homosexual," *Esquire*, December 1969, 178.

53. Robert McRuer, "Gay Gatherings: Reimagining the Counterculture," in *Imagine Nation: The American Counterculture of the 1960s and '70s*, ed. Peter Braunstein and Michael William Doyle (New York: Routledge, 2002), 216, 221.

54. John Knoebel, "Somewhere in the Right Direction: Testimony of My Experience in a Gay Male Living Collective," in *Out of the Closets: Voices of Gay Liberation*, ed. Karla Jay and Allen Young (New York: New York University Press, 1992), 301–315.

55. Lemke-Santangelo, *Daughters of Aquarius*, 163.

56. Cleaver quoted in Peck, *Uncovering the Sixties*, 257–258; additional quote in Robert Greenfield, *Timothy Leary: A Biography* (New York: Harcourt, 2006), 419–420; Jezer, *Abbie Hoffman*, 219–220; Simon Hall, *Peace and Freedom: The Civil Rights and Antiwar Movements in the 1960s* (Philadelphia: University of Pennsylvania Press, 2005), 190–191.

57. Myron B. Bloy Jr., "The Counter-Culture: It Just Won't Go Away," *Commonweal*, October 8, 1971, 29.

58. "Speak Out," *Rebirth* (Phoenix) vol. 1, no. 6 (1969).

59. Andrew E. Hunt, *The Turning: A History of Vietnam Veterans against the War* (New York: New York University Press, 1999), 94–107, *Washington Post* quoted on 107; Ron Kovic, *Born on the Fourth of July* (New York: Akashic Books, 2005), 169–170.

60. Michael T. Kaufman, "Many Students Are Turning away from Protest to Seek Own Goals," *New York Times*, May 9, 1971, 29; Gregory Wierzynsk, "All Quiet on the Campus Front," *Time*, February 22, 1971, 26–27.

61. Yankelovich, *Changing Values on Campus*, 51, 59, 62; Wierzynsk, "All Quiet on the Campus Front," 26–27.

62. Allyn, *Make Love, Not War*, 71–77.

63. Miller, *Hippies and American Values*, 27.

64. Harrison Pope Jr., *Voices from the Drug Culture* (Boston: Beacon, 1971), 5.

65. Juicy Lucy, "Rock Prevue," *Great Speckled Bird* (Atlanta), January 11, 1971.

66. James E. Perone, *Music of the Counterculture Era* (Westport, CT: Greenwood, 2004), 62, 133–135.

67. Perone, *Music of the Counterculture Era*, 30; David Szatmary, *Rockin' in Time: A Social History of Rock and Roll* (Upper Saddle River, NJ: Prentice Hall, 1996), 193.

68. "Down to Old Dixie and Back," *Time*, January 12, 1970, 43; Perone, *Music of the Counterculture Era*, 144–146.

69. Santelli, *Aquarius Rising*, 204–213, biker quoted on 210.

70. David Hepworth, *Never a Dull Moment: 1971—The Year That Rock Exploded* (New York: Henry Holt, 2016), 167–181.

71. Susan Sands, "Backpacking: 'I Go to the Wilderness to Kick the Man-World Out of Me,'" *New York Times*, May 9, 1971, xxl, 7, 9–10.

72. Robert A. Jones, "National Parks: A Report on the Range War at Generation Gap," *New York Times*, July 25, 1971.

73. "This Organic World," *Ecolog* no. 19, July 15, 1970, newsletter, Social Protest Collection, BANC MSS 86/157 c; BANC FILM 2757, reel 89, Bancroft Library, University of California, Berkeley; "Food for Thought," *All You Can Eat* (New Brunswick, NJ), July 20, 1970; Maitreya, "Diet," *Home Cookin'* (Oklahoma City), September 1, 1972.

74. Laura J. Miller, *Building Nature's Market: The Business and Politics of Natural Foods* (Chicago: University of Chicago Press, 2017), 150.

75. Dale, "Our New Age," *Hundred Flowers* (Minneapolis), January 13, 1972.

76. "The Kosher of the Counterculture," *Time*, November 16, 1970, 59–60, 63.

77. Sonya Rudikoff, "O Pioneers!: Reflections on the Whole Earth People," *Commentary*, July 1972, 62.

78. Rudikoff, "O Pioneers!," 63–64; Andrew G. Kirk, *Counterculture Green: The Whole Earth Catalog and American Environmentalism* (Lawrence: University Press of Kansas, 2007), 1–12.

79. "Callin' All Freekcommunards," *Free Press of Louisville*, September 14, 1970; "Tripping Down Hippie Highway," *Newsweek*, July 27, 1970, 22; Steven V. Roberts, "Youth

Seeking Freedom on the Road," *New York Times*, July 15, 1971, 33, 51; Erwin Baker, "300 Shouting Hippies Protest Hitchhiking Ban," *Los Angeles Times*, October 15, 1970, C1.

80. "The Knapsack Nomads," *Time*, July 19, 1971, 66–67.

81. "Youth Unrest—What Worldwide Survey Shows," *U.S. News & World Report*, October 26, 1970, 76; "Knapsack Nomads," 66–67.

82. "Hippies Find India Is Not So 'Groovy,'" *New York Times*, January 2, 1972, 4; Sharif Gemie and Brian Ireland, *The Hippie Trail: A History, 1957–78* (Manchester: Manchester University Press, 2017), 50–52.

83. Dale D. Morsch, "Hippies Invade Himalayas," *Dallas Morning News*, November 20, 1967, 4; Richard Horn, "Letter from Kathmandu," *East Village Other* (New York), October 4, 1968; Gemie and Ireland, *Hippie Trail*, 5, 33.

84. "Thailand Places Official Ban on Admitting Flower Children," *Dallas Morning News*, May 11, 1968, 2; Charles Mohr, "Hippies Find Laos a Tolerant Haven," *New York Times*, October 19, 1967, 7; Lee Elbinger, "Hitch-Hiking in Laos," *Fifth Estate* (Detroit), November 28–December 11, 1968; "Hippies in Indonesia," *Washington Post*, October 25, 1967, D15; "Airline Told to Keep Hippies off Planes," *Los Angeles Times*, September 8, 1968, 13.

85. Sydney H. Schanberg, "U.S. Envoy Scores Hippies in Kabul," *New York Times*, November 16, 1969, 8; Gemie and Ireland, *Hippie Trail*, 5, 52.

86. Dial Torgerson, "Mexico's Harsh Message: Hippies Not Wanted," *Los Angeles Times*, March 30, 1969, A1; "Mexico Cuts Invasion by U.S. Hippies," *Chicago Tribune*, March 26, 1970, 18.

87. Gemie and Ireland, *Hippie Trail*, 67–72, 75–76, 87.

88. Gemie and Ireland, 84.

89. "Kenya to Ban Hippies," *New York Times*, March 12, 1972, 19.

90. Doug Rossinow, "Letting Go: Revisiting the New Left's Demise," in *The New Left Revisited*, ed. John McMillian and Paul Buhle (Philadelphia: Temple University Press, 2003), 244; "Telegraph Avenue's Flower Children Have Gone Underground," *New York Times*, March 27, 1971, 26; Sinclair, *Guitar Army*, 318.

91. Daniel Zwerdling, "The Uncertain Revival of Food Cooperatives," in *Co-ops, Communes and Collectives: Experiments in Social Change in the 1960s and 1970s*, ed. John Case and Rosemary C. R. Taylor (New York: Pantheon, 1979), 89–91; Harvey Davis Jr., "Food Coop Grows," *Dallas News*, August 12, 1970; "Food Co-op," *Big Muddy Gazette* (Carbondale, IL), 1970; "Co-op," *Head Lines* (Memphis) vol. 1, no. 2 (1973); "Food Co-ops," *New York City Star*, October 1973; "People Food Co-op," *Lincoln Gazette*, September 12, 1972; "Food Co-ops," *Outlaw* (Saint Louis), March 10–30, 1972.

92. Joshua Clark Davis, *From Head Shops to Whole Foods: The Rise and Fall of Activist Entrepreneurs* (New York: Columbia University Press, 2017), 176–223, quote on 208.

93. See *Great Speckled Bird* (Atlanta), January 11, 1971; "Photography Cooperative," *Kudzu* (Jackson, MS), March 1970.

94. See *Omaha Kaleidoscope*, February 10, 1970; "Craftspeople," *Spare Change* (Washington, DC), February 27, 1971; ad, *All You Can Eat* (New Brunswick, NJ), April 1, 1972; ad, *Peach* (Wausau, WI), January 3, 1972; ad, *Black Hills Free Press* (Rapid City, SD), January–February 1972.

95. Joshua Clark Davis, "The Business of Getting High: Head Shops, Countercultural Capitalism, and the Marijuana Legalization Movement," *Sixties* 8, no. 1 (2015): 27–35, head shop owner quoted on 33; Davis, *From Head Shops to Whole Foods*, 100.

96. Davis, "Business of Getting High," 27–35; Davis, *From Head Shops to Whole Foods*, 4, 85.

97. Terry H. Anderson, "The New American Revolution: The Movement and Business" in *The Sixties: From Memory to History*, ed. David Farber (Chapel Hill: University of North Carolina Press, 1994), 193–194.

98. "Austin Echoes," *Glyptodon News* (Austin), March 19–April 2, 1973; "People News," *Berkeley Tribe*, September 11–18, 1970; Dennis Fitzgerald, "Survive to Struggle," *Space City!* (Houston), September 19–October 3, 1970; "Crashes," *Spare Change* (Washington, DC), February 27, 1971; "Switchboard," *Augur* (Eugene, OR), January 6–20, 1972.

99. Rosemary C. R. Taylor, "Free Medicine," in *Co-ops, Communes and Collectives*, 20–22; "Free Clinic," *Big Muddy Gazette* (Carbondale, IL), 1970; "Community Services," *Berkeley Tribe*, March 13–20, 1970; "Free Clinics' Funding In," *Berkeley Barb*, April 7–13, 1972; "To Be Healthy Is to Be Free," *Nashville Rag*, November 1972; see *Rag* (Austin), March 6, 1972.

100. "Survival," *Helix* (Seattle) vol. 11, no. 13 (1970); "People News," *Berkeley Tribe*, September 11–18, 1970; newsletter, *Street Sheet* (Madison), 1972, Social Action Vertical File, box 60, Wisconsin Historical Society Library, University of Wisconsin, Madison.

101. "Hippie-Type Crusade Battles Drug Scene," *Los Angeles Times*, June 10, 1970, 16; "An Easy Way to Kill a Movement," *Paper* (Stamford, CT), July 1972.

102. "Save Open City—A Service or a Rip-Off?" *Fifth Estate* (Detroit), December 10–23, 1970; "Crossroads," *Black Hills Free Press* (Rapid City, SD), January–February 1972.

103. Irwin Unger, *The Sixties* (New York: Pearson, 2011), 178–179.

104. Allyn, *Make Love, Not War*, 242; bulletin, January 1970, box 3, folder 32; letter to *Berkeley Tribe*, November 1969, box 3, folder 31; "The Psychedelic Venus Church Invites You to Our Celebration," bulletin, July 1970, box 3, folder 32; Sexual Freedom League Papers, BANC MSS 83/181 c, Bancroft Library, University of California, Berkeley; Miller, *Hippies and American Values*, 34.

105. W. J. Rorabaugh, *Berkeley at War: The 1960s* (New York: Oxford University Press, 1989), 152.

106. Quote from Polina Olsen, *Portland in the 1960s: Stories from the Counterculture* (Charleston, SC: History Press, 2012), 78.

107. Matthew Levin, *Cold War University: Madison and the New Left in the Sixties* (Madison: University of Wisconsin Press, 2013), 142–143, 177–179.

108. James T. Wooten, "The Life and Death of Atlanta's Hip Strip," *New York Times Magazine*, March 14, 1971, 34–35; Rick Briant Dandes, "Where Did All the Hippies Go?" *Atlanta Weekly*, December 5, 1982.

109. Miller, *60s Communes*, 67.

110. Pamphlet, *Twin Oaks*, 1973, David L. Rice Library, University of Southern Indiana, Evansville; Taub quoted in Miller, *60s Communes*, 151; MNS in Miller, *60s Communes*, 129–130.

111. Pamphlet, *The Revolution is Over: We Won!*, 1969, and *Journal of a Walden Two Commune*, 39, David L. Rice Library, University of Southern Indiana, Evansville; Robert Strand, "'67 Flower Children Lose Ardor," *Los Angeles Times*, December 14, 1971, B4.

112. Miller, *60s Communes*, 151–158.

113. The Farm Report, September 1973 and 1971, Center for Communal Studies, University of Southern Indiana, Evansville; Miller, *60s Communes*, 118; Lemke-Santangelo, *Daughters of Aquarius*, 68–69.

114. Brochure, What Is East Wind?, 1976, David L. Rice Library, University of Southern Indiana, Evansville; Miller, *60s Communes*, 160–164.

115. "Preliminary General Plan for Harvest Hills," September 1970; Liz Williams, "Aquarians Working Together," *Evansville Courier*, August 24, 1970; *Springtree Newsletter*, April 1972; What Is East Wind?, 1976; and "We Can Envision A New Society"; all David L. Rice Library, University of Southern Indiana, Evansville. Farm Report, September 1973.

116. Williams, "Aquarians Working Together."

117. Larry Eskridge, *God's Forever Family: The Jesus People Movement in America* (New York: Oxford University Press, 2013), 2, 14–15, 18–19, 28–31.

118. Eskridge, *God's Forever Family*, 2–3, 5.

119. Phil Tracy, "The Jesus Freaks: Savagery and Salvation on Sunset Strip," *Commonweal*, October 30, 1970, 122–125; "The New Rebel Cry: Jesus Is Coming!" *Time*, June 21, 1971, 56; Jesus Person in Edward B. Fiske, "New Youth Groups 'Freaked Out' on Jesus," *Chicago Tribune*, February 22, 1970, 64.

120. Eskridge, *God's Forever Family*, 287–292; Miller, *60s Communes*, 93–95; Tracy, "Jesus Freaks," 122–125; "Street Christians: Jesus as the Ultimate Trip," *Time*, August 3, 1970.

121. Eskridge, *God's Forever Family*, 87–89; "Street Christians"; "New Rebel Cry," 61.

122. Karen M. Staller, *Runaways: How the Sixties Counterculture Shaped Today's Practices and Policies* (New York: Columbia University Press, 2006), 97–98, 109–110; Ann Blackman, "Youth Centers Set Up to Aid Social Outcasts," *Los Angeles Times*, December 6, 1971, C6, 7.

123. Robert Reinhold, "New Campus Problem: Young Drifters," *New York Times*, November 10, 1970, 1, 34.

CHAPTER 5. CHANGING THE WORLD

1. Rubin quoted in Peter Doggett, *There's a Riot Going On: Revolutionaries, Rock Stars, and the Rise and Fall of the '60s* (Edinburgh: Canongate, 2007), 469.

2. Tom Fels, *Buying the Farm: Peace and War on a Sixties Commune* (Amherst: University of Massachusetts Press, 2012), 15.

3. Fels, 17–20.

4. Fels, 20–25.

5. Michael Corr and Dan MacLeod, "Getting It Together," *Environment* 14, no. 9 (November 1972): 3; Timothy Miller, *The 60s Communes: Hippies and Beyond* (Syracuse, NY: Syracuse University Press, 1999), 118.

6. Nancy Zaroulis and Gerald Sullivan, *Who Spoke Up? American Protest against the War in Vietnam, 1963–1975* (Garden City, NY: Doubleday, 1984), 379.

7. John Kendall, "War Protests Flare in Southland Cities," *Los Angeles Times*, May 9, 1972, 2.

8. Rex Weiner and Deanne Stillman, *Woodstock Census: The Nationwide Survey of the Sixties Generation* (New York: Viking, 1979), 115, 197, 247.

9. Terry H. Anderson, *The Movement and the Sixties* (New York: Oxford University Press, 1995), 394, 397.

10. Doggett, *There's a Riot Going On*, 497–504.

11. Zippie leaflet, High!, 1972, and Zippie leaflet, Paradise Now!, 1972, both Social Action Vertical File, box 60, Wisconsin Historical Society Library, University of Wisconsin, Madison.

12. Tom Headly, "Info Gap," *Lincoln Gazette*, August 31, 1972; Paul Valentine, "Friction Splinters Protesters' Camp," *Washington Post*, August 21, 1972, A3.

13. Michael Allen, "'I Just Want to Be a Cosmic Cowboy': Hippies, Cowboy Code, and the Culture of a Counterculture," *Western Historical Quarterly* 36, no. 3 (Autumn 2005): 275–299; Doug Rossinow, *The Politics of Authenticity: Liberalism, Christianity, and the New Left in America* (New York: Columbia University Press, 1998), 289.

14. Rossinow, *Politics of Authenticity*, 290.

15. Sarah Eppler Janda, *Prairie Power: Student Activism, Counterculture, and Backlash in Oklahoma, 1962–1972* (Norman: University of Oklahoma Press, 2018), 138–162, Terry Allen quoted on 161.

16. Michael S. Foley, *Confronting the War Machine: Draft Resistance during the Vietnam War* (Chapel Hill: University of North Carolina Press, 2003), 360.

17. "This You Deserve . . . ?" *Joint Issue* (East Lansing, MI) vol. 4, no. 7 (April 1973); "Boycotts," *New York City Star*, May 1, 1973; "Let Us Not Lettuce," *Joint Issue* (East Lansing, MI) vol. 4, no. 7 (April 1973); "Long Beach Workers Strike," *Seed* (Chicago), May 18, 1972; "Strike," *Great Speckled Bird* (Atlanta), July 10, 1972; "Strike Continues," *Pure Corn* (Evansville, IN), December 1972; Tom Headly, "Lettuce Boycott," *Lincoln Gazette*, September 12, 1972.

18. Gavan Duffy, "Electoral Politics," *Rag* (Austin), March 6, 1972.

19. David Larry, 'We Share Each Other's Lives," *Augur* (Eugene, OR), December 1972.

20. Doggett, *There's a Riot Going On*, 496.

21. "Attica Never Ends," *Seed* (Chicago), May 18, 1972; Gary Friedman, "Leary Asks for Closing of California Prisons," *Los Angeles Weekly News*, August 10–17, 1973.

22. Ruth Rosen, *The World Split Open: How the Modern Women's Movement Changed America* (New York: Penguin, 2000), 157–158; Maralee, "Our Bodies, Our Lives, Our Right to Decide!" *Seed* (Chicago), May 18, 1972.

23. Sherry L. Smith, *Hippies, Indians, and the Fight for Red Power* (New York: Oxford University Press, 2012), 4, 8, 79–81.

24. Smith, 87–93, 97.

25. Smith, 175.

26. Suzan Shown and Bruce Soloway, "Wounded Knee," *New York City Star*, May 1, 1973; "Wounded Knee!" *Breakdown* (Klamath Falls, OR), March 16–20, 1973; Fred Duisberg Jr., "An American Tragedy," *Caravan* (Sarasota, FL), May 17, 1973; Smith, *Hippies, Indians, and the Fight for Red Power*, 191–193.

27. Philip Deloria, "Counterculture Indians and the New Age," in *Imagine Nation: The American Counterculture of the 1960s and '70s*, ed. Peter Braunstein and Michael William Doyle (New York: Routledge, 2002), 159–188.

28. "Impeach the President," *Head Lines* (Memphis) vol. 1, no. 2 (1973).

29. Red Bear, "May Daze," *Joint Issue* (East Lansing, MI) vol, 4, no. 7 (April 1973).

30. Yippie leaflet, Statement of the YIP Tribal Council in Iowa City, May 4, 1973, Social Action Vertical File, box 60, Wisconsin Historical Society Library, University of Wisconsin, Madison.

31. "Don't Tread on Me," *Saint Louis New Times*, February 17, 1972.

32. Paul Valentine, "Pro-Pot, Anti-Nixon Rally," *Washington Post*, July 5, 1973, E3.

33. Travis D. Stimeling, *Cosmic Cowboys and New Hicks: The Countercultural Sounds of Austin's Progressive Country Music Scene* (New York: Oxford University Press, 2011), 117–132; Patrick Carr, "It's So 'Progressive' in Texas," *New York Times*, July 22, 1973, 97.

34. "Woodstock Matured," *Time*, August 6, 1973, 8; Judy Klemesrud, "Bigger Than Woodstock, but Was It Better?" *New York Times*, August 5, 1973, 97.

35. Gregg Kilday, "Balkanizing the Woodstock Nation at Watkins Glen," *Los Angeles Times*, August 19, 1973, O16.

36. "Woodstock Matured," 8; Kilday, "Balkanizing the Woodstock Nation at Watkins Glen," O16; Klemesrud, "Bigger Than Woodstock, but Was It Better?" 97.

37. Mary Harper, "'Great Guts Award' at Women's Festival," *Los Angeles Weekly News*, August 24, 1973.

38. "No More Sex Ads in Berkeley Barb," *Los Angeles Weekly News*, August 10–17, 1973.

39. "Male Role Workshop," *Joint Issue* (East Lansing, MI), October 1–15, 1973; Pink Floyd and Bowie in Doggett, *There's a Riot Going On*, 496; Michael A. Messner, "Radical Feminist and Socialist Feminist Men's Movements in the United States," in *Feminism and Men: Reconstructing Gender Relations*, ed. Steven Schacht and Doris Ewing (New York: New York University Press, 1998), 69.

40. Blake Slonecker, *A New Dawn for the New Left: Liberation News Service, Montague Farm, and the Long Sixties* (New York: Palgrave Macmillan, 2012), 127–135.

41. Slonecker, 137–146.

42. Slonecker, 159–166.

43. Miller, *60s Communes*, 129–130; Andrew Cornell, "The Movement for a New Society: Consensus, Prefiguration, and Direct Action," in *The Hidden 1970s: Histories of Radicalism*, ed. Dan Berger (New Brunswick, NJ: Rutgers University Press, 2010), 231–235.

44. Frank Zelko, "On Earth Day, Remembering Counterculture Environmentalists," *Oxford University Press Blog*, April 22, 2013, https://blog.oup.com/2013/04/earth-day-environmentalism-counterculture-greenpeace/; Frank Zelko, *Make It a Green Peace! The Rise of Countercultural Environmentalism* (New York: Oxford University Press, 2013).

45. Andrew Radolf, "Haight Street: Six Blocks in Search of a New Identity," *New York Times*, April 22, 1973, 381; Kilday, "Balkanizing the Woodstock Nation at Watkins Glen," O16.

46. Thomas Frank, *The Conquest of Cool: Business Culture, Counterculture, and the Rise of Hip Consumerism* (Chicago: University of Chicago Press, 1997), 16, 178.

47. Craig Karpe, "Das Hip Kapital," *Esquire*, December 1970, 185.

48. Michael Lydon, "Rock for Sale," *Ramparts*, June 1969, 19–24.

49. Reebee Garofalo, *Rockin' Out: Popular Music in the U.S.A.* (Upper Saddle River, NJ: Prentice Hall, 2008), 220–222; David Szatmary, *Rockin' in Time: A Social History of Rock and Roll* (Upper Saddle River, NJ: Prentice Hall, 1996), 219–220.

50. Jann Wenner, "A Letter from the Editor: On the Occasion of Our Fourth Anniversary Issue," *Rolling Stone*, November 11, 1971, 34.

51. "Radical Chic," *Submarine Church Press* (Northampton, MA), 1972; Timothy Tyler, "The Cooling of America: Out of Tune and Lost in the Counterculture," *Time*, February 22, 1971, 16; Conklin quoted in Peter Maguire and Mike Ritter, *Thai Stick: Surfers, Scammers, and the Untold Story of the Marijuana Trade* (New York: Columbia University Press, 2014), 32; Sonya Rudikoff, "O Pioneers!: Reflections on the Whole Earth People," *Commentary*, July 1972, 62.

52. Thomas Borstelmann, *The 1970s: A New Global History from Civil Rights to Economic Inequality* (Princeton, NJ: Princeton University Press, 2012), 163–164.

53. "The Knapsack Nomads," *Time*, July 19, 1971, 67.

54. "Letters," *All You Can Eat* (New Brunswick, NJ), July 20, 1970.

55. Miller, *60s Communes*, 225–227.

56. Larry Zink, "A Better World," *Lincoln Gazette*, September 12, 1972.

CONCLUSION

1. Bernard Von Bothmer, *Framing the Sixties: The Use and Abuse of a Decade from Ronald Reagan to George W. Bush* (Amherst: University of Massachusetts Press, 2010), 221.

2. Von Bothmer, *Framing the Sixties*, 221; Roger Kimball, "Virtue Gone Mad," *New Criterion*, December 16, 1997: 4–11.

3. Thomas Borstelmann, *The 1970s: A New Global History from Civil Rights to Economic Inequality* (Princeton, NJ: Princeton University Press, 2012), 122–133.

4. Maurice Isserman and Michael Kazin, *America Divided: The Civil War of the 1960s*, 5th ed. (New York: Oxford University Press, 2015), 293–294.

5. Mark Oppenheimer, "The Sixties' Surprising Legacy," *Chronicle of Higher Education*, October 3, 2003, B11–12.

6. Gerald L. Zelizer, "Should Clergy Endorse 'Living in Sin,'" *USA Today*, July 24, 2003, 13A.

7. "Same-Sex Relations Get Record-High Approval," *Christian Century*, June 28, 2011, 16.

8. Linda Feldmann, "Support for Legal Marijuana May Have Reached a Tipping Point," *Christian Science Monitor*, April 4, 2013; Joel Stein, "The New Politics of Pot: Can It Go Legit?" *Time*, November 4, 2002, 57–61.

9. Morris Dickstein, "After Utopia: The 1960s Today," in *Sights on the Sixties*, ed. Barbara L. Tischler (New Brunswick, NJ: Rutgers University Press, 1992), 14, 19; Terry H. Anderson, *Bush's Wars* (New York: Oxford University Press, 2011), 124.

10. Daren Fonda, "Organic Growth," *Time*, August 12, 2002.

11. Richard Corliss, "The Power of Yoga," *Time*, July 9, 2001.

12. Fred Turner, *From Counterculture to Cyberculture: Stewart Brand, the Whole Earth Network, and the Rise of Digital Utopianism* (Chicago: University of Chicago Press, 2006), 4–5; W. J. Rorabaugh, *American Hippies* (New York: Cambridge University Press, 2015), 221–223, Brand quoted on 221.

13. Ali Lorraine, "The New Invasion," *Newsweek*, February 26, 2001, 68; Richard Corliss, "I Am the Walrus," *Time*, September 14, 2009, 59–61.

14. Mikal Gilmore, "Soul Survivors," *Rolling Stone*, May 23, 2013, 46–82; Steve Knopper, "Stones Rule the Road," *Rolling Stone*, January 25, 2007, 12.

15. David Browne, "Business Booming for the Dead," *Rolling Stone*, February 2, 2012, 15–18; Ray Waddell, "Dead Live on in Touring Legacy," *Billboard*, May 11, 2002.

16. Jules Archer, *The Incredible Sixties: The Stormy Years That Changed America* (New York: Harcourt, 1986), 200–201.

17. R. U. Sirius, "The New Counterculture," *Time*, November 9, 1998, 88–89.

18. Jim Rutenberg, "McCain Reflects on P.O.W. Past, and Goes after Clinton," *New York Times*, October 25, 2007.

19. Yuval Levin, "Conservatism in an Age of Alienation," *Modern Age* (Spring 2017): 12–17; Greg Jones, "Conservatism is the New Counterculture," *Federalist*, October 22, 2018, https://thefederalist.com/2018/10/22/conservatism-new-counterculture/.

20. Crumb quoted in Abe Peck, *Uncovering the Sixties: The Life and Times of the Underground Press* (New York: Pantheon, 1985), 51; Robert Merry, "Hippies Find Afghanistan a Hellish Drug Haven," *Chicago Tribune*, August 9, 1971, A9; Nicholas Schou, *Orange Sunshine: The Brotherhood of Eternal Love and Its Quest to Spread Peace, Love, and Acid to the World* (New York: Thomas Dunne Books, 2010), 113.

21. Timothy Miller, *The 60s Communes: Hippies and Beyond* (Syracuse, NY: Syracuse University Press, 1999), 233–234; Mark Matthews, *Droppers: America's First Hippie*

Commune, *Drop City* (Norman: University of Oklahoma Press, 2010), 206; Taylor quoted in Gretchen Lemke-Santangelo, *Daughters of Aquarius: Women of the Sixties Counterculture* (Lawrence: University Press of Kansas, 2009), 32.

22. Peter Coyote, *Sleeping Where I Fall: A Chronicle* (Washington, DC: Counterpoint, 1998), 349; Andrea Sachs, "Rock Survivor," Time, October 22, 2006; Kantner in "My Generation," *The History of Rock and Roll*, prod. Andrew Solt (Chicago: Time-Life Video, 1995), DVD.

BIBLIOGRAPHY

PRIMARY SOURCES

Manuscript Collections

Bancroft Library, University of California, Berkeley
    Chester Anderson Papers
    Sexual Freedom League Papers
    Social Protest Collection
Bentley Historical Library, University of Michigan, Ann Arbor
    John and Leni Sinclair Papers
San Francisco Public Library
    Hippies Collection
University of Southern Indiana, Evansville
    David L. Rice Library Communal Documents
    Center for Communal Studies
Wisconsin Historical Society Library, University of Wisconsin, Madison
    Social Action Vertical File
    Underground Newspaper Collection

Underground Newspapers Methodology

The Bell and Howell Underground Newspaper Collection, available on microfilm, constituted the bulk of the underground papers I examined. I collected others at the Wisconsin Historical Society Library on the University of Wisconsin campus. Because I sought to demonstrate that the counterculture was truly national in scope, I made a point of selecting papers from every region of the country. Some underground presses published one, two, or three issues; in such instances, I studied them all. The better-established newssheets—*Los Angeles Free Press, Berkeley Barb, East Village Other, Chicago Seed*—published regularly from the mid-1960s to the early 1970s. For these titles, I investigated issues from the beginning, middle, and end of the year. For example, I might select papers from January, June, and December, or February, July, and November. I maintained this methodology for every year a given title was published. Beyond this approach, I collected additional issues that reported on an important counterculture event such as Monterey Pop, Human Be-In, and Altamont.

Underground Newspapers

All You Can Eat (New Brunswick, NJ)
Aquarian (Tampa)
Aquarian Herald (Nyack, NY)
Asterisk (Omaha)
Astral Projection (Albuquerque)
Augur (Eugene, OR)
Avatar (Boston)
Bauls (West Lafayette, IN)

Berkeley Barb
Berkeley Citizen
Berkeley Tribe
Big Muddy Gazette (Carbondale, IL)
Black Hills Free Press (Rapid City, SD)
Black Panther (Oakland, CA)
Breakdown (Klamath Falls, OR)
Buddhist Third Class Junkmail Oracle (Cleveland)
Buffalo Insighter
Cahoots! (Joplin, MO)
Caravan (Sarasota, FL)
Chinook (Denver)
Dallas News
Der Zeitgeist (Phoenix)
Distant Drummer (Philadelphia)
East Village Other (New York)
Electric News (Salt Lake City)
Extra! (Providence)
Fifth Estate (Detroit)
Free Press of Louisville
Free Statesman (Saint Cloud, MN)
Free Student (New York)
F.T.E.! (Los Angeles)
Glyptodon News (Austin)
Great Speckled Bird (Atlanta)
Haight-Ashbury Maverick (San Francisco)
Head Lines (Memphis)
Helix (Seattle)
Home Cookin' (Oklahoma City)
Hundred Flowers (Minneapolis)
In Arcane Logos (New Orleans)
Indian Head (Santa Ana, CA)
Intercourse: A Journal of Sexual Freedom (Berkeley)
Joint Issue (East Lansing, MI)
Kaleidoscope (Milwaukee)
Kudzu (Jackson, MS)
Liberator (Morgantown, WV)
Lincoln Gazette
Los Angeles Free Press
Love (Reno, NV)
Madison Kaleidoscope
Minisink Bull (Dingman's Ferry, PA)
Modern Utopian (San Francisco)
Nashville Rag
News from Nowhere (Dekalb, IL)
New York City Star
Northwest Passage (Bellingham, WA)

Notes from the Underground (Dallas)
Old Mole (Boston)
Omaha Kaleidoscope
Open City (Los Angeles)
Open City Press (San Francisco)
Oracle of Southern California (Los Angeles)
Outlaw (Saint Louis)
Paper (East Lansing, MI)
Paper (Mendocino, CA)
Peach (Wausau, WI)
Pure Corn (Evansville, IN)
Rag (Austin)
Rat (New York)
Rebirth (Phoenix)
San Francisco Express Times
San Francisco Oracle
Sanity (Madison)
Screw (Lawrence, KS)
Seed (Chicago)
Seventy-Nine Cent Spread (Carmel, CA)
Solid Muldoon (Denver)
Space City! (Houston)
Space City News (Houston)
Spare Change (Washington, DC)
Spokane Natural
Submarine Church Press (Northampton, MA)
Sunshine Aura (Erie, PA)
Underground (Washington, DC)
Washington Free Press
Western Activist (Kalamazoo, MI)
Willamette Bridge (Portland)

Magazines

Billboard
Businessweek
Christian Century
Christian Science Monitor
Commentary
Commonweal
Ebony
Esquire
Life
Nation
Newsweek
New Yorker
Ramparts
Rolling Stone

Time
Trans-Action
U.S. News & World Report

Newspapers

Baltimore Sun
Boston Globe
Chicago Tribune
Chronicle of Higher Education
Dallas Morning News
Los Angeles Times
New York Times
New York Times Magazine
San Francisco Chronicle
USA Today
Washington Post

Published Primary Sources

Ald, Roy. The Youth Communes. New York: Tower, 1970.
Berke, Joseph, ed. Counter Culture. London: Peter Owen, 1969.
Boone, Pat. A New Song. Carol Stream, IL: Creation House, 1970.
Carey, James T. The College Drug Scene. Englewood Cliffs, NJ: Prentice Hall, 1968.
Cavan, Sherri. Hippies of the Haight. Saint Louis: New Critics, 1972.
Cleaver, Eldridge. Soul on Ice. New York: Dell, 1968.
del Renzio, Toni. The Flower Children. London: Solstice Productions, 1969.
Dragonwagon, Crescent. The Commune Cookbook. New York: Simon and Schuster, 1972.
Draper, Hal. Berkeley: The New Student Revolt. New York: Grove, 1965.
Eisen, Jonathan, ed. Altamont: Death of Innocence in the Woodstock Nation. New York: Avon
    Books, 1970.
Fairfield, Richard. Communes USA: A Personal Tour. Baltimore: Penguin, 1972.
Ginsberg, Allen. Collected Poems, 1947–1980. New York: Harper & Row, 1988.
Goodman, Mitchell, ed. The Movement toward a New America: The Beginnings of a Long
    Revolution (A Collage)—A What? New York: Alfred A. Knopf, 1970.
Gross, Henry. The Flower People. New York: Ballantine Books, 1968.
Hoffman, Abbie. Revolution for the Hell of It. New York: Dial Books, 1968.
———. Woodstock Nation: A Talk-Rock Album. New York: Vintage Books, 1969.
Hopkins, Jerry, ed. The Hippie Papers: Trip-Taking, Mind-Quaking, Scene-Making Word from
    Where It's At. New York: New American Library, 1968.
Kanter, Rosabeth Moss. Commitment and Community: Communes and Utopias in Sociological
    Perspective. Cambridge, MA: Harvard University Press, 1972.
Katzman, Allen, ed. Our Time: An Anthology of Interviews from the East Village Other. New
    York: Dial, 1972.
Keats, John. The Crack in the Picture Window. Boston: Houghton Mifflin, 1956.
Kesey, Ken. Kesey's Garage Sale. New York: Viking, 1973.
Kornbluth, Jesse, ed. Notes from the New Underground: An Anthology. New York: Viking,
    1968.
Leary, Timothy. The Politics of Ecstasy. New York: Putnam, 1968.

Marks, J. "The Dream Is Over." In *The Eloquence of Protest: Voices of the 70's*, edited by Harrison E. Salisbury, 227–231. Boston: Houghton Mifflin, 1972.

McNeill, Don. *Moving through Here*. New York: Alfred A. Knopf, 1970.

Melville, Keith. *Communes in the Counter Culture: Origins, Theories, Styles of Life*. New York: Morrow, 1972.

Morgan, Robin, ed. *Sisterhood Is Powerful: An Anthology of Writings from the Women's Liberation Movement*. New York: Random House, 1970.

Mungo, Ray. *Famous Long Ago: My Life and Hard Times with Liberation News Service*. Boston: Beacon Press, 1970.

Noebel, David A. *Communism, Hypnotism and the Beatles: An Analysis of the Communist Use of Music, The Communist Master Music Plan*. Tulsa, OK: Christian Crusade, 1965.

Perry, Helen Swick. *The Human Be-In*. New York: Basic Books, 1970.

Pope, Harrison, Jr. *Voices from the Drug Culture*. Boston: Beacon, 1971.

Romm, Ethel Grodzins. *The Open Conspiracy: What America's Angry Generation Is Saying*. New York: Giniger, 1970.

Rubin, Jerry. *Do It! Scenarios of the Revolution*. New York: Simon and Schuster, 1970.

Simmons, J. L., and Barry Winograd. *It's Happening: A Portrait of the Youth Scene Today*. Santa Barbara, CA: Marc-Laird, 1966.

Sinclair, John. *Guitar Army: Street Writings/Prison Writings*. New York: Douglas Book, 1972.

Stearn, Jess. *The Seekers*. Garden City, NY: Doubleday, 1969.

Stevenson, Adlai. "Commencement Address." In *America in the Sixties—Right, Left, and Center: A Documentary History*, edited by Peter B. Levy. Westport, CT: Praeger, 1998.

Stewart, Jon. "Communes in Taos." In *Conversations with the New Reality: Readings in the Cultural Revolution*, edited by Editors of Ramparts, 206–220. San Francisco: Canfield, 1971.

Thompson, Hunter S. *The Great Shark Hunt: Strange Tales from a Strange Time*. New York: Summit, 1979.

von Hoffman, Nicholas. *We Are the People Our Parents Warned Us Against*. Chicago: Quadrangle, 1968.

Watkins, Paul. *My Life with Charles Manson*. With Guillermo Soledad. New York: Bantam Books, 1979.

Wein, Bibi. *The Runaway Generation*. New York: McKay, 1970.

Wolf, Leonard, and Deborah Wolf, eds. *Voices from the Love Generation*. Boston: Little, Brown, 1968.

Wolfe, Burton H. *The Hippies*. New York: Signet, 1968.

Wolfe, Tom. *The Electric Kool-Aid Acid Test*. New York: Farrar, Straus and Giroux, 1968.

Yablonsky, Lewis. *The Hippie Trip*. New York: Pegasus, 1968.

Yankelovich, Daniel. *The Changing Values on Campus: Political and Personal Attitudes of Today's College Students*. New York: Washington Square, 1972.

Zablocki, Benjamin. *The Joyful Community*. Baltimore: Penguin Books, 1971.

SECONDARY SOURCES

Allen, Michael. "'I Just Want to Be a Cosmic Cowboy': Hippies, Cowboy Code, and the Culture of a Counterculture." *Western Historical Quarterly* 36, no. 3 (Autumn 2005): 275–299.

Allyn, David. *Make Love, Not War: The Sexual Revolution: An Unfettered History*. Boston: Little, Brown, 2000.

Anderson, Terry H. *Bush's Wars.* New York: Oxford University Press, 2011.

———. *The Movement and the Sixties.* New York: Oxford University Press, 1995.

———. "The New American Revolution: The Movement and Business." In *The Sixties: From Memory to History,* edited by David Farber, 175–201. Chapel Hill: University of North Carolina Press, 1994.

———. *The Sixties.* 4th ed. New York: Pearson, 2012.

Anthony, Gene. *Magic of the Sixties.* Layton, UT: Gibbs Smith, 2004.

———. *The Summer of Love: Haight-Ashbury at Its Highest.* Milbrae, CA: Celestial Arts, 1980.

Archer, Jules. *The Incredible Sixties: The Stormy Years That Changed America.* New York: Harcourt, 1986.

Bailey, Beth. *Sex in the Heartland.* Cambridge, MA: Harvard University Press, 1999.

———. "Sexual Revolution(s)." In *The Sixties: From Memory to History,* edited by David Farber, 235–262. Chapel Hill: University of North Carolina Press, 1994.

Bates, Tom. *Rads: The 1970 Bombing of the Army Math Research Center at the University of Wisconsin and Its Aftermath.* New York: HarperCollins, 1992.

Beatles. *The Beatles Anthology.* San Francisco: Chronicle Books, 2000.

Belz, Carl. *The Story of Rock.* New York: Oxford University Press, 1972.

Blum, John Morton. *Years of Discord: American Politics and Society, 1961–1974.* New York: W. W. Norton, 1991.

Bradley, Doug, and Craig Werner. *We Gotta Get Out of This Place: The Soundtrack of the Vietnam War.* Amherst: University of Massachusetts Press, 2015.

Brands, H. W. *The Devil We Knew: Americans and the Cold War.* New York: Oxford University Press, 1993.

Borstelmann, Thomas. *The 1970s: A New Global History from Civil Rights to Economic Inequality.* Princeton, NJ: Princeton University Press, 2012.

Braunstein, Peter, and Michael William Doyle, eds. *Imagine Nation: The American Counterculture of the 1960s and '70s,* edited by Peter Braunstein and Michael William Doyle. New York: Routledge, 2002.

———. "Introduction: Historicizing the American Counterculture of the 1960s and '70s." In Braunstein and Doyle, *Imagine Nation,* 5–14.

Bryan, John. *Whatever Happened to Timothy Leary?* San Francisco: Renaissance, 1980.

Bugliosi, Vincent. *Helter Skelter: The True Story of the Manson Murders.* With Curt Gentry. New York: W. W. Norton, 1994.

Burner, David. *Making Peace with the 60s.* Princeton, NJ: Princeton University Press, 1996.

Burns, Stewart. *Social Movements of the 1960s: Searching for Democracy.* Boston: Twayne, 1990.

Candida-Smith, Richard. *Utopia and Dissent: Art, Poetry, and Politics in California.* Berkeley: University of California Press, 1995.

Caute, David. *The Great Fear: The Anti-Communist Purge under Truman and Eisenhower.* New York: Simon and Schuster, 1978.

———. *Year of the Barricades: A Journey through 1968.* New York: Harper & Row, 1988.

Chafe, William H. *The Unfinished Journey: America since World War II.* 6th ed. New York: Oxford University Press, 2007.

Chalmers, David. *And the Crooked Places Made Straight: The Struggle for Social Change in the 1960s.* Baltimore: Johns Hopkins University Press, 1991.

Chepesiuk, Ron. *Sixties Radicals, Then and Now: Candid Conversations with Those Who Shaped the Era*. Jefferson, NC: McFarland, 1995.

Coleman, Ray. *Lennon: The Definitive Biography*. New York: HarperPerennial, 1992.

Coontz, Stephanie. *The Way We Never Were: American Families and the Nostalgia Trap*. New York: Basic Books, 1992.

Cornell, Andrew. "The Movement for a New Society: Consensus, Prefiguration, and Direct Action." In *The Hidden 1970s: Histories of Radicalism*, edited by Dan Berger, 231–249. New Brunswick, NJ: Rutgers University Press, 2010.

Corr, Michael, and Dan MacLeod. "Getting It Together." *Environment* 14, no. 9 (November 1972): 2–9.

Cottrell, Robert C. *Sex, Drugs, and Rock 'n' Roll: The Rise of America's 1960s Counterculture*. Lanham, MD: Rowman and Littlefield, 2015.

Cox, Craig. *Storefront Revolution: Food Co-ops and the Counterculture*. New Brunswick, NJ: Rutgers University Press, 1994.

Coyote, Peter. *Sleeping Where I Fall: A Chronicle*. Washington, DC: Counterpoint, 1998.

Crowley, Walt. *Rites of Passage: A Memoir of the Sixties in Seattle*. Seattle: University of Washington Press, 1995.

Cruikshank, Margaret. *The Gay and Lesbian Liberation Movement*. New York: Routledge, 1992.

Curl, John. *Memories of Drop City: The First Hippie Commune of the 1960's and the Summer of Love*. Lincoln, NE: iUniverse, 2007.

Davis, Joshua Clark. "The Business of Getting High: Head Shops, Countercultural Capitalism, and the Marijuana Legalization Movement." *Sixties* 8, no. 1 (2015): 27–49.

———. *From Head Shops to Whole Foods: The Rise and Fall of Activist Entrepreneurs*. New York: Columbia University Press, 2017.

Davis, Stephen. *Old Gods Almost Dead: The 40-Year Odyssey of the Rolling Stones*. New York: Broadway Books, 2001.

DeGroot, Gerard J. *The Sixties Unplugged: A Kaleidoscopic History of a Disorderly Decade*. Cambridge, MA: Harvard University Press, 2008.

Deloria, Philip. "Counterculture Indians and the New Age." In Braunstein and Doyle, *Imagine Nation*, 159–188.

D'Emilio, John, and Estelle B. Freedman. *Intimate Matters: A History of Sexuality in America*. 2nd ed. Chicago: University of Chicago Press, 1997.

Dickstein, Morris. "After Utopia: The 1960s Today." In *Sights on the Sixties*, edited by Barbara L. Tischler, 13–23. New Brunswick, NJ: Rutgers University Press, 1992.

Diggins, John Patrick. *The Proud Decades: America in War and Peace, 1941–1960*. New York: W. W. Norton, 1988.

Dodgson, Rick. *It's All a Kind of Magic: The Young Ken Kesey*. Madison: University of Wisconsin Press, 2013.

Doggett, Peter. *There's a Riot Going On: Revolutionaries, Rock Stars, and the Rise and Fall of the '60s*. Edinburgh: Canongate, 2007.

Dufton, Emily. *Grass Roots: The Rise and Fall and Rise of Marijuana in America*. New York: Basic Books, 2017.

Echols, Alice. "Nothing Distant about It: Women's Liberation and Sixties Radicalism." In *The Sixties: From Memory to History*, edited by David Farber, 149–174. Chapel Hill: University of North Carolina Press, 1994.

———. *Shaky Ground: The '60s and Its Aftershocks.* New York: Columbia University Press, 2002.

Ellwood, Robert S. *The Sixties Spiritual Awakening: American Religion Moving from Modern to Postmodern.* New Brunswick, NJ: Rutgers University Press, 1994.

Eskridge, Larry. *God's Forever Family: The Jesus People Movement in America.* New York: Oxford University Press, 2013.

Evans, Sara. *Personal Politics: The Roots of Women's Liberation in the Civil Rights Movement and the New Left.* New York: Vintage, 1979.

Farber, David. *The Age of Great Dreams: America in the 1960s.* New York: Hill and Wang, 1994.

———. "Building the Counterculture, Creating Right Livelihoods: The Counterculture at Work." *Sixties* 6, no. 1 (2013): 1–24.

———. *Chicago '68.* Chicago: University of Chicago Press, 1988.

———. "The Counterculture and the Antiwar Movement." In *Give Peace a Chance: Exploring the Vietnam Antiwar Movement,* edited by Melvin Small and William D. Hoover, 7–21. Syracuse, NY: Syracuse University Press, 1992.

———. "The Intoxicated State/Illegal Nation: Drugs in the Sixties Counterculture." In Braunstein and Doyle, *Imagine Nation,* 17–40.

Farrell, James J. *The Spirit of the Sixties: The Making of Postwar Radicalism.* New York: Routledge, 1997.

Fels, Tom. *Buying the Farm: Peace and War on a Sixties Commune.* Amherst: University of Massachusetts Press, 2012.

Fischer, Klaus P. *America in White, Black, and Gray: The Stormy 1960s.* New York: Continuum, 2006.

Foley, Michael S. *Confronting the War Machine: Draft Resistance during the Vietnam War.* Chapel Hill: University of North Carolina Press, 2003.

Frank, Thomas. *The Conquest of Cool: Business Culture, Counterculture, and the Rise of Hip Consumerism.* Chicago: University of Chicago Press, 1997.

Fried, Richard. *Nightmare in Red: The McCarthy Era in Perspective.* New York: Oxford University Press, 1990.

Garofalo, Reebee. *Rockin' Out: Popular Music in the U.S.A.* Upper Saddle River, NJ: Prentice Hall, 2008.

Gemie, Sharif, and Brian Ireland. *The Hippie Trail: A History, 1957–78.* Manchester: Manchester University Press, 2017.

Gillett, Charlie. *The Sound of the City: The Rise of Rock and Roll.* New York: Outerbridge & Dienstfrey, 1970.

Gitlin, Todd. *The Sixties: Years of Hope, Days of Rage.* New York: Bantam, 1987.

Goffman, Ken, and Dan Joy. *Counterculture through the Ages: From Abraham to Acid House.* New York: Villard, 2004.

Goldman, Eric F. *The Crucial Decade and After: America, 1945–1960.* New York: Vintage Books, 1960.

Goulden, Joseph C. *The Best Years, 1945–1950.* New York: Atheneum, 1976.

Greene, John Robert. *America in the Sixties.* Syracuse, NY: Syracuse University Press, 2010.

Greenfield, Robert. *Timothy Leary: A Biography.* New York: Harcourt, 2006.

Halberstam, David. *The Fifties.* New York: Random House, 1993.

Hale, Grace Elizabeth. *A Nation of Outsiders: How the White Middle Class Fell in Love with Rebellion in Postwar America*. New York: Oxford University Press, 2011.

Hale, Jeff A. "The White Panthers' 'Total Assault on the Culture.'" In Braunstein and Doyle, *Imagine Nation*, 125–156.

Hall, Simon. *Peace and Freedom: The Civil Rights and Antiwar Movements in the 1960s*. Philadelphia: University of Pennsylvania Press, 2005.

Hamby, Alonzo L. *Man of the People: A Life of Harry S. Truman*. New York: Oxford University Press, 1995.

Hansen, Emmanuel. *Frantz Fanon: Social and Political Thought*. Columbus: Ohio State University Press, 1977.

Henke, James, and Parke Puterbaugh, eds. *I Want to Take You Higher: The Psychedelic Era, 1965–1969*. San Francisco: Chronicle Books, 1997.

Hepworth, David. *Never a Dull Moment: 1971—The Year That Rock Exploded*. New York: Henry Holt, 2016.

Herring, George C. *America's Longest War: The United States and Vietnam, 1950–1975*. New York: Alfred A. Knopf, 1986.

Hicks, Michael. *Sixties Rock: Garage, Psychedelic, and Other Satisfactions*. Urbana: University of Illinois Press, 1999.

Hinckle, Warren. "A Social History of the Hippies." In *The American Experience: A Radical Reader*, edited by Harold Jaffe and John Tytell, 262–284. New York: Harper & Row, 1970.

Hodgdon, Tim. *Manhood in the Age of Aquarius: Masculinity in Two Countercultural Communities, 1965–83*. New York: Columbia University Press, 2008.

Hodgson, Godfrey. *America in Our Time: From World War II to Nixon—What Happened and Why*. New York: Doubleday, 1976.

———. *The World Turned Right Side Up: A History of the Conservative Ascendancy in America*. New York: Houghton Mifflin, 1996.

Hofmann, Albert. *LSD: My Problem Child*. New York: McGraw-Hill, 1980.

Hunt, Andrew E. *The Turning: A History of Vietnam Veterans against the War*. New York: New York University Press, 1999.

Isserman, Maurice, and Michael Kazin. *America Divided: The Civil War of the 1960s*. 5th ed. New York: Oxford University Press, 2015.

Jackson, Andrew Grant. *1965: The Most Revolutionary Year in Music*. New York: Thomas Dunne Books, 2015.

Janda, Sarah Eppler. *Prairie Power: Student Activism, Counterculture, and Backlash in Oklahoma, 1962–1972*. Norman: University of Oklahoma Press, 2018.

Jezer, Marty. *Abbie Hoffman: American Rebel*. New Brunswick, NJ: Rutgers University Press, 1992.

Jones, Landon Y. *Great Expectations: America and the Baby Boom Generation*. New York: Coward, McCann & Geoghegan, 1980.

Kessler, Lauren. *After All These Years: Sixties Ideals in a Different World*. New York: Thunder's Mouth, 1990.

Kimball, Roger. "Virtue Gone Mad." *New Criterion*, December 1997, 4–11.

Kirk, Andrew G. *Counterculture Green: The Whole Earth Catalog and American Environmentalism*. Lawrence: University Press of Kansas, 2007.

Kirkpatrick, Rob. *1969: The Year Everything Changed*. New York: Skyhorse, 2009.

Klatch, Rebecca. *A Generation Divided: The New Left, the New Right, and the 1960s.* Berkeley: University of California Press, 1999.

Knoebel, John. "Somewhere in the Right Direction: Testimony of My Experience in a Gay Male Living Collective." In *Out of the Closets: Voices of Gay Liberation*, edited by Karla Jay and Allen Young, 301–315. New York: New York University Press, 1992.

Kovic, Ron. *Born on the Fourth of July.* New York: Akashic Books, 2005.

Kramer, Michael J. *The Republic of Rock: Music and Citizenship in the Sixties Counterculture.* New York: Oxford University Press, 2013.

Leamer, Laurence. *The Paper Revolutionaries: The Rise of the Underground Press.* New York: Simon and Schuster, 1972.

Leary, Timothy. *Flashbacks: An Autobiography.* New York: G. P. Putnam, 1990.

Lee, Martin A., and Bruce Shlain. *Acid Dreams: The Complete Social History of LSD: The CIA, the Sixties, and Beyond.* New York: Grove, 1985.

Lemke-Santangelo, Gretchen. *Daughters of Aquarius: Women of the Sixties Counterculture.* Lawrence: University Press of Kansas, 2009.

Leuchtenburg, William E. *The American President: From Teddy Roosevelt to Bill Clinton.* New York: Oxford University Press, 2015.

——. *A Troubled Feast: American Society since 1945.* Boston: Little, Brown, 1979.

Levin, Matthew. *Cold War University: Madison and the New Left in the Sixties.* Madison: University of Wisconsin Press, 2013.

Li-Marcus, Moying. *Beacon Hill: The Life and Times of a Neighborhood.* Boston: Northeastern University Press, 2002.

Lyons, Paul. *The People of This Generation: The Rise and Fall of the New Left in Philadelphia.* Philadelphia: University of Pennsylvania Press, 2003.

Lytle, Mark Hamilton. *America's Uncivil Wars: The Sixties Era from Elvis to the Fall of Richard Nixon.* New York: Oxford University Press, 2006.

Maguire, Peter, and Mike Ritter. *Thai Stick: Surfers, Scammers, and the Untold Story of the Marijuana Trade.* New York: Columbia University Press, 2014.

Marcus, Eric. *Making Gay History: The Half-Century Fight for Lesbian and Gay Equal Rights.* New York: Perennial, 2002.

Marwick, Arthur. *The Sixties: Cultural Revolution in Britain, France, Italy, and the United States.* Oxford: Oxford University Press, 1998.

Matthews, Mark. *Droppers: America's First Hippie Commune, Drop City.* Norman: University of Oklahoma Press, 2010.

Matusow, Allen J. *The Unraveling of America: A History of Liberalism in the 1960s.* New York: Harper & Row, 1984.

McBride, David. "Counterculture." In *A Companion to Los Angeles*, edited by William Deverell and Greg Hise, 327–345. Oxford: Wiley-Blackwell, 2010.

——. "Death City Radicals: The Counterculture in Los Angeles." In *The New Left Revisited*, edited by John McMillian and Paul Buhle, 110–138. Philadelphia: Temple University Press, 2003.

McCleary, John Bassett. *The Hippie Dictionary: A Cultural Encyclopedia (and Phraseicon) of the 1960s and 1970s.* Berkeley, CA: Ten Speed, 2002.

McCormick, John. *Reclaiming Paradise: The Global Environmental Movement.* Bloomington: Indiana University Press, 1989.

McMillian, John. *Smoking Typewriters: The Sixties Underground Press and the Rise of Alternative Media in America.* New York: Oxford University Press, 2011.

———. "'You Didn't Have to Be There': Revisiting the New Left Consensus." In *The New Left Revisited*, edited by John McMillian and Paul Buhle, 1–8. Philadelphia: Temple University Press, 2003.

McNally, Dennis. *A Long Strange Trip: The Inside History of the Grateful Dead*. New York: Broadway Books, 2002.

McWilliams, John C. *The 1960s Cultural Revolution*. Westport, CT: Greenwood, 2000.

Mele, Christopher. *Selling the Lower East Side: Culture, Real Estate, and Resistance in New York City*. Minneapolis: University of Minnesota Press, 2000.

Messner, Michael A. "Radical Feminist and Socialist Feminist Men's Movements in the United States." In *Feminism and Men: Reconstructing Gender Relations*, edited by Steven Schacht and Doris Ewing, 67–85. New York: New York University Press, 1998.

Michals, Debra. "From 'Consciousness Expansion' to 'Consciousness Raising.'" In Braunstein and Doyle, *Imagine Nation*, 41–68.

Miles, Barry. *Hippie*. New York: Sterling, 2004.

———. *Paul McCartney: Many Years from Now*. New York: Owl Books, 1997.

Miller, Douglas T., and Marion Nowak. *The Fifties: The Way We Really Were*. Garden City, NY: Doubleday, 1975.

Miller, James. *Flowers in the Dustbin: The Rise of Rock and Roll, 1947–1977*. New York: Simon and Schuster, 1999.

Miller, Laura J. *Building Nature's Market: The Business and Politics of Natural Foods*. Chicago: University of Chicago Press, 2017.

Miller, Timothy. *The Hippies and American Values*. Knoxville: University of Tennessee Press, 1991.

———. *The 60s Communes: Hippies and Beyond*. Syracuse, NY: Syracuse University Press, 1999.

Mitchell, Robert Cameron. "From Conservation to Environmental Movement: The Development of the Modern Environmental Lobbies." In *Government and Environmental Politics: Essays on Historical Developments since World War Two*, edited by Michael J. Lacey, 81–114. Baltimore: Johns Hopkins University Press, 1989.

Moore, LeRoy, Jr. "From Profane to Sacred America: Religion and the Cultural Revolution in the United States." *Journal of the American Academy of Religion* 39, no. 3. (September 1971): 321–338.

Moretta, John Anthony. *The Hippies: A 1960s History*. Jefferson, NC: McFarland, 2017.

Morgan, Edward P. *The 60s Experience: Hard Lessons about Modern America*. Philadelphia: Temple University Press, 1991.

Morrison, Joan, and Robert K. Morrison. *From Camelot to Kent State: The Sixties Experience in the Words of Those Who Lived It*. New York: Oxford University Press, 2001.

Mumford, Lewis. *The City in History: Its Origins, Its Transformation, and Its Prospects*. New York: Penguin, 1961.

Nettler, Gwynn. "A Measure of Alienation." *American Sociological Review* 22 (1957): 670–677.

Nisbet, Robert. *The Quest for Community: A Study in the Ethics of Order and Freedom*. Wilmington, DE: ISI Books, 2010.

Norman, Philip. *Shout! The Beatles in Their Generation*. New York: Simon and Schuster, 1981.

Oakley, J. Ronald. *God's Country: America in the Fifties*. New York: Barricade Books, 1990.

Olsen, Polina. *Portland in the 1960s: Stories from the Counterculture*. Charleston, SC: History Press, 2012.

O'Neill, William L. *Coming Apart: An Informal History of America in the 1960s*. Chicago: Quadrangle, 1971.

Oram, Matthew. *The Trials of Psychedelic Therapy: LSD Psychotherapy in America*. Baltimore: Johns Hopkins University Press, 2018.

Oshinsky, David M. *A Conspiracy So Immense: The World of Joe McCarthy*. New York: Oxford University Press, 1983.

Palmer, Robert. *Rock and Roll: An Unruly History*. New York: Harmony Books, 1995.

Peck, Abe. *Uncovering the Sixties: The Life and Times of the Underground Press*. New York: Pantheon, 1985.

Perone, James E. *Music of the Counterculture Era*. Westport, CT: Greenwood, 2004.

Perry, Charles. *The Haight-Ashbury: A History*. New York: Random House, 1984.

Perry, Paul. *On the Bus: The Complete Guide to the Legendary Trip of Ken Kesey and the Merry Pranksters and the Birth of the Counterculture*. New York: Thunder's Mouth, 1990.

Persico, Connell. "Live and Let Live." In *To Make a Difference: A Student Look at America: Its Values, Its Society and Its Systems of Education*, edited by Otto Butz, 110–124. New York: Joanna Cotler Books, 1967.

Petrovic, G. "Alienation." In *Encyclopedia of Philosophy*, 2nd ed., edited by Donald M. Borchert. Farmington Hills, MI: Thomson Gale, 2006.

Pichaske, David. *A Generation in Motion: Popular Music and Culture in the Sixties*. New York: Schirmer Books, 1979.

Raskin, Jonah. *For the Hell of It: The Life and Times of Abbie Hoffman*. Berkeley: University of California Press, 1996.

Richardson, Peter. *No Simple Highway: A Cultural History of the Grateful Dead*. New York: St. Martin's, 2015.

Roose-Evans, James. *Experimental Theatre: From Stanislavsky to Peter Brook*. New York: Universe Books, 1989.

Rorabaugh, W. J. *American Hippies*. New York: Cambridge University Press, 2015.

———. *Berkeley at War: The 1960s*. New York: Oxford University Press, 1989.

Rosen, Ruth. *The World Split Open: How the Modern Women's Movement Changed America*. New York: Penguin, 2000.

Rossinow, Doug. "Letting Go: Revisiting the New Left's Demise." In *The New Left Revisited*, edited by John McMillian and Paul Buhle. Philadelphia: Temple University Press, 2003, 241–256.

———. *The Politics of Authenticity: Liberalism, Christianity, and the New Left in America*. New York: Columbia University Press, 1998.

———. "'The Revolution Is about Our Lives': The New Left's Counterculture." In Braunstein and Doyle, *Imagine Nation*, 99–124.

Roszak, Theodore. *The Making of a Counter Culture: Reflections on the Technocratic Society and Its Youthful Opposition*. Garden City, NY: Doubleday, 1969.

Roxon, Lillian. *Rock Encyclopedia*. New York: Grosset & Dunlap, 1978.

Sager, Anthony P. "Radical Law: Three Collectives in Cambridge." In *Co-ops, Communes and Collectives: Experiments in Social Change in the 1960s and 1970s*, edited by John Case and Rosemary C. R. Taylor, 136–150. New York: Pantheon Books, 1979.

Sale, Kirkpatrick. *The Green Revolution: The American Environmental Movement, 1962–1992*. New York: Hill and Wang, 1991.

Santelli, Robert. *Aquarius Rising: The Rock Festival Years*. New York: Dell, 1980.

Scaduto, Anthony. *Bob Dylan*. New York: Grosset & Dunlap, 1971.

Schaffner, Nicholas. *The Beatles Forever*. New York: McGraw-Hill, 1978.

Schou, Nicholas. *Orange Sunshine: The Brotherhood of Eternal Love and Its Quest to Spread Peace, Love, and Acid to the World*. New York: Thomas Dunne Books, 2010.

Schulman, Bruce J. *The Seventies: The Great Shift in American Culture, Society, and Politics*. New York: Free Press, 2001.

Shelton, Robert. *No Direction Home: The Life and Music of Bob Dylan*. New York: William Morrow, 1986.

Shires, Preston. *Hippies of the Religious Right*. Waco, TX: Baylor University Press, 2007.

Shorr, Catherine O' Sullivan. *Andy Warhol's Factory People*. Scotts Valley, CA: Create Space Independent Publishing, 2014.

Sitkoff, Harvard. *The Struggle for Black Equality, 1954–1992*. New York: Hill and Wang, 1993.

Skolnick, Arlene. *Embattled Paradise: The American Family in an Age of Uncertainty*. New York: Basic Books, 1991.

Sloman, Larry. *Steal This Dream: Abbie Hoffman and the Countercultural Revolution in America*. New York: Doubleday, 1998.

Slonecker, Blake. "The Columbia Coalition: African Americans, New Leftists, and Counterculture at the Columbia University Protest of 1968." *Journal of Social History* 41, no. 4 (Summer 2008): 967–996.

———. *A New Dawn for the New Left: Liberation News Service, Montague Farm, and the Long Sixties*. New York: Palgrave Macmillan, 2012.

Smith, Sherry L. *Hippies, Indians, and the Fight for Red Power*. New York: Oxford University Press, 2012.

Sounes, Howard. *Down the Highway: The Life of Bob Dylan*. New York: Grove, 2001.

Spitz, Bob. *The Beatles: The Biography*. New York: Back Bay Books, 2005.

Spitz, Robert Stephen. *Barefoot in Babylon: The Creation of the Woodstock Music Festival, 1969*. New York: Viking, 1979.

Staller, Karen M. *Runaways: How the Sixties Counterculture Shaped Today's Practices and Policies*. New York: Columbia University Press, 2006.

Steigerwald, David. *The Sixties and the End of Modern America*. New York: Bedford/St. Martin's, 1995.

Stephens, Jay. *Storming Heaven: LSD and the American Dream*. New York: Atlantic Monthly Press, 1987.

Stephens, Julie. *Anti-disciplinary Protest: Sixties Radicalism and Post-modernism*. New York: Cambridge University Press, 1998.

Stimeling, Travis D. *Cosmic Cowboys and New Hicks: The Countercultural Sounds of Austin's Progressive Country Music Scene*. New York: Oxford University Press, 2011.

Suri, Jeremi. "The Rise and Fall of an International Counterculture, 1960–1975." *American Historical Review* 114, no. 1 (February 2009): 45–68.

Szatmary, David P. *Rockin' in Time: A Social History of Rock and Roll*. Upper Saddle River, NJ: Prentice Hall, 1996.

Tanner, Stephen L. *Ken Kesey*. Boston: Twayne, 1983.

Taylor, Rosemary C. R. "Free Medicine." In *Co-ops, Communes and Collectives: Experiments in Social Change in the 1960s and 1970s*, edited by John Case and Rosemary C. R. Taylor, 17–48. New York: Pantheon Books, 1979.

Torgoff, Martin. *Can't Find My Way Home: America in the Great Stoned Age, 1945–2000*. New York: Simon and Schuster, 2004.

Turner, Fred. *From Counterculture to Cyberculture: Stewart Brand, the Whole Earth Network, and the Rise of Digital Utopianism.* Chicago: University of Chicago Press, 2006.

Unger, Irwin. *The Sixties.* New York: Pearson, 2011.

Von Bothmer, Bernard. *Framing the Sixties: The Use and Abuse of a Decade from Ronald Reagan to George W. Bush.* Amherst: University of Massachusetts Press, 2010.

Walker, Michael. *Laurel Canyon: The Inside Story of Rock-and-Roll's Legendary Neighborhood.* New York: Farrar, Straus and Giroux, 2006.

Ward, Ed, Geoffrey Stokes, and Ken Tucker. *Rock of Ages: The Rolling Stone History of Rock and Roll.* New York: Rolling Stone, 1986.

Weiner, Rex, and Deanne Stillman. *Woodstock Census: The Nationwide Survey of the Sixties Generation.* New York: Viking, 1979.

Whalen, Jack, and Richard Flacks. *Beyond the Barricades: The Sixties Generation Grows Up.* Philadelphia: Temple University Press, 1989.

Whitfield, Stephen J. *The Culture of the Cold War.* Baltimore: Johns Hopkins University Press, 1991.

Wiener, Jon. *Come Together: John Lennon in His Time.* New York: Random House, 1984.

Williamson, Joel. *A Rage for Order: Black-White Relations in the American South since Emancipation.* New York: Oxford University Press, 1986.

Wittner, Lawrence S. *Cold War America: From Hiroshima to Watergate.* New York: Praeger, 1974.

Woodward, C. Vann. *The Strange Career of Jim Crow.* New York: Oxford University Press, 1955.

Wynkoop, Mary Ann. *Dissent in the Heartland: The Sixties at Indiana University.* Bloomington: Indiana University Press, 2002.

Young, Ralph. *Dissent: The History of an American Idea.* New York: New York University Press, 2015.

Zablocki, Benjamin David. *Alienation and Charisma: A Study of Contemporary American Communes.* New York: Free Press, 1980.

Zaroulis, Nancy, and Gerald Sullivan. *Who Spoke Up? American Protest against the War in Vietnam, 1963–1975.* Garden City, NY: Doubleday, 1984.

Zelko, Frank. *Make It a Green Peace! The Rise of Countercultural Environmentalism.* New York: Oxford University Press, 2013.

Zimmerman, Nadya. *Counterculture Kaleidoscope: Musical and Cultural Perspectives on Late Sixties San Francisco.* Ann Arbor: University of Michigan Press, 2008.

Zwerdling, Daniel. "The Uncertain Revival of Food Cooperatives." In *Co-ops, Communes and Collectives: Experiments in Social Change in the 1960s and 1970s,* edited by John Case and Rosemary C. R. Taylor, 89–111. New York: Pantheon Books, 1979.

INDEX

consumer culture: co-opting of counterculture, 272–274; counterculture rejection of, 19; in 1950s, 18–19

contraception, and sexual freedom, 47

Cooperative League of the USA (CLUSA), 232

coops, in countersociety of 1970s, 232–235

CORE. See Congress of Racial Equality

counterculturalists: as champions of civil liberties, 12; vs. hippies, xv–xvi; as largely liberal/left wing, 253–254; mainstream public's dislike of, 86; number of, xviii, 100, 126; principles of, xvi; types of people included in, xvi; See also hybrid counterculturalists

counterculture: as anarchistic, 28, 48–49, 68, 149–150; apogee of, as 1971, 187; aspects deserving of criticism, 287–288; vs. Beats, differences between, 27–28; blooming of, in late 1960s, 99; broad categories of, xviii–xix; cities with enclaves of, 156–158; comprehensive history of, need for, x; dark side of, ix–x; as decentralized, 28; definition of, xv–xvii; developments and themes, 1965–1967, 37–38; dissipation by 1974, 250; emergence of, 38; factional struggles of late 1960s, 100; fragmentation of, 204; impact on mainstream culture, 274–275, 278, 281–289; as leaderless, 127–128; legacy of, as matter of debate, 287–288; long-term influence of, 250; microsocieties within cities, xiii, xiii–xiv; as mostly middle- and upper-class whites, 111; origins and growth of, xvi–xvii; peaking of, in early 1970s, 220–221; as positive experience for many, 288–289; rise to political power, and conservatives as the new rebels, 287; spread across nation, xii, 100, 156–158; thriving of, in late 1960s–early 1970s, 120; types of groups included in, xvii–xviii; victory in culture wars, 279, 281; See also end of counterculture; goals of counterculture; origins of counterculture

counterculture, vs. New Left, xix, xx, 76–80 animosity between, 77–79 blurring of line between, in late 1960s, 136–139 and campus occupations, brief unity for, 138 counterculturalists' perception of, 142–143 as distinct despite overlaps, 137

and dope, different views on, 79–80 dress and hair styles, differences in, 79 efforts to unite in mid-1960s' Los Angeles, 121 fusion of, in early 1970s, 195–202; and counterculture flavor of political protests, 197–199; in opposition to Vietnam War, Nixon, and establishment, 195–199, 200, 202; and shift toward cultural radicalism, 199–200; and union of cultural and political struggle, 197–198; violence by Leftists and, 200–202 hippies' rejection of political action, xviii, 29–30, 76, 77–79, 95, 145–146, 150 Leftists' perception of, 143 merging of, in 1970s, 187–188, 193 partial blending of, in late 1960s, 99–100 People's Park episode and, 160–161 philosophical differences, 143 public's failure to distinguish, 77 scholarship on, 136 union in antiwar protests, 167 values shared by, 138–139

counterculture in late 1960s, developments in, 100–101

counterculture in 1968: groups constituting, 137; and political unrest, 135–136

counterculture in 1970s activism through electoral politics, 259–260 changed focus of, 187–188 coalition of groups constituting, 196–197 differences from 1960s version, xii efforts to revitalize, 249 gatherings and events, 265–268, 270 issues of concern to, 250, 254, 258; abortion rights, 261–262; American Indian rights, 262–264; environmentalism, 187–188, 191–192, 271–272; prison reform/elimination, 259–260; workers' rights, 258 as national phenomenon, xii notable events shaping, 187–188 pivot to local politics, 258–260 and polarization of U.S. society, 196 pro-dope activism, 266–267 turn to political activism, xi–xiii, 249–250, 265–266 as under-studied, x Watergate scandal and, 264–265

women of color, limited interest in counterculture, 20
Women's Culture celebration (1973), 268
women's liberation movement. *See* feminism
Women's Strike for Equality, 206
Women Strike for Peace, 77
Woodstock (1970 film), 203–204
Woodstock Music and Art Fair, 162–164: as blueprint for new society, 99, 162–163, 164; conservative views on, 286–287; criticisms of, 165–166, 167; and cultural revolution, hope for, 164; and drug use, 51, 57; as frame of mind, 276; and Hog Farm commune, 84; number attending, 162; performers at, 162; political activists at, as ignored or silenced, 163; presidential campaign of 2008 and, 286–287; problems at, 162; promoters' losses on, 203; scholarship on, ix; as supreme moment of counterculture history, 163–164, 171
Woodstock Nation (Hoffman), 4, 148
Worchester, Mass, head shops in, 235
workers' rights, counterculture support for, in 1970s, 258–259
World War II: as good war, in U.S. view, 5, 12–13; prosperity following, 5; spread of capitalism and democracy as U.S. postwar goal, 5; and U.S. foreign policy, 7
Wright, Gridley, 121, 146

Yippies (Youth International Party): and African Americans, militant, admiration for, 111; anti-Nixon protests, 266–267; beliefs and practices, 144; call for revolution, xii, 144; conflict with New Left, 145; criticisms of, from hippies and New Left, 145, 165; criticisms of hippies, 148; demonstration at Democratic National Convention (1968), 144–145, 146–147, 151; Diggers' opposition to, 147; dope legalization activism, 266–267; founding of, 143–144; hippies' rejection of, 145, 146, 147–148; as hybrid counterculturalists, 144; and Lake Villa Conference, 145; as one type of counterculturalist, 100, 137; protests at Nixon's inauguration, 179; and rift within counterculture, 145; on rock festivals, 204; zippies as offshoot of, 255
yoga: counterculture interest in, 130; public interest in, as legacy of counterculture, 284
York, Richard L., 239–240
Yosemite National Park, hippies camping in, 225–226
Young, Neil, 222, 255
youth culture, spread of, in 1970s, 197; *See also* countersociety in 1970s

Zappa, Frank, 87, 121
Zippies: activism by, 255, 256; as offshoot of Yippies, 255